LEARN TO

Drive

© Robert Davies 2011

Crown copyright material has been reproduced by permission of the Driving Standards Agency which does not accept any responsibility for the accuracy of the reproduction.

First published in 2003
Reprinted and updated in 2004 and 2005
2nd Edition published 2005
Reprinted and updated in 2007
3rd Edition published 2008
Reprinted in 2008 and 2010
4th Edition published 2011

A catalogue record for this book is available from the British Library

ISBN 978 0 85733 149 6

Published by Haynes Publishing,
Sparkford, Yeovil, Somerset BA22 7JJ, UK

Tel: +44 (0)1963 442030 Fax: +44 (0)1963 440001
E-mail: sales@haynes.co.uk
Website: www.haynes.co.uk

Haynes North America, Inc.,
861 Lawrence Drive, Newbury Park,
California 91320, USA

Printed in the USA by Odcombe Press LP,
1299 Bridgestone Parkway, La Vergne, TN 37086

Author	Robert Davies
Project Manager	Louise McIntyre
Design and Layout	Lee Parsons James Robertson Dominic Stickland
Technical Advisors	John Farlam Jason Youé
Photographer	Simon Clay
Learner Driver	Zara Sparkes, LMP Models

LEARN TO
Drive
ALL IN **ONE** BOOK

Haynes

L

L YG60 UGX

- Theory Test
- Practical Test
- Official DSA Revision Questions

learn to drive

contents

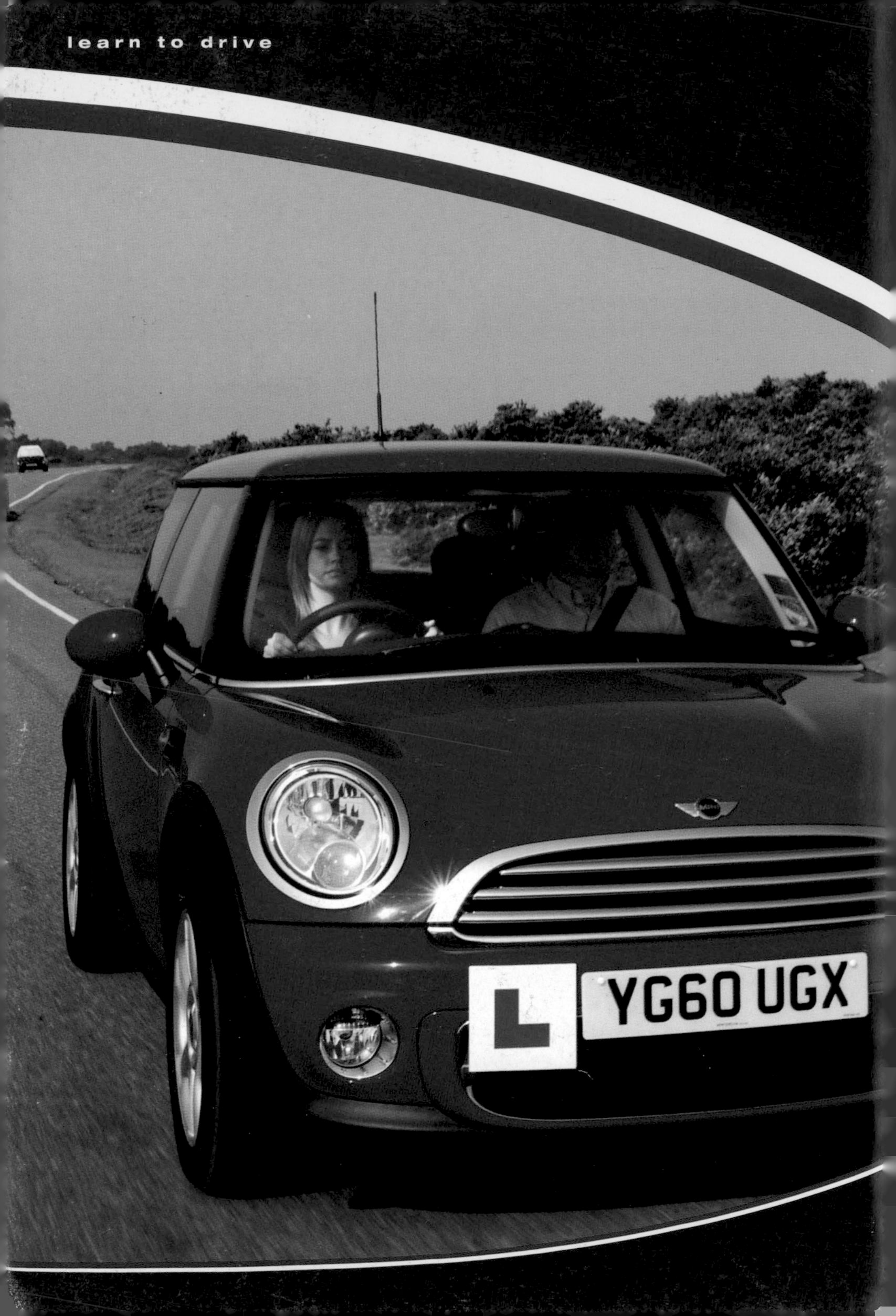
learn to drive
YG60 UGX

introduction

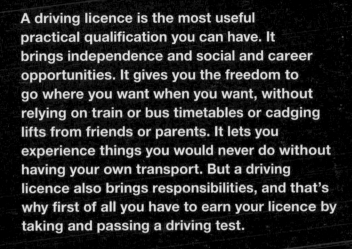

A driving licence is the most useful practical qualification you can have. It brings independence and social and career opportunities. It gives you the freedom to go where you want when you want, without relying on train or bus timetables or cadging lifts from friends or parents. It lets you experience things you would never do without having your own transport. But a driving licence also brings responsibilities, and that's why first of all you have to earn your licence by taking and passing a driving test.

Driving isn't so difficult – well over half a million people pass their driving test each year. But it's a fact that over half of those who take their driving test fail. In most cases the reason is simply lack of preparation.

That's where this book comes in. *Learn To Drive* brings together all the information you need to pass your theory and practical driving tests. It's important to prepare for the two tests side by side. Despite their titles, you can't pass the practical driving test without a thorough knowledge of driving theory, and you'll struggle to succeed in the theory test without getting some practical driving experience under your belt first.

Learning to drive is a great adventure and it can be a lot of fun too. We hope this book helps to put you on the road towards a long and safe driving career.

1 first steps

There's more to starting to drive than reaching your 17th birthday and jumping behind the wheel. You need to make sure you're licensed and insured to drive, and that you are legally supervised while on the road. You also need to think about your own fitness to drive, so get your eyesight checked and make sure you are physically and mentally prepared for the challenge of getting behind the wheel. As a first step, it's best to arrange some driving lessons to get you started. Even if you have access to the family car (and this is a good way to build up extra experience) it's important to get some professional tuition too.

1

preparing for the test

Being able to drive brings independence, freedom and exciting new work and social opportunities. Getting the driving licence that brings these benefits involves hard work, determination, and inevitably, money. Don't try to rush the process. Driving examiners complain that the main reason test candidates fail is lack of practice. Put in the time and effort to prepare really thoroughly for your test, and your investment will certainly be worthwhile.

learners and the law

As a learner driver using a car on public roads you must:

- be at least 17 years old (except if you receive the highest rate of mobility allowance when you may start learning at 16)
- hold a provisional driving licence
- have at least minimum insurance cover
- be accompanied by a supervising driver
- ensure that your car is roadworthy, taxed and if it is over three years old has a current MOT certificate
- display L-plates on your car front and rear
- not drive on motorways.

As a learner driver you are not allowed to use a motorway or drive without proper supervision

getting a driving licence

Driving licences are issued by the Driver and Vehicle Licensing Agency (DVLA). Apply online, or with form D1 from the post office. The fee for a provisional licence is £50. (In Northern Ireland the licensing authority is Driver and Vehicle Licensing Northern Ireland.)

L-plates

The size, shape and colour of L-plates is laid down by law, so don't try to economise by making your own. Make sure the plates are positioned on the front and rear of the vehicle so they are clearly visible. Fix the plates to the car bodywork, not on the front or rear screen where they could obscure the driver's vision. Remove or cover the plates when someone who is not a learner is driving the car. In Wales a D-plate can take the place of an L-plate.

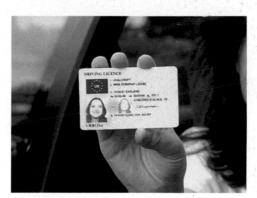

You must get your provisional driving licence before you can get behind the wheel as a learner

insurance

If you drive a friend's or relative's car make sure they check with their insurance company that you are insured to drive it. You must have at least the legal minimum of third party insurance cover. For more information about arranging insurance cover, as well as tax and MOT requirements, see pages 198-201.

Fix L-plates where they can be clearly seen, but not where they might impair your own vision

preparing for the test

There are two parts to the driving test – theory and practical.

The theory test is itself split into two elements. First is a touch-screen multiple-choice exam which takes 57 minutes. This is followed after a three-minute break by a video-clip based hazard perception test, which takes up to half an hour.

The practical test consists of a 40-minute drive accompanied by a driving examiner.

You must pass the theory test before you can take your practical test. Despite this, it's not a good idea to put off starting to drive until you've passed your theory test. The theory element of the test will make much more sense – and be a lot easier to master – if you can relate it to the real experience of driving on the road.

The theory and practical driving tests are covered in detail in Chapter 14.

You must pass your theory test before you are allowed to take the practical driving test

driving lessons

Driving lessons may seem expensive but there is no substitute for expert one-to-one tuition. If you have access to a family or friend's car, this can be a useful way of getting extra experience behind the wheel. But it makes sense to start out under the expert supervision of an Approved Driving Instructor (ADI). Once your instructor is happy that you've mastered the basics of car control, then you can think about getting extra practice sessions with a friend or relative supervising. Practice is the key to passing the driving test: the more miles you cover before taking your test, the greater the variety of driving situations you'll encounter and the less likely it is that you will be caught out by an unfamiliar situation during your test.

choosing an instructor

Only an Approved Driving Instructor (ADI) registered with the Driving Standards Agency (DSA) can accept money in return for giving driving lessons. All ADIs have to pass a strict driving test and they undergo regular assessments. However, as with all teachers, some are better than others.

The DSA grades driving instructors. A grade 4 ADI is classed as competent, grade 5 is good and grade 6 is a very high standard. All ADIs must display a green certificate on the windscreen. Trainee driving instructors are permitted to give driving lessons, in which case the certificate they display is pink instead of green.

As well as looking at your instructor's qualifications, it's just as important to choose one who you get along with and have confidence in. Ask friends who have been preparing for the test if they know an instructor who they would recommend.

practice makes perfect

Get in as much practice as you can in the run up to your driving test. Try to experience as many different driving situations as possible: drive in the country as well as in town, on dual carriageways, at night and in wet weather. Thoroughly practise the reversing manoeuvres required in the driving test (but don't spend too much time reversing round the same quiet back streets or you may irritate local residents).

Fully-qualified Approved Driving Instructors are allowed to display a green certificate in their car windscreen (top); Trainee Driving Instructors are also authorised to give tuition to learners, and they display a pink certificate (bottom)

driver's record

The Driver's Record is a handy free official guide that will help you to monitor your progress as you gain experience on the road. You can get one from your ADI or download it from direct.gov.uk/driversrecord.

Most test failures are caused by lack of practice, so get in as much driving as you can before your test

it's the law

supervisors

By law the person who supervises you when you are learning to drive must:

➜ be at least 21 years old

➜ hold a full driving licence for the type of car being driven (a licence valid for cars with automatic transmissions isn't adequate if the car being driven is a manual)

➜ have held their driving licence for at least three years.

fit to drive

Driving a car demands a high degree of alertness, concentration, quick reactions and a sober, safety-conscious state of mind. Many forms of illness or disability, alcohol or drug use, or simply tiredness can affect your ability to the point where you are not safe to be on the road. Remember: it doesn't matter how important it seems to get to a job appointment or friend's party – if you're not fit to drive, stay off the road.

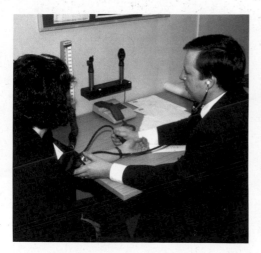

You must by law contact the DVLA if you develop a serious illness which may affect your driving

Even everyday medicines can impair your ability to drive, so always check the packet for warnings

health and safety

How you feel affects how you drive. If you develop a serious illness (see *It's the law* overleaf) then you must inform the DVLA. This won't necessarily mean you'll lose your licence, but the DVLA may ask you to undergo a medical check-up to ensure you are still fit to drive.

Less serious medical problems can also affect your safety behind the wheel. Even a severe cold or flu can lower your concentration and reactions and make you unfit to drive. If you're feeling unwell enough to need medication, then ask yourself if you are really fit enough to drive.

medicines

Many medicines can affect your ability to drive. Some of these are available without a prescription across the counter at a chemists.

Certain drugs prescribed to treat depression cause drowsiness and impair concentration. Driving should be avoided while taking these and for some months afterwards. Some tranquillisers and sleeping pills have similar side-effects.

Drugs available at a chemists without a prescription which impair driving include certain hayfever treatments and cold remedies. These can reduce concentration, slow reaction times and promote drowsiness, and they make driving particularly dangerous when taken with any amount of alcohol.

Whenever you take a medicine, carefully check the label for a warning – sometimes not as prominent as it might be – that you should not drive while using it. If prescribed a drug by your doctor, always ask if it will affect your driving.

If you drive to the pub, either don't drink any alcohol at all, or arrange to go home by taxi

alcohol

Drinking and driving don't mix. It's a message that has been rammed home by endless publicity campaigns in the last 30 years, but still around one in five drivers killed on the road is under the influence of alcohol.

When a driver has been drinking alcohol it makes them less in control of their vehicle, slows their reactions and impairs their ability to concentrate and judge speed accurately. It also gives them a false sense of confidence which can lead them to take dangerous risks.

The police treat drink-driving very seriously. Drivers involved in an accident are now routinely breathalysed; if convicted they face at least a one-year driving ban, as well as higher insurance premiums when they get back on the road.

Remember:

- ⊙ you must not drive if your breath alcohol level is higher than 35µg per 100ml (equivalent to a blood-alcohol level of 80mg per 100ml)
- ⊙ alcohol takes time to be broken down by the body and if you have had a heavy night's drinking session the chances are that you will still be over the limit the next morning
- ⊙ any amount of alcohol impairs your ability to drive safely, even if you're still under the legal limit. So if you plan to drink anything at all, the safest option is to leave your car at home.

Don't mix driving with drugs or alcohol: it's dangerous, illegal and the penalties are severe

Pay a visit to an optician and get your eyesight checked before you start learning to drive

illegal drugs

Outlawed drugs such as cannabis, ecstasy, cocaine and heroin have the potential to impair your driving and it is an offence to drive under their influence. These drugs can have unpredictable effects and users may remain affected for up to 72 hours after taking them. The police are cracking down on drug-driving and introducing roadside tests to identify drivers who are under the influence of drugs.

eyesight

You must be able to read the current style of numberplate (introduced in September 2001) at a distance of 20 metres (66 feet). If you need to wear contact lenses or spectacles to do this then you must wear them at all times when driving (it makes sense to keep spares in the car too, in case you lose or damage your usual pair). Other eye defects such as tunnel vision can also affect your driving so it's a good idea to take a full eye test before you start to learn, and again at regular intervals throughout your driving career.

it's the law

fit to drive?

You must by law inform the DVLA if you suffer any of the following:

→ epilepsy

→ giddiness, fainting or blackouts

→ a severe mental handicap

→ diabetes

→ heart pain while driving

→ Parkinson's disease

→ any chronic neurological condition

→ a serious memory problem

→ a stroke

→ brain surgery, a brain tumour or a severe head injury

→ severe psychiatric illness or mental disorder

→ long-term problems with your arms or legs

→ dependence on alcohol or drugs or chemical substances in the past three years

→ any visual disability which affects both eyes (not short/long sightedness or colour blindness)

→ have a pacemaker, defibrillator or anti-ventricular tachycardia device fitted.

2 behind the wheel

You've signed your provisional licence, you're sitting in a roadworthy car with a lawful supervisor beside you, you've checked your eyesight and health and you can't wait to start the engine and head off down the road. But try to be patient. You're in a complex piece of machinery and before you go anywhere you need to take a good look around and make sure you know exactly what all those switches do, how the controls work and what the warning lights mean. Remember, you could run into a patch of fog for the first time in the middle of your driving test – and the examiner won't be impressed if you have to search high and low to locate the switch that works the foglights.

instrument panel

speedometer

On most cars the speedometer shows both miles per hour (mph) and kilometres per hour (km/h). The kilometre scale is marked in smaller figures on the inner ring of the dial and should be ignored unless the car is driven overseas. Some cars have digital speedometers, or show the speed in km/h as a separate digital display. It is a legal requirement to have a working speedometer and it must not show a reading lower than the actual speed. If you ever fit a different size of wheel or tyre, you should get the speedometer checked as doing so may affect its accuracy.

fuel gauge

The fuel gauge gives a rough indication of how much fuel remains in the fuel tank. As this reaches the lower limit a fuel warning light may illuminate, indicating that only a few litres (check the car handbook for the exact amount) of fuel remains.

water temperature gauge

Until it is thoroughly warm the engine does not operate efficiently. Avoid working the engine hard until the dial reaches its normal working temperature, or you will waste fuel and cause extra engine wear.

The instrument panel is fitted with dials and warning lights which give you visual information while you drive. Only a few dials – such as the speedometer and fuel gauge – are truly essential. Some car makers deliberately keep the instrument panel simple to minimise distraction, and rely on warning lights to alert the driver if something goes wrong. Others take the view that the more information the driver has the better, and add a profusion of extra dials. Whatever is fitted to the car you're driving, you must make sure you know what all the dials and warning lights mean before driving off.

rev counter

Many cars are fitted with a rev counter (or tachometer) which shows the engine speed in revolutions per minute (rpm). Most engines tick over at around 1000rpm. The maximum engine speed permitted is usually indicated by a red line, marked on the dial at around 6000–7000rpm on a petrol engine. (Most cars also have a rev limiter which prevents the engine running too fast.)

other gauges

Additional gauges may be fitted to indicate oil temperature, oil pressure and battery charge. In some cars a trip computer gives a digital read-out of information including fuel consumption, journey time and average speed, and the distance the car will be able to cover on the fuel remaining (bear in mind that if fuel consumption increases, for instance on joining a motorway, this figure may drop alarmingly). Before driving, consult the car handbook for a full explanation of all the gauges fitted.

warning lights

Warning lights are fitted to alert you to serious faults and remind you about items which are switched on.

Lights monitoring your car's systems (such as the ignition, oil and ABS lights) should come on when you turn on the ignition, then extinguish. If they come on while you are driving, stop the car and investigate.

Reminder lights (such as fog lamps, heated rear window, headlight main beam) will illuminate when these items are in use.

other lights

Depending on the make or model of car there may be extra warning lights in addition to those explained here. These include low windscreen washer fluid level, service needed, clogged fuel filter, immobiliser fault and fasten seat belt reminder. Make sure that you know what all the warning lights in your car mean. If a light comes on that you don't recognise, stop at the first safe opportunity and consult your car handbook to see if it is safe to continue.

oil pressure
If this light comes on when driving
it means the oil pressure is low.
Stop as soon as possible to avoid
serious engine damage. Check the
oil level and top up if necessary, but
do not drive if the light stays on.

 ignition
If lit when the engine is running
this indicates there is a problem
with the battery charging system.

 **water (coolant)
temperature/level**
If lit when the engine is running the
engine is overheating or water level
is low. Stop as soon as possible and
investigate.

 ABS
If this lights up when driving it
indicates a problem with the anti-
lock brakes (see p46). Stop and
consult the handbook to see if
the car is still safe to drive, and
get the braking system checked
immediately.

 **handbrake/
brake warning**
Make sure the parking brake is
fully disengaged when the car is in
motion. If this light comes on while
driving, it may indicate low brake
fluid or a serious brake fault: stop
and consult the handbook.

 door/boot open
Warns if one of the doors or the
boot is not shut properly.

 left/right indicator
The warning light is accompanied
by an audible ticking when the
indicators are activated.

 air bag
If this lights up when driving it
indicates a fault with the airbag.
Get the car professionally checked
as soon as possible.

 **diesel
pre-heating**
Some diesel engines require pre-
heating and will not start after
turning on the ignition until this
light goes out.

 **heated rear
window**
Lights while the heated rear window
element is active.

 hazard warning
There is an audible ticking as well
as an in-car flashing light when
the hazard warning lights are
operating (see p58 for advice on
when to use them).

 side/headlamp on
Reminds that these lights are
switched on.

 **headlamp main
beam**
Warns that headlamps are on
main beam setting which may
dazzle other road users.

 fog light
Reminds that the rear fog lamp
is switched on. There may be a
separate warning light for front
fog lamps if fitted (see p190 for
advice on using fog lights).

 choke warning
In older cars only, this reminds
that the manual choke is out (see
p27 for how to use the choke).

All cars have lights, wipers, a horn and a heater. But the switches which operate them may be located in different places depending on the model of car. There may be a confusing variety of extra switchgear too. Some cars now have wipers and headlamps which work automatically, radar to help you park and an electronic voice to guide you to your destination using satellite navigation. Your driving instructor's car may not feature such refinements, but you must be prepared to cope with unusual switches whenever you get into an unfamiliar car. Before driving off you must know where each switch is, so when you need to sound the horn, flash the headlamps or flick on your windscreen wipers, you can do so instantly without having to take your eyes off the road.

windscreen wipers

These are usually activated by the right-hand stalk. Most offer a choice of intermittent, slow and fast settings. It is often possible to change the wiping frequency on the intermittent setting. Some cars have an automatic setting for rain-sensing windscreen wipers, but you should be prepared to override this if necessary.

windscreen washers

The windscreen washer jets are activated by pulling the stalk or pressing the end of it. Use them to clean mud or spray off the windscreen. Using the washers should automatically trigger several passes of the wipers to clear the windscreen.

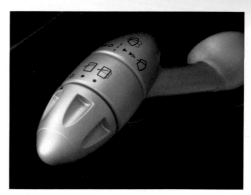

rear wiper/washer

Most hatchback and estate cars have a rear wiper and washer which should be used whenever rear visibility becomes obscured by dust or spray on the back window. Usually the switch for the rear wiper and washer is on the same stalk that operates the front windscreen wipers.

lights

Usually the lights are switched on by rotating the left-hand stalk. The first setting turns on the rear lights, number plate lights, and side lights (unless permanently-lit daytime running lights are fitted). In the second position the dipped headlights come on. For main beam, move the stalk either backwards or forwards.

direction indicators

Press the left-hand stalk up to activate the right indicators, down for the left indicators. The indicators are self-cancelling, and should stop automatically when you have turned a corner. In a few models the indicator stalk is on the right of the steering wheel and the wiper stalk on the left.

heating and ventilation

Basic heating/ventilation systems have a fan, a dial to control the temperature and another to direct the airflow onto the feet, face, or windscreen.

If fitted, air conditioning is useful for providing cooling air in hot weather (the windows must be kept shut to allow it to work effectively). Air conditioning also helps keep the windows free of mist in wet weather. Run the system regularly to keep it working properly.

Where fitted, climate control allows you to select a temperature at which the interior of the car will be automatically maintained whatever the weather outside.

Air recirculation shuts off air entering from outside and recirculates the air already in the car. This is useful when starting in icy conditions, as the inside of the car heats up more quickly with no cold air coming in. You can also use it to prevent unpleasant smells and exhaust fumes entering the cabin. But don't leave air recirculation on for too long: it makes the windows more prone to misting up, and the lack of fresh air can make you sleepy.

The heated rear window keeps the rear screen clear of mist and ice. Do not leave the rear screen heater on once the screen is clear as it drains a lot of power from the battery. Some models also have a front screen heating element.

For maximum demisting, select the highest temperature and fan setting, direct the airflow to the windscreen, and switch the screen heaters on.

Make sure you know how to set the heating to its maximum setting for demisting the windscreen

 ### headlamp adjustment

This adjusts the angle of the dipped headlamp beam to prevent it dazzling other road users when the car is heavily laden (see p211).

 ### fog lights

Cars must by law have at least one rear fog lamp. Front fog lamps are optional (see p190 for advice on using fog lights).

 ### electric windows

Use this switch to lower or raise the windows. Some feature one-touch operation. Where rear windows are electric, there may be a switch which you can use to deactivate them when young children are in the rear seats. Some cars have an electrically operated sunroof with switches usually located above the mirror.

 ### horn

Usually sounded by pressing part of the centre of the steering wheel. Make sure you know where the horn is before you have to use it in an emergency.

 ### central locking

Locks and unlocks the doors independently of the keyfob.

 ### traction/skid control

Abbreviations such as TSC, ASC or ESP refer to traction/skid control systems (see p195). Where fitted, it may be possible to switch off traction/skid control, but it is safer to leave it permanently engaged.

 ### cruise control

This allows the driver to set a constant speed at which the car cruises automatically. If fitted, use cruise control only in light traffic and read the manual to make sure you fully understand how it works.

 ### choke

Many older cars (from the mid-1980s or earlier) have a manual choke lever which needs to be pulled out before starting the car and for the first few miles of driving. Once the engine is warm make sure the choke is pushed all the way back in or fuel is wasted and engine damage may result.

 ### other switches

Depending on the model, various other switches may be fitted. Always consult the car handbook for a full explanation of all the switches before driving.

controls

Unlike the minor switchgear, the major controls are laid out in a similar fashion whatever the make of car. The pedals, from left to right, are the clutch, brake and accelerator, and they are in this order whether the car is right-hand drive (like a British car) or left-hand drive like those from mainland Europe. Operate the accelerator and brake with your right foot and the clutch with your left. In a right-hand drive car the gear lever is operated with the left hand, as is the parking brake which usually sits between the front seats.

steering wheel

Most cars have power-assisted steering which means less effort is needed to turn the wheel, though this assistance is only provided when the engine is running. A lever beneath the steering column may allow the position of the steering wheel to be adjusted up or down, and in or out. Most cars have a steering lock fitted as an anti-theft precaution. This means the steering locks into place if the wheel is turned without the key in the ignition. Once locked, it may be necessary to jiggle the wheel to allow the key to be turned in the ignition to release it.

parking brake

The parking or handbrake is a lever, usually between the front seats, which activates the rear brakes. Use your thumb to press in the button at the end of the lever and pull it up to engage it; after releasing the button push down on the lever to check it has secured properly. To release the handbrake, hold in the button and let down the lever. A few cars have foot-operated parking brakes, and some are now equipped with electronic parking brakes. These are operated by a switch or button, and some are designed to release automatically when you move off.

gear lever

Most cars have a gear lever next to the driver's left thigh, although in some the gear stick sprouts from the dashboard.

There will be five or six forward gears in addition to a reverse gear. The gears are laid out in an H pattern. The central bar of the H is the neutral position, and when the lever is in this position no gear is selected. This means the engine can idle with no power going to the wheels.

Reverse gear is normally on a dog leg to the left or right. Usually there's a device fitted to prevent reverse being selected by accident: depending on the model of car, you may have to lift a ring beneath the gear lever, or press the gear lever downwards, before reverse gear will engage.

Always fully depress the clutch pedal before engaging any gear.

You may need to lift the gear knob upwards or press it downwards to engage reverse gear

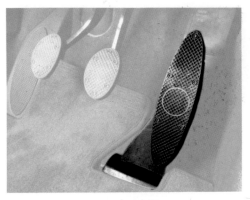

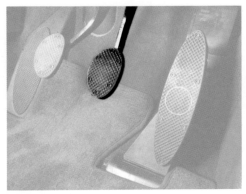

accelerator pedal

Pressing your right foot on the accelerator pedal (also called the gas pedal or throttle) increases the flow of fuel to the engine, giving extra power when you need to increase the speed of the car or climb hills. Light and gentle use of the accelerator improves fuel economy and ensures a smooth driving style.

brake pedal

Use your right foot to operate the brake pedal, which applies the brakes on all four wheels. On most cars the brakes are servo-assisted, which means no more than a gentle pressure is needed to slow the car. Pressing the brake pedal also operates the rear brake lights, giving a warning to following traffic that you are slowing.

how the clutch works

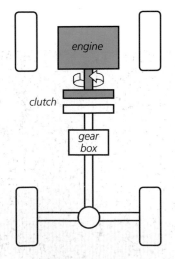

Clutch pedal fully depressed: the gear box is separated from the engine, no power is being transmitted to the wheels and the car is stationary

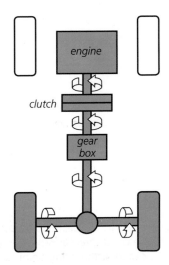

Clutch pedal fully released: the gear box is joined to the engine, power is being transmitted, to the wheels and the car is now in motion

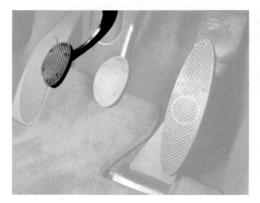

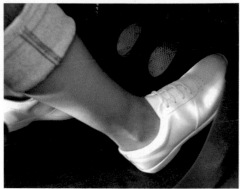

Wear sensible, flat-soled shoes when driving to prevent your feet slipping off the pedals

clutch pedal

The left-hand pedal in a manual car operates the clutch. When the clutch pedal is pressed down, it disconnects the engine from the wheels. This allows the car to stop without stalling the engine.

The clutch consists of a pair of friction plates which are pulled apart when the clutch pedal is pressed down.

As you let the clutch pedal up, the two plates touch and power starts to be transmitted to the wheels. This is termed the 'biting point'. The further you release the clutch pedal, the more power is transmitted. Once the clutch pedal is fully released the clutch plates lock together and all the power from the engine is delivered to the wheels. When you hold the pedal so the clutch is only half engaged, it is called 'slipping the clutch' or 'clutch control'. Clutch control is useful when you want to drive very slowly – for instance when carrying out low-speed manoeuvres – but you should take care not to slip the clutch for too long or premature wear to the clutch plates will result.

Never:

- ⊖ rest your foot on the clutch pedal while you are driving as this causes unnecessary wear to the clutch mechanism
- ⊖ hold the clutch at the biting point to prevent the car from rolling back on a slope. Always apply the handbrake when you come to a halt on a hill.

know the code

highway code rule 122

Coasting This term describes a vehicle travelling in neutral or with the clutch pressed down. It can reduce driver control because:

- ➔ engine braking is eliminated
- ➔ vehicle speed downhill will increase quickly
- ➔ increased use of the footbrake can reduce its effectiveness
- ➔ steering response will be affected, particularly on bends and corners
- ➔ it may be more difficult to select the appropriate gear when needed.

safety checks

Airline pilots carry out a detailed routine of instrument checks before they even think of heading for the runway. Driving a car doesn't involve quite such a complex cockpit drill, but it is essential that you always run through a short series of checks to ensure that you are sitting comfortably and safely before driving off. Get in the habit of carrying out these checks every time you get into the car.

cockpit drill

Before turning the key in the ignition, you must always:

- ⊙ check that the doors and boot are fully closed
- ⊙ adjust your seat and steering wheel to give you the correct driving position
- ⊙ check that your head restraint is in the right position
- ⊙ put on your seatbelt
- ⊙ check your mirrors are properly adjusted
- ⊙ check the handbrake is on
- ⊙ ensure the gear lever is in neutral (or in Park [P] or Neutral [N] in an automatic).

sitting comfortably

Finding a comfortable driving position is vital. You need to be able to reach all the controls without stretching. At the same time you don't want to sit too close to the wheel – which could be dangerous in a crash – or adopt an awkward posture which will put a stain on your back. Follow these steps to achieve a comfortable driving position:

- ⊙ raise the seat as high as possible without your head making contact with the roof
- ⊙ move the seat forwards until you can easily depress the clutch pedal and accelerator fully
- ⊙ tilt the base of the seat so that it provides support along the length of your thighs
- ⊙ recline the seat back to the point where your shoulders and upper back are resting comfortably on the seat and your arms are slightly bent when you hold the steering wheel in the 'ten-to-two' position. Avoid sitting too upright, as this can put a strain on your wrists and shoulders as you lean forward to grip the wheel, or reclining too far back, as this means your neck muscles have to work harder to support your head

Adjust the seat and steering wheel to give yourself a comfortable driving position

- ⊙ adjust the height and reach of the steering column so your hands are resting comfortably a little lower than your shoulders, and you can see the instrument panel clearly
- ⊙ if fitted, lumbar support can give extra support for the lower part of your back and help prevent backache on a long journey. But too much lumbar support does more harm than good. Only if you feel a lack of support should you slowly turn the knob on the side of the seat back until you feel a slight, even pressure.

A correctly adjusted head restraint can significantly reduce the risk of neck injury in a crash

Adjust the door mirrors so that the side of your car can just be seen in the edge of the mirror

seatbelt

You must by law wear your seatbelt at all times while driving a car, except:

- when carrying out reversing manoeuvres
- if you have a medical exemption certificate.

Most cars have a seatbelt height adjuster on the door pillar by your right shoulder. Move this down until the belt gives a firm but not excessive pressure over the top of your right shoulder, with no gap between the belt and the front of your shoulder. Do not position the adjuster any lower than shoulder height.

head restraint

It's sometimes called a head rest, but it's not there to rest your head on. The head restraint performs an important safety function. If a vehicle collides with the rear of your car, your head may be jerked abruptly backwards, causing your neck to suffer whiplash injuries. The head restraint helps prevent this, but only if it is correctly adjusted, so check it before driving off. The base of the head restraint should be level with the base of your skull where it meets the top of the neck, and the restraint should be about an inch away from the back of your head while driving.

mirrors

Your mirrors should be positioned so that you can see what is happening behind you at a glance, without moving your head unnecessarily. Adjust the interior rear view mirror while you are in your normal driving position with your seatbelt fastened. A lever beneath the mirror shifts the angle of the mirror at night to reduce the glare from following headlamps (some cars have mirrors which react automatically to reduce glare at night). Side mirrors are adjustable from inside the car, either manually or by an electric switch. Adjust them so just a sliver of the side of the car is showing in the mirror, and there is a roughly equal proportion of road and sky visible.

handbrake

Check this is securely engaged by pulling the lever upwards slightly.

gears in neutral

Always check the gear lever is in neutral before starting the engine. If it is in gear then the engine will not start when you turn the key in the ignition. Instead, the car will lurch forwards (or backwards if it is in reverse gear), causing a potential hazard.

Twist the key all the way to start the engine but remember to release it the instant the engine fires

A growing number of cars now have keyless ignition with a separate starter button

starting the engine

The ignition switch usually has four positions:

0: the ignition is switched off

I: disengages the steering lock and operates some electrical systems, such as the radio

II: turns on the ignition and activates the warning lights and dials

III: activates the starter motor.

Once started the engine should settle to a steady tickover at around 1000rpm (revs per minute)

To start the engine, turn the key all the way to position III. You will hear a whirr as the starter motor activates and turns the engine. Release the key as soon as the engine fires or the starter motor may be damaged. The switch is spring loaded so the key returns to position II automatically.

In some cars an ignition button rather than a key is used to activate the starter motor.

In a modern car fitted with fuel-injection you should not press the accelerator pedal while starting the engine (though it may be necessary to do this with older vehicles).

When the engine starts, let it settle to a steady tickover. Make sure the ignition and oil pressure lights have gone out.

3 car control

Mastering the car's main controls is the first step in learning to drive. It's a lot easier than it used to be because today's cars have light, smooth controls designed for ease of use. Power steering is fitted to just about all new cars, taking the effort out of turning the wheel even in tight parking spaces. Brakes are servo-assisted and need only a light pressure to bring the car to a swift halt. It can take a bit longer to get the knack of clutch control and smooth gear changing, but this too should soon become second nature.

moving off

Turning a stationary car into a moving one demands careful co-ordination of clutch and accelerator pedals. Everyone takes a bit of time to master this, and you can expect your fair share of jerky starts and the occasional stall. Don't despair – keep practising and you'll soon get the hang of it. In these early days of driving you can't expect to be in full control of the car, so it's best to start out on a quiet, clear piece of road, with an experienced driving instructor sitting beside you.

moving off on the level

- press the clutch pedal to the floor
- engage first gear
- press the accelerator pedal gently until the engine revs rise
- let the clutch up gradually until you can feel the biting point
- release the handbrake
- bring the clutch pedal smoothly upwards while gradually increasing the pressure on the accelerator.

Extra power is needed to prevent the engine stalling when you are moving off uphill

stalling

If you bring up the clutch too quickly or don't apply enough power, the engine may cut out. This is called stalling. A common reason for stalling is trying to start in third gear instead of first by mistake – so check that you're in the right gear before you try again to move off after stalling.

moving off at an angle

Often you need to move off and at the same time steer round an obstacle such as a parked car. This means moving off very slowly to give yourself time to check all around your car while you pull out. To do this you need to use clutch control: lift the clutch pedal just past the biting point and press on the accelerator until the car starts to creep forward. Keep looking all around for other vehicles, pedestrians or cyclists as you pull out.

hill starts

Uphill Moving off uphill needs more power to prevent the engine stalling. It's vital not to let the car roll backwards, which could be dangerous. To hold the car steady, press more firmly on the accelerator and hold the clutch a little further past the biting point than you would on the level. After releasing the handbrake, apply a little more power to move off while releasing the clutch fully.

Downhill Keep your right foot on the brake, not the accelerator. Find the clutch biting point, release the handbrake, then ease off the brake pedal. As the car rolls forward, release the clutch fully and apply some power. On a steep downhill slope, moving off in second gear instead of first can give a smoother start.

know the code

highway code rule 159

Before moving off you should

→ use all mirrors to check the road is clear

→ look round to check the blind spots (the areas you are unable to see in the mirrors)

→ signal if necessary before moving out

→ look round for a final check.

Move off only when it is safe to do so.

test tips

do

- remember to carry out the cockpit drill (p32–5) before moving off at the start of your test

- stay cool if you stall the engine. This isn't normally considered a serious fault – but if you panic, restart the engine and drive off without rechecking your mirrors and blind spot, it will be

don't

→ let the car roll back on a hill start

→ block the path of oncoming traffic when pulling out from behind a parked car on a narrow road.

changing gear

If you've ridden a bicycle fitted with gears you'll understand the effect that choice of gear has on speed, as well as on the amount of work the rider has to do. Try to move off in too high a gear and you'll struggle to turn the pedals. Stay in a low gear on a level stretch of road and you'll find yourself pedalling furiously for no extra forward velocity. It's the same in a car, except that the engine does the work instead of the rider. The low gears provide lots of acceleration but run out of steam before the car is travelling very quickly. Higher gears provide plenty of road speed, but not much acceleration. Your job is to match the gears to the speed of the car, moving up the gearbox as your speed rises, and to select a lower gear when more power is needed, for instance when overtaking or approaching a steep hill.

It can be easier to select the right gear if you cup your palm round the gear knob on the opposite side to the gear you want, rather than placing your hand directly on top of the gear knob

how to change gear

- ⊃ release the accelerator pedal and at the same time press down the clutch to disengage the engine from the gearbox
- ⊃ cup your hand around the gearknob and move the lever gently but positively from one position to another
- ⊃ re-engage the clutch and simultaneously apply the power.

Although it sounds straightforward, changing gear requires careful co-ordination of foot and hand movements, so don't be surprised if your gear changes feel clumsy at first. Practice makes perfect, and by the time you are ready for your test you should not be having to concentrate to make smooth gear changes.

Don't use unnecessary force when changing gear. Ease the lever from one position to another, and try not to rush your changes.

To make even smoother changes down the gearbox, keep your foot slightly on the accelerator as you shift the gear lever. The engine revs rise to match the gear selected – which means that with practice you can make your changes down the gearbox almost seamless.

selecting the right gear

You don't have to use the gears in exact sequence. Where appropriate, you can skip a gear, which is called 'block changing'. For instance, when overtaking a slower vehicle you might accelerate in third gear from 40mph to 60mph, then change directly from third into fifth once you are safely past.

When approaching a hazard such as a road junction or roundabout, you should first reduce your speed, then select the appropriate gear to negotiate the hazard. This may mean changing directly from fifth gear into second gear. Changing sequentially down through the gear box in this situation would be pointless, making your progress less smooth and causing unnecessary clutch wear.

test tips

do
- ⊃ make smooth, unhurried gear changes
- ⊃ change down in good time when approaching a hazard or road junction
- ⊃ carry out block changing where appropriate

don't
- → rest your hand on the gear lever while not changing gear
- → look at the gear lever while changing gear, keep your eyes on the road
- → race the engine unnecessarily, especially in the lower gears
- → coast when approaching a hazard (see know the code, p31).

automatics

Don't ignore this section just because you're preparing for the test in a manual car – you are sure to find yourself behind the wheel of an automatic at some stage in your driving career. Automatic transmissions have always been less popular than manuals for three reasons: they give less precise control over gear selection, they are thirstier on fuel and they add extra cost to a new car. But automatics are getting increasingly sophisticated and economical. Don't be surprised if in 20 years time a manual gearbox has become an unusual option and automatics are the norm.

taking your test

It makes a lot of sense to take your test in a manual even if you intend to drive an automatic, because passing in a manual qualifies you to drive both manual and automatic cars. If you pass in a car which isn't fitted with a clutch pedal, your licence won't cover driving a manual.

how an auto works

In an automatic there are just two pedals – the accelerator and brake. When the transmission is put into Drive (D) the car changes gears automatically according to the load on the engine and the road speed. A CVT automatic uses pulleys and belts to change the gearing continuously, giving a smoother drive and better economy.

Semi-automatic transmissions are becoming more common. They give the driver the choice of leaving the gearbox in automatic – though gearshifts may not be as smooth as in a true auto – or changing gear manually by way of an electronic gear selector such as paddles mounted on the steering wheel. Various different systems exist so consult the car handbook carefully before driving.

Semi-automatic transmissions are becoming more popular; they give all the control of a manual without the effort of operating a clutch pedal

driving an automatic

Automatic transmissions vary from car to car, so it's important to read the handbook to get the best out of each system. In general, follow this advice:

⊘ check the gear shift is in Park (P) and your foot firmly on the brake pedal before trying to start the ignition. Most autos are designed not to start unless these precautions are taken

⊘ when you are ready to drive away, move the lever out of Park and into Drive (D). To do this you will need to push in the security button mounted on the gear lever. Hold down the footbrake as the car will try to creep forward as soon as Drive is engaged

⊘ do not use your left foot for braking. You could confuse which foot you should be using if you have to brake in an emergency

⊘ when coming to a brief halt, for instance at traffic lights, there is no need to move the gear shift out of Drive, but you must always use the parking brake to ensure the car is safely immobilised

⊘ if you need to accelerate quickly while the gearbox is in Drive, for instance to overtake another vehicle, press down firmly on the accelerator. This causes the gearbox to kick down automatically to a lower gear.

⊘ on steep downhill sections engage a lower gear manually to give extra engine braking. The lower gears are marked with numbers equivalent to the intermediate gears on a manual (first gear is sometimes marked L for Low). You should also select these positions to give extra control over the gears when overtaking or cornering, in heavy traffic, or to stop the gearbox changing gear unnecessarily when climbing uphill

⊘ on stopping the car at the end of the journey, put the gear shift into Park and engage the parking brake before switching off the ignition.

steering

Turning the steering wheel causes the front wheels to change direction, which makes the car alter course. But because only the front wheels do the steering, you must remember to leave extra room on tight turns to stop the rear wheels clipping the kerb. Just about every car on sale nowadays has power-assisted steering, which is light and easy to use. If you drive a car without power assistance you will find it needs much more effort to turn the wheel at low speeds and when parking.

holding the wheel

Imagine the steering wheel is a clock face and keep your hands in the 'ten-to-two' or 'quarter-to-three' position, whichever you find more comfortable. Grasp the wheel firmly but not tightly and keep both hands on the wheel except when you have to take one hand off to operate another control. Never take both hands off the wheel while you are driving.

turning the wheel

For small steering movements you can keep your hands in the ten-to-two position. However, when turning a sharp corner you will need to feed the wheel smoothly through your hands. You should also do this as you straighten the wheel after a turn – allowing the wheel to spin back can lead to loss of control.

When turning the wheel, it's important to look in the direction that you want the car to turn. Looking where you want the car to go helps your brain to send the right messages to your arms and hands about just how much to turn the wheel and when to start straightening up.

dry steering

Turning the steering wheel when the car isn't moving is called dry steering. It's not a good idea because it puts unnecessary strain on the steering mechanism, and causes premature wear to the front tyres. When carrying out a low-speed manoeuvre, get the car moving before you start to steer.

steering lock

When you turn the steering wheel as far as it will go it is at full steering lock. This is the maximum angle the front wheels will reach, and on full lock the car's turning circle – the space it needs to turn around in the road – is at its smallest.

Avoid crossing your hands on the wheel – this could prevent you keeping control of the steering

The greater the steering lock, the easier it is to manoeuvre the car in and out of tight spaces

braking

Modern cars have extremely effective brakes and you may be surprised
when you carry out your first emergency stop just how powerful the
brakes can be. But in everyday driving you should aim to use the
brakes as little as possible by anticipating the need to slow down well
in advance. Harsh, late braking is a sign of poor driving and it will not
impress the examiner on your driving test.

using the brakes

Apply the brakes gently at first, then progressively increase the pressure. Never brake harshly, or you risk making the wheels 'lock up' – stop rotating – and the car will skid. Once the front wheels start skidding you lose the ability to steer the car and will not be able to avoid obstacles in the road ahead. Special care is needed when the roads are wet or icy as the risk of skidding becomes much higher.

Try to brake only when the car is travelling in a straight line. Tyres have a limited amount of grip. They can use this grip to help the car go around a corner, or to help it stop. If you ask your tyres to do both these things at once there may not be enough grip to go round, causing a skid.

anti-lock brakes

An anti-lock braking system (ABS) works electronically to prevent the wheels from locking up and skidding under emergency braking. This means that you can still steer the car, which you would not be able to do with the wheels locked.

ABS works by sensing when the wheels are on the point of locking up. At this point it releases the brakes momentarily and reapplies them, then repeats this cycle several times a second.

Even with ABS fitted it still takes longer to stop on a wet or slippery surface, and ABS may not prevent skidding on a loose surface or where there is standing water on the road.

test tips

do
- brake smoothly and progressively
- find out if your car is fitted with ABS well before your driving test

don't
- leave your braking to the last moment
- forget after the excitement of the emergency stop to carry out proper observation before moving off again.

emergency stop

You may be required to carry out an emergency stop during your driving test. The technique depends on whether or not your car is fitted with ABS.

Without ABS: Keep both hands firmly grasping the steering wheel. Brake firmly, but not so hard that the wheels lock up and you start to skid. If the wheels do lock, ease off the brake until they start to rotate again then reapply the brake less harshly. Press the clutch down just before you come to a halt to prevent the engine stalling.

With ABS: Keep both hands firmly grasping the steering wheel. Press as hard as you can on the brake pedal and keep full pressure applied until you come to a stop. Don't be put off by any noise or pulsating sensation you feel through the brake pedal – this is a normal feature of ABS. Press the clutch down just before you come to a halt to prevent the engine stalling.

brake fade

Overuse of the brakes can cause them to overheat and lose efficiency – known as brake fade. This is most likely when driving down a steep hill, when heavily laden or towing, or if the brakes are worn. If brake fade occurs, stop and let the brakes cool before continuing, and get the braking system checked as soon as possible.

engine braking

When you lift off the accelerator the engine slows the car even if you don't put your foot on the brake pedal. Engine braking is hardly noticeable in top gear, but in the lower ratios it is much more effective. Make use of engine braking by selecting a lower gear to give more control when descending a steep hill.

handbrake

Apply the handbrake to secure the car whenever you are stationary for more than a few seconds. The handbrake should never be used while the car is moving.

car control

stopping

There's more to stopping than just pressing the brake pedal and bringing the car to a halt. First you have to select a suitable place to stop, where you won't be endangering or inconveniencing any other road users.

stopping

When stopping at the side of the road, you should aim to pull up close and parallel to the side of the road.

To do this, lift off the power and gently steer towards the kerb, braking smoothly and progressively as you do so. As you get near to the kerb, steer away from it and then straighten the steering wheel. Just before the car stops, press the clutch pedal down to prevent the engine stalling. Easing off the brake pedal as you come to a halt will prevent the car stopping with a jerk.

Avoid letting the wheels touch the kerb as this might damage the wheels and tyres.

where to stop

During your test your examiner will ask you to pull up at a convenient place on the left to carry out a manoeuvre. This doesn't necessarily mean you are expected to pull immediately to the side of the road. You must use your judgement to select an appropriate place to stop where you will not be endangering, inconveniencing or obstructing anyone.

Don't stop or park:

- near a school entrance
- where you would prevent emergency access
- at or near a bus stop or taxi rank
- on the approach to a level crossing
- opposite or within ten metres of a junction
- near the brow of a hill or hump bridge
- opposite a traffic island
- opposite another parked vehicle if it would cause an obstruction
- where you would force other traffic to enter a tram lane
- where the kerb has been lowered to help wheelchair users
- in front of an entrance to a property
- on a bend
- where you would obstruct cyclists from using cycle facilities

Places where you must not stop include level crossings (left) and school entrances (right)

learn to drive

4 reading the road

When you start to drive you may be surprised by how much information there is on the road to help you drive safely. Road markings and signs warn of a whole range of hazards as well as giving you instructions and information. Then there are the signals coming from other drivers. Their indicators, brake lights and even how they position themselves on the road tell you a lot about what they are going to do. Meanwhile you need to communicate to everyone else what you intend to do by giving clear and accurate signals yourself.

mirrors

You need to use your mirrors to observe what is happening all around your car. Modern cars have three mirrors – an interior mirror and two exterior or door mirrors. Use all three to stay aware of what traffic around you is doing, and be sure to always check your mirrors before changing your speed or position on the road.

adjusting mirrors

Always make sure your mirrors are correctly adjusted and clean before starting the engine (see p34). Check again after going through a car wash in case the door mirrors have been knocked out of position.

On frosty mornings make sure you de-ice your door mirrors along with all the windows before driving off. If your car has heated door mirrors, switching them on will help stop condensation forming on the mirrors.

Don't hang anything from your interior mirror. It will restrict your view and distract your attention

image distortion

Compare the images in your interior and exterior mirrors. You may find the image on the exterior mirrors is smaller because these mirrors use convex curved glass. This means you get a greater field of view, but it will also make following vehicles look like they are further away than they really are.

blind spot

Even with your mirrors perfectly adjusted there are areas around the car which do not appear in any of your mirrors. The most dangerous of these blind spots is the one behind your right shoulder. If you check your mirrors frequently you can reduce the chance of a vehicle creeping unseen into this blind spot but there are times – such as before pulling out from the kerb or joining a motorway or dual carriageway from a slip road – when it is essential to glance over your right shoulder to make sure there is nothing hidden in your blind spot.

Some door mirrors have curved glass which makes vehicles seem further away than they really are

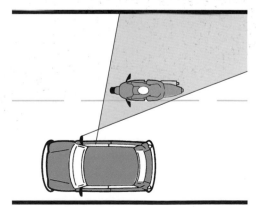

nearside and offside

These terms are sometimes used when referring to door mirrors. The nearside mirror is the one nearest the kerb (that is, on the left-hand side of the car); the offside door mirror is the one on the right-hand side.

Always remember the blind spot between your mirrors where a vehicle may be hidden from view

using your mirrors

You need to keep alert to what is happening behind you at all times when you are driving. Get into the habit of glancing frequently in your interior mirror to monitor what following traffic is doing. That way you will never be caught out by a car or motorbike overtaking unexpectedly.

You must always check your mirrors before carrying out any manoeuvre that affects your speed or position on the road. This includes:

Use your door mirrors to check for vehicles which are alongside you or about to overtake

- **moving off**
  Check your mirrors, and back this up with a glance over your right shoulder to confirm that nothing is in your blind spot
- **changing lanes**
  Use your mirrors plus a shoulder glance to check the blind spot
- **overtaking**
  Use your mirrors, especially your right door mirror, to check no one is about to overtake you before you begin the manoeuvre
- **turning right or left**
  Check the appropriate door mirror before turning. Never forget to check the left-hand mirror when turning left in town – a cyclist may be passing on the inside

It's vital to glance over your shoulder before pulling out to make sure your blind spot is clear

- **slowing down or stopping**
  A vehicle following too closely may not be able to stop in time when you brake. Check your mirror in good time so you can lose speed more gently if necessary
- **increasing speed**
  Check your mirrors before accelerating, for instance when leaving a lower speed limit, in case a following vehicle is about to overtake you
- **leaving the car**
  Always check your mirrors and blind spot before opening the door in case a vehicle is passing.

Check your nearside door mirror before turning left in case a cyclist is passing on the inside

mirror-signal-manoeuvre

The mirror-signal-manoeuvre routine is fundamental to safe driving. Every time you intend to change your speed or position you must first check your mirrors. Next give a signal if it might help other road users. Only then can you start to carry out the manoeuvre.

The mirror-signal-manoeuvre routine must become an automatic part of your driving. But be careful not to let yourself fall into the trap of doing it without considering *why* you are doing it.

You must start the sequence sufficiently in advance of your planned manoeuvre to allow yourself plenty of time to act on what you see in the mirror.

For instance, suppose you are planning to move from the left to the right-hand lane of a dual carriageway. A mirror check shows a car about to overtake you in that lane. You need to act on this information and delay giving a signal until the car has gone past – if you signal too early the message you are sending to the overtaking car is that you haven't noticed it's there.

1 mirror

2 signal

3 manoeuvre

test tips

do
- ➲ ensure your mirrors are properly adjusted before driving off
- ➲ check your mirrors frequently even on a straight clear road

don't
- ➲ gaze in the mirror for seconds at a time: your mirror checks should be frequent but brief
- ➲ emphasise your mirror checks by turning your whole head towards the interior mirror – the examiner can see you are using your mirrors without you having to do this.

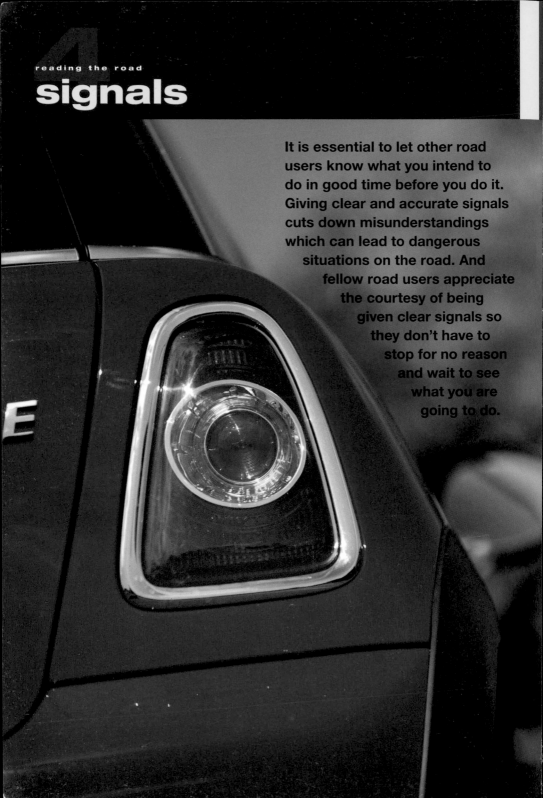

signals

It is essential to let other road users know what you intend to do in good time before you do it. Giving clear and accurate signals cuts down misunderstandings which can lead to dangerous situations on the road. And fellow road users appreciate the courtesy of being given clear signals so they don't have to stop for no reason and wait to see what you are going to do.

Give a signal well in advance when you have to change lanes so that other road users have plenty of time to see and react to your signal

indicators

Use your indicators – the flashing amber lights situated at each corner of the car – to signal that you intend to move out or change direction. Always:

- give a signal in good time so other road users have time to react to it before you start changing your speed or position. If a road user shows no sign of reacting to your signal, don't carry out the manoeuvre until you're sure they have seen you
- think before using your indicators. Identify who may benefit from a signal and make that signal as clear as possible. There's no point indicating if there is no one in the vicinity to see your signals
- avoid making ambiguous signals. For instance, if you want to pull into the kerb just after a left turn, don't indicate until you are past the turning, or other drivers may think you're turning left
- make sure your indicator is cancelled after carrying out a manoeuvre, or you could mislead other road users.

Don't signal where it might confuse other road users. For instance, if you want to turn left into a driveway immediately after this junction, you should wait until you are past the junction before signalling. If you signal too early, the driver waiting to emerge might pull out in front of you, thinking you intend to turn into the side road

Brake signals give a useful advanced warning that traffic ahead is slowing down or stopping

Engaging reverse gear activates your reversing light which helps indicate your intentions to others

brake signal

Each time you press the brake pedal the rear warning lights come on, giving a signal to traffic behind that you are slowing down. You can also press gently on the brake pedal to warn following drivers that you intend to slow for a hazard which they may not yet have noticed.

There are other situations where the brake lights can give a useful warning. For instance, pressing the brake pedal as well as engaging the handbrake while you are stopped at roadworks or traffic lights can help alert approaching drivers that you are stationary. But remember to release the brake pedal once a vehicle has pulled up behind you or your brake lights may dazzle and irritate the driver.

hazard warning lights

Use these:

⊙ when you have broken down

⊙ when your car is temporarily obstructing traffic

⊙ while driving on a dual carriageway or motorway to warn other road users of a hazard ahead.

Do not use them:

⊙ as an excuse for dangerous or illegal parking

⊙ while towing or being towed.

reversing signal

White reversing lights come on at the back of the car when you engage reverse gear. This can be useful to signal to other road users or pedestrians that you intend to reverse into a parking space or around a corner. But avoid engaging reverse where it could worry approaching drivers, who might think you're about to back out in front of them without giving way.

headlamp flash

This signal has only one meaning, which is to alert another road user to your presence. A headlamp flash is useful in situations where a horn may not be heard, such as at high speed on a motorway, or at night when horn use is not permitted.

Don't flash your headlamps for the wrong reason. It must never be done to intimidate a slower driver or to give instructions to another driver – you might know what *you* mean when you flash your lights, but the other driver may not, with potentially dangerous consequences.

The same reasoning applies if another car flashes its headlights at you. Don't assume this is an invitation to drive on – the driver may intend it to mean 'stop, I'm coming through'. Always wait until you are certain what the other driver is doing before proceeding.

Treat signals from other drivers with caution: they may not necessarily mean what you think they do

Make sure you know where the horn button is so that you can find it instantly in an emergency

acting on signals

Imagine you are waiting to emerge from a T-junction. The road is clear to the left, and a car is approaching from the right with its left-hand indicator flashing. Does it mean that the driver is about to turn into your junction so it's safe for you to pull out ahead of it? Or does it mean that the driver:

- ◯ is hard of hearing and has forgotten to cancel the indicator since their last manoeuvre
- ◯ has knocked on the indicators by mistake while reaching for the radio
- ◯ intends to pull left into a driveway immediately past your junction
- ◯ has a faulty indicator switch?

The answer, of course, is any of the above. Never assume another driver is about to do something simply because they are indicating. Always wait for them to confirm the signal, for instance by slowing down or starting to turn, before making any manoeuvre in front of them.

Be cautious if you see another driver signalling for no apparent reason. Never overtake a vehicle that is indicating right, even if you think that the driver has left on their indicator by mistake.

horn

The horn is one of the most misused items on the car. Never sound the horn to tick off another driver who you think has driven badly. This achieves nothing, and it may provoke an aggressive response. Use the horn only to alert another road user who you think may not have noticed that you are there. Give a short toot and consider raising your hand to show there was no aggressive intent on your part.

It is illegal to sound the horn when you are stationary, or in a built-up area between 11.30pm and 7.00am except when another moving vehicle poses a danger to you.

test tips

do

- ◯ give an arm signal if it will make the meaning of your indicators more obvious
- ◯ use your horn in a dangerous situation where you think another driver hasn't seen you

don't

- ➜ give a signal when there is nobody to benefit from it
- ➜ give any signals which are not in the Highway Code
- ➜ use your horn or lights to reprimand other road users.

Never wave pedestrians across the road. You could put them in danger if they walk out without checking for themselves that the road is clear

A police officer (or other authorised person) may direct you with arm signals. Make sure you know what these signals mean as you must obey them

arm signals

Although arm signals are rarely used nowadays, there are certain situations when an arm signal can be really useful to confirm a signal given by your indicator. For instance:

- ⊃ a right turn arm signal emphasises that you are turning right and not just passing a parked car
- ⊃ a slowing down arm signal makes your intention clear when you want to show you are pulling in to the kerb, not turning left
- ⊃ a slowing down arm signal is clearly visible when your indicators are hard to see because of strong sunlight
- ⊃ pedestrians waiting at a crossing can't see your brake lights. Giving the slowing down arm signal tells them you are about to stop.

You will not be asked to give arm signals in your test but you must be able to recognise what the different arm signals mean.

arm signals given by drivers and riders

| *I intend to move to the left or turn left* | *I intend to move to the right or turn right* | *I intend to slow down or stop* |

police directing traffic

When traffic lights fail or when traffic is unusually heavy, a police officer may use arm signals to direct the traffic flow.

Familiarise yourself with these signals, and also the signals you should give to tell the officer which way you want to go. You must by law obey arm signals given by authorised persons – police officers, Highways Agency traffic officers and traffic wardens – as well as signs displayed by school crossing patrols.

Consider making an arm signal where it would be helpful, for example to show waiting pedestrians you are slowing as you approach a zebra crossing

You must by law stop and wait whenever a school crossing patrol signals you to do so

arm signals given by authorised persons

Traffic coming from the front must stop	Traffic approaching from behind must stop	Traffic from both front and behind must stop

Traffic from the side may proceed	Traffic from the front may proceed	Traffic from behind may proceed

arm signals to persons controlling traffic

I want to go straight on	I want to turn left	I want to turn right

road signs

Road signs give drivers vital information and you must obey them to stay safe and within the law. Many signs show simplified pictures instead of written instructions, which makes it easier to take in the message at a glance. You must be able to recognise and understand the meaning of all road signs. More importantly, you must act on the information given by signs. If there's a sign warning of a hazard ahead – such as an uneven road surface, no footway, slippery road or traffic queues – you should consider adjusting your speed and position on the road so that you are ready to deal safely with the hazard when you encounter it.

shapes and colours

You'll know that some signs are round, some square and some triangular, and that they come in different colours, but you may not realise why. In fact, all these shapes and colours have distinct meanings.

Circular signs give orders.

Those with a red border tell you what you must not do. For example:

Triangular signs warn of a hazard on the road ahead.

For example:

Blue rectangular signs give information.

For example:

no motorcycles   *no overtaking*

children crossing   *low bridge*

no through road   *end of motorway*

Blue circular signs tell you what you must do. For example:

minimum speed 30 mph   *turn left ahead*

unique shapes

Two particularly important traffic signs have unique shapes: the give way sign is an upside down triangle, and the stop sign is an octagon.

The reason? So that even if these signs are obscured by snow and can't be read, drivers can still recognise them by their shape alone.

give way sign is an inverted triangle

stop sign is octagonal

directions

Direction signs use different colours depending on what sort of road they are on. Signs on motorways are blue, those on primary routes are green, those on other roads are white with a black border, diversion signs are yellow and signs showing local attractions are brown.

MORDEN PARK CORNER
Dorchester A35
Weymouth (A353)
Bere Regis

Morden
B3075
Blandford
(A350)

Sandford
B3075
Wareham
(A352)

YG60 UGX

route finding

On unfamiliar roads it is vital to be able to use road signs to find the right route. You must be able to read and interpret signs to enable you to position your car in good time to make a turning. This is an ability that will be tested during the independent driving section of your practical test.

Generally, the more important the road, the more warning you get of the turning. Minor roads often have no advance warning sign at all, with just a small finger signpost to show where to turn. Major roads provide more warning, with a sign in advance of the turning and also a sign to confirm the route you're on after the junction. On motorways, junctions are numbered, and signposted at one mile and half a mile before the exit.

motorways (blue signs)

left-hand lane leads to a different destination (the arrows pointing downwards mean 'get in lane')

inclined arrow indicates the destinations that can be reached by leaving motorway at next junction

sign placed at a junction leading onto a motorway

on approach to motorway junction ('25' is the junction number)

route confirmed after the junction

diversions (yellow signs)

when you encounter a diversion, follow the signs or the symbols that indicate the alternative route

non-primary and local routes (white signs)

signs on the approach to the junction. Route numbers on a blue background show the way to a motorway; those on green show the way to a primary road

sign at the junction

primary routes (green signs)

on the approach to the junction

at the junction (symbol warns of a hazard on this route)

blue panel indicates that the motorway starts at the next junction; motorways in brackets can also be reached along the route indicated

bilingual sign in Wales

route confirmed after junction

local attractions (brown signs)

tourist attraction *camp site* *picnic site*

other direction signs

ring road (by-passes town)

ring road (non-primary road)

holiday route

road markings

Road markings are a vital source of information for drivers. They are often placed alongside road signs, and have the advantage of being visible when the signs are hidden by traffic. Or they may be used without other signs to give a continuous message as you drive along the road. Remember the general rule that the more paint there is on the road, the greater the danger. When you approach an area criss-crossed with white lines and warnings, take note, slow down and prepare to negotiate a serious hazard ahead.

types of road marking

There are a number of different types of road marking which each have distinct meanings. The main types are (with specific examples):

Lane arrows tell you in advance which lane to get into, and are often accompanied by road numbers or place names.

traffic lane directions

Lines across the road separate traffic at road junctions, telling you where you must stop or give way to other vehicles.

give way

Written warnings on the roads give specific commands or warnings of hazards ahead.

do not block entrance to side road

Lines along the road divide lanes of traffic, give information about hazards on the road ahead and tell you when you are not permitted to overtake.

do not cross centre line

Parking restrictions are shown by yellow lines running alongside the kerb. They indicate that waiting restrictions are in force.

no waiting

Speed reduction lines are raised yellow lines across the road at the approach to a hazard such as a lower speed limit. They make drivers aware of their speed so they will slow down well in time. Rumble strips are red and give an audible warning too.

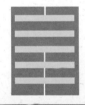

slow down for hazard ahead

traffic lights

Traffic lights automatically control busy junctions. They ease traffic flow by switching priorities in sequence, allowing vehicles from one direction to flow freely while vehicles from another direction are held back to wait their turn. Approach junctions controlled by traffic lights with caution and be prepared for the lights to change.

approaching traffic lights

Use the mirror-signal-manoeuvre routine as you approach a junction controlled by traffic lights. Slow down and be prepared to stop. Never speed up to try and get through while the lights are still green.

Remember that green means go only if the road is clear and it is safe to do so. Always check the road is clear before you proceed when the lights go green. Serious collisions occur at junctions controlled by traffic lights when one car moves off through a green light at the same time that a driver from the other direction has left it too late to stop after the lights have changed.

When a green filter arrow is illuminated you may proceed only in the direction it indicates

traffic light sequence

1 RED means stop. Wait at the stop line.

2 RED AND **AMBER** also means stop. Do not start to move off until the lights change to green.

3 GREEN means go if it is clear and safe to do so. Give way to pedestrians who are crossing.

4 AMBER means stop. You may only continue if the amber light appears after you have crossed the stop line or if you are so close to it that it might be dangerous to pull up. (Red then follows amber and the sequence repeats itself.)

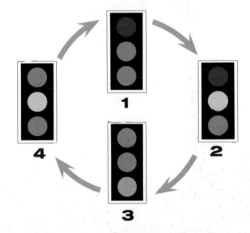

traffic light failure

If a set of traffic lights is not working, you should treat the intersection as an uncontrolled one where no one has priority. Be prepared to stop as traffic from other directions may assume they have right of way. If a police officer is controlling the junction, follow the signals you are given (see p61). When signalled to stop by a police officer, wait at the stop line.

Proceed with great care when traffic lights are out of order

(see p61)

know the code — highway code rule 178

Advanced stop lines Some signal-controlled junctions have advanced stop lines to allow cycles to be positioned ahead of other traffic. Motorists, including motorcyclists, MUST stop at the first white line reached if the lights are amber or red and should avoid blocking the way or encroaching on the marked area at other times, e.g. if the junction ahead is blocked. If your vehicle has proceeded over the first white line at the time that the signal goes red, you MUST stop at the second white line, even if your vehicle is in the marked area. Allow cyclists time and space to move off when the green signal shows.

5 in traffic

You may find this hard to believe at first, but controlling the car – making it start and stop, and go round corners and up hills – is the easy bit. On today's busy roads, the real driving skill is interacting with other road users. Good drivers blend in with the traffic flow, watch what other drivers are doing, communicate their own intentions clearly, make good progress without needing to brake or accelerate harshly, and arrive at their destination relaxed and unruffled. Bad drivers fail to observe what other drivers are doing, get into misunderstandings, drive too close and too fast on congested roads, and arrive feeling angry and tired and blaming everyone but themselves. Learning to cope with traffic requires concentration and self-discipline, but it's a skill you must master to pass your test.

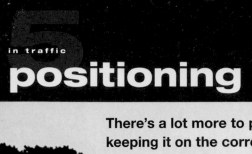

There's a lot more to positioning your car than just keeping it on the correct side of the road. By always being in the right place you will make your intentions clearer to other road users, maximise your vision, facilitate the free flow of traffic and increase your margin of safety when approaching hazardous situations.

lane discipline

Always keep within the road markings indicating your lane unless you are changing lane or direction. Try to anticipate when lanes will have to split, and get ready to move across into the correct lane. Don't change lanes at the last moment if you find you have got into the wrong lane: instead carry on and find another way back onto your route. Never straddle lanes or weave in and out of lanes.

Get into the correct lane in good time when arrows indicate that lanes are changing direction

lane markings

A broken white line marks the centre of the road

Longer broken white lines indicate a hazard ahead. Never cross a hazard warning line unless you are sure it is safe

Lane lines divide the lanes on dual carriageways and motorways: keep between them except when changing lane

You may cross the centre lines where there are double white lines and the line nearest to you is broken, if it is safe to do so

You must not cross the centre lines where the line nearest to you is solid. You also must not park on a road with double white lines whether broken or solid

Where there are double solid white lines, vehicles from either direction are prohibited from crossing the lines

An edge line marks the left-hand side of the carriageway

Diagonal hatching is used to separate lanes of traffic and to protect vehicles waiting to turn off the road. If the area is bordered by a broken white line you can enter it, but only if it is necessary and safe to do so; if it is bounded by a solid white line then you must not enter it except in an emergency

it's the law

crossing white lines

You are permitted to cross a central solid white line only if it is safe and necessary to do so in order to:

➔ enter or leave a side turning or driveway

➔ pass a stationary vehicle

➔ avoid an accident

➔ pass a working road maintenance vehicle displaying a keep left/right arrow and moving no faster than 10mph

➔ pass a pedal cycle or horse moving no faster than 10mph

➔ comply with the direction of a police constable or traffic warden.

If it is safe to do so, position your car towards the centre of the road when turning right

Leave enough room for a door to open unexpectedly when passing parked cars

road position

Normally you should position your car in the centre of your half of the road. Avoid getting too close to the kerb: the road surface is more uneven near the gutter and if you accidentally clip the kerb you may lose control of the car. However, there are times when it is useful to move a little nearer to the kerb. For instance to:

- ⊘ make space for oncoming traffic through a narrow gap
- ⊘ let a vehicle overtake
- ⊘ let motorbikes pass in congested traffic
- ⊘ increase your vision and safety when approaching a right-hand bend.

Conversely, you should move out towards the centre of the road, if it is safe to do so, when:

- ⊘ making a right-hand turn; this confirms your intentions to other road users and gives following vehicles space to overtake you on the left
- ⊘ the pavement is busy with pedestrians.

passing parked vehicles

When passing parked vehicles, leave plenty of space in case a car starts pulling out, or a car door opens unexpectedly. Making more space also helps you to see children coming out from between parked cars to cross the road. If you have to pass closer to parked cars, then reduce your speed and be ready to stop.

When passing a series of parked cars, don't weave in and out between them: maintain a straight course which clearly indicates your intentions to other road users.

know the code

highway code rule 143

One-way streets Traffic MUST travel in the direction indicated by signs. Buses and/or cycles may have a contraflow lane. Choose the correct lane for your exit as soon as you can. Do not change lanes suddenly. Unless road signs or markings indicate otherwise, you should use:

- ➜ the left-hand lane when going left
- ➜ the right-hand lane when going right
- ➜ the most appropriate lane when going straight ahead. Remember – traffic could be passing on both sides.

Take care to observe lane markings in one-way streets, and beware of vehicles passing on your left

Bus lanes are marked by a solid white line. You must not use them except when signs say you can

one-way systems

In a one-way street select the most appropriate lane in good time before you have to turn at the end of the street.

It is legal to overtake on either the left or the right on a one-way street, so take particular care when changing lanes. If you drive down a one-way street by mistake, you must continue to the end of the road – don't try to turn round or reverse out again.

One-way streets may have contra-flow bus or cycle lanes, allowing these vehicles to proceed against the direction of traffic flow.

keep out

Remember that you must not drive in a bus lane, cycle lane, tram lane or high-occupancy vehicle lane unless signs state otherwise. (Only vehicles containing the minimum number of people indicated on the accompanying traffic signs can use a high-occupancy vehicle lane.)

You must also not drive on the pavement except to cross it when using a driveway into a property, or where signs specifically permit parking on the pavement.

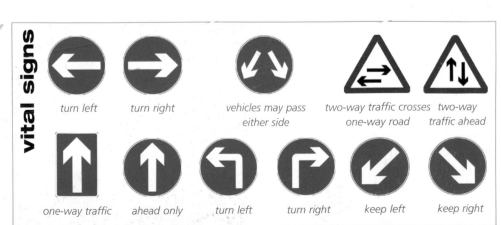

vital signs

turn left   turn right   vehicles may pass either side   two-way traffic crosses one-way road   two-way traffic ahead

one-way traffic   ahead only   turn left   turn right   keep left   keep right

5
following

On our busy roads much of your driving time will be spent following the vehicle in front. You'll find that many drivers commit the serious error of following too closely. They get away with this until one day the vehicle ahead brakes unexpectedly and they end up careering into the back of it. Most serious collisions – such as motorway pile-ups – could be avoided if drivers left more space between their vehicles.

how close?

When you are following another vehicle, ask yourself: 'if it suddenly slams on its brakes, have I left myself enough space to be able to react and stop without hitting it?'

If the answer is no, pull back until you have created a safe gap. A useful way to ensure you are keeping a safe distance in dry, bright conditions is to use the two-second rule. Watch as the vehicle in front goes by a lamp post or driveway, then count how long it takes for your car to pass the same point. If you can slowly count 'one thousand – two thousand' (or repeat the apt phrase 'only a fool breaks the two-second rule') before your car reaches the marker then you are keeping a safe distance.

wet roads

On wet, greasy or icy roads you will take much longer to stop in an emergency. When it rains, double the two-second rule and leave a four-second gap. If the road is slippery or icy you should leave up to ten times the distance in which to stop.

Wet roads mean you will need further to stop in an emergency, so leave at least a four-second gap

large vehicles

Another time you should leave extra space is when you're following a large truck or bus. If you are too close to it your view past will be obscured and you won't be able to anticipate what is happening on the road ahead. Keeping well back also means you don't have to breathe in the truck's diesel exhaust fumes, or get your windscreen smeared by spray thrown up from its rear wheels on a wet road.

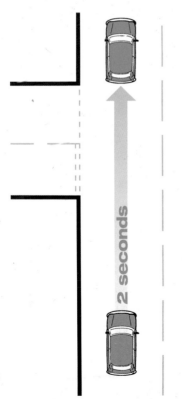

Use a fixed point on the road side to measure a two-second gap from the vehicle in front

Keep well back when following a bus or you won't be able to see past to overtake it when it stops

Many drivers cause unnecessary risk by tailgating on the motorway – don't become one of them

Leave enough space from the vehicle ahead to give following drivers room to overtake you safely

tailgating

This is the dangerous habit of following too closely behind the vehicle in front. When someone is tailgating you, it means that if you have to stop in an emergency they may not be able to avoid running into the back of your car. Reduce this risk by easing off the accelerator and increasing your following distance from the vehicle in front. Because you have created more space in front of you, you won't have to slow so abruptly in an emergency, which in turn gives the driver behind extra time to react.

Often drivers tailgate because they are impatient to get past. If this is the case, let the driver overtake at the first opportunity. Never try to retaliate to a tailgating driver by putting on your brakes or driving obstructively. The fact that they are driving dangerously means that you have to take even more care to drive responsibly to ensure everyone's safety.

queues

When in a slow-moving traffic queue, hold back if keeping up with the queue would mean obstructing the exit of a junction or straddling a pedestrian crossing or level crossing. Wait till the traffic in front has moved forward far enough for you to be able to clear the junction or crossing before proceeding.

stopping in traffic

Avoid getting too close to the vehicle in front when it stops at traffic lights or a junction. Leave enough space so you can see where its rear tyres touch the tarmac. That way, if it stalls or breaks down you have enough room to manoeuvre safely past without getting stuck behind it. On a slope leaving this gap also gives room for the car in front to roll back if the driver performs a bad hill start.

being overtaken

When you're in a line of traffic on the open road, remember that even if you don't intend to overtake, drivers behind may want to overtake you. Leave enough space for them to do so safely.

If another driver is trying to overtake, you should help them get past quickly and safely. Keep a steady course, slow down if necessary and leave plenty of space from the vehicle in front for the overtaking car to move into. But leave the decision to overtake to the other driver – don't beckon them to pass, or indicate left, as there may be hazards which you haven't spotted.

Don't ever try to obstruct or prevent someone from overtaking, even if you are already driving at the speed limit. Let the other driver get by and concentrate

Leave a gap when approaching side turnings in queuing traffic so you don't obstruct access to them

Leave plenty of space behind the vehicle in front, or you could get stuck if it stops unexpectedly

on ensuring your own safety. Slow down if someone overtakes where there is not enough forward vision for them to carry out the manoeuvre safely, or to assist a large vehicle which is taking a long time to pull past you.

Never be the cause of a tailback of traffic. If you are driving a slow-moving vehicle on a narrow road with little opportunity for overtaking, pull over as soon as it is safe and let the traffic pass before resuming your journey.

When leaving a safe gap you may find that other drivers pull in front of you, especially when you are driving on a dual carriageway or motorway. Don't think of this as a problem – simply ease off the power and pull back until you open up a safe gap again. Even if ten vehicles pull in front of you during the course of a journey you'll still get where you're going only a few seconds later – and more importantly, you'll get there safely.

know the code

highway code rule 151

In slow moving traffic you should:

➔ reduce the distance between you and the vehicle ahead to maintain traffic flow

➔ never get so close to the vehicle in front that you cannot stop safely

➔ leave enough space to be able to manoeuvre if the vehicle in front breaks down or an emergency vehicle needs to get past

➔ not change lanes to the left to overtake

➔ allow access into and from side roads, as blocking these will add to congestion

➔ be aware of cyclists and motorcyclists who may be passing on either side.

Rule 151: Do not block access to a side road

meeting

If you meet an oncoming vehicle where an obstruction such as a parked car reduces the width of the road so there is only room for one vehicle to pass, one of you has to give way. Forward thinking and anticipation make all the difference when dealing with this sort of situation. You need to anticipate, and adjust your speed and position well in advance so that if it is necessary for you to give way you can do so smoothly and safely.

A hump bridge is a potentially dangerous meeting place because the brow of the bridge restricts your forward view. Hump bridges are often narrow so you may encounter oncoming vehicles or pedestrians in the middle of the road. Slow right down and consider sounding your horn to give a warning of your approach

giving way

Where the obstruction is on your side of the road you should be prepared to stop and give way to oncoming traffic. But don't assume you necessarily have priority if the obstruction is on the other side of the road. If an oncoming car carries straight on through, you must be able to stop safely and give way to it. Thinking in terms of 'right of way' in this sort of situation isn't helpful: drivers who insist on always taking what they see as their 'right of way' end up in a collision sooner or later.

judging the gap

As you approach a meeting situation use the mirror-signal-manoeuvre routine. The oncoming vehicle may pull nearer to the kerb to create enough space for you to continue through the gap. But if you are not absolutely certain there is enough room, hold back until the other vehicle is through. Never pull past an obstruction expecting the oncoming vehicle to move over to make space for you.

hills

It's courteous to stop and give way to vehicles, particularly large lorries and buses, which are coming towards you up a steep hill. If a heavily-laden truck loses momentum on a hill it has to work hard to regain it.

Where a parked car causes an obstruction ahead, stop and give way to oncoming traffic

Use passing places to pull in and give way to oncoming vehicles on single track roads

vital signs

give way to vehicles from other direction

you have priority over oncoming vehicles

road narrows on both sides

road narrows on right (left if symbol reversed)

know the code

highway code rule 155

Single-track roads
These are only wide enough for one vehicle. They may have special passing places. If you see a vehicle coming towards you, or the driver behind wants to overtake, pull into a passing place on your left, or wait opposite a passing place on your right. Give way to vehicles coming uphill whenever you can. If necessary, reverse until you reach a passing place to let the other vehicle pass. Slow down when passing pedestrians, cyclists and horse riders.

5

overtaking

Overtaking is a vital driving skill. When drivers lack the confidence to overtake where it would be safe to do so, long queues of slow traffic can build up, causing congestion and frustration among following drivers. But overtaking is also one of the most potentially dangerous driving manoeuvres, and it demands careful judgement and a full assessment of the risks involved. Always remember the golden rule: if you're not absolutely sure it is safe to overtake, don't.

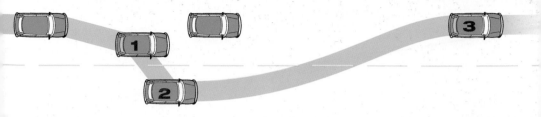

how to overtake

1 Maximise your observation of the road ahead before overtaking. Don't get too close or you will reduce your view past the vehicle you want to overtake. Position yourself towards the centre of the road so you can see past. (When following a large vehicle it can also be useful to move towards the kerb to get a view along its nearside.) Check your mirrors and give a signal before pulling out. Make sure you are in a lower gear that gives enough power to get past quickly, but try to avoid having to change gear in the middle of an overtaking manoeuvre.

2 Move to the other side of the road to make a final check of the road ahead. If it is clear then apply full power and drive past as swiftly as possible.

3 Don't cut in too early after overtaking. Check your mirrors to ensure that it is safe to pull back in.

when to overtake

The only reason to overtake is when it will help you to make progress. There's no point overtaking when you are approaching a built-up area or if you intend to turn off the road soon. Don't try to overtake when you are in heavy traffic and overtaking will achieve nothing but putting you a couple of places up the traffic queue. If there are signs indicating the distance to a stretch of dual carriageway, take note of them and wait till you get there before overtaking.

Check your mirrors to ensure you don't cut back in too soon after overtaking another vehicle

it's the law

no overtaking

It is illegal to overtake:

- → if you would have to cross or straddle double white lines with a solid line nearest to you (apart from the exceptions mentioned on p73)

- → if you would have to enter an area surrounded by a solid white line that is designed to divide traffic streams

- → the nearest vehicle to a pedestrian crossing

- → if you would have to enter a lane reserved for buses, trams or cycles during its hours of operation

- → after a 'no overtaking' sign until you pass the sign cancelling it.

A white arrow in the middle of the road is warning you to move back to the left when overtaking. Never overtake where you see this marking

Don't try to squeeze past a cyclist or motorcyclist: hold back and wait until it is safe to pass, leaving as much room as you would to overtake a car

dangers from other vehicles

If you overtake at 60mph while an oncoming car approaches at the same speed, it means you are closing at a combined speed of 120mph. This leaves little margin for error. Make sure you spend the minimum amount of time exposed to danger on the wrong side of the road when overtaking. Select a gear that will give you plenty of power and use the full acceleration of your car to get past quickly. Never overtake where you may force another vehicle to swerve or slow down.

While you are deciding whether to overtake, be aware that the driver behind may be thinking about overtaking you. Check your mirrors, and give a signal to indicate your intentions both to following traffic and to the vehicle being overtaken.

Make sure there is no possibility that the vehicle you intend to overtake is about to make a right turn or swerve across the road to overtake a cyclist or pedestrian you haven't seen. Take care before overtaking at the start of a downhill stretch or when leaving a lower speed restriction in case the vehicle in front speeds up. If you are unsure that the vehicle you want to overtake is aware of your presence consider sounding your horn or flashing your headlamps briefly to warn that you are about to overtake.

If the driver in front waves or indicates left to encourage you to overtake, don't rely on their judgement: overtake only if you can see to your own satisfaction that it is safe to do so.

It is very dangerous to follow straight after another overtaking vehicle as your view ahead will be obscured and oncoming vehicles may not be able to see you. Hold back and make sure the road is clear before overtaking.

overtaking hazards

Overtaking is potentially dangerous because there are so many different hazards to assess before making the manoeuvre. Never overtake:

- where there are road junctions or driveways from which a vehicle may emerge in front of you
- where the road narrows
- where you cannot see the road ahead to be clear, such as on the approach to a bend, a hump bridge, the brow of a hill or a dip in the road
- when approaching a school crossing patrol
- between the kerb and a bus or tram when it is at a stop
- where traffic is queuing at junctions or road works
- at a level crossing.

Caution is required when overtaking on three-lane roads, especially where traffic from either direction is allowed to overtake on the same stretch

Overtaking on the left is permitted in certain situations, but take extra care as other drivers may not be expecting you to do so

three-lane roads

Take special care when overtaking on a road divided into three lanes so that traffic from either direction may use the middle lane to overtake. Don't pull out unless you are certain there is no risk of an oncoming vehicle trying to overtake at the same time.

overtaking on the left

You must normally overtake on the right only. However, there are a few situations where you are permitted to pass slower moving vehicles on the left-hand side:

- ➲ where a vehicle is signalling to turn right
- ➲ where traffic is moving slowly in queues on a multi-lane road
- ➲ in a one-way street
- ➲ in a lane turning left at a junction.

know the code

highway code rule 164

Large vehicles Overtaking these is more difficult. You should

- ➜ drop back. This will increase your ability to see ahead and should allow the driver of the large vehicle to see you in their mirrors. Getting too close to large vehicles, including agricultural vehicles such as a tractor with a trailer or other fixed equipment, will obscure your view of the road ahead and there may be another slow-moving vehicle in front

- ➜ make sure that you have enough room to complete your overtaking manoeuvre before committing yourself. It takes longer to pass a large vehicle. If in doubt do not overtake

- ➜ not assume you can follow a vehicle ahead which is overtaking a long vehicle. If a problem develops, they may abort overtaking and pull back in.

vital signs

*side winds:
take special care
when overtaking
cyclists, motorbikes
or high-sided
vehicles*

Hidden dip

*hidden dip in road:
don't overtake as
oncoming traffic
may be obscured*

no overtaking

6 junctions

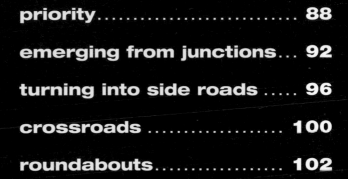

A road junction is where two or more roads meet. Traffic has to merge and with this comes the risk that mistakes may lead to collisions. At junctions you need to signal clearly and position your car accurately to give a clear indication to other road users of what you intend to do. Good all-round observation is needed to make sure that when you pull out at a junction, you do so without endangering or inconveniencing other road users. However, in today's busy traffic you can't afford to wait until the road is clear as far as the eye can see before moving out. Judging when to cross a junction takes skill and confidence which can only be acquired by getting in lots of experience at all types of road junction.

If no one knew who had priority where two roads meet the result would be chaos. To promote a smooth traffic flow, most junctions are organised so that traffic on the major road has priority and traffic on the minor road must wait until it is clear to proceed. Although there are few basic types of junctions, individual circumstances make each junction unique and they need to be negotiated with care. Assess each junction as you approach it by looking at such things as bends, visibility, obscured sightlines, the amount of traffic, road markings and signs.

Give way to oncoming vehicles

types of junction

There are five main types of junction:
- T-junctions
- Y-junctions
- staggered junctions
- crossroads
- roundabouts.

priorities at junctions

Priorities at junctions are indicated by give way signs and markings, stop signs and markings, and traffic lights – or there may be no priority marked. Remember that even if you are on the road that has priority, you need to be ready to slow down or stop for vehicles which pull out in front of you, or for vulnerable road users such as cyclists or pedestrians who you may need to give priority to whatever the road signs say.

give way sign

A give way sign means you must stop at the line to give priority to traffic on the road you are joining. You do not need to stop if the road is clear and it is safe to proceed. A give way junction is indicated by double broken white lines across your half of the road, or a single broken white line at the entrance to a roundabout.

know the code

highway code rule 170

Take extra care at junctions You should:

- watch out for cyclists, motorcyclists, powered wheelchairs/mobility scooters and pedestrians as they are not always easy to see. Be aware that they may not have seen or heard you if you are approaching from behind
- watch out for pedestrians crossing a road into which you are turning. If they have started to cross they have priority, so give way
- watch out for long vehicles which may be turning at a junction ahead; they may have to use the whole width of the road to make the turn
- watch out for horse riders who may take a different line on the road from that which you would expect
- not assume, when waiting at a junction, that a vehicle coming from the right and signalling left will actually turn. Wait and make sure
- look all around before emerging. Do not cross or join a road until there is a gap large enough for you to do so safely.

vital signs

STOP
100 yds

distance to stop line ahead

GIVE WAY
50 yds

distance to give way line ahead

GIVE
WAY

give way to traffic on major road

side turning

T-junction (the road with priority is shown by the broader line)

stop and give way

roundabout

mini-roundabout

crossroads

staggered junction

stop sign

A stop sign is used instead of a give way sign where reduced visibility means it would be dangerous to proceed through a junction without stopping. You must come to a complete halt at the line and check that the road is clear before proceeding. A stop junction is indicated by a single continuous white line across your side of the road. This type of line also shows where you should stop at traffic lights, level crossings, swing bridges and ferries.

box junctions

Box junctions are designed to prevent the junction being blocked by queuing traffic. It is illegal to enter the area of yellow criss-cross lines marked on the road at a box junction unless your exit road is clear. But remember the important exception to this rule: you *can* enter a box junction when you want to turn right and your exit road is clear but you are prevented from proceeding by oncoming traffic or right-turning vehicles in front of you.

traffic lights

At junctions controlled by traffic lights the priorities change with the lights. See p69 to remind yourself of the sequence and meaning of traffic lights.

road markings at junctions

This marking appears on the road just before a give way sign

Give way to traffic on a major road

Stop line at stop sign

Give way to traffic from the right at a roundabout

Give way to traffic from the right at a mini-roundabout

Stop line at signals or police control

Stop line for pedestrians at a level crossing

highway code rule 174

Box junctions These have criss-cross yellow lines painted on the road. You MUST NOT enter the box until your exit road or lane is clear. However, you may enter the box and wait when you want to turn right, and are only stopped from doing so by oncoming traffic, or by other vehicles waiting to turn right. At signalled roundabouts you MUST NOT enter the box unless you can cross over it completely without stopping.

know the code

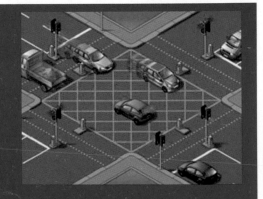

uncontrolled junctions

On minor roads some junctions may not have road signs or markings. This means all vehicles approaching the junction have equal priority. Slow down, look for traffic coming from all directions and be prepared to stop and give way if necessary.

approaching junctions

You are already familiar with the mirror-signal-manoeuvre routine. When approaching a road hazard such as a junction you need to take this procedure a step further by developing a structured approach to carrying out the manoeuvre.

   After checking your mirror and signalling, you need to:

- ◯ check your position on the road and adjust it if necessary
- ◯ check your speed and adjust to suit
- ◯ select the appropriate gear
- ◯ take one last good look all around to check it is safe to proceed
- ◯ make the manoeuvre if it is safe to do so.

The diagram opposite shows how this procedure works when making a right turn.

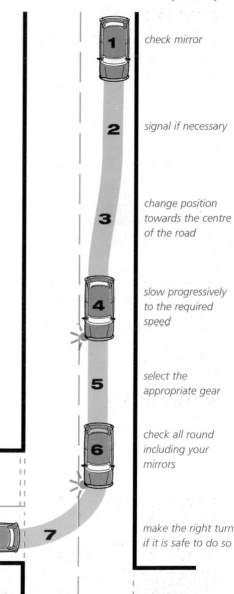

1 — *check mirror*

2 — *signal if necessary*

3 — *change position towards the centre of the road*

4 — *slow progressively to the required speed*

5 — *select the appropriate gear*

6 — *check all round including your mirrors*

7 — *make the right turn if it is safe to do so*

test tips

do

- ◯ scan each junction as you approach to get as much information as possible about approaching traffic and the junction layout
- ◯ make progress by proceeding straight through a give way junction without coming to a complete stop when it is safe to do so

don't

- ➔ assume that because you are on the major road you will not have to give way to other road users
- ➔ creep across a stop line, however slowly. Make sure you always come to a complete halt.

6

emerging from junctions

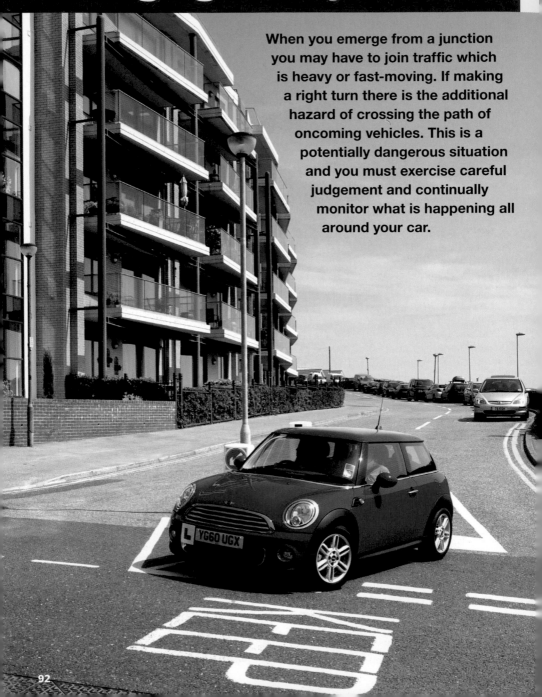

When you emerge from a junction you may have to join traffic which is heavy or fast-moving. If making a right turn there is the additional hazard of crossing the path of oncoming vehicles. This is a potentially dangerous situation and you must exercise careful judgement and continually monitor what is happening all around your car.

Careful all round observation is essential when you are emerging from a road junction

emerging left from a junction

Follow this general procedure:

- ⮑ check your mirrors as you approach the junction
- ⮑ if other road users would benefit from a signal give it in good time
- ⮑ position your car to the left of the road, about one metre from the kerb
- ⮑ slow down and be prepared to give way or stop at the junction
- ⮑ look in all directions before pulling out. Check your left door mirror for bicycles or motorbikes passing on your nearside
- ⮑ pull onto the main road, then check your mirrors again, make sure your indicator is cancelled and accelerate to a safe speed for the road you have joined.

emerging right from a junction

Carry out the same procedure, but position your car as near to the centre of the road as possible (although if the road is narrow, you must leave enough space for other vehicles to turn into the junction). Take extra care when pulling out as you have to give way to traffic coming from both directions.

When stopping at a junction make sure that you pull right up to the give way or stop line (above). Do not stop short of the line (below) or you will restrict your view out of the junction

maximising vision

Sometimes you will find that your view out of a junction is obscured, for instance by parked vehicles. If this is the case, stop at the junction and then edge carefully forward until you can get a good view down the road in both directions.

Large vehicles may also obscure your view. Before pulling out in front of a bus or lorry, ask yourself if there might be a hidden motorcycle overtaking it. Remember that motorcyclists and cyclists are particularly vulnerable at junctions because they are smaller and harder to see, and can easily be hidden behind your windscreen pillars.

judging traffic speed

Judging when to emerge from a junction requires great care: on the one hand, you must be able to emerge from the junction without forcing other vehicles to slow down or change position; on the other, you should not be over-cautious so that you fail to take advantage of safe opportunities while a queue of frustrated drivers forms behind you. As a rough guide, if you would feel happy about walking across the road in front of an oncoming vehicle, then there should be space for you to emerge. Once you have joined the main road accelerate briskly to match your speed to that of other traffic.

staggered junctions

This is where two minor roads join a major road not quite opposite each other. When you are on a minor road and wish to pass across the major road you should usually treat this as two manoeuvres: first join the major road, then make a second turn into the minor road. If the junctions are very close together you may proceed across the major road in one manoeuvre, but check carefully that the road is clear in both directions.

When approaching a staggered junction on the major road you should treat it with caution. Be prepared to slow down and give way to vehicles emerging.

When parked cars obstruct your view out of a junction, edge cautiously forward until you can see if the road is clear for you to pull out

Y-junctions

At a Y-junction the minor road meets the major road at an angle. When turning right at a Y-junction you may need to pull up at a right angle to the major road to prevent your view to your left being obscured.

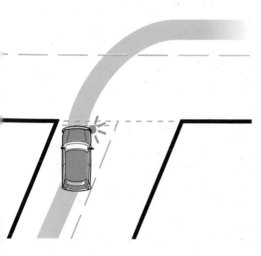

Pulling up at a right angle to the major road at a Y-junction means that you can get a clear view in both directions through your side windows

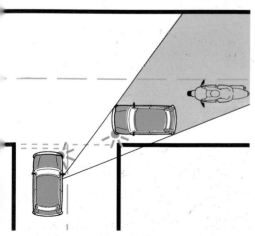

Be alert for overtaking vehicles – particularly motorbikes – which can easily be hidden from view behind other vehicles at junctions

turning right across a dual carriageway

Crossing a dual carriageway needs extra care because of the high speed of traffic. There are two types of right turn across a dual carriageway:

> **where there is a waiting area within the central reservation**

You should cross the road in two stages. First, check that the road to your right is clear of oncoming traffic and drive into the waiting area. Stop here and check if the road is clear to the left before joining the carriageway. You must not not join the right-hand lane and expect approaching traffic to pass you on the left. Wait until both lanes are clear so you are able to cross safely to the left-hand lane.

Take care if you are driving a longer vehicle or pulling a trailer. Check before emerging that there is enough space for your whole vehicle to fit into the central reservation without obstructing traffic already on the dual carriageway.

> **where there is no waiting area within the central reservation**

You must cross the dual carriageway in a single manoeuvre. This calls for careful observation in both directions before pulling out.

Where there is a central reservation wide enough to wait in, split a right turn across a dual carriageway into two separate manoeuvres

turning into side roads

Careful observation is needed when turning into a minor road. Try not to concentrate your attention on the danger from just one direction – for instance, oncoming traffic when you are turning right – as you may overlook other hazards, such as motorbikes overtaking you, or pedestrians crossing the road you are turning into.

turning left

Follow this general procedure:

- check mirrors as you approach the junction
- if other road users would benefit from a signal give it in good time
- position your car to the left of the road, about one metre from the kerb. Don't move too far to the left or following drivers may think you are pulling up, not turning left
- slow down, then select the appropriate gear. Your speed must reflect how sharp the corner is and how clearly you can see round it. Remember that a vehicle could be parked just round the corner out of sight, or an oncoming vehicle may be in the middle of the road passing parked cars
- check your mirrors again, especially your nearside mirror in case a cyclist or motorcyclist is passing on your nearside. Look all round, and check that the road you are turning into is clear. You must stop and give way to any pedestrians crossing the road
- turn the corner, making sure you stay well on your side of the road, and that your rear wheel does not clip the kerb. Remember the rear wheels don't exactly follow the front wheels, but take a short cut which brings them closer to the kerb.
- check your mirrors again, make sure your indicator is cancelled and build up speed if it is safe to do so.

Keep close in when turning left, but don't cut round so tightly that your rear wheel hits the kerb

know the code

highway code rule 182

Turning left Use your mirrors and give a left-turn signal well before you turn left. Do not overtake just before you turn left and watch out for traffic coming up on your left before you make the turn, especially if driving a large vehicle. Cyclists, motorcyclists and other road users in particular may be hidden from your view.

rule 183

When turning

- keep as close to the left as is safe and practicable
- give way to any vehicles using a bus lane, cycle lane or tramway from either direction.

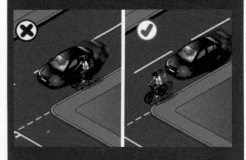

RULE 182: Do not cut in on cyclists

test tips

do

- take care to check that the road you are driving into is clear before starting to turn
- judge your positioning carefully when turning right on a road which has no centre line

don't

- swing back to the left before turning right, or swing out to the right before making a left turn
- cut the corner on a left turn so your rear wheel hits the kerb

Continuous observation is vital when turning right. As well as checking for oncoming traffic, look for vehicles overtaking you and hazards – such as pedestrians – in the road you are turning into

turning right

Follow this general procedure:

- check your mirrors as you approach the junction
- if other road users would benefit from a signal give it in good time
- position your car towards the centre of the road, keeping as close as you can to the white line. This helps other road users see what you are intending to do, and also lets following traffic pass on your nearside while you are waiting to turn. If there is a waiting area marked on the road for traffic turning right, follow the road markings into this
- slow down and be prepared to stop if you need to give way to oncoming traffic or if the entrance of the road you are turning into is blocked
- look out for vehicles waiting to turn right from the road you are driving into – they may try to pull out ahead of you. If there is not enough space for you to manoeuvre around them and enter the road then hold back and wait for them to emerge. But don't beckon or flash them to come out
- check your mirrors before turning, especially your right-hand mirror in case a vehicle is overtaking you. Be particularly alert for motorbikes
- do not start to turn unless you are sure you can enter the side road and will not be forced to stop in a dangerous position halfway across the main road
- take care not to cut the corner as you make the turn
- check your mirrors after completing the turn, make sure your indicator is cancelled and build up speed if it is safe to do so.

Never cut a corner like this. Steer so that you stay on your own side of the road when turning right or you risk colliding with an emerging vehicle

stopping at junctions

Whenever you have to halt at a junction for more than a few seconds, always apply your handbrake. This is a safety measure which will help stop your car being pushed into the path of other traffic if it is hit from behind while you are stationary at the junction. The impact could easily knock your foot off the brake pedal if you were holding the car on the footbrake alone.

When waiting to make a right turn, do not turn the steering wheel before you are ready to move off. If you were hit from behind while waiting in the middle of the road with your front wheels already turned, the impact could push you across the road into the path of oncoming traffic

vital signs

no motor vehicles except motorcycles without sidecars

no vehicles except bicycles being pushed

no entry for vehicular traffic

no left turn

no motor vehicles

no right turn

These signs all mean that you must not drive into a road. Sometimes there will be a plate giving exceptions – for instance, you may be able to enter outside certain hours, or if you need to gain access to a property in the road

crossroads

At a crossroads there are two T-junctions opposite each other. Serious collisions can occur at crossroads when one vehicle pulls out in front of another travelling at high speed. Take special care when you are on a major road and see a crossroads ahead. Slow down and be prepared to give way in case another driver proceeds straight across without seeing you.

turning right

When turning right at the same time as another vehicle wants to turn across you, you have two choices:

⊙ turn right side to right side

This is the safer option. It has the advantage of giving you a clear view of approaching traffic.

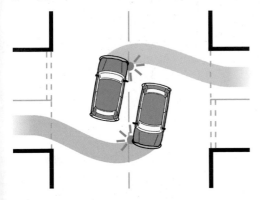

⊙ turn left side to left side

This method can be useful when turning against a long vehicle, or where the side roads are slightly offset. But because the other vehicle is passing in front of you, it blocks your view of oncoming traffic, so take extra care.

Sometimes there are road markings which direct which course you should take. Where there are no markings, watching the course of the other vehicle and establishing eye contact with its driver may help you decide.

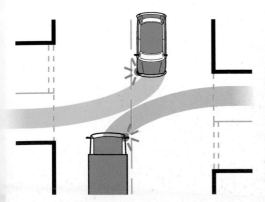

emerging

When you are emerging from one minor road at a crossroads and another vehicle is waiting to emerge from the minor road opposite, what you should do depends on the circumstances:

⊙ if you are turning right and the other vehicle is turning left or going ahead, you should wait for the other vehicle to proceed before you emerge, otherwise you would be cutting across its path

⊙ if you are turning left or going ahead you should proceed with caution in case the other vehicle emerges and cuts across your path

⊙ if you are turning right and the other driver is turning right, neither of you has priority and you should proceed with extra care.

In practice you will find that many drivers are unfamiliar with these priorities. It is usually helpful to establish eye contact with the other driver to help determine what they intend to do. The other driver may gesture you to come out first – but do so only if you are completely certain that their meaning is clear and it is safe to do so. You should not wave or flash at another driver across a crossroads – it could be dangerous if they pull out without checking for themselves that the road is clear.

Extra caution is needed when emerging from a crossroads at the same time as another vehicle

101

Roundabouts are designed to allow vehicles to merge smoothly and keep the overall traffic stream flowing. A driver who is looking well ahead and anticipating traffic movements may be able to traverse a string of roundabouts safely and smoothly without once having to come to a complete halt. But negotiating roundabouts correctly does demand a high degree of concentration, anticipation and accurate signalling.

Signal clearly at roundabouts to let other road users know which direction you intend to take

roundabout safety

Fewer serious crashes occur on roundabouts than at crossroads. Yet paradoxically there are more collisions in total at roundabouts. That's because roundabouts slow down the traffic flow so when accidents happen they tend to be less severe. But the give and take nature of roundabouts means that minor shunts are more common. Careful observation, anticipation and signalling are needed to stay out of trouble.

Take care when anticipating what other road users intend to do on roundabouts. Some drivers have strange ideas about the correct lane or signalling to use, others don't bother signalling at all and some may simply be lost and unsure of which exit to take. So look out for vehicles:

- ⊘ turning right without indicating
- ⊘ indicating right but going straight on
- ⊘ using the right-hand lane to go straight ahead even if the left lane is clear
- ⊘ making a U-turn at the roundabout.

Beware also of cyclists, horse riders and long vehicles, all of which may take an unusual course at roundabouts.

negotiating a roundabout

As you approach the roundabout, scan all the approach roads to spot vehicles which may arrive at the same time as you do. Aim to make progress by adjusting your speed so you can join the traffic flow, but be prepared to stop and give way if necessary. Use the mirror-signal-manoeuvre routine on the approach to a roundabout, and always check your nearside mirror before taking your exit road in case someone – especially a cyclist or motorcyclist – is trying to pass on your left.

lanes and signalling

On some roundabouts, particularly larger roundabouts with multiple exits, white arrows painted on the approach road indicate which lane you should get into for the exit you intend to take. Where there are no arrows or signs indicating which lane to take, follow these guidelines:

Turning left:
- ➲ indicate left as you approach
- ➲ take the left-hand lane
- ➲ keep left on the roundabout
- ➲ continue to indicate left until you have exited the roundabout.

Turning right:
- ➲ indicate right as you approach
- ➲ take the right-hand lane
- ➲ keep right on the roundabout
- ➲ after passing the exit before the one you intend to take, indicate left
- ➲ check your nearside mirror before taking your exit road.

Going straight ahead:
- ➲ do not indicate on approach
- ➲ take the left-hand lane
- ➲ keep left on the roundabout
- ➲ after passing the exit before the one you intend to take, indicate left
- ➲ check your nearside mirror before taking your exit road.

It is also acceptable to use the right-hand lane when going straight ahead if the left-hand lane of the roundabout is blocked, for instance by vehicles turning left. In this case you should stay in the right-hand lane as you drive through the roundabout. You will need to check your nearside mirror carefully before taking your exit, in case a vehicle is moving up on your inside.

It is perfectly legal to carry out a U-turn by going all the way round a roundabout, but other drivers may not be expecting you to do this so take special care and signal clearly.

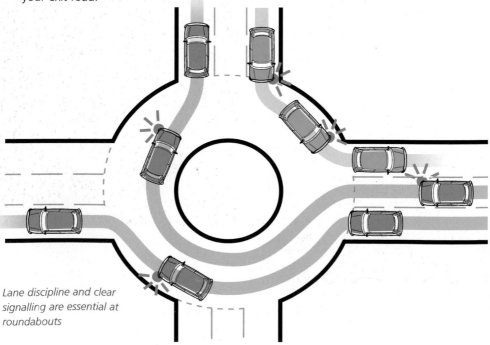

Lane discipline and clear signalling are essential at roundabouts

Where there are mini-roundabouts close together, you must treat them as separate junctions

If lanes are marked on approaching a roundabout, get into the correct lane as soon as possible

Avoid driving alongside large vehicles on roundabouts as they may need to take up more than one lane to make their turn

mini-roundabouts

Treat mini-roundabouts in the same way as larger roundabouts. You must by law pass around the white central circle (but watch out for other drivers who may cut straight across without slowing down).

When turning right at a mini-roundabout you should indicate right as you approach but the small size of the roundabout means it is usually not practical to indicate left before exiting.

Some junctions consist of a series of mini-roundabouts. Treat each separately and give way if necessary as you approach each one in turn.

test tips

do

- give special caution to cyclists: they can find it difficult to pull across the traffic stream and may stay in the left-hand lane even when they want to turn right

- take extra care in the wet, as the road surface on roundabouts can become polished and slippery, causing your wheels to spin if you try to move off in a hurry

don't

- creep forward when waiting to join the roundabout. Drivers on the roundabout may think you are about to pull out in front of them. It could also lead to someone driving into the back of your car because they assume you are pulling onto the roundabout

- drive alongside a long vehicle – it may need more than one lane when negotiating a roundabout, so hold back and leave it room.

7 on the road

As a driver you have to deal with constantly changing situations on the road. In a single day you could find yourself negotiating busy city back streets, cruising on an empty motorway, tackling a twisting country lane and queuing in head to tail traffic at roadworks. You need to be ready to adapt your driving style to meet these changing conditions, and be aware of the specific hazards you are likely to encounter in different driving situations.

bends

A car weighing around a tonne and a half and travelling at 50mph has a lot of momentum. This means that when you want to change course, you have to persuade the car to turn even though the forces acting on it are trying to make it carry straight on. Because of their sophisticated suspension systems, modern cars are reassuringly surefooted. But never forget that ultimately all that gets your car round a bend is the contact of four patches of tyre tread – each no bigger than a handprint – on the tarmac.

cornering

Road signs and markings give advance warning when you approach some bends ahead, but not all sharp bends have warnings. Remember that the bend sign not only warns you of a corner ahead, it also tells you which direction the road turns.

Carry out the mirror-signal-manoeuvre routine on the approach to a bend. Take care nothing is hidden from view behind your windscreen pillars. On a right-hand bend, move a little nearer to the kerb to improve your view through the bend. But don't move towards the centre of the road at the start of a left-hand bend: this could put you in danger from oncoming traffic, particularly if an oncoming vehicle cuts the corner.

If you need to change down a gear do this before you enter the bend. Steer gently into the bend, and apply some power to help balance the car. Once you see the bend start to open out, progressively apply more power and build up to the appropriate speed.

speed and grip

The golden rule when driving through a bend is that you must be able to stop, on your side of the road, in the distance you can see to be clear. Most bends are blind – your view through them is obscured by hedges or walls. At every bend ask yourself what might be hidden from your view halfway round. A horse rider? Stationary traffic? A fallen branch? Some drivers get into the habit of cornering a little too fast because experience tells them that most of the time there is nothing hidden round a bend. Until one day their luck runs out and they cause a serious accident.

Corner at a speed that keeps you well within the limit of grip of your tyres on the road. On a damp or greasy road the amount of grip you have is greatly reduced. If you try to take a corner too fast, the tyres will start to slide, putting you in danger of skidding off the road or into the path of another vehicle.

Another factor which influences how quickly a car can corner is the camber – the way the road slopes to one side to allow rainwater to drain off. On an adverse camber a car will start to slide at a lower speed.

Remember that if you have to carry out an emergency stop while cornering, your car will not stop as quickly or smoothly as if you were travelling in a straight line, and if you brake too harshly it may skid.

Never stop or park on a bend. If you are forced to stop on a bend, for instance by meeting stationary traffic, put on your hazard warning lights to warn other vehicles.

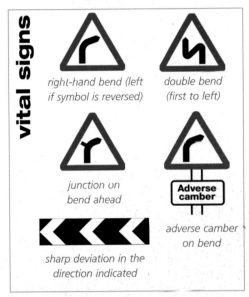

vital signs

right-hand bend (left if symbol is reversed)

double bend (first to left)

junction on bend ahead

Adverse camber

adverse camber on bend

sharp deviation in the direction indicated

Slow down when approaching a bend and be ready to stop in the distance you can see to be clear

hills

On hills you have to take into account the force of gravity. Going uphill, the car needs more power to maintain its speed, so you may have to change down the gearbox. Downhill, the car will pick up speed and you may need to use the brakes and gearbox to restrain it. Hills affect the feel of the controls: harder braking is needed to slow a car when it is going downhill, and in a high gear the car may lose speed up a steep hill even with the accelerator pedal flat to the floor.

hill warnings

Steep hills often have warning signs shown as a percentage: 25% indicates a steep one-in-four gradient, where the road rises one metre for every four metres travelled horizontally; 10% means a less severe one-in-ten slope.

driving uphill

You will need to apply more power when climbing a hill, and your car will slow more quickly than when driving on the level. When approaching an uphill gradient don't wait until the engine starts to labour before changing down. Anticipate the need for more power and select the appropriate gear before the car starts losing momentum.

Look out for slow-moving heavy vehicles going uphill. If you want to overtake, remember that your car will feel more sluggish than on the level, and you will need more space to get past safely.

Slow vehicles may be directed to use a special crawler lane on uphill sections of motorway.

driving downhill

You need to prevent your car picking up unwanted speed when going downhill. Doing this with the brakes alone isn't a good idea as they may overheat and lose effectiveness. Use engine braking as well by engaging a lower gear to help slow the car. The steeper the hill, the lower the gear: as a rule of thumb, you should use the same gear to go down a hill as you would to come up it.

Always apply the brakes carefully when driving downhill as harsh use may provoke a skid, especially if the road is wet or slippery.

Leave extra space between your car and the vehicle in front when going downhill, as you will need a greater distance to stop in an emergency. On very steep hills an escape lane is sometimes provided, filled with loose gravel which will bring a vehicle to a halt if its brakes fail.

When parking on a hill take extra precautions to make sure your car cannot run away. Check the handbrake is firmly engaged. Then, if facing uphill, turn the front wheels so they are pointing away from the kerb (above) and leave the car in first gear; if facing downhill, turn the front wheels into the kerb and leave the car in reverse gear

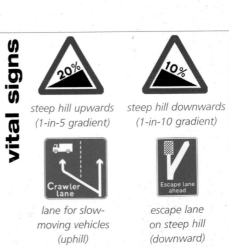

vital signs

steep hill upwards (1-in-5 gradient)

steep hill downwards (1-in-10 gradient)

lane for slow-moving vehicles (uphill)

escape lane on steep hill (downward)

in town

Driving in a built-up area poses an extra challenge because of the sheer number of hazards. You are sharing the road with vulnerable road users such as cyclists, pedestrians and children, there are numerous traffic signs and speed limits to observe, and your view of the road ahead is often obscured by parked vehicles. It means that extra concentration, anticipation and observation is required to stay safe in town.

speed

Because they are so hazardous, town streets have lower speed limits – usually 30mph. Remember that there is no requirement for 30mph repeater signs to be displayed on roads with street lighting. Where buildings are less dense a 40mph limit is often posted, while in town centres 20mph zones are becoming more common. Often you will need to drive below the posted speed limit to ensure the safety of other road users. Take special care:

- ⦿ on busy high streets where pedestrians may not have their mind on traffic
- ⦿ in zones with a 20mph speed limit where there are pedestrians or children playing
- ⦿ near schools, especially around school opening and closing times. Roads outside schools can become chaotic when parents are dropping off and picking up their children so slow down and give way to manoeuvring vehicles. You must not park or stop to drop off passengers where road markings indicate a school entrance.

traffic calming

Features such as humps, road narrowings and mini-roundabouts are becoming more common in urban streets, often in conjunction with a 20mph speed limit. Their purpose is to slow down traffic in residential areas, and discourage drivers from using 'rat-runs' – short cuts through backstreets.

Drive smoothly and slowly through these areas. Don't accelerate and then brake harshly between humps, and don't try to overtake a slower-moving vehicle. Not all humps are of uniform size so be prepared to slow to a walking pace to pass over them without causing discomfort to your passengers or damage to your car.

Road narrowings will be accompanied by warning signs showing which side the road narrows and from which direction vehicles have priority. You must give way to oncoming vehicles at road narrowings where signs and road markings indicate.

confidence

Drivers in busy cities can be assertive to the point of seeming aggressive – which can be intimidating to anyone not used to city driving. You need to be alert and decisive when joining a busy stream of traffic, or you could end up waiting for ages and holding up a queue of frustrated drivers. It helps to get some experience of city driving with your instructor beside you, and to avoid the rush hour the first time you drive into a city.

The fact is that driving on busy, congested city streets is no fun, and with congestion charging and high parking fees it is costly too. Wherever possible, park on the outskirts of town and use public transport instead.

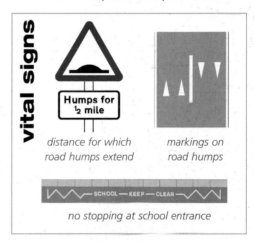

vital signs

distance for which road humps extend

markings on road humps

no stopping at school entrance

Drive slowly where traffic calming measures are in force and be prepared to give way where indicated

7 country roads

Country roads may look open, traffic free and safe, but appearances can be deceptive. That country bend could hide a horse and rider, a slick of mud left by a tractor, or a sudden sharp turn onto a narrow hump bridge. Although you should make progress where it is safe to do so on country roads, always be ready to encounter slow-moving vehicles, cyclists and pedestrians.

narrow lanes

On country roads wide enough for only one vehicle, be prepared to pull over where there is a passing place to let an oncoming vehicle through, or to let a following vehicle overtake. If the passing place is on your right-hand side then wait opposite it. If you meet a vehicle in between two passing places you may need to reverse back to the nearest passing place to let the other vehicle through. Never park in a passing place.

Use extreme caution when approaching a blind bend on a single-track road. In this situation you should be able to stop in half the distance you can see to be clear, which allows space for an approaching vehicle to stop too.

On narrow country roads be prepared to stop in half the distance you can see to be clear

special hazards

Take care when overtaking slow-moving agricultural vehicles as the driver may have difficulty seeing or hearing you.

Look out for pedestrians who may be approaching on your side of the road.

Animals – both domestic and wild – are another hazard on country roads (see p148).

Look out for slow-moving agricultural vehicles – and the slippery mud they leave on the road

vital signs

agricultural vehicles

falling or fallen rocks

hump bridge

uneven road

opening or swing bridge ahead

quayside or river bank

know the code

highway code rule 154

Country roads Take extra care on country roads and reduce your speed at approaches to bends, which can be sharper than they appear, and at junctions and turnings, which may be partially hidden. Be prepared for pedestrians, horse riders, cyclists, slow-moving farm vehicles or mud on the road surface. Make sure you can stop within the distance you can see to be clear. You should also reduce your speed where country roads enter villages.

115

dual carriageways

On dual carriageways the lanes in either direction are separated by a central reservation. Driving on a dual carriageway is similar to driving on a motorway, with a speed limit of 70mph unless otherwise signed, but there can be extra hazards such as slow-moving vehicles and right turns across the carriageway which would not be encountered on a motorway.

joining a dual carriageway

At many dual carriageway junctions you join by using a slip road. The purpose of the slip road is to let vehicles build up speed so they can merge smoothly with the traffic on the main carriageway.

As you drive onto the slip road try to assess the speed at which traffic in the inside lane of the dual carriageway is moving and accelerate to match it. Use the mirror-signal-manoeuvre routine, signal right to show that you intend moving across from the slip road and glance over your right shoulder just before you join the main carriageway to make sure there is nothing in your blind spot.

When joining from a slip road you must be prepared to give way to vehicles already on the dual carriageway. Adjust your speed and position to blend in smoothly with the traffic flow

Don't expect traffic to make space for you and be prepared to use the full length of the slip road to merge safely. You should not have to stop and wait at the end of the slip road unless traffic on the main dual carriageway is very slow moving.

Where there is no slip road you join the dual carriageway as you would a normal road at a stop or give way junction. Be sure to take into account the higher speed of vehicles on the dual carriageway before moving out.

Exit slip roads may be short and busy so watch your speed when leaving a dual carriageway

leaving a dual carriageway

Where there is a long slip road at the exit to a dual carriageway you can use this to lose speed. But some slip roads are short and end in a sharp bend, so be prepared to start losing speed before you leave the main carriageway. Where no slip road is provided you should start signalling and slowing early to give following traffic plenty of warning that you are turning off.

test tips

do
- ➲ use the length of the slip road to build up your speed to match that of traffic on the dual carriageway
- ➲ take into account higher traffic speeds on dual carriageways and check your mirrors frequently

don't
- ➲ get too close to vehicles you intend to overtake. Remember the two-second rule
- ➲ leave it till the last moment before returning to the left-hand lane when you see that the dual carriageway is about to end

right turns

Keep in the left lane of the dual carriageway unless you are overtaking slower-moving traffic or turning right. If you want to carry out a right turn, you need to consider the high speed of traffic and start planning your turn at an early stage. Check your mirror carefully, signal well in advance, and consider a gentle pressure on the brake pedal at an early stage to signal to following traffic that you are slowing. Position your car accurately inside the turning bay in the central reservation, and take care to check that the road you are entering is clear before turning across the right-hand carriageway.

Be careful when overtaking large vehicles as your car may be obscured in the driver's blind spot

dual carriageway ends

When you see the dual carriageway ends sign, check your speed because, unless signposted otherwise, the speed limit is about to drop back from 70 mph to 60 mph – the national speed limit for single carriageway roads. If you are overtaking, make sure you get back into the left-hand lane in good time before the dual carriageway ends. Be alert for other vehicles cutting past to pull in front of you at the last moment, and leave plenty of room from the vehicle in front so they have space to pull in safely.

When approaching a roundabout on a dual carriageway, reduce speed in good time, look at the signs and follow the 'get in lane' instruction

Finish overtaking and return to the inside lane in good time when you see the 'dual carriageway ends' sign

overtaking

On dual carriageways you need to plan your overtaking manoeuvres well in advance and give clear signals in good time because other vehicles may be coming up fast behind you.

1 Carry out the mirror-signal-manoeuvre routine and look well down the road to check for hazards in front of the vehicle you will be overtaking. Let the indicator flash at least three times before you start to move out to give other road users time to respond to your signal. Give a signal even if there is no one behind as it indicates your intentions to the driver you are overtaking.

2 When it is safe to move out, pull across into the right-hand lane of the dual carriageway. This should be carried out as a smoothly flowing manoeuvre – don't steer harshly or change lanes abruptly.

(Remember that on a dual carriageway you may overtake only on the right, unless traffic is moving slowly in queues and your queue is quicker than the one in the right-hand lane).

3 Accelerate and overtake briskly, always keeping within the speed limit. Avoid lingering in the blind spot of the vehicle you are overtaking where the driver may not be able to see you, especially when you are overtaking a large vehicle.

4 Don't cut in sharply once you're past the front of the vehicle you've overtaken – you mustn't leave it with less than a two-second separation distance once you've pulled back in. Check your mirrors to make sure you've left enough room before pulling back into the inside lane.

motorways

You aren't permitted to drive on motorways until you get your full driving licence, but the theory test includes plenty of questions about motorways, so don't overlook this section. Motorways are great for covering long distances quickly, but driving on them demands discipline and responsibility. Although motorways are statistically the safest of all roads, because of their higher speeds and volume of traffic, when accidents do occur they are often serious ones.

Keep in the left-hand lane of the motorway unless you need to pull out to overtake slower traffic

planning your journey

Motorways are laid out to avoid sharp bends or steep hills, and there are no stop or give way junctions to halt the traffic flow. This means it's possible to make swift progress, and if you're planning a long journey it makes sense to use the motorway.

You must make sure you are prepared before setting out, because long high-speed journeys put extra strain on both car and driver. Check the car's lights, fluid levels and tyre pressures before setting out. If you do break down, recovery from a motorway is expensive so it pays to be a member of a breakdown recovery service. Don't travel long distances if you are ill or haven't slept well. The hard shoulder is only for stopping in a real emergency – not just if you feel tired – so plan frequent rest stops at service areas.

it's the law

motorway access

These road users are not permitted on motorways:

- ➜ learner drivers and riders
- ➜ pedestrians
- ➜ cyclists
- ➜ horse riders
- ➜ motorcycles under 50cc
- ➜ slow-moving vehicles, agricultural vehicles and invalid carriages.

lane discipline

Keep in the left-hand lane unless you need to overtake slower-moving vehicles. Where there is a stream of slower-moving traffic, don't weave in and out of the left-hand lane. It's better to stay in the middle lane until the left-hand lane clears (but do keep an eye on your mirror and be prepared to move over to let faster-moving vehicles pass).

Use the outer lane to overtake when the inner and middle lanes are occupied with slower traffic, but again be ready to move back as soon as it is clear to do so.

If a vehicle which is clearly exceeding the speed limit comes up behind you, never try to make it slow down or hold it up: pull over at the first safe opportunity and let it overtake. If you are held up by a slower vehicle, never try to intimidate your way past: wait patiently until it pulls over.

Large goods vehicles, buses, coaches and vehicles towing a trailer or caravan are not allowed to use the outer lane of a motorway, so take care not to block their progress by neglecting to pull back into the left-hand lane as soon as it is clear for you to do so.

junctions

As you approach a junction be prepared for vehicles exiting the motorway to cut across in front of you at the last moment.

There is usually a slip road entering the motorway immediately after you pass an exit. Anticipate that vehicles may be joining here. If there is space to do so then pull into the middle lane to give vehicles joining the motorway room to move across from the slip road into the inside lane.

stopping

Stopping is not permitted on a motorway except in an emergency, or if you are directed to by a sign with flashing red lights or by the police. If you need a break or want to use a mobile phone, go to the next exit or service station. You must not pick up or put down hitch hikers, even on a slip road.

joining and leaving

When joining a motorway, use the slip road as you would when joining a dual carriageway. Once you have joined, keep in the left-hand lane until you have adjusted to traffic conditions on the motorway.

Motorway exits are signposted at one mile and half a mile, with countdown markers at 300, 200 and 100 yards (270, 180 and 90 metres) before the slip road. Don't pull across to the exit at the last second. You should aim to be in the left-hand lane by around the half-mile warning sign. Where other traffic might benefit from a signal, start indicating left at the 300 yard marker. If you go past your junction by mistake you must continue to the next junction and leave the motorway to rejoin in the opposite direction. You must never reverse on a motorway or slip road.

Keep an eye on your speedometer after leaving a motorway, as it may feel you are driving more slowly than you really are.

traffic officers

Highways Agency traffic officers now work alongside police officers on motorways to manage incidents and keep traffic moving. It is an offence not to comply with directions given by a traffic officer.

ATM schemes

Active Traffic Management (ATM) schemes are in place on some motorways to reduce congestion. They use variable mandatory speed limits to promote a more constant traffic flow and reduce delays. In congested conditions the hard shoulder comes into use as an extra traffic lane. Emergency refuge areas are provided every 500m and should be used in the event of a breakdown, whether or not the hard shoulder is open to traffic. When the ATM is operating, speed limits are shown in red circles on electronic overhead signs: a speed limit shown above the hard shoulder means it is open to traffic; a red cross or blank sign means the hard shoulder is for emergency use only.

anticipation

Anticipating what is happening far ahead of your vehicle is vital when driving at high speed on the motorway. Too often, drivers follow too closely behind the vehicle in front. When one brakes, it sends a chain reaction of panic braking back down the motorway. Leave at least a two-second gap between your car and the vehicle in front – more in wet weather or poor visibility. Keep looking well ahead and ease off the accelerator if you see brake lights in the distance. Be ready to slow down or stop if you see hazard warning lights flashing ahead, and if you encounter slow or stationary traffic consider switching on your hazard warning lights briefly to warn the drivers behind you.

It is illegal (except in an emergency) to enter the triangular chevrons within a solid white line that separate the slip road from the main carriageway

Take special care when entering service stations as slip roads can be shorter than normal, and you will need to slow to a walking pace in the car park

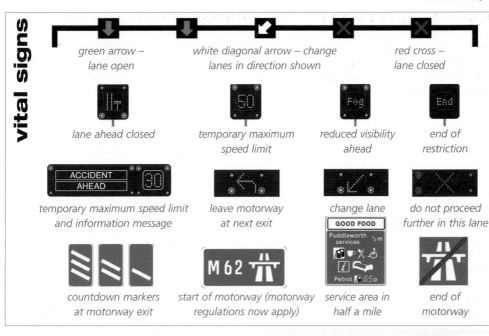

vital signs

green arrow – lane open

white diagonal arrow – change lanes in direction shown

red cross – lane closed

lane ahead closed

temporary maximum speed limit

reduced visibility ahead

end of restriction

temporary maximum speed limit and information message

leave motorway at next exit

change lane

do not proceed further in this lane

countdown markers at motorway exit

start of motorway (motorway regulations now apply)

service area in half a mile

end of motorway

bad weather

Because of the high traffic speeds it is essential to make yourself visible on the motorway. Always use your headlights at night and in rain or poor light, even when the motorway is well lit.

In wet conditions, beware of spray thrown up from the road, particularly as you overtake large goods vehicles and coaches. Look out also for the effect of crosswinds on exposed stretches of motorway. Be prepared for the wind to drop as you come alongside a high-sided vehicle, then increase violently as you pass it.

Use your fog lights whenever visibility falls below 100 metres – but remember to turn them off again as soon as the fog clears. Patches of fog are a special danger on motorways as you may run into them at high speed with little warning. Reduce your speed in conditions where fog patches may be likely to form and take heed of fog warning signs, even if it is still clear where you are.

know the code

highway code rules 255-58
Motorway signals

255. Motorway signals are used to warn you of a danger ahead. For example, there may be an incident, fog, a spillage or road workers on the carriageway which you may not immediately be able to see.

256. Signals situated on the central reservation apply to all lanes. On very busy stretches, signals may be overhead with a separate signal for each lane.

257. Amber flashing lights. These warn of a hazard ahead. The signal may show a temporary maximum speed limit, lanes that are closed or a message such as 'Fog'. Adjust your speed and look out for the danger until you pass a signal which is not flashing or one that gives the 'All clear' sign and you are sure it is safe to increase your speed.

258. Red flashing lights. If red lights on the overhead signals flash above your lane and a red 'X' is showing, you MUST NOT go beyond the signal in that lane. If red lights flash on a signal in the central reservation or at the side of the road, you MUST NOT go beyond the signal in any lane.

roadworks

Roadworks are an occupational hazard for drivers, and the delays they cause can be frustrating. For safety's sake, stay calm and follow all signs to the letter. You may have to merge with other traffic where lanes are closed off, follow a deviation over an uneven temporary road surface, and give way to workmen and machinery crossing in front of you. Take particular care on motorway contraflows.

roadwork precautions

- take care when you see the roadworks ahead sign, and look out for further signs
- temporary speed limits posted at roadworks are mandatory and you must obey them, even if there is no work taking place
- if one or more lanes are closed, carry out the mirror-signal-manoeuvre routine and get into the correct lane in good time. Leave plenty of space and be alert for vehicles cutting across at the last moment
- do not switch lanes to overtake queuing traffic. When queuing in lines of traffic, obey merge in turn signs where posted
- lanes may narrow through roadworks so look for width restriction warnings. Use the hard shoulder if signs direct you to
- be prepared to stop where traffic at roadworks is controlled by a stop-go board, a police officer or temporary traffic lights
- do not enter areas cordoned off by cones
- try not to be distracted by work going on around you, but be prepared to give way to works vehicles or staff
- slow down for ramps, rough road surfaces or loose chippings
- at the end of motorway roadworks there may be a national speed limit sign or an end of roadworks sign: both indicate that the speed limit has returned to the national limit (70mph for cars)
- where the pavement is closed due to street repairs, look out for pedestrians walking in the road.

contraflows

On motorway contraflow systems traffic from both directions share the same carriageway. Lanes are separated by temporary red and white marker posts, and may be narrower than usual. You may need to select a lane some way in advance if you intend leaving at the next junction. Make sure you:

- reduce speed in good time and obey any speed limit signposted
- get into an appropriate lane early
- keep a generous separation distance.

---

vital signs

roadworks

loose chippings

manually operated temporary stop and go signs

temporary hazard at roadworks

roadworks one mile ahead

lane restrictions at roadworks ahead

temporary lane closure

one lane crossover at contraflow roadworks

Mandatory reduced speed limit ahead

end of roadworks and any temporary restrictions

When minor roadworks are carried out on motorways and dual carriageways these signs may be shown on the back of a slow-moving or stationary works vehicle blocking a traffic lane. The four amber lamps flash in alternate horizontal pairs. Pass the vehicle in the direction shown by the arrow. Where a lane is closed there will be no cones to separate it off

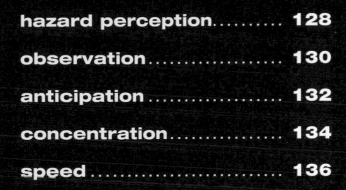

8 road sense

Unfortunately there's no equivalent to an aircraft's auto-pilot when you're driving a car. Every moment you are behind the wheel, you need to concentrate one hundred per cent on your driving. Not only do you need to observe what is happening on the road all around you, you need to think hard about what you're seeing too, identifying hazards and assessing what sort of risk they represent. That way you can anticipate risks in advance, not react to them at the last moment. You must also watch your speed on the road: speeding is both illegal and responsible for many serious road accidents.

hazard perception

SLOW
DOWN

One reason why inexperienced drivers have a higher accident rate is that they take more time – up to two seconds longer – to detect a hazard as it is developing on the road ahead. Hazard perception is tested in a special video-clip based exam that forms part of the theory test. Get into the habit of trying to identify potential hazards every time you are on the road, even as a passenger, and ask yourself what action you would need to take to deal with them safely.

what is a hazard?

Simply any potential danger you encounter on the road which may cause you to change your speed or direction.

There are three types of hazard:

◆ static hazards

These are stationary features such as bends, junctions, traffic lights and crossings. They are the easiest type of hazard to recognise, as they do not change as you approach them, but you often have to deal with them while concentrating on what other road users – such as pedestrians using a zebra crossing – are doing as well

◆ moving hazards

These may be pedestrians, cyclists, animals, horse riders, motorcyclists and large vehicles as well as other cars. Each type of road user is likely to react differently to situations on the road, and you need to understand why this is in order to anticipate how they are likely to react and so share the road safely with them

◆ road and weather hazards

Rain, ice or snow, mud or loose gravel on the road all make it more likely that harsh steering, braking or acceleration will cause a skid. Bright sunshine can dazzle, and darkness makes it harder to spot hazards. Fog dangerously reduces visibility and high winds make it more hazardous to drive near cyclists, motorcyclists and high sided vehicles.

prioritising hazards

Hazards on the road don't come neatly one at a time. It's important to assess how serious each hazard is so you can decide which one takes priority. For instance, a parked car on a wide road with no oncoming traffic is a minor hazard. But if you spot that there is a driver sitting in the car and exhaust fumes show that the engine is running, then it becomes a more serious hazard, and you must anticipate that the driver might pull out in front of you.

The sooner you recognise a hazard, the sooner you are able to take the action needed to negotiate it safely. If ever you have to take emergency action to avoid a collision on the road, ask yourself whether you could have recognised and anticipated the hazard earlier, and what steps could you take to avoid the same thing happening again in the future.

Effective observation is a vital
driving skill to develop. You can
only react to what you see
happening on the road around
you, and the sooner you see
a hazard, the more time
you will be able to give
yourself to deal
with it safely.

looking or seeing?

If you let your attention wander you may find yourself looking at hazards without really seeing them. Or driving past a road sign without actually taking in what it means. Try to train your sense of observation so you really are seeing and thinking about everything on the road around you.

scanning

Keep your eyes moving, so you are seeing what is happening in all directions. Scan to the left and right of the road, then shift the focus of your eyes into the far distance. By looking well ahead of the vehicle in front you can see any hazards that its driver may react to, and anticipate in advance that you will need to slow down. Don't wait till you see the brake lights of the car in front come on before starting to take action.

Keep your eyes constantly moving and shifting focus from the foreground into the far distance

Remember to use your mirrors to keep an eye on what is happening behind your vehicle too; carry out the mirror-signal-manoeuvre routine every time you meet a hazard.

improve your view

- ⊙ following too closely behind the vehicle in front can drastically reduce your view. Keep well back, especially when behind a large vehicle, so you can see around it
- ⊙ scan to your left and right as you approach a crossroads or roundabout to see if you can spot other vehicles which will arrive there at the same time you do
- ⊙ look at rows of trees or lamp posts along the road ahead to see if they curve to indicate a bend in the road
- ⊙ look underneath parked cars to spot the feet of pedestrians who may be about to cross the road
- ⊙ where parked vehicles restrict your view at a junction, look for traffic reflected in shop windows
- ⊙ don't rely just on your eyes. In fog or where high hedges obscure a junction, wind down your window and listen for the sound of approaching vehicles.

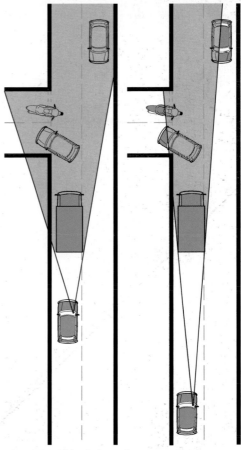

Keeping well back from the vehicle in front can dramatically improve your view and give you much earlier warning of hazards ahead

Some people think that a good driver is one who has the quick reactions to get out of trouble. This isn't true. The good driver is the one who anticipates trouble and avoids getting into it in the first place. Ask yourself 'what if?' as you drive along the road. What if that pedestrian walks onto the zebra crossing? What if that taxi does a U-turn? What if that driver waiting to pull out hasn't seen me? If you always anticipate the worst that may happen, you won't be taken unawares when it does.

Anticipating hazards

Hazards on the road come in all sorts, shapes and sizes. The situations pictured opposite illustrate the sort of questions you need to ask yourself in order to anticipate what hazards might develop on the road ahead.

Approaching pedestrian crossing
Scan the pavements on either side and ask yourself whether any of the pedestrians may be about to use the crossing ahead

Cyclist approaching junction
Ask yourself if this cyclist might suddenly swerve across the road to turn right at the junction. Hold back until you are certain what he intends to do

Car waiting to pull out
You have to slow down to let the pedestrian cross. Ask yourself if the car driver might think you are slowing to let him pull out of the junction

Car following slow truck on motorway
Ask yourself if the driver is likely to pull out in front of you in order to overtake the slow truck, with or without giving a signal beforehand

Stationary vehicle on hard shoulder
Ask yourself whether this vehicle may start to move out without warning, or if the driver may open the door and jump out without looking. This situation needs particular care as most of your attention is focused on joining the motorway

vital signs

stationary traffic is likely ahead (always make sure that you can stop in the distance you can see to be clear)

danger ahead

REDUCE SPEED NOW

reduce speed warning shown beneath some signs

concentration

Driving is a serious business. If you walk along a footpath chatting to a friend and not concentrating on where you're stepping, you may trip on a fallen branch and stub your toe. It's irritating but no disaster. But if you're driving along lost in conversation, or fiddling with the radio, or daydreaming about your next holiday, and you fail to see a cyclist pull out in front of you, then the outcome could be devastating.

staying alert

To maintain your concentration:

⊘ don't drive when you are feeling distracted or emotional. Delay setting out until you have calmed down, or take a cab instead

⊘ keep your eyes on the road. At 70mph you travel over 30 metres (100 feet) every second – so if you glance away for three seconds to fiddle with the car stereo, you have covered nearly 100 metres (330 feet) without looking where you're going

⊘ avoid eating, drinking or smoking while driving. On a long journey you need to take regular breaks, so plan a lunch stop into your itinerary

⊘ don't listen to excessively loud music

⊘ avoid arguing with passengers

⊘ if you need to consult a map, or use a satellite navigation system, find a safe place to pull over first

⊘ never use a mobile phone while driving – it's illegal and dangerous, making you four times more likely to have a crash. Even hands-free phones are a serious distraction – you can't concentrate on a telephone conversation and driving at the same time. And never try to send or receive text messages while driving.

⊘ don't drive when you are tired, or when under the influence of drugs or alcohol.

fatigue

Driving when tired is a major cause of death on the road. Crashes involving drivers who doze off at the wheel are usually serious, because a sleeping driver isn't able to slow down or take avoiding action. But no one falls asleep without warning. As soon as you start to feel drowsy and lose concentration you should:

⊘ make sure there is plenty of fresh air coming into the car – but remember that if you are really tired then opening a window will not stop you falling asleep

⊘ pull over as soon as you can into a lay-by or service area (but not the hard shoulder of a motorway) and take a break

⊘ have a drink high in caffeine, such as two cups of strong coffee

⊘ recline your seat and take a short nap.

You can reduce the risk of becoming sleepy while you are driving by:

⊘ avoiding long drives during your body's natural sleep periods (the early hours of the morning and just after lunch)

⊘ taking regular breaks during a long drive. Stop for at least 15 minutes for every two hours you are on the road

⊘ not driving a long distance after a poor or interrupted night's sleep.

Using a hand-held mobile while driving is illegal, so park up safely before making or receiving calls

Take regular breaks when driving long distances to avoid losing concentration behind the wheel

135

speed

Most cars are capable of exceeding 100mph. Many could easily double the maximum speed permitted on the motorway. With so much power on tap it takes discipline to keep your speed under control. But using speed safely is one of the most vital driving skills. The stark truth is that if you have to stop in an emergency and you are driving too quickly then you will crash. The higher your speed, the more serious that crash will be.

speed limits

You must always keep your speed below the maximum speed limit for the road and vehicle you are driving. These general rules govern the speed limit for cars on most roads:

- ◐ the national speed limit on single carriageway roads is 60mph
- ◐ the national speed limit on dual carriageways and motorways is 70mph
- ◐ the speed limit on roads with street lighting is 30mph.

These speed limits apply at all times unless signs indicate otherwise. There will not usually be repeater signs to remind you that one of these speed limits is in force.

These limits are overridden if there are signs which indicate a different speed limit, such as 50mph on a dual carriageway. Some stretches of motorway have variable speed limits, which allow a lower speed limit to be set during busy periods to smooth traffic flow and prevent vehicles bunching.

Where different speed limits apply there will be regular speed limit repeater signs placed along the road.

safe speeds

Speed limits represent the maximum speed permitted. They are not targets to be achieved at all costs. There are many occasions where it is not safe to drive as fast as the speed limit. For instance, when driving near children running along the pavement, or where parked cars obscure your vision on either side, 30mph could be recklessly fast.

Too many drivers routinely ignore the speed limit in town. It's true that 30mph feels slow from inside a car, but you must always put the safety of pedestrians and cyclists first. The fact is that if a car hits a pedestrian while travelling at 20mph, nine times out of ten the pedestrian will live through the impact; in a collision at 40mph, the pedestrian is unlikely to survive.

In busy town centres (above) or on narrow country lanes (below) you may need to keep your speed well below the speed limit to stay safe

national speed limits

Type of vehicle	Built-up area	Single carriageway	Dual carriageway	Motorway
Cars & motorcycles	30	60	70	70
Cars towing caravans or trailers	30	50	60	60
Buses & coaches	30	50	60	70
Goods vehicles * 60 if articulated or towing a trailer	30	50	60	70*
Goods vehicles (exceeding 7.5 tonnes maximum laden weight)	30	40	50	60

20 mph	6 metres	6 metres		3 car lengths or	**12** metres
30 mph	9 metres	14 metres		6 car lengths or	**23** metres
40 mph	12 metres	24 metres		9 car lengths or	**36** metres
50 mph	15 metres	38 metres		13 car lengths or	**53** metres
60 mph	18 metres	55 metres		18 car lengths or	**73** metres
70 mph	21 metres	75 metres		24 car lengths or	**96** metres

Thinking distance   Braking distance   Average car length = 4 metres

stopping distances

The diagram above gives typical stopping distances from varying speeds. There are a number of important points to bear in mind when you are considering these stopping distances:

- it takes a long way to bring a car to a complete halt even from a low speed: six car lengths are needed from 30mph, which is a lot more space than most drivers allow when driving in town
- it takes time to react and press the brake pedal before you even start to slow down. At 40mph you will travel three car lengths during the time it takes you to react. This assumes that it takes about 0.7 seconds to react before braking, a time that could easily treble if you aren't concentrating
- stopping distance doesn't increase uniformly with speed: double your speed from 30mph to 60mph, and you need not twice but three times the distance in which to stop
- these are stopping distances on a dry road in good weather: in the wet, allow twice the distance to stop; on icy roads, ten times further may be needed
- a car with worn brakes or tyres may take much further to stop, particularly on a wet road, even if the tyre tread depth is still above the legal minimum
- always remember the driving rule which cannot be repeated too often: **you must be able to stop in the distance you can see to be clear**.

how fast?

Sometimes your senses can trick you into thinking you are driving more slowly than you really are. A speed of 40mph feels much slower on an open road than it does through an avenue of trees, because the objects flashing past on the edge of your vision give you a sensation of speed. This means it is particularly difficult to judge your speed when the reference points around you are obscured, for instance at night or in foggy weather.

Take particular care to monitor your speed at times when you may feel you are going more slowly than you really are, such as:

- at night or in poor visibility
- on long, open stretches of road, especially motorways
- when you enter a speed limit after a spell of fast driving on the open road
- when driving an unusual car, particularly if it is quieter and more powerful than the one you are used to.

other vehicles

Remember that drivers of other vehicles are not necessarily permitted to travel as quickly as you are in your car. Make allowance for this and don't get frustrated when you are following, for instance, a caravan doing 50mph on the open road – it's going as fast as it is allowed.

minimum speed

Minimum speed limits are not common, but are sometimes posted on roads where it is important for traffic to keep flowing smoothly.

Don't race up to hazards and brake at the last moment: anticipate them and lose speed smoothly

It's good driving to make progress when it is safe to do so, but you must stay within the speed limit

acceleration sense

Never accelerate towards a hazard. If you spot brake lights coming on ahead, or see advance warning for a give way sign, lift your foot off the accelerator pedal. The sooner you start to lose speed as you approach a hazard the more time you give yourself to deal with it. Accelerating up to a hazard and braking at the last minute is bad practice for other reasons too: it wastes fuel and causes unnecessary brake wear, as well as being unnerving for passengers (including your driving examiner) who may think you haven't noticed there's a hazard ahead.

making progress

If safety is the most important consideration when driving, and the higher your speed the greater the potential danger, wouldn't the best plan be to drive everywhere at 10mph? Unfortunately this would be a sure route to failing your driving test. Although you must at all times drive safely, you should also make progress when it is safe to do so. Drivers who crawl along the road when it would be safe to drive at the speed limit obstruct other road users, making them feel frustrated and more likely to take risks to overtake. Where it is safe to drive at the indicated speed limit, then it is good driving practice to do just that.

vital signs

maximum speed limit

national speed limit applies

end of 20 mph zone

maximum speed limit within traffic calming scheme

minimum speed limit

end of minimum speed limit

area with traffic enforcement cameras

9 other road users

From the smooth, warm, quiet comfort of your car, it can be hard to put yourself in the position of other road users who are exposed to harsher conditions. Such as the pedestrian hurrying to get home through blinding rain, the cyclist swerving to avoid a broken drain cover, or the rider trying to calm a horse spooked by a tin can rattling across the road. But you should never forget that you are at the wheel of a potentially lethal weapon and it is your responsibility to look out for the safety of these more vulnerable road users.

pedestrians

Cars and pedestrians make an uneasy mix and where the two come into conflict it's the pedestrian who comes off worst. You simply cannot take risks where pedestrians are around. That means slowing down when there are people on the pavement and always being prepared to give way for pedestrians crossing the road.

vulnerable people

Take special care around those pedestrians who may fail to be aware of your presence, such as:

- ⊃ elderly pedestrians, who can find it harder to judge the speed of approaching vehicles
- ⊃ children, who may run into the road unexpectedly
- ⊃ blind and deaf pedestrians, who may be unaware of your approach. If a person is holding a white stick, or leading a guide dog on a harness, it means they are blind. If the white stick has a red band around it, they are deaf as well. There are guide dogs for the deaf too, and these usually wear a burgundy-coloured coat
- ⊃ wheelchair users. Be patient when a wheelchair user needs to cross the road, and don't obstruct them by parking where the kerb is lowered to allow wheelchair access.

Look out for powered vehicles used by disabled people. These small vehicles travel at a maximum speed of 8mph. When used on a dual carriageway they must by law have a flashing amber light, but on other roads you may not be given any such warning of their presence

pedestrian crossings

Pedestrian crossings are points designed to allow pedestrians to cross the road in safely. Always be prepared to stop when approaching a crossing, and take special care if your view as you approach the crossing is obscured by queuing traffic or badly parked vehicles.

Treat pedestrians using a crossing courteously. Consider giving a slowing down arm signal as you approach to let waiting pedestrians know you are stopping, but do not beckon them to cross – this may be dangerous if other vehicles are approaching. Wait patiently while they are crossing, especially for elderly or disabled pedestrians who may not be able to get across before the lights change.

Never park on a crossing or in the area marked by zig-zag lines. When approaching a crossing in a slow-moving queue, hold back so you do not stop where you would obstruct the crossing. It is illegal to overtake the moving vehicle nearest to a pedestrian crossing or a vehicle which has stopped to give way to pedestrians at the crossing.

Pedestrians don't always use crossings, so drive carefully wherever there are people on foot

know the code

highway code rule 5

Organised walks Large groups of people walking together should use a pavement if available; if one is not, they should keep to the left. Look-outs should be positioned at the front and back of the group, and they should wear fluorescent clothes in daylight and reflective clothes in the dark. At night, the look-out in front should show a white light and the one at the back a red light. People on the outside of large groups should also carry lights and wear reflective clothing.

Approach zebra crossings with caution and be prepared to stop and give way to pedestrians

zebra crossings

Be ready to slow down or stop as you approach a zebra crossing. You must by law give way when someone has stepped on to a crossing, but you should also be prepared to stop and let waiting pedestrians cross. Scan the pavements as you approach for anyone who looks like they might want to cross and slow down well before you get to the crossing. If a pedestrian does not cross immediately, be patient and remain stationary until they do. Be prepared for pedestrians to change their mind halfway across and walk back in front of you.

Where the zebra crossing is divided by a central island you should treat each half as a separate crossing.

pelican crossings

Pelican crossings are controlled by lights. Unlike normal traffic lights, these have a flashing amber phase in between red and green. When the amber light is flashing, you must give way to pedestrians who are on the crossing. If there are no pedestrians on the crossing when the amber light is flashing, you may proceed across it with caution. If pedestrians are still crossing after the lights have changed to green you should continue to give way to them.

Pelican crossings which go straight across the road are one crossing, even when there is a central island. This means you must wait for pedestrians who are crossing from the other side of the island. However, if the crossings are staggered on either side of the central island they should be treated as separate crossings.

Pelican crossings (above), toucan crossings and puffin crossings are all controlled by traffic lights

Always be courteous to school crossing patrols and be prepared to stop if requested to do so

toucan crossings

These are also used by cyclists, who are permitted to ride across a toucan crossing. They are operated by push buttons and follow the normal traffic light sequence, with no flashing amber phase. Take care when preparing to move off when the lights turn green, in case a pedestrian has left it late to cross or is an elderly person crossing slowly.

school crossings

You must stop when a school crossing patrol shows a stop for children sign. Always be courteous to school crossing patrols.

There may be a flashing amber signal below the school warning sign to alert you that children may be crossing the road ahead. Drive very slowly until you are clear of the area. Be cautious also when passing a stationary bus showing a school bus sign. You may have to give way to children running across the road to and from the bus.

equestrian crossings

These are designed to allow horse riders to cross the road safely and are controlled by red and green lights. They have wider crossing areas, pavement barriers, and may be alongside pedestrian or cycle crossings.

puffin crossings

These have automatic sensors which detect when pedestrians are on the crossing and delay the green light until they have safely reached the other side. Like the toucan crossing, puffins have a normal traffic light sequence with no flashing amber.

vital signs

pedestrian crossing

Patrol
school crossing patrol ahead

elderly people (or blind or disabled as shown) crossing road

No footway for 400 yds
no footway (there may be pedestrians walking in the road)

STOP
stop at school crossing patrol

horse riders

Horses are easily alarmed and unpredictable. When you encounter a horse rider on the road, slow right down and be prepared to stop. Don't become irritated with horse riders for slowing your journey – they aren't riding on the road for the fun of it, but have no other option to get to and from local bridleways.

horses on the road

Treat all horses as a potential hazard. Slow to a walking pace as you approach a horse being ridden on the road and give it plenty of space. Be prepared to stop and wait if other vehicles are approaching, as you will need to move well onto the other side of the road to pass a horse rider. Never try to squeeze by when a vehicle is coming the other way. Remember that horses are easily startled and may shy into the middle of the road if it is surprised by something – even just a rustling crisp packet in the hedge.

Be prepared to stop for horses crossing the road at equestrian crossings, which are controlled by lights showing red or green.

avoid noise

Never sound your horn or rev your engine while approaching a horse. If the horse looks skittish, pull over and turn off your engine until it has gone by.

Take extra care if you are driving a larger and more noisy vehicle such as a van or car and trailer which may be more likely to alarm the horse. More caution is also needed in wet weather when your tyres make more noise, and you need to avoid startling the horse by splashing it with spray.

inexperienced riders

Be particularly careful when horses are being ridden by children, or where there is a line of inexperienced riders. Riders may be in double file when escorting a young or inexperienced horse rider. Look out for signals from horse riders, and always heed a request to slow down or stop.

right turns

Take care when following a horse and rider at the approach to a right-hand turn or roundabout. The rider may signal right but stay on the left of the road at the approach to the turn, so slow down and be prepared to stop and wait to let the rider cross the road in front of you and make the right turn.

Slow right down when passing horse riders and always leave them plenty of space

Take special care when you encounter horse riders who may be young or inexperienced

know the code

highway code rule 215

Horse riders and horse-drawn vehicles. Be particularly careful of horse riders and horse-drawn vehicles especially when overtaking. Always pass wide and slowly. Horse riders are often children, so take extra care and remember riders may ride in double file when escorting a young or inexperienced horse or rider. Look out for horse riders' and horse drivers' signals and heed a request to slow down or stop. Take great care and treat all horses as a potential hazard; they can be unpredictable, despite the efforts of their rider/driver.

animals

Animals – both wild and domestic – are unpredictable and represent a serious hazard when they stray onto the road. Observe signs warning of animals, and keep your speed down, especially where there are no fences to keep cattle, sheep or ponies off the road.

domestic animals

In country areas, especially moorland, there may be no fences keeping cattle, sheep and horses from straying onto the road. Exercise great caution in these areas and keep your speed down, especially at night or in misty conditions. Where there are animals on or near the road, drive past them at walking pace. Do not sound your horn, flash your lights, or rev your engine loudly as this may cause them to panic. Bear in mind that if an animal such as a sheep crosses the road in front of you then several others may follow it, and that young animals will run to their mother if they feel threatened, even if that means darting in front of your car.

Sometimes sheep or cattle have to be led across the road. If your way is blocked by a herd of animals, stop, switch off your engine and wait until they have left the road.

wild animals

Colliding with a large wild animal like a deer is distressing, and can cause serious damage to your car and possibly you too. Keep your speed down wherever there is likely to be wildlife near the road, and slow down when you see warning signs. Take special care at dawn and dusk when deer are most active.

Cattle grids are often placed at the entrance to areas of open country: cars can cross them but cattle cannot. Slow down when driving across a grid as they can be loose and slippery

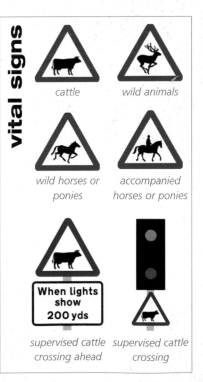

vital signs

cattle

wild animals

wild horses or ponies

accompanied horses or ponies

supervised cattle crossing ahead

supervised cattle crossing

cyclists

If you have ever cycled on a busy road you'll know how intimidating it is when cars speed by leaving only a couple of feet to spare. Cyclists have every much right to use the road as car drivers – maybe more right, as they are doing so at less cost to the environment – so treat them with courtesy, and be conscious of their extra vulnerability compared with a motor vehicle.

overtaking cyclists

Leave as much room when overtaking a cyclist as you would when overtaking a car. Remember that a cyclist may swerve to avoid something you can't see, such as a pothole or rubbish in the road. Never try to squeeze past a cyclist when another vehicle is coming towards you, and slow right down when passing a cyclist on a narrow road.

Be prepared for cyclists to do the unexpected. Although most cyclists are responsible road users, remember that no training is needed to ride a bicycle and riders of any age are allowed to use the road. Situations where you should be particularly alert for cyclists include:

- **slow-moving traffic**
  Cyclists may overtake on your inside, so check your nearside mirror before pulling into the kerb or turning left
- **junctions and roundabouts**
  Cyclists can find it daunting to pull across the road to turn right in busy traffic, and may feel safer keeping to the left when turning right at a roundabout. Be cautious whenever you see a cyclist looking over their shoulder as they could be about to turn right. Give them time and space to do so safely
- **left turns**
  Never overtake a cyclist just before a left turn so you have to cut in front to make the turn. Slow down and hold back until the cyclist has passed the turning
- **country lanes**
  You may encounter slow-moving cyclists around any bend
- **at night or dusk**
  Cyclists may not be showing lights, or their lights may be hard to spot among other vehicle lights
- **windy weather**
  In strong winds cyclists may find it hard to keep a straight course and you should leave more space when overtaking them

Take special care around young cyclists who may not be aware of the dangers of riding on the road

vital signs

cycle route ahead

no cycling

route for cycles only

route for pedestrians and cyclists

recommended route for cycles

with-flow cycle lane

know the code

highway code rule 140

Cycle lanes These are shown by road markings and signs. You MUST NOT drive or park in a cycle lane marked by a solid white line during its times of operation. Do not drive or park in a cycle lane marked by a broken white line unless it is unavoidable. You MUST NOT park in any cycle lane whilst waiting restrictions apply.

motorbikes

Motorcyclists are seriously vulnerable road users. They are twenty times more likely than car drivers to be killed or seriously injured in a road accident. Many collisions involving bikers are caused by car drivers who aren't thinking about motorbikes approaching. Always look out for motorbikes, give them plenty of room and do what you can to let them get past easily and safely.

check your mirrors

Motorcyclists use the small size, acceleration and manoeuvrability of their machine to make progress by overtaking streams of slower vehicles. This means you need to be alert at all times to the possibility of a motorbike overtaking, especially when you are making a right turn.

junctions

Motorbikes aren't always easy to see. Many riders wear bright clothing and use a dipped headlamp during the day to make themselves more visible, but even so it can be easy to overlook a motorbike on the road. Be vigilant at junctions. Before pulling out in front of a large vehicle or bus, always consider the possibility that an overtaking motorbike may be hidden from your view by the larger vehicle.

overtaking

When you overtake a motorbike allow as much room as you would when overtaking a car. Bear in mind that the rider may swerve to avoid debris or potholes. Take special care in the wet when a rider may swerve to avoid skidding on a metal drain cover or tram lines, and in windy weather when a strong gust could blow the bike across the road in front of you.

Make sure before overtaking a slow-moving motorbike that it is not about to make a turn, or quickly pick up speed again. Motorcyclists often look over their right shoulder to check their blind spot just before turning right, so if you see a rider doing this, hang back and give them room.

traffic queues

It is perfectly legal for a motorcyclist to filter between lanes of queueing traffic. Keep an eye on your mirrors when queueing, consider edging to one side to give motorcyclists space to get past safely, and leave enough room for them to cut in front of you. Be extra vigilant for filtering motorbikes before you change lanes in slow-moving traffic.

Use your mirrors to look out for motorcyclists who may be filtering past queues of slower traffic

large vehicles

If you have any difficulty with manoeuvring your car, you can't fail to be impressed by the skills demonstrated by drivers of large articulated vehicles as they thread their vehicles through narrow streets and reverse into tight spaces. But LGV drivers can't work miracles, and there are times when they need extra space and consideration from other road users.

take care

Driving situations where you need to take extra care around large vehicles include:

- **left turns**: a long vehicle may need to pull on to the right side of the road to be able to make a sharp left turn without cutting the corner. Don't overtake until it has completed the manoeuvre
- **roundabouts**: a long vehicle may not be able to keep entirely inside its own lane markings on a tight roundabout. Don't pull alongside it or you may get squashed
- **low bridges**: a high lorry or bus may have to pull into the middle of the road to squeeze under a low bridge. Slow down and be prepared to stop at a bridge with a height restriction
- **overtaking**: it can be difficult to see past large vehicles to overtake. Keep well back to improve your view, and look past the nearside of the vehicle as well as the offside. Remember you will need extra space to overtake a long vehicle. Be cautious about overtaking a heavily laden truck after it crests a hill – it may pick up speed quickly when heading downhill
- **blind spots**: you may be hidden in the driver's blind spot while driving past a truck or coach, particularly if it's a left-hand drive vehicle. Remember, if you cannot see the driver's eyes in their offside mirror, they cannot see you. Don't linger in this blind spot: get past trucks on multi-lane roads briskly. You will also be hidden from the driver's view if you get too close behind a large vehicle, so always maintain a generous separation distance
- **bad weather**: in the wet take care to avoid being blinded by spray thrown up by large vehicles. Be careful when passing high vehicles in windy weather as wind gusting around them may cause your car to veer off course.

vital signs

no goods vehicles over maximum weight shown in tonnes

risk of grounding

markers displayed on a vehicle with an overhanging load

low bridge – beware of oncoming high vehicles in middle of road

vehicles more than 13 metres long must display these warnings to the rear. The vertical markings are also required to be fitted to builders' skips left in the road

know the code

highway code rule 221

Large vehicles. These may need extra road space to turn or to deal with a hazard that you are not able to see. If you are following a large vehicle, such as a bus or articulated lorry, be aware that the driver may not be able to see you in the mirrors. Be prepared to stop and wait if it needs room or time to turn.

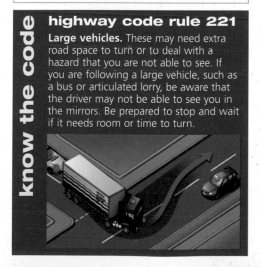

One thing you know for sure when following a bus is that it's soon going to stop to let down or pick up passengers. Keep well back so when the bus does pull in you are not held up behind it but are in a position to see beyond and pass it if it is safe to do so.

bus stops

Exercise great care when passing a stationary bus as passengers getting on or off may walk into the road without checking for traffic. Take care when a bus has stopped on the other side of the road too: passengers may run across to get on it, and oncoming vehicles may pull onto your side of the road to overtake it.

As you approach a bus at a bus stop try and assess whether it is about to move off. (If there is a long queue waiting, it will probably be stopped for a while; if no-one is queueing, it may have loaded its passengers and be ready to leave.) Be ready to slow down and give way to a bus which indicates that it wants to pull out.

Do not park at or near a bus stop.

bus lanes

These are special lanes at the side of the road which only buses (and taxis, motorbikes or cycles if indicated) are permitted to use. Check if there is a sign showing times of operation because the lane may be restricted at rush hours only; outside the times indicated, you are allowed to drive in the lane. Where there are no signs it means the lane is reserved for buses 24 hours a day.

If you have to turn across a bus or cycle lane to enter a side road or driveway, always give way to vehicles using it.

Slow down and give way when you see a bus at a bus stop with its right-hand indicator flashing

vital signs

school bus: take extreme care passing a stationary school bus as children may run from or towards it without looking

bus lane on road at junction ahead

with-flow bus and cycle lane

other vehicles may use this bus lane outside the times shown

no buses (over eight passenger seats)

bus lane road markings

bus stop road markings

buses and cycles only

contra-flow bus lane

Tram or Light Rapid Transit (LRT) systems have been established in several cities. They are an environmentally efficient public transport system which runs on electricity and helps to reduce noise and traffic congestion in town. Trams move quickly and quietly, and cannot steer to avoid you, so they need to be treated with special caution. Be particularly careful the first time you drive where there are trams, and anticipate the unexpected from other road users who may be coming across trams for the first time.

tram lanes

Do not enter a lane reserved for trams and indicated by white lines, yellow dots or a different colour or texture of road surface.

Always give way to trams and do not try to overtake a moving tram – wait until it is stationary at a tram stop. Take extra care where a tram track crosses from one side of the road to the other and where the road narrows and the tracks come close to the kerb.

Where a tram line crosses the road, treat it in the same way as a railway level crossing.

Take care when driving across tram rails. They can be slippery when wet so avoid braking or steering while crossing them. Look out for cyclists and motorcyclists who may swerve suddenly to avoid tram rails.

traffic signals

Tram drivers usually have their own traffic signals. These may give a different instruction to the signal for other road users, and a tram may be permitted to move when cars are not. Diamond-shaped road signs give instructions to tram drivers only.

tram stops

Follow the route indicated by signs and road markings where the tram stops at a platform, either in the middle or at the side of the road. Do not drive between a tram and the left-hand kerb when it has stopped to pick up passengers at a stop with no platform. Look out for pedestrians, especially children, running to catch a tram which is at or approaching a stop.

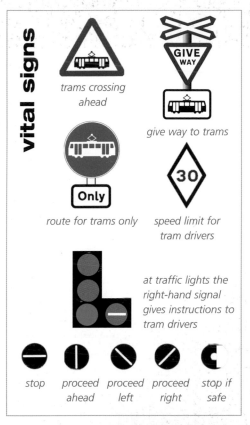

vital signs

trams crossing ahead

give way to trams

route for trams only

speed limit for tram drivers

at traffic lights the right-hand signal gives instructions to tram drivers

stop

proceed ahead

proceed left

proceed right

stop if safe

it's the law

tram rules

It is illegal to:
→ park your vehicle where it would get in the way of trams or where it would force other drivers to do so
→ drive in a lane reserved for trams
→ drive between the left-hand kerb and a tram which has stopped to pick up passengers.

Extra care is needed near a tramway, especially where trams are stopping or crossing the road

159

level crossings

Level crossings are situated where a railway line crosses the road. Trains approach them at high speed, which means accidents involving vehicles on a crossing are serious ones. Never take risks when approaching a level crossing, and make sure you do not get stranded on a level crossing when a train is approaching. Only drive onto a crossing if you can see the exit is clear on the other side, and never stop or park on or near the crossing.

controlled crossings

Most crossings have traffic light signals with a steady amber light, twin flashing red stop lights and an audible alarm for pedestrians. They may have full, half or no barriers. Never try to zig-zag around half-barriers or drive over a crossing without barriers when the lights show.

When a train approaches, the amber light will show, followed by the red lights. If the amber light comes on after you have passed the stop line you should keep going. Otherwise, stop and wait at the line. Turn off your engine as you may be waiting for a few minutes. If a train goes by and the red lights continue to flash, or the alarm changes tone, you must carry on waiting as this means another train is approaching. Only cross when the lights go out and the barriers open.

Some crossings do not have warning lights. In this case you should stop and wait at the barrier or gate when it begins to close, and wait until it opens again before crossing.

user-operated crossings

These crossings have stop signs and small red and green lights. Only cross if the green light is on, and wait when the red light shows. To cross, open the gates or barriers on both sides of the crossing, check that the green light is still on and drive quickly across. Then pull up well clear of the crossing, walk back and close the gates or barriers.

If there are no lights, stop, look both ways and listen before you cross. If there is a railway telephone, use it to contact the signal operator to make sure it is safe to cross. Inform the signal operator again when you are clear of the crossing.

open crossings

These require special care as they have no gates, barriers, attendant or traffic lights (but do have a give way sign). Look both ways, listen and make sure there is no train coming before crossing.

vital signs

countdown markers placed on approach to concealed level crossing

level crossing warning lights (also used at lifting bridges, airfields and fire stations)

STOP when lights show

light signals ahead

level crossing with barrier or gate

level crossing without barrier or gate

level crossing without barrier

accidents and breakdowns

If your vehicle breaks down or you have an accident on a level crossing you should get everyone out of the vehicle and clear of the crossing immediately.

If there is a railway telephone then use it to tell the operator what has happened. Follow any instructions you are given. If there is time before a train arrives then try to move your car clear of the crossing. If you are on your own and cannot push the car clear, you may be able to move it by putting it in first gear with the handbrake off and engaging the starter motor repeatedly. Take care as the engine may start unexpectedly. If the alarm sounds, or the amber light comes on, leave the vehicle and get clear of the crossing immediately.

emergency vehicles

It's easy to panic when you see an emergency vehicle bearing down on you with lights flashing and siren blaring. In this situation it's important to stay calm and do your best to help the driver of the emergency vehicle get past quickly and safely.

warning lights

In an emergency, drivers of police, fire and ambulance vehicles are permitted to use flashing blue lights and sirens. They are also exempt from certain road regulations and may lawfully exceed the speed limit and drive through red traffic lights.

Certain other organisations, including mountain rescue, coastguard, mines rescue, bomb disposal, blood transfusion, lifeboat and medical transplant services are also permitted to drive under blue lights. A doctor answering an emergency call may display a flashing green beacon.

(A flashing amber beacon indicates a slow-moving vehicle.)

giving way

When you see an emergency vehicle in your rear-view mirror it's important to keep your cool and not slam on the brakes. This will only make it more difficult for the driver to get by quickly. Look ahead and find a safe space where you can pull over, and signal clearly to let the driver of the emergency vehicle know what you are doing.

If you see an emergency vehicle coming from the other direction, pull over to make room for it to drive on your side of the road if it needs to. If you are approaching a

You must pull over and stop if signalled to do so by a police officer, and produce your driving documents for inspection on request

junction and can hear the emergency vehicle but are uncertain where it is coming from, hold back till you can see it.

Remember that several vehicles may attend the same emergency. Don't pull straight out after letting an emergency vehicle pass without checking there isn't another one following it. It makes sense anyway to pause for a few moments after having an emergency vehicle rush by to calm your nerves before continuing your journey.

stop – police

You must by law stop your car if signalled to do so by a police officer. The officer will usually signal you to stop by flashing headlights and indicating and pointing to the left. Stop in the first safe place, then switch off your engine. Stay calm and courteous, listen carefully to what the officers have to say, and be prepared to produce your driving documents for inspection (see p198).

Vehicle & Operator Services Agency officers and Highways Agency traffic officers are also empowered to stop vehicles. They will direct you to pull over by flashing amber lights.

10 manoeuvring

During your driving test you will be asked to perform two of the following manoeuvres:
→ turning in the road
→ reversing into a side street
→ reverse parking at the side of the road or into a parking bay.

For many candidates, performing these manoeuvres under the watchful eye of the examiner is the most nerve-racking part of the driving test. The only way to build up your confidence is practice. Try these manoeuvres in as many different locations as possible. Remember that this is a test not just of technical skill but of safety. It's essential to keep looking out for other vehicles and pedestrians at all times when manoeuvring.

manoeuvring

reversing

Reversing isn't a difficult skill to master, although it takes a bit of practice to get used to the different way a car responds to the steering when going backwards. The key to carrying out reversing manoeuvres is to do them slowly, giving yourself plenty of time to make any steering adjustments needed to keep on course.

steering

Find a comfortable position to adopt while reversing. You may need to shift your body around in your seat so you can see clearly over your left shoulder. Adjust your grip on the steering wheel so you are holding it with your right hand at the top of the wheel and your left hand low down on the wheel. If it feels more natural, you may prefer to keep just your right hand on the wheel and rest your left arm on the back of the seat while reversing in a straight line. However, when you are changing direction while reversing, you will probably find that keeping both hands on the wheel gives you more accurate control over your steering.

seatbelt

You are permitted by law to undo your seatbelt while you are carrying out a manoeuvre that involves reversing, and you may wish to do this if you find your belt restricts your movements. However, it is easy to forget to put the seatbelt back on when you have finished reversing – particularly during your driving test when you have so much else to think about – and for this reason it is advisable to keep your seatbelt fastened wherever possible.

Be prepared to stop and give way to other vehicles or pedestrians when you are reversing

Continual all-round observation is essential when carrying out any sort of reversing manoeuvre

observation

Reversing is a potentially dangerous manoeuvre which needs to be carried out with care. This is partly because your view when going backwards is restricted, but also because when you steer the front of the car swings outwards, posing a hazard for oncoming traffic. Take these precautions when reversing:

- look all round your car before starting to reverse to check for approaching vehicles, cyclists or pedestrians
- stop and give way to pedestrians crossing the road while you are reversing
- be alert for children, who may be harder to see when you are reversing
- don't reverse using your mirrors alone – you need to perform continual all round observation when reversing
- never reverse anywhere if you cannot clearly see what's behind you. If necessary get out of your car and have a look, or ask someone else to guide you.

vital signs

no U-turns permitted

*no through road
(If you drive down a road with this sign on it, you will have to turn round and come out again, which may be difficult if you are towing a trailer)*

A car is easier to manoeuvre when reversing so it is almost always better to reverse into a parking space than to try driving straight into it

Remember when reversing that the front of your car will swing out as you start to turn. Look forwards up and down the road as well as behind you to check that this will not cause an obstruction or endanger other road users

reversing manoeuvres

Always choose a safe, legal and convenient place to carry out any reversing manoeuvre. Consider whether you really need to reverse or if there might be a simpler alternative. For instance, if you need to turn around, and there is a roundabout ahead, drive all the way around that to turn round.

A car is easier to manoeuvre when reversing, which is why it usually makes sense to reverse into parking spaces and parking bays.

Never reverse from a side road into a main road. This includes your driveway at home – always reverse in at night so you can drive out forwards in the morning.

U-turns

Where the road is very wide and there is no traffic, it may be easier to carry out a U-turn instead of turning by reversing in the road or reversing into a side street. You should only carry out a U-turn where it is safe and legal to do so, with no signs or road markings prohibiting it. Take special care to make sure the road is clear in both directions, and don't forget to look over your shoulder for a final check before starting the U-turn.

test tips

do
- be prepared to stop and give way if other road users want to go by. If drivers have clearly stopped to let you finish your manoeuvre then continue with it – but don't rush what you are doing because they are waiting or you may end up making mistakes
- if you have taken off your seatbelt to carry out a reversing manoeuvre, remember to put it back on once you have finished

don't
- stop where you would inconvenience or endanger another road user when asked by your examiner to pull over to carry out any manoeuvre
- dry steer, by turning the steering wheel while the car isn't moving

169

turning in the road

Turning in the road using forward and reverse gears is one of the reversing manoeuvres that you may be required to perform during your driving test. This is sometimes called the three-point turn. In fact, on a narrow road you may need to make five or even seven turns, though you should always aim to make as few turns as possible.

turning in the road

1 Stop by the kerb in a safe, legal and convenient place and apply the handbrake. Avoid stopping where trees or lamp posts by the kerb make the manoeuvre more difficult.

2 Engage first gear. Check it is clear all round. Release the handbrake and slowly move forward using clutch control. Once the car is moving apply full right steering lock.

3 As you drive over the centre of the road be careful not to let the car run away if there is a downhill camber. Apply the footbrake gently if necessary. Keep looking all round.

4 Just before you reach the other kerb, apply as much left steering lock as possible. Stop before your front wheels touch the kerb and apply the handbrake.

5 Select reverse gear and check the road is clear in all directions. Remember you may be making an uphill start against the slope of the road camber. Use clutch control to keep the car moving slowly and steer quickly to your left. Keep looking all round.

6 Look over your right shoulder as you near the other kerb and apply right steering lock. Stop before the rear wheels touch the kerb and apply the handbrake. Engage first gear. Check it is clear all round. Drive forward into a normal position on the left side of the road.

reversing into side roads

Reversing into a side road is often the safest and most convenient way to turn round. But it requires great caution: not only are you reversing against traffic emerging from the junction, but once you start reversing the front of your car will swing out into the road. This means you must continually check not only what's behind your car but also what is happening to the front and side as you carry out the manoeuvre.

reversing to the left

1 As you drive past the road you want to reverse into take a good look down it for potential hazards. Pull up about half a metre from the kerb in a safe, legal and convenient place at least two car lengths past the corner and apply the handbrake.

2 Engage reverse gear. Check the road is clear in all directions and take note of any pedestrians or cyclists approaching on the pavement. Release the handbrake and use clutch control to move slowly backwards.

reversing to the right

Reversing to the right is useful when your rear view is restricted, for instance if you're driving a van. It gives you a clearer view down the side road through the driver's door window. All round observation is especially important because you are on the wrong side of the road facing oncoming traffic. Look out for vehicles wanting to turn into the junction while you are reversing. Once you straighten up after turning, reverse back about twice as far as you would when reversing to the left. This gives you space to cross to the left of the road before emerging at the junction.

Make sure you also practise reversing to the right, which can be easier if your rear view is restricted

3 As your rear wheels come level with where the road starts to curve, begin to steer to the left. Look in all directions, not just behind, as the front of the car will swing out as you turn.

4 Keep looking all around. If a vehicle wants to emerge from the junction as you are reversing, be prepared to stop, drive back to your original position, and wait for the road to clear before continuing.

5 As the road straightens begin to wind off the steering lock, ensuring that the car stays parallel to the kerb.

6 Continue reversing back about three car lengths, then and stop and apply the handbrake, taking care not to block any driveways or other entrances.

reverse parking

Parking in the gap between two vehicles is an essential driving skill. Although it might look easier to drive straight into the space, it's almost impossible to park neatly this way. What you need to do is take advantage of your car's increased manoeuvrability when going backwards by driving past the space and then reversing into it. If you are required to carry out this manoeuvre on your driving test, you will not necessarily be required to park between two vehicles, but may be asked to park behind a single vehicle as though you are reversing into a space of about two car lengths.

reverse parking

1 Stop slightly ahead of the front vehicle and no more than a metre away from it. Don't get too close or it will make reversing into the space more difficult. Apply the handbrake if necessary and engage reverse gear (your reversing lights will help to signal to other road users what you intend to do).

Don't park so close to other vehicles that they have difficulty getting out of the space you have left

2 Check in all directions before you start to turn because the front of your car will swing out, posing a hazard for other road users. Pause and wait if you need to give way to other vehicles or pedestrians.

3 Looking over your left shoulder, use clutch control to move backwards slowly. Quickly apply left steering lock as your rear wheels pass the back of the car. Aim for an angle of around 45 degrees to the kerb.

4 Check that the front nearside of your car is going to clear the back of the vehicle in front, then apply full right steering lock. Just before you come parallel to the kerb, straighten the wheels by steering left. If you find that you have misjudged the angle, pull forward and correct the steering – don't wait until your rear wheels hit the kerb.

5 Adjust the position of your car so you are close to and parallel to the kerb, and not too near to the vehicles in front or behind.

reversing into parking bay

Most car parks have rows of parking bays neatly marked out with white lines. Reversing into a bay is normally the best option as it's easier to manoeuvre in reverse, and it's also safer to drive out forwards than backwards. But there are occasions when it makes more sense to drive straight in – for instance, when you're visiting the DIY store and need easy access to the boot to load bulky items.

reversing into a parking bay

1 After checking all round to make sure it is clear, stop in front of the parking bay. This manoeuvre is easier to perform if you turn away from the parking bay before pulling up as you will then be steering into the bay at an easier angle.

2 Release the handbrake and use clutch control to reverse slowly back while steering to the left. Aim to make the sides of the car line up parallel to the white lines that mark out the parking bay.

Pull up neatly in the middle of the parking space and parallel to the white lanes that mark out the bay

3 You can use your mirrors or glance out of the driver's window to check your position as you are reversing, but don't forget to keep observing all around as well. Remember that the front of your car will swing out as you turn, causing a possible hazard for other vehicles and pedestrians.

4 Park squarely in the middle of the parking bay and apply the handbrake. If you find that you are not entering the space straight, pull forwards to straighten the steering before trying again. Don't leave your car with its front or rear end sticking out of the parking space.

When you need to park your car you must make sure you find a safe and legal place. Parking regulations can be complicated, so if you plan to leave your car for any length of time check road markings and signs to make quite sure that it is permitted. If you park where you shouldn't the penalties can be severe – including points on your licence for an offence such as parking on the zig-zag lines at a pedestrian crossing.

where to park

When looking for somewhere to leave your car, try to use a secure off-street car park. If you have to park in the street use a marked parking bay wherever possible. Do not park on the pavement unless there are signs which specifically permit this.

If you do have to park on the road, stop so that passengers, especially children, can get out of the vehicle on the side next to the kerb. Always check your door mirror for approaching vehicles before opening your door.

You must by law apply the handbrake and switch off the engine, headlights and foglights when leaving your car on the roadside, even if you're just popping into a shop for a couple of minutes.

Always lock your car securely and remove the key, even if you're leaving it for just a few moments

parking at night

When leaving your car at night, remember the following rules:

- ➲ you are not allowed to leave your car facing against the direction of traffic flow on a road at night
- ➲ vehicles must display parking lights when parked on a road (or a lay-by on a road) with a speed limit over 30mph
- ➲ cars, small vans and motorcycles may be parked without lights on a road (or a lay-by on a road) with a speed limit of 30mph or less as long as they are at least ten metres away from any junction, close to the kerb and facing in the direction of the traffic flow, or in a recognised parking place or lay-by
- ➲ trailers must not be left on a road at night without lights.

Parking on the road against the direction of traffic flow is permitted only during daytime

signs and markings

Whenever you park your car, check signs and road markings to ensure you are legally entitled to do so.

On a clearway you are not permitted to stop at any time. On an urban clearway, you may stop only to set down and pick up passengers.

Double yellow lines along the edge of the road mean no waiting at any time (although in places such as seaside towns this restriction may be eased out of season). A single yellow line indicates no waiting during the times shown on the nearby yellow plate. If no days are shown on the plate, then the restrictions are in force every day including sundays and bank holidays.

You may stop on yellow lines for a short time to load and unload, or to let passengers on and off, unless yellow lines on the kerb and accompanying black and white plates indicate that no loading is allowed.

Red routes have been introduced in some cities to improve the traffic flow. These have red lines in place of yellow lines along the side of the road. You must not stop even to unload or drop off passengers on a red route except in marked bays or at the times indicated by accompanying signs.

Leave enough space when parking: even if you can squeeze out of your car, the occupants of the other car may not be able to get back into theirs

disabled parking

You must display a Blue Badge to park in a space reserved for disabled people. If you do not have a badge, you must not park there even if all other spaces are occupied. Leave extra space if you park next to a car displaying a disabled badge. The driver may need more room to get a wheelchair alongside the car.

car parks

Car parks are full of hazards such as manoeuvring vehicles, pedestrians walking to and from their cars and excited children running around.

The golden rule in car parks is to drive dead slow. Observe what is going on all around and look out for children running out from between parked cars. Show courtesy when parking – don't leave your car so close to another vehicle that it will be difficult for its driver or passengers to get in.

it's the law

no parking

It is illegal to stop or park on:

➔ the carriageway or hard shoulder of a motorway (except in an emergency)

➔ a pedestrian crossing (including the area marked by zig-zag lines)

➔ a clearway

➔ an urban clearway, or a bus stop clearway within its hours of operation (except to pick up or set down passengers)

➔ a road marked with centre double white lines (except to pick up or set down passengers)

➔ a bus, tram or cycle lane during its hours of operation

➔ a cycle track

➔ red routes, unless otherwise indicated by signs

➔ school entrance markings (see p49).

vital signs

no stopping
(clearway)

no waiting

no stopping at times shown
(except to set down or pick up
passengers)

controlled
parking zone
(pay at meter at
times shown)

end of
controlled
parking zone

distance to
parking place
ahead

vehicles may
park fully on
the verge or
footway

parking place
for solo
motorbikes

parking
restricted to
permit holders

direction to
car park

direction to
park and ride
car park

No loading at
any time

no loading at
times shown

no waiting
at any time

no waiting at times
shown

loading allowed only
at times shown

parking limited as
indicated by sign

no stopping
at any time

no stopping
at times shown

waiting limited as
indicated by sign

loading bay

parking space reserved
for vehicles named

11 adverse conditions

Driving is easiest in clear, bright weather on dry roads. Once night falls, it starts to rain, or the thermometer drops below zero, the hazards start to multiply alarmingly. You need to slow down, concentrate harder and sharpen your anticipation skills to stay safe. Inside a warm car you can become insulated from what's happening outside. It's easy to keep driving at the same pace while conditions deteriorate, only to discover when an emergency develops that you have no safety margin left. Recognise that in atrocious weather conditions it is best to avoid driving altogether. If you wake up to find the roads covered in snow, ask yourself whether your journey is really worth risking an accident to accomplish, and stay at home instead until conditions improve.

driving at night

Night driving can feel strange and unnerving at first. It's a good idea to get your first taste of night driving with your instructor alongside you. If you're learning to drive in winter time then you may get plenty of opportunity to drive at night. But if you start in the summer when daylight hours are longer, it's worth trying to arrange a special late evening lesson.

night vision

On unlit roads at night, what we can see is limited to the range of our car headlights. Reduce speed to compensate, and never drive so fast that you are unable to stop within the distance your lights show to be clear. If you find driving at night particularly difficult this can be a sign that your eyesight needs checking, so arrange a visit to an optician.

using lights

Car lights serve two purposes: they help you to see at night, and they help other road users to see you. Put your headlights on anytime light levels are low, even if street lamps are not yet lit and most other drivers are not yet using lights. Put them on earlier still if you are driving a dull coloured car which doesn't stand out against the background.

Check and clean your lights regularly, and remember it is a requirement for your side lights and numberplate light as well as your headlights to function properly.

Use the main beam setting on unlit roads at night. Main beam headlights will dazzle oncoming drivers, so dip your headlights as soon as you see another vehicle approaching. Road users such as cyclists or pedestrians will also be dazzled by main beam lights so dip your headlights for them too.

Just before you dip your lights look along the left-hand verge to check that there is nothing on the road ahead. Immediately the oncoming vehicle has passed, switch back to main beam. If there is a stream of traffic approaching you will need to leave your headlights dipped until the road clears.

Main beam headlights can also cause discomfort for drivers you are following, so switch to dipped beam when you approach a vehicle ahead. When following at night, you should adjust your following distance so that your lights are not shining on the vehicle in front.

overtaking at night

If you need to overtake at night, exercise great caution. Switch your lights to main beam as soon as you have pulled past the car you are overtaking so you get the maximum view of the road ahead. Beware of bends and dips in the road ahead which may hide an oncoming vehicle.

If a driver wants to overtake you, help them see the road ahead by keeping your lights on main beam while the driver is preparing to overtake, and dip them only as the overtaking vehicle comes level with you.

avoiding dazzle

- don't stare at oncoming headlights, or you may be dazzled. Look slightly towards the left-hand side of the road. Slow down and if necessary stop if you cannot see. Keeping your windscreen clean will help reduce dazzle
- anticipate when your vision may be reduced by oncoming lights. When a car approaches round a bend, slow down in advance if you think that you may be dazzled by its lights
- following headlights reflected in your rear-view mirror can be dazzling. Flick the lever beneath the mirror to adjust its angle and reduce dazzle. Some cars have photochromatic mirrors which react automatically to reduce dazzle
- turning down the instrument panel illumination and switching off any interior lights can also help reduce distraction
- never wear tinted glasses to try to reduce dazzle at night.

noise at night

Remember that people are trying to sleep at night. Avoid revving your engine and slamming car doors.

It is illegal to use your horn in a built-up area between 11.30pm and 7.00am, except in an emergency. Flash your headlights instead if you need to give a warning signal.

adverse conditions

bad weather

Bad weather makes driving more hazardous in many ways. Winter is a time to be especially cautious on the road, as it brings a number of hazards including icy roads, snow, fog, heavy rain and high winds. When bad weather threatens check the forecast before leaving and if possible postpone your journey until conditions improve.

driving in winter

Make sure you and your car are prepared for wintry conditions before setting out:

- get your antifreeze and battery checked. Flat batteries are the main cause of breakdowns in winter
- check your screenwash. The cleaning solution you put in your washer reservoir acts as anti-freeze as well as helping to clean the windscreen. Fill it with screenwash to the concentration recommended on the bottle
- inspect your tyres to ensure they have plenty of tread: to be sure of staying safe on winter roads you need more than the legal 1.6mm minimum
- carry windscreen de-icer, a scraper and a brush for sweeping snow off the car. In very wintry conditions make sure you have plenty of warm clothes, a spade, some emergency food and a mobile phone in case you get stranded
- if you do a lot of driving on snow-covered roads, consider buying a set of winter tyres, designed to give more grip on frozen surfaces. Alternatively, you can fit snow chains which help to improve grip
- never start driving before your car is completely defrosted. When the windows are covered in ice, start the engine and switch the heater to maximum defrost. Scrape the ice off the windows all round the car – not just the windscreen – and make sure the lights, door mirrors and numberplates are clear too. If your windscreen wipers can't keep the screen clear of falling snow when you are driving then stop and clear it by hand.

Driving in snow is extremely hazardous: try to postpone your journey until conditions improve

know the code

highway code rule 230

When driving in icy or snowy weather:

- ➜ drive with care, even if the roads have been treated
- ➜ keep well back from the vehicle in front as stopping distances can be ten times greater than on dry roads
- ➜ take care when overtaking vehicles spreading salt or other de-icer, particularly if you are riding a motorcycle or cycle
- ➜ watch out for snowploughs which may throw out snow on either side. Do not overtake them unless the lane you intend to use has been cleared
- ➜ be prepared for the road conditions changing over relatively short distances
- ➜ listen to travel bulletins and take note of variable message signs that may provide information about weather, road and traffic conditions ahead

wet weather

Driving is more dangerous when it's raining for several reasons:

⊙ reduced vision

Rain makes it more difficult to see, and other road users may find it harder to see you too. Windows become obscured by raindrops, and they mist up more readily. As a general rule you should switch on your dipped headlights whenever it is raining. Keeping your windows clean makes it easier to see clearly in wet weather. Make sure you keep your windscreen washer bottle topped up and use the washers whenever your screen becomes dirty. Don't forget that most cars have a washer jet and wiper to keep the rear screen clear too. If the windows mist up, switch your heater fan to maximum, and if you have air conditioning, turn it on. If necessary open a window to get the air moving and reduce misting.

⊙ slippery roads

Water on the road acts as a lubricant which reduces tyre grip, making it easier to skid and lose control. If you have to brake in an emergency you will take further to stop than in the dry, even if your car has anti-lock brakes. Reduce your speed in wet weather, and increase your separation distance from the car in front, leaving at least a four-second gap. Be careful when cornering, especially where the road surface is worn or greasy, such as on roundabouts.

⊙ spray

In wet weather vehicles send up spray from their tyres which can drastically reduce your vision. Use dipped headlights in these conditions. Keep well back from other vehicles, particularly large vehicles which can throw up huge quantities of spray. Flick your wipers to full speed before you start to overtake so they can cope with the spray thrown on your windscreen as you go past the other vehicle.

⊙ standing water

Aquaplaning can occur on standing water – the tyres surf on the water and lose their grip. You may feel a tug at the steering wheel as you start to aquaplane, then the wheel will feel strangely light. Don't attempt to steer or brake which could cause loss of control. Ease off the accelerator, and as the car loses speed the wheels will regain contact with the road surface. The higher your speed on a wet road, the more likely you are to aquaplane, so slow down in conditions where aquaplaning is likely. Be careful too when driving through puddles at the side of the road – the drag of the water can tug at the steering and cause you to swerve.

Put on your headlights as soon as it starts to rain

Drive through a ford only if you are certain the water level is low enough to allow safe passage

⊙ flooding

You may have to drive through water either where the road has flooded, or at a ford (where a river runs across the road). Driving through deep water can cause your engine to stall if water blocks the exhaust, and if water enters the engine air intake it can cause serious damage.

Fords may deepen after heavy rain or in winter and become unsafe to cross. Never attempt to drive through water unless you are certain how deep it is. Watch another vehicle make the attempt first, or check the depth on the gauge located beside many fords. If the water is too deep, turn round and find another route.

When you are driving through standing water, try to choose the shallowest route. This is usually the middle of the road, because the camber makes the edges slope away. Don't rush at the water – you want to avoid creating a wave that could flood your engine. Proceed slowly and steadily in first gear but keep the engine revs high by slipping the clutch (this helps prevent water entering the exhaust).

Once out the other side, drive slowly while applying the brakes gently to make sure they are dry and working properly.

know the code

highway code rule 227

Wet weather In wet weather, stopping distances will be at least double those required for stopping on dry roads. This is because your tyres have less grip on the road. In wet weather

➔ you should keep well back from the vehicle in front. This will increase your ability to see and plan ahead

➔ if the steering becomes unresponsive, it probably means that water is preventing the tyres from gripping the road. Ease off the accelerator and slow down gradually

➔ the rain and spray from vehicles may make it difficult to see and be seen

➔ be aware of the dangers of spilt diesel that will make the surface very slippery

➔ take extra care around pedestrians, cyclists, motorcyclists and horse riders.

Driving in fog is dangerous, so slow down and leave plenty of extra time to complete your journey

Foglights should be used only when visibility falls below 100 metres, and switched off once it clears

fog

Fog is a major road hazard. Serious motorway pile-ups occur most winters because motorists carry on driving too fast and too close in foggy conditions. If you can avoid making your journey, stay off the road when it is foggy.

If you do have to drive in fog:

- ➲ leave more time for your journey as you will have to reduce your speed to stay safe
- ➲ make sure your windows are clean and your lights – including your foglights – are working properly
- ➲ use your windscreen wipers and keep the windows demisted
- ➲ switch on your dipped headlights, plus your foglights when visibility falls below 100 metres (328 feet). Avoid using main beam headlights as they reflect off the fog and can make it harder to see. Remember that your rear foglights are designed to alert following drivers to your presence. Keeping them switched on when you are in dense traffic will just dazzle the driver behind you. Don't leave your foglights on once visibility improves – it's illegal, it makes your brake lights less clear and it dazzles and annoys other drivers

- ➲ keep your speed down and leave more space between your car and the vehicle in front
- ➲ always make sure you can stop in the distance you can see to be clear. With all usual reference points outside the car obscured it can be harder to gauge how quickly you're travelling, so keep an eye on your speedometer
- ➲ don't overtake unless you can be absolutely sure nothing is coming
- ➲ when waiting to emerge at a junction it can help to wind down the window and listen for the sound of approaching vehicles which may not be visible till the last moment
- ➲ remember that in dense fog the reflective studs separating lanes on a motorway can help you tell which lane you are in:
  red studs to left, white studs to right mean you are in the left-hand lane
  white studs to both left and right mean you are in a middle lane
  white studs to left, amber studs right mean you are in the right-hand lane
  green studs to left mean you are passing a slip road

⊙ avoid parking your car on the road on a foggy day. If you have to do this, then leave the side lights on

⊙ be alert to the possibility of encountering unexpected fog patches. Slow down in conditions where fog might occur, and anticipate that fog may form on higher ground, or in valleys on cold winter mornings. Always slow down on the motorway when you see a fog warning sign, even if it is clear where you are.

high winds

Windy conditions can make driving hazardous. Take care on exposed sections of road where crosswinds may gust across the road. On country lanes expect fallen branches or even trees in the road.

Leave more room when overtaking cyclists and motorcyclists who could be blown in front of you by a fierce gust. Choose a sheltered place to pass high-sided vehicles, and as you pass anticipate that you may need to correct your steering to compensate for eddying wind currents.

If you are towing a trailer or caravan your vehicle may be unstable in high winds and you should stay off the road till conditions improve.

sunshine

Wear tinted glasses to reduce dazzle in bright sunshine, particularly when the sun is low in the sky in the morning and evening, and in winter time. If you need corrective lenses to drive, make sure your sunglasses are made up to match your prescription.

Pull your windscreen visor down to reduce dazzle from the sun. The visor can also be twisted around to shield the side window if the sun is causing you discomfort from that direction. But be prepared to slow down and if necessary stop if you are so dazzled that you cannot see properly.

When driving with the sun setting behind you, be aware that oncoming drivers may find it harder to see you, although from your perspective you can still see clearly. Put your headlights on to make yourself more visible.

hot weather

Keep your car well ventilated in hot weather to avoid getting drowsy. When it's very hot the road surface can become soft, reducing the grip of the tyres and affecting the steering and braking. Take particular care when it rains after a period of dry weather: the water can combine with the film of grease, rubber and oil deposited on the road to make the surface slippery.

Be careful when driving with the sun low in the sky, as it can dazzle you and obscure other vehicles

Skidding is more likely in bad weather, but it's important to understand that the fundamental cause of a skid is the driver. A car only skids if it's being driven too fast for the conditions, or if a skid is provoked through harsh steering, braking or acceleration.

avoiding skids

Skids can be avoided by never asking your car to do more than it can with the grip available from its tyres in the prevailing road conditions. This means that in poor weather you must:

- slow down
- increase your stopping distance, so if the vehicle in front of you stops unexpectedly you have enough space to brake to a halt without skidding
- take extra care when approaching a bend which may be slippery
- be gentle and progressive in your use of the steering, accelerator and brakes.

The best way to avoid a skid is to read the road and slow down wherever grip might be reduced

slippery roads

Just as you're more likely to slip when walking on frosty pavements, when the roads are icy or it is snowing your car is more likely to skid. You need to slow right down, steer and brake very gently and leave a much greater stopping distance – up to ten times further than normal.

Be alert for ice forming on roads whenever you drive on a winter evening with clear skies. Look for signs of frost forming on verges or parked cars. Take special care where the road is exposed, such as on motorway bridges, because ice often forms here first. If your car has an outside temperature gauge, take extra care as this nears zero.

Beware of rain falling in freezing conditions and forming black ice, which is particularly treacherous because it is invisible.

On icy roads you may notice a reduction in tyre noise, and the steering will feel unusually light. Do not attempt to brake or steer. Lift gently off the accelerator and let your car slow down gradually. Drive slowly and cautiously, stay in a high gear and avoid harsh acceleration which could cause the wheels to spin.

You may need to leave up to ten times more distance to stop when braking on an icy road

vital signs

risk of ice   *slippery road*

Too much power can cause the wheels to spin if you try to pull away from a junction in a hurry

Start slowing down well before a hazard to reduce the risk of skidding while braking

skidding when accelerating

If you accelerate too hard when moving off on a slippery road, the driven wheels will spin frantically with little or no forward motion. This can be dangerous when you are trying to move out into a stream of traffic, or on a bend or slope when it can cause the car to slide across the road.

On an icy surface you may find it difficult to avoid wheel spin however gentle you are with the accelerator. It may help to engage a higher gear before moving off. Spinning the wheels in snow can cause the car to dig itself in. Try using reverse then forward gears in quick succession to free it. Fitting skid chains will improve traction on snow-covered roads.

If you have to stop on an uphill slope in icy conditions you may find it difficult to get moving again. Leave a long separation distance from the car in front so if it slows you you have a better chance to keep moving.

skidding when braking

If you brake hard on a slippery surface the wheels may lock up and you will slide onwards with little or no braking effect. With the wheels locked you are also unable to steer the car. If the wheels lock up, release the brake pedal so they start to rotate again, then reapply the brake less harshly.

If your car has ABS fitted it will prevent the wheels locking up (see p47). But even ABS can't work miracles on snow or ice. You still need to allow a much longer stopping distance than you would if you were driving on dry tarmac.

Be extra cautious when heading downhill on a slippery road. Engage a low gear and approach the incline very slowly, as you may find it difficult to slow down again if your car starts to pick up speed.

skidding when steering

If you approach a corner too fast on a slippery road there is a danger that the car will skid. This is even more likely if you brake or use the accelerator harshly while cornering.

In a front-wheel drive car (most small cars), the most common skid is caused when the front wheels lose grip. You turn the steering wheel on the approach to a bend but there is no response and the car carries straight on no matter how much steering lock you apply. If this starts to happen, come off the power. This throws the weight balance of the car forwards and helps the front wheels find more grip. Don't touch the brake pedal. As the car slows you should feel the tyres start to regain grip, and you can carefully steer the car back on course.

A rear-wheel skid can be more dramatic and if uncontrolled may develop into a spin. This type of skid is normally caused when the car is unbalanced mid-corner by lifting off the power or harsh braking, or by excessive acceleration in a rear-wheel drive car. If you feel the rear of the car starting to slide round, take your foot off the accelerator and brake, and steer in the direction that the rear of the car is sliding. This should bring the rear of the car back into line, but take care not to overcorrect so that it starts to slide the other way.

four-wheel drive

Some high-performance cars are fitted with four-wheel drive which improves traction in slippery conditions, but they are not suitable for off-road use. True off-roaders are designed specifically to tackle rough or muddy conditions, though their higher centre of gravity makes them less stable than a conventional car on the road. Special tuition is recommended to get the most out of driving a 4x4 off-road. Remember that 4x4s can cause extensive damage to the countryside and should be used responsibly and only where it is legal to do so.

anti-skid devices

Electronic traction and skid control systems are now often fitted. Traction control senses when a wheel starts to lose grip, and automatically cuts the power or applies the brake to stop that wheel spinning. Skid control is a more sophisticated version which uses sensors to anticipate the onset of a skid and cuts the power or brakes individual wheels to counter it. If your car has traction or skid control, always leave it switched on.

Even the best skid control system cannot overcome the laws of physics and will not prevent a crash if a car is driven too fast for the conditions. Stay within the limits of your car's grip so that even if skid control is fitted you never give it cause to activate.

highway code rule 119

Skids Skidding is usually caused by the driver braking, accelerating or steering too harshly or driving too fast for the road conditions. If skidding occurs, remove the cause by releasing the brake pedal fully or easing off the accelerator. Turn the steering wheel in the direction of the skid. For example, if the rear of the vehicle skids to the right, steer immediately to the right to recover.

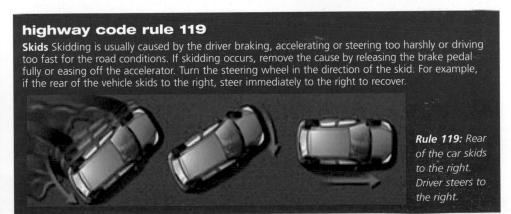

Rule 119: Rear of the car skids to the right. Driver steers to the right.

12 you and your car

As a driver you have legal responsibilities. You must ensure that you have a valid signed driving licence, that you are insured for the car you are driving, and that the car is properly registered and taxed. It is your responsibility to keep the car in a roadworthy condition, and ensure it is not overloaded. You should keep your vehicle secure from theft, and take steps to minimise its impact on the environment. And if you take your car abroad you are responsible for making sure you remain safe and legal whatever the local driving conditions.

documents

There are a number of documents required to keep you and your car legal on the road. You must by law produce your driving licence and counterpart, a valid insurance certificate and (if appropriate) a valid MOT certificate if requested to do so by the police. If you can't produce these documents on the spot, you will be asked to take them to a police station of your choice within seven days. You must also ensure your car is taxed and that the tax disc is clearly displayed.

driving licence

You must have a valid signed driving licence for the category of vehicle you are driving.

The photocard driving licence consists of a photo ID card and a counterpart. You will need to show both parts if you are asked to produce your licence by a police officer.

You must by law inform the Driver and Vehicle Licensing Agency (DVLA) if you change your name or address – there is a section on the licence to fill in and return to the DVLA to do this.

The photograph on your photocard licence is valid for ten years, after which you need to renew it. You can renew online, providing you have a valid UK passport issued within the last five years.

registration document

Every car has a registration document (sometimes called a logbook or V5C) which lists identification details including the name and address of its registered keeper, year of first registration, make, model, colour, engine size, and identifying marks such as registration, chassis and engine numbers.

As the registered vehicle keeper, you are responsible for taxing the vehicle and you must by law notify the DVLA if you change any of the details listed on the V5C, including your name or permanent address, or the car's colour or engine size. When a car is sold, both buyer and seller must complete the top part of the V5C and the seller must forward this immediately to the DVLA.

The V5C is not proof of ownership of a car – something worth bearing in mind when you buy a second-hand car privately.

insurance certificate

There are three types of motor insurance:

⊙ **third party insurance** is the minimum legal requirement. It means that if you injure or cause damage to the property of a third party (that is, another person), your insurance will cover the cost of their repairs and medical treatment – but you will receive nothing for your own injuries or damage to your own car

⊙ **third party fire and theft insurance** means that in addition to having third party cover you will be compensated if your car is stolen or damaged by fire

⊙ **comprehensive insurance** means that your costs, as well as those of any third party, will be covered if you have an accident, even if it is your own fault. Comprehensive is the most common type of insurance cover. When looking for insurance quotes it is always worth considering comprehensive insurance as it provides much more protection, often at little or no extra cost.

You must notify the DVLA of any changes to your car's details on the registration document (V5C)

By law you must keep your car insured at all times. If you ever want to keep your car uninsured off the road, then you must make a SORN (Statutory Off Road Notification), using the reference number shown on your V5C registration certificate.

When you take out motor insurance you will be given a detailed policy document, plus an insurance certificate which acts as legal confirmation of your insurance cover (you may initially receive a cover note, which is legally recognised as a substitute for your certificate until this reaches you).

Check your insurance cover if you wish to drive someone else's car. Your insurance may not cover you and even if it does, a comprehensive policy usually limits you to third party cover in another car.

You must always inform your insurer of any changes to your circumstances, or modifications to your car, otherwise you may invalidate your insurance policy. Telling lies when taking out insurance – for instance by claiming that an older person is the car's

main driver in order to reduce the premium you have to pay – gives the insurer the right to void the policy. This would leave you uninsured, a serious offence punishable by a fine of up to £5000, 6–8 penalty points and possible confiscation of your car.

Various factors affect the cost of motor insurance. You will pay more:
- to insure a high-performance car
- if you live in a high-risk area such as an inner city
- if you are a young driver – premiums fall significantly for drivers over 25
- if you have penalty points on your licence – insurance is particularly expensive and difficult to get after a drink-driving conviction.

Unfortunately, new drivers have a higher accident rate than more experienced motorists, which means that insurace premiums are expensive when you are starting to drive. Shop around by using a broker or online comparison site to get the best deal.

You may cut your insurance premium by:
- completing the Pass Plus scheme after passing your driving test
- avoiding accidents – every year that you don't claim on your insurance earns you a no-claims bonus, which knocks a percentage off your premium. If you have to make a claim you lose a year's no-claims bonus
- opting for a higher excess (this is an amount you have to pay when you make a claim. If you have an excess of £100, it means you have to pay the first £100 of any claim you make).

Modified or performance cars cost a lot more to insure. All car models are given insurance ratings, from 1 to 50, so be sure to buy a car from one of the lowest groups to get the best insurance deal

MOT certificate

Your car must take an MOT test three years after the date it was first registered. The MOT test checks that the car is safe to use on the road, and that exhaust noise and emissions are within specified limits. Items examined include bodywork, suspension, steering, brakes, lighting, tyres, indicators, windscreen wipers and washers, horn and seatbelts. If your car passes you will be given an MOT certificate which is valid for one year. You can get your car tested up to one month before its current MOT expires, and the new certificate will still run from the original expiry date. Remember that an MOT certificate shows simply that the items examined were found to be satisfactory on the day the test was carried out, and it is no guarantee of roadworthiness.

You are breaking the law if you drive a car without a current MOT certificate when it requires one (the only exception is if you are driving it to an MOT test which you have already booked). If you drive a car without a current MOT it could invalidate your insurance cover.

Vehicle Excise Duty

This is better known as road tax. You must by law display a tax disc on the left-hand side of the windscreen of any car which is used or parked on the public road. You can apply for a tax disc at the post office. You will need to take along your motor insurance certificate, MOT certificate (if applicable) and either the DVLA road tax reminder form V11, or the registration document (V5). It's also possible to apply online at www.taxdisc.direct.gov.uk.

Tax discs are available for six months or one year. The cost varies on a graduated scale depending on the car's exhaust emissions.

If you intend to keep your car off the road you must use the road tax reminder form (V11) or form V890 to make a SORN (Statutory Off Road Notification). This exempts you from paying road tax but it must be renewed annually if the car is kept off-road for over a year.

Cars first registered before 1973 are exempt from road tax but must still display a current nil tax disc.

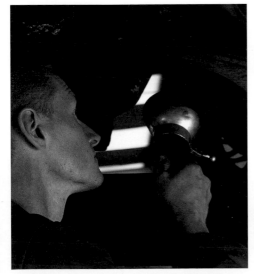

MOT test examines components which could affect safety, such as suspension and steering

If you don't tax your car you risk having it clamped, or even confiscated and scrapped

motoring law

The consequences of breaking the law on the road can be severe.
Serious offences, such as drink-driving, result in automatic
disqualification or even a jail sentence – up to ten years for causing
death by dangerous driving. Being convicted for even a minor motoring
offence is an unpleasant and expensive experience. It's worth
remembering that it is easy to avoid ever coming into conflict with the
law, simply by driving in a safe, sensible and responsible manner.

penalty table

OFFENCE	Imprisonment	Fine	Disqualification	Penalty points
			MAXIMUM PENALTIES	
Causing death by dangerous driving	14 years	Unlimited	Obligatory 2 years minimum	3–11 (if exceptionally not disqualified)
Dangerous driving	2 years	Unlimited	Obligatory	3–11 (if exceptionally not disqualified)
Causing death by careless driving under the influence of drink or drugs	14 years	Unlimited	Obligatory 2 years minimum	3–11 (if exceptionally not disqualified)
Careless or inconsiderate driving	–	£5000	Discretionary	3–9
Driving while unfit through drink or drugs or with excess alcohol; or failing to provide a specimen for analysis	6 months	£5000	Obligatory	3–11 (if exceptionally not disqualified)
Failing to stop after an accident or failing to report an accident	6 months	£5000	Discretionary	5–10
Driving when disqualified	6 months (12 months in Scotland)	£5000	Discretionary	6
Driving after refusal or revocation of licence on medical grounds	6 months	£5000	Discretionary	3–6
Driving without insurance	–	£5000	Discretionary	6–8
Speeding	–	£1000 (£2500 for motorway offences)	Discretionary	3–6 or 3 (fixed penalty)
Traffic light offences	–	£1000	Discretionary	3
No MOT certificate	–	£1000	–	–

driving offences

Some examples of driving offences and their maximum penalties are shown in the table above. For serious offences, the courts can impose a range of penalties including imprisonment, a fine, disqualification from driving and endorsing the offender's driving licence with penalty points. Minor offences, such as speeding slightly in excess of the limit, may be dealt with by a fixed penalty fine and licence endorsement which can be settled without a court hearing.

penalty points

Under the penalty point system, drivers who break the law have their licence endorsed with points, the number depending on the severity of the offence. A driver who accumulates 12 or more penalty points within a three-year period will be disqualified from driving for a minimum of six months.

For every offence which carries penalty points the court has a discretionary power to order the licence holder to be disqualified. This may be for any period the court thinks fit, but is usually between one week and a few months. For serious offences there is a mandatory period of disqualification – 12 months in the case of drink-driving. Serious or repeat offenders may face longer periods of disqualification, and in some cases the offender has to pass an extended driving test before being allowed back on the road.

New Driver Act

Special rules apply to drivers within two years of passing their driving test. If the number of penalty points on their licence reaches six or more as a result of offences they commit before the two years are over (including any they committed before passing their test) their licence is revoked. They revert to learner status and must reapply for a provisional licence and retake both theory and practical driving tests to get their full licence back again.

maintenance

You can't expect your car to function safely with no attention outside its stated service intervals. This is more important than ever now that recommended service intervals are being stretched to 20,000 miles or more. Running a car with worn or wrongly inflated tyres, or which is low on oil or coolant, is dangerous and illegal, as well as being likely to incur serious expense rectifying problems caused by neglect.

regular checks

Every time you drive your car you should ensure that its windows, lights and numberplates are clean. Make sure that everything that is needed to make the car roadworthy is in good working order, including the lights, horn, speedometer, windscreen, wipers/washers and seatbelts.

To avoid expensive breakdowns, make sure your car is regularly serviced in accordance with the schedule laid down in the handbook.

As part of the practical driving test, candidates are required to show that they can perform basic vehicle safety checks (see pp253–255 for the specific questions you may be asked). Your answers should be relevant for the car you are driving. So as well as reading the advice outlined in this section, you should consult the handbook of the car in which you will be taking your practical test for specific information on the maintenance checks applicable to that model.

Make sure your windows are always kept clean

fault finding

Keep an eye open for any faults your car may develop. Look out for problems such as those listed below, and get the car checked by a garage as soon as possible:

- car pulls to one side under braking. This may indicate a puncture or fault in the braking system
- smell of petrol or burning rubber. Stop and investigate immediately
- loud or unusual knocking or rubbing noises. Any noise indicates that wear is taking place and it needs to be checked
- poor roadholding or body control on bumpy roads may point to worn shock absorbers. Check by pressing down on a wing and releasing. If the car keeps bouncing then the shock absorbers may need replacing
- if the windscreen picks up a chip or crack get it repaired or replaced
- vibration through the steering wheel may mean that the wheels are out of balance.

Washers and wipers must be kept in working order

know the code

highway code annex 6

Vehicle maintenance Take special care that lights, brakes, steering, exhaust system, seat belts, demisters, wipers and washers are all working. Also:

- lights, indicators, reflectors, and number plates MUST be kept clean and clear
- windscreens and windows MUST be kept clean and free from obstructions to vision
- lights MUST be properly adjusted to prevent dazzling other road users. Extra attention needs to be paid to this if the vehicle is heavily loaded
- exhaust emissions MUST NOT exceed prescribed levels
- ensure your seat, seat belt, head restraint and mirrors are adjusted correctly before you drive
- items of luggage are securely stowed.

under the bonnet

Open the bonnet regularly and inspect the fluid levels. The levels you need to check are:

- brake fluid
- engine oil
- engine coolant
- windscreen washer bottle
- battery.

to open the bonnet:

- pull the bonnet release handle (usually located under the dashboard)
- release the bonnet latch under the front edge of the bonnet
- raise the bonnet and secure it on its support.

to close the bonnet:

- remove the support and secure it
- lower the bonnet and press down firmly on the leading edge
- check that it is securely shut.

brake fluid

Never let this drop below the minimum mark on the brake fluid reservoir or braking could be dangerously impaired. Get a garage to investigate if there is any loss of fluid. Brake fluid becomes contaminated with age and must be replaced at the intervals stated in your car's service schedule.

windscreen washer bottle

Never let the windscreen washer reservoir run dry. Add a mixture of water and washer solution made up to the concentration indicated on the bottle – this helps clean the screen and prevents the washers freezing in winter. Always use proper washer solution, not washing-up liquid which won't do the job and could damage paintwork.

engine coolant

The engine cooling system is pressurised when hot, so never try to take off the filler cap straight after the engine has been running or you could be scalded. Do not let the coolant level fall below the minimum indicated on the coolant reservoir or the engine may overheat and be damaged. Ask a garage to investigate if you have to keep topping up the coolant level, and get the concentration of anti-freeze checked so the system won't freeze solid in winter, causing expensive damage.

⟳ engine oil

It is especially important to check the oil before a long journey. If the engine runs short of oil expensive wear may result. With the car on a level surface, take out the dip stick, wipe it clean with a rag, reinsert it and then remove it again. Check that the oil is above the minimum mark on the stick. If necessary, undo the oil filler cap and add more oil (a little at a time so you do not overfill, which could overpressurise the system and cause oil leaks). Some cars have a gauge on the instrument panel which shows the oil level without having to open the bonnet, though it's also a good idea to occasionally double-check the level using the dip stick. Never pour old engine oil down the drain – take it to a local authority waste disposal site.

⟳ battery

Most batteries are sealed and need no maintenance apart from keeping the terminals secure, clean and greased. If there is a filler cap, remove it and check the fluid level – it should cover the plates in each cell. Use distilled water to top it up if necessary. At the end of its life dispose of a battery by taking it to a local authority site or a garage.

In your practical test you will be asked how you would carry out two vehicle safety checks, such as checking that your indicators are working

Check the tread depth of your tyres regularly; 1.6mm is the legal minimum but you should replace them before they get this worn

lights

To check that lights such as indicators or headlamps are working, switch them on and walk round the car so you can check them visually (you may need to turn the ignition on first).

The easiest way to check the brake lights is to get someone to help you; alternatively, reversing up to a reflective surface (such as a window) and applying the brakes will show you if the lights are operating correctly. Some cars have a warning light which illuminates in the event of a bulb failure.

horn

Test the horn at regular intervals, but remember to do this somewhere off the highway as it is illegal to sound the horn while the car is stationary on the road.

brakes

As soon as you can after moving off press the brake pedal gently to ensure that the braking system is working properly.

You can also get an indication that the brake servo-assistance is functioning properly if you press your foot on the brake while starting the engine: as the servo activates you should feel a pulse through the pedal.

Make sure that the parking brake is working effectively. The car should not roll on a gradient with the handbrake firmly applied. Check that the travel needed to apply the handbrake does not exceed the amount specified in the car's handbook.

steering

Try the steering once you have moved off to check that the power-assistance is working correctly (if it has failed then the steering wheel will feel heavy and hard to turn). As with checking the brakes, you can confirm that the power-assistance is working by putting a little pressure on the steering wheel as you start the engine: you should feel the wheel move slightly when the assistance activates.

tyre care

Your tyres are your only contact with the road, so don't skimp on their maintenance or you could regret it. Get in the habit of glancing at your tyres every time you use your car to check for obvious defects such as cuts or bulges.

At least once a week check that the tyres are correctly inflated to the pressures laid down in the car handbook. Do this before a journey, when the tyres are cold, or you may get an inaccurate reading. Having underinflated tyres affects the braking and handling of the car, makes the steering feel heavy, and causes increased fuel consumption and tread wear. Overinflated tyres also affect handling, give a harsh ride and cause increased tread wear.

Tyres fitted to cars, vans and trailers must have a tread depth of at least 1.6mm across the central three-quarters of the width of the tread and around the entire circumference. But you should regard this as the absolute legal minimum. Worn tyres greatly reduce roadholding on damp, flooded or icy roads. For safety's sake you should start thinking about replacing a tyre when its tread gets below 3mm, especially if winter is approaching. A deep cut in the sidewall also makes a tyre unsafe and illegal.

If your tyres are wearing excessively or unevenly it may indicate that the wheels are out of alignment or that there is a fault with the braking or suspension systems. Get them checked as soon as possible.

Most everyday road tyres are the radial type. It illegal to mix cross-ply and radial tyres on the same axle.

Some cars have a space saver spare tyre which is narrower then the normal tyre. If you have a space saver fitted after a puncture, remember that it will affect your car's handling and braking performance, and restrict you to a lower maximum speed. Check the car handbook for further information and get the space saver replaced by a proper tyre as soon as you can.

reducing tyre wear

To get the best use from your tyres:

- ⊙ keep them correctly inflated
- ⊙ avoid fierce braking, hard cornering and harsh acceleration
- ⊙ steer around pot holes and slow down on poorly surfaced roads
- ⊙ don't drive over kerbs or scrape your tyres along them while parking. This could weaken the wall of the tyre. Hitting the kerb can also put the wheels out of alignment, leading to uneven tread wear.

It's essential to check tyre pressures regularly to keep your car safe on the road and to prevent unnecessary tyre wear and fuel consumption

loading and towing

It is your responsibility to ensure that you do not overload your car. For larger loads you should consider using a trailer. Towing is not difficult but there are important rules to be aware of, and if you intend to tow a trailer or caravan you would be well advised to take some expert instruction in towing. Reversing in particular is something that towing novices find difficult, and it pays to practise first somewhere safe off the road.

loading

- ⊃ you, the driver, are responsible for making sure that your vehicle is not overloaded. Overloading can seriously affect a car's steering and handling
- ⊃ check your car handbook to see if you need to increase tyre pressures when driving with a heavy load
- ⊃ don't load the rear of the car higher than the top of the rear seats, or heavy items could fly forward dangerously during an emergency stop
- ⊃ distribute any load as evenly as possible
- ⊃ take care when loading a roof rack. The load must be securely fastened when driving. A heavy load on the roof rack can reduce stability, so take special care when cornering
- ⊃ if anything falls from your vehicle on to the road, retrieve it only if it is safe to do so. If you are on a motorway, do not try to remove the obstruction yourself. Go to the next emergency telephone and call the police
- ⊃ the front of a heavily laden car can be angled upwards so that its headlights are likely to dazzle other road users even on dipped beam. Adjust the headlamp angle to compensate, from its normal setting (0) to 1, 2 or 3 depending on the load
- ⊃ if carrying domestic pets such as dogs, make sure they are properly restrained in a cage or behind bars in the rear.

Use a special rack for bicycles. If a rear-mounted carrier is used it must not obscure the numberplate

Make sure pets are securely restrained while they are carried in the car, for their safety and yours

know the code

highway code rule 98

Vehicle towing and loading As a driver

- → you MUST NOT tow more than your licence permits. If you passed a car test after 1 Jan 1997 you are restricted on the weight of trailer you can tow
- → you MUST NOT overload your vehicle or trailer. You should not tow a weight greater than that recommended by the manufacturer of your vehicle
- → you MUST secure your load and it MUST NOT stick out dangerously. Make sure any heavy or sharp objects and any animals are secured safely. If there is a collision, they might hit someone inside the vehicle and cause serious injury
- → you should properly distribute the weight in your caravan or trailer with heavy items mainly over the axle(s) and ensure a downward load on the tow ball. Manufacturer's recommended weight and tow ball load should not be exceeded. This should avoid the possibility of swerving or snaking and going out of control. If this does happen, ease off the accelerator and reduce speed gently to regain control
- → carrying a load or pulling a trailer may require you to adjust the headlights.

In the event of a breakdown, be aware that towing a vehicle on a tow rope is potentially dangerous. You should consider professional recovery.

Towing is a specialised skill and taking some training before setting out is highly recommended

caravans and trailers

Before starting your journey, check that:

⊃ your car is capable of towing the trailer. The maximum weight of the laden caravan/trailer should be no more than 85% of the towcar's kerbside weight

⊃ the caravan/trailer is loaded evenly. Stow heavy items low down over the axle. With the caravan/trailer hitched up, run your eye along the outfit from the side: if properly loaded, it should be level or make a slight V-shape towards the coupling

⊃ the caravan/trailer is correctly hitched up and the breakaway cable (which applies the trailer brakes if the towbar fails) is connected

⊃ the noseweight is correct. This is the weight at the front towbar coupling and it plays an important role in maintaining stability. The noseweight is generally around 7% of the caravan or trailer's laden weight, and you need to check in your vehicle handbook that this doesn't exceed your car's noseweight limit

⊃ all lights on the car and caravan/trailer are working correctly

⊃ the caravan/trailer brakes are working

⊃ the handbrake of the caravan/trailer is off, corner steadies are up, jockey wheel fully retracted, gas cylinders turned off and all windows and skylights closed

⊃ any trailer load is securely fastened and not protruding dangerously

⊃ your door mirrors give a good view down the side of the caravan/trailer. If not, fix a set of extension mirrors (but remember these must be removed when you are not towing)

⊃ all tyres are in good condition and inflated to the correct pressure.

towing licence

A car driving licence allows you to use your car to tow a small caravan or trailer. However, for combinations exceeding 3.5 tonnes (or where the weight of the laden trailer exceeds the unladen weight of the car) you need to obtain a category B+E licence by taking a separate towing test (this does not apply to drivers who passed their driving test before January 1997).

towing guidelines

- passengers are not permitted to travel in a moving caravan
- speed limits are lower when towing: 50mph on single carriageways, 60mph on dual carriageways and motorways
- you are not allowed to use the right-hand lane of a motorway with more than two lanes when towing, unless other lanes are closed
- remember the extra size of your vehicle when towing and look out for warning signs, especially when entering a car park or lay-by with height/width restrictions
- consider the extra length of your vehicle when emerging from junctions and overtaking
- allow extra space for braking and watch your speed on corners
- avoid obstructing other traffic. If a queue of vehicles forms behind you, pull over somewhere safe and let them pass
- beware of crosswinds on bridges and exposed motorway sections which can cause the outfit to sway or 'snake'. If this happens don't try to brake or correct the steering. Instead, ease off the accelerator gently to reduce speed. Fitting a stabiliser to the towbar can help improve handling and stability, but don't use one to compensate for poor weight distribution
- when reversing, begin by steering in the opposite direction to where you want the caravan/trailer to go.

vital signs

no towed caravans

no vehicle or combination of vehicles over length shown

overhead electric cable: no vehicles over height shown

no vehicles over width shown

no vehicles over maximum gross weight shown (in tonnes)

no vehicles over height shown

Caravans can become unstable in high winds so stay off the road during bad weather conditions

Check first that your driving licence is legally valid for the size of trailer that you want to tow

12 environment

In the last hundred years the motor car has transformed the way we live. It allows us to go where we want when we want, and to travel long distances for work and leisure. The downside is that this mobility has been achieved at a considerable cost to the environment we live in.

environmental issues

The growth in motor traffic has had wide-ranging effects on the environment. These include:

- ⊘ production of carbon dioxide (CO_2), which contributes to global warming: road transport accounts for about 20% of the UK's CO_2 emissions
- ⊘ depletion of natural resources such as oil reserves
- ⊘ air pollution which causes health problems and damages historic buildings
- ⊘ road building which degrades the natural landscape
- ⊘ traffic congestion
- ⊘ noise pollution.

CO₂ emissions

Every time you drive a car it emits carbon dioxide (CO_2), a gas linked to the atmospheric greenhouse effect and global warming. More efficient cars such as smaller-engined superminis produce less CO_2 than large executive cars and off-roaders. Automatic cars generally use 10% or so more fuel than a manual, although modern automatic designs are becoming more efficient. The government has taken several steps to encourage motorists to produce less CO_2, including:

- ⊘ car manufacturers must publish CO_2 emission figures for all their models
- ⊘ road tax (Vehicle Excise Duty) rates are linked to CO_2 emissions, so that cars with lower emissions are taxed less
- ⊘ company car drivers pay less tax on cars with lower CO_2 emissions
- ⊘ the MOT test includes a strict emissions test to check that older cars are not producing unnecessary pollution.

Increasing car ownership has raised environmental issues such as traffic congestion and pollution

Exhaust emissions are checked as part of the annual MOT test for cars older than three years

215

fuel types

You can reduce the negative effect you have on the environment by choosing to drive a more efficient car with lower emissions. Higher efficiency means better economy, so you will also be saving yourself money. The type of fuel your car uses influences how polluting it is, and you need to know the characteristics of different engines so you can choose the one that's most appropriate for your driving style. The common fuel types are:

⊘ petrol

Petrol is the most usual car fuel in the UK. Modern cars use unleaded petrol and have exhaust systems with a catalytic converter which helps to remove certain toxic gases including carbon monoxide, nitrogen oxide and hydrocarbons. However, the catalytic converter does not reduce CO_2 emissions.

Petrol and diesel are still the usual fuels but less-polluting electric cars are getting more common

⊘ diesel

Modern diesels are quiet and powerful. Diesels are more efficient than petrol engines, typically consuming around 20% less fuel than petrol models and producing 20% less CO_2. But diesels also produce more particulates, which can aggravate breathing disorders where they build up in urban areas.

⊘ gas

Cars powered by Liquefied Petroleum Gas (LPG) and Compressed Natural Gas (CNG) are available. LPG, which is the more widely available of the two, is less polluting than petrol or diesel, although a car running on it will produce more CO_2 than a typical diesel equivalent. It is possible to get a petrol-engined car converted to run on LPG.

⊘ hybrid

Hybrid cars combine a conventional engine with battery power. The battery is kept topped up using energy produced by braking that would otherwise be wasted. This reduces emissions and pollution, especially in urban areas, as hybrids are able to cover short low-speed trips using electric power alone. Hybrid cars do tend to be more expensive to purchase, though.

⊘ electric

A fully electric car emits no pollution and low levels of noise, and so is particularly suitable for use in cities. It still does emit some CO_2, produced at the power station which generates the electricity the car runs on, though this can be reduced by using electricity from a renewable source. Electric cars still suffer from a limited range (typically under 100 miles) and lengthy recharging times, though manufacturers are trying to improve this. They are also expensive.

⊘ fuel cell

Fuel cell cars combine hydrogen with oxygen to generate electricity, giving zero-emissions operation. Several manufacturers are currently developing fuel cell models.

environmental costs

Running a more environmentally-friendly car can be good for your pocket, in terms of lower running costs. An efficient car uses less fuel, and less powerful cars are cheaper to insure too. A number of other financial incentives, such as lower car tax, company car tax and congestion charging rates, also favour running a car that emits less CO_2.

congestion charging

Drivers must pay a congestion charge to enter central London between 7am and 6.30pm, Monday to Friday (excluding Bank Holidays). The congestion charging zone is clearly signposted; if you drive into it, then you must pay the congestion charge by midnight the following day, or face an automatic fine. The charge is currently £12, with discounts if paying in advance, and can be paid at by telephone or at www. cclondon.com. There is a Greener Vehicle Discount of 100% for cars that emit 100g/km or less CO_2 and that meet the Euro 5 standard for air quality. To qualify you need to register and pay an annual fee.

Some cars that emit low levels of carbon dioxide are exempt from London's congestion charge

refuelling

Keep an eye on your fuel gauge so you never risk running out during a journey. Always check the gauge when you start a journey and anticipate when you may need to fill up. Where few fuel stations are available, such as on the motorway or when driving at night, don't wait for the fuel warning light to come on before stopping for fuel.

There should normally be no need to carry spare fuel with you, but if you do, it must be in an approved container.

When you visit a fuel station, remember that petrol is highly flammable. Smoking is strictly forbidden on fuel station forecourts. You must also never use a mobile phone in the vicinity of a fuel station.

If you're driving an unfamiliar car, check whether it uses petrol or diesel before filling up. If you confuse the two you may need to get the fuel tank flushed out. Petrol can cause expensive damage to a diesel engine so do not run a diesel engine if you mistakenly put petrol in the tank. In a modern petrol-engined car you must only use unleaded petrol or you risk damaging the catalytic converter.

When refuelling a diesel, take care not to spill any fuel as it will make the ground slippery and hazardous. Check your filler cap is securely fitted before driving off so there's no danger of diesel splashing onto the road.

Make sure you know what type of fuel your car runs on and use the right pump to fill it up

217

By adopting eco-safe driving techniques you can reduce the impact your car has on the environment

eco-safe driving

Eco-safe driving is about applying good, safe driving techniques such as anticipation and smoothness to help reduce your fuel consumption and emissions. As well as being good for the environment, studies have shown that eco-safe driving can save up to one month's worth of fuel each year through reduced fuel consumption.

Although you will not lose marks during your practical driving test if you fail to drive in an environmentally responsible manner, your examiner will be monitoring your driving style and at the end of your test will brief you on how you have performed. Follow these eco-safe driving tips to make your driving greener:

⊗ drive smoothly

By anticipating and planning ahead, you can reduce the need to brake and accelerate, saving fuel. Avoid harsh acceleration wherever possible, and don't carry on accelerating when you can see you will soon have to slow for a hazard ahead. Pick up speed gently, and don't race the engine through the lower gears. Block changing (missing out gears where conditions allow – see p41) can save fuel by reducing the time spent accelerating.

Stick to the speed limits too. The higher your speed, the more fuel your car uses. At 70mph fuel consumption is up to 30% higher than at 50mph. If fitted, cruise control can help you save fuel by maintaining a steady speed.

When stationary while waiting in a traffic queue or to pick up a passenger, don't leave you engine idling pointlessly. Switch it off and start up again only when you're ready to drive off.

⊗ maintain your vehicle

Stick to your car's maintenance schedule – an unserviced engine can waste fuel and produce unnecessary emissions, and catalytic converters need checking regularly to ensure they're working effectively.

Make sure you keep your tyres correctly inflated. Running tyres at the wrong pressure can cause fuel consumption and tread wear to increase. You can save money when you buy new tyres too, if you choose a low rolling-resistance brand which helps to cut fuel consumption.

❍ travel light

Remove unnecessary items from the boot to reduce weight and improve fuel consumption. Avoid adding heavy accessories or wider tyres that increase rolling resistance. A fully loaded roof rack increases fuel consumption by up to 30%. Even an unladen rack causes extra drag, so remove it when it's not in use. Keep windows closed too, but remember that air conditioning also consumes power so use it only when necessary.

❍ plan your journey

Work out your best route in advance, make sure you know the way so you don't waste time and fuel by getting lost, and try to travel off-peak to avoid congestion. There are now plenty of resources on-line to help you plan the best route and check for roadworks and traffic congestion before you set out. Print off your route or write it down clearly, and plan an alternative route too, in case your first choice is blocked. If you have satellite navigation, enter your destination before you start your journey. Allow plenty of time to get where you are going, especially when travelling a long distance. If you can avoid busy times you'll have an easier journey and be less likely to be delayed by heavy traffic – and you won't be adding to traffic congestion yourself.

❍ share your car

Sharing a car for commuting or the school run halves your fuel costs and reduces urban pollution and congestion.

❍ use public transport

The best way to reduce the impact of your car on the environment is to leave it at home and take public transport instead, particularly if you're travelling in towns and cities. Short journeys – less than two miles – don't let the exhaust catalyst warm up which means they cause a disproportionate amount of pollution. If there's no bus available, why not walk or cycle these short journeys instead? It will be good for you as well as for the environment.

Avoid revving your engine unnecessarily, as it increases fuel consumption and mechanical wear

know the code

highway code rule 123

The Driver and the Environment

You MUST NOT leave a parked vehicle unattended with the engine running or leave a vehicle engine running unnecessarily while that vehicle is stationary on a public road. Generally, if the vehicle is stationary and is likely to remain so for more than a couple of minutes, you should apply the parking brake and switch off the engine to reduce emissions and noise pollution. However, it is permissible to leave the engine running if the vehicle is stationary in traffic or for diagnosing faults.

car theft

A car is many people's most valuable possession. Treat yours accordingly. Always be alert to the possibility of it being stolen or broken into. Even if you have fully comprehensive insurance, car theft is still a costly, inconvenient and unpleasant experience. And don't think that if you car is older and not of great value it won't interest thieves – they often target older cars because these are easier to steal.

beat the car thief

- if you have a garage always keep your car locked inside it overnight
- look after your car keys. Don't leave them near the front door at night where they are accessible to burglars
- if you don't have a garage, park your car where a thief would draw attention to himself. Leave it under a lamp post on the main road and not in a dark side street where the thief could work uninterrupted
- lock your car and remove the key, even if you are leaving it for just a few seconds outside your home or at a petrol station
- most cars have an engine immobiliser and often an alarm too. Check what is fitted to your car and consider extra deterrents – such as fitting a manual steering lock, or getting the registration number etched on the windows
- make sure you always activate any anti-theft devices you have, and ensure the steering column lock is engaged by twisting the wheel until it clicks
- If you have a portable satellite navigation device, remove it and take the whole unit, including support cradle and suction pads, with you when you leave the car
- Fit a security coded radio. If your radio has a removable front section, always take this with you or lock it securely in the boot when you park your car
- check that you know how your central locking works – you may have to press the remote control button twice to activate deadlocks if fitted
- never leave valuables on display in the car, or even items such as jackets or briefcases which look as though they might contain something of value. If you can't remove these items when parking, conceal them in the boot
- don't leave your vehicle paperwork (such as the registration document or MOT certificate) in the car when it is left unattended
- consider joining a vehicle watch scheme. This means you place a sticker in your car which informs the police they should flag it down if they see it being driven by someone who looks under 25 years old, or (depending on the scheme) if it is being driven between midnight and 5am.

Always make sure you lock your car even if you are leaving it unattended for just a few seconds

Don't leave valuables on display in the car. Lock up everything securely in the boot out of sight

driving abroad

Although questions about driving in other countries aren't included in the driving test, it's important to be aware of the issues involved. Many of us now routinely hire a car when on holiday, or take our own car across the channel, and you should prepare yourself before you set out for the different laws and driving conditions you will encounter overseas.

driving on the right

In Europe, America and much of the rest of the world, traffic travels on the right-hand side of the road and local vehicles are left-hand drive. Adapting to driving on the right isn't difficult, but you must be alert for situations – such as emerging from a lay-by or petrol station – where you may drive onto the wrong side of the road without thinking.

accessories

In many countries it is a legal requirement to carry in the car a:
- warning triangle
- set of spare light bulbs
- first aid kit
- fire extinguisher
- reflective waistcoat.

Carrying spare fuel in a can is illegal in some countries.

You will also need to obtain headlamp converters, or get your headlamps adjusted so they will not dazzle oncoming traffic when driving on the right.

documents

You must take your full valid UK driving licence and keep it with you at all times in case the police ask to see it. For some countries outside the EU you also need an International Driving Permit. When taking your car abroad make sure you also have the registration document, written authorisation that you are permitted to drive the car if it is a lease, hire or company car, and an MOT certificate if the car is over three years old.

Unless your car has 'Europlate' style numberplates (which show the letters GB below the Euro symbol) you must display a GB sticker on your car, as near as possible to the rear number plate.

Well in advance of leaving check with your insurance company that you will be covered to drive your car abroad. A green card may be required if you are visiting a country outside the EU.

local laws

Speed limits and drink-drive laws vary from country to country. For instance, in France the maximum motorway speed limit is 130km/h (81mph), while in Norway it is 90km/h (56mph). The maximum blood-alcohol limit varies from 0.08% in Switzerland through 0.05% in France to 0.02% in Sweden. To stay safe, always keep to the speed limit, and do not drink at all when you are driving.

In many countries the police are empowered to hand out a fine which must be paid on the spot. Local laws include:
- where two roads meet and there is no priority sign, in many countries you must automatically give way to the right
- in Austria and Switzerland you must purchase and display a vignette (tax disc) before driving on the motorway
- if you need to wear spectacles when driving, in Spain and Switzerland you must keep a spare pair in the car
- in Scandinavian countries you must keep your headlamps switched on at all times
- in the US, vehicles may use any lane to overtake on multi-lane highways, and they are permitted to turn right through a red traffic light if it is safe to do so.

For more advice on driving techniques and regulations overseas see the Haynes book, **Driving Abroad** *by Robert Davies.*

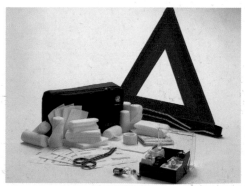

Check which accessories you will need to carry with you when driving your car overseas

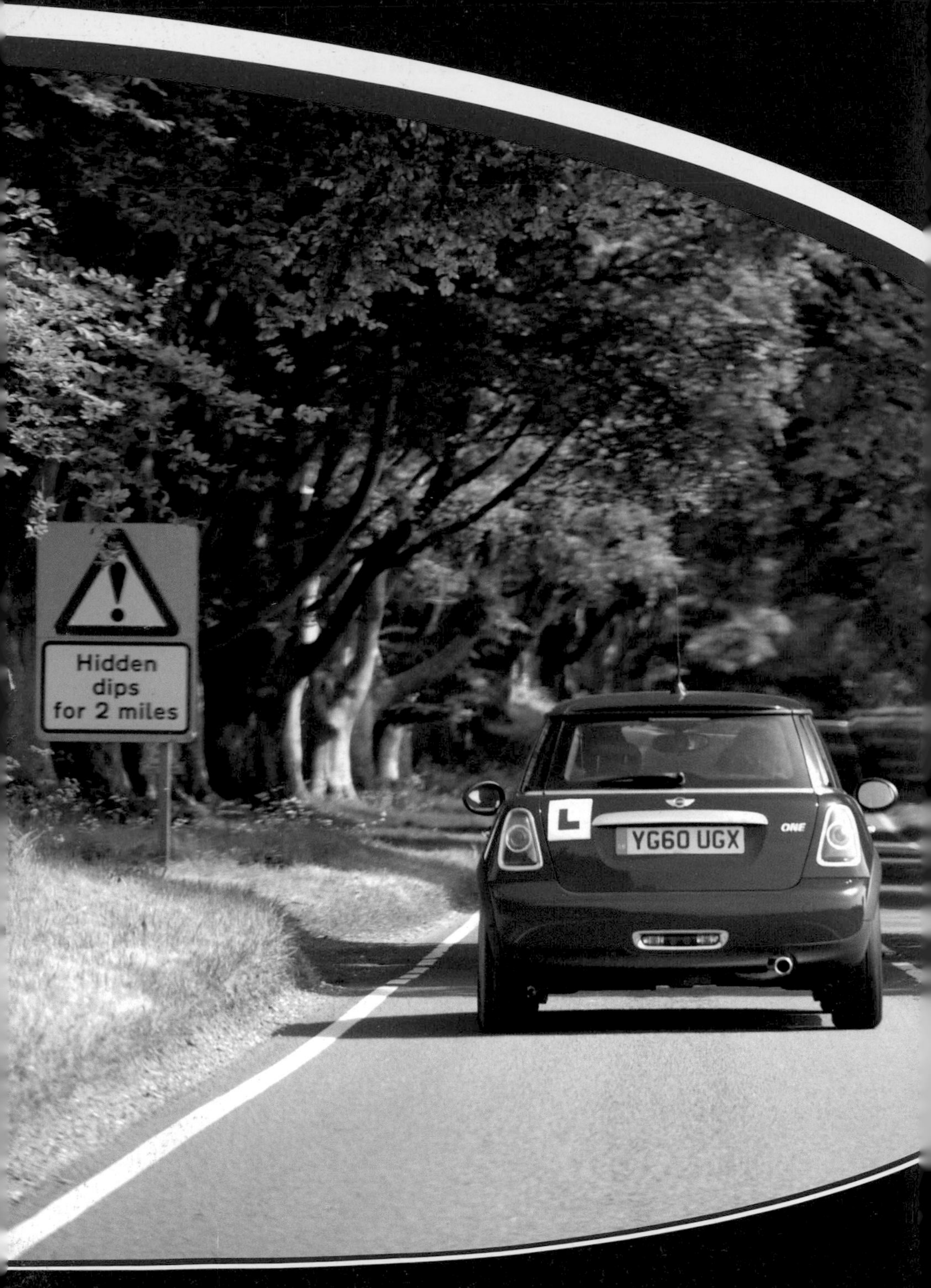
Hidden
dips
for 2 miles
YG60 UGX
ONE

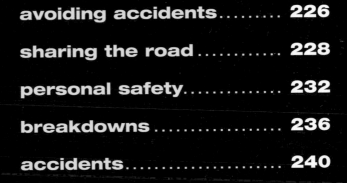

13 staying safe

Driving is the most dangerous thing most people do. Each of us has about a 1 in 200 chance of being killed in a road accident. You probably know of someone who has been killed or badly hurt on the road. And as a driver you don't just put yourself at risk. A car is a lethal weapon and every time you take to the road you have the capability to kill or maim. But it is reassuring to know that crashes don't happen for no reason. The overwhelming majority of road accidents are caused by bad driving. If you follow the advice in this book and become a good driver who always puts safety first, there is no reason why you should not enjoy an accident-free driving career.

avoiding accidents

Society has a blind spot about road casualties. When a train or plane crashes, it makes headline news, yet the toll of death on the roads goes largely unreported. Ten people die on British roads every day. In total each year over 300,000 people – equivalent to the population of a large town – are killed or injured on the road. And the sad truth is that the vast majority of the crashes that cause these deaths and injuries are caused by bad driving and are completely avoidable.

causes of accidents

Something like 95% of road accidents are caused by driver error. These are all crashes which could have been avoided.

You might think that the way to avoid accidents is to have highly developed car control skills. This is actually not the case. The sort of abilities which make a good racing driver – quick reactions, the ability to corner a car at its limits of grip and so on – are of little value when it comes to staying safe on the road. What really counts is having the right mental attitude. On the road good drivers are those who put safety first. They always drive within their limits and do not let their emotions influence their behaviour behind the wheel.

Driving a car quickly and competitively can be exciting. But the public road is not the place to do it. If you'd like to find out what it's like to push your car to its limits, then take it along to a track day at a racing circuit where you can drive quickly without endangering anyone.

risk taking

One in five drivers involved in an accident in which someone is injured is aged under 25. Young drivers, particularly men, are more likely to be involved in car crashes because they take more risks on the road. Sometimes young drivers take risks to try to impress their friends. Research has shown that young male drivers are much more likely to crash when they have other young men in the car with them.

Drivers of all ages are more likely to take risks when they're in a bad mood. If they've just fallen out with a friend, or are anxious because they're running behind schedule, they may allow this to cloud their judgement, become aggressive towards other road users and overtake when it isn't safe. It's important to realise how your mood can affect your driving and try to stay cool behind the wheel even when you're feeling under pressure.

bad habits

When drivers do something wrong and get away with it they start to develop bad habits. They may get too close to the car in front on the motorway, or not bother to signal when turning right at a roundabout. They keep doing this and getting away with it so it becomes part of their everyday driving. Until the day that the car in front on the motorway slams on its brakes unexpectedly, or a lorry pulls onto the roundabout thinking they are heading straight ahead.

Research shows that even when these drivers have a crash it may not be enough to break their bad habits. Drivers who crash tend to have the same sort of crash again and again.

To prevent yourself developing bad habits, you need to:

● realise that driving is a life-long skill which you should never stop trying to improve. Don't fall into the trap of getting two or three years' experience after passing your test and thinking you have no room for improvement. The best drivers – such as police class 1 drivers – recognise that however well trained they are, they are not perfect and are always working to improve their driving

● be critical towards your own driving. If you have to slam on the brakes to avoid another vehicle, or have a close shave when overtaking, ask yourself what you could do to avoid such a situation happening again in the future

● put your imagination to work when you are driving. Continually ask yourself 'what if?' What if a car pulls out of that driveway? What if there's a queue of stationary traffic round this bend? What if a child runs out between those two cars? If the answer is that there would be a nasty accident, then you're going too fast for the conditions and you need to slow down.

sharing the road

There are more than 32 million vehicles on our increasingly congested road system, and the only place you're likely to see an empty road nowadays is in a car advert. In the real world, whenever you get behind the wheel you need to interact with other road users. As in any other sphere of life, you can't expect these people to think or act exactly like you do – but you should make it your aim to get along with them courteously and harmoniously.

road rage

It's strange how some of the most mild-mannered people undergo a Jekyll-and-Hyde personality change when they get behind the wheel. They swear at other drivers, curse their stupidity, and generally get hot and bothered. This seriously compromises their ability to drive safely, as well as being unpleasant for their passengers.

Why does this happen? Visualise this scenario. An elderly lady walking along the pavement stops suddenly because she's just forgotten she meant to go to the greengrocers. A young man following behind has to stop and walk around her. She apologises for getting in his way; he smiles back and says 'no problem'.

Now imagine the same scene on the road. The lady realises she has missed her turning so slows down and looks for somewhere to turn. The young man in the car behind starts swearing under his breath, pulls right up behind her and flashes his lights. The lady complains to her passenger about the irresponsible young hooligan following and slows down even more to teach him a lesson. Finally he blasts past at the approach to a blind corner, honking his horn and waving his fist furiously.

The explanation for such different responses to an essentially similar situation is that driving a car has an unfortunate effect on the way we interact with other people. We have a strong sense of our car being an extension of our personal space, and become threatened and angry if we think others are encroaching on this space. We can't hear other drivers or see their facial expressions, so we stop seeing them as human beings and start treating them like mere objects which have the annoying habit of getting in our way.

Losing your cool on the road can lead to potentially lethal situations. However irritating other drivers seem, you must always put safety first and keep your emotions under control

Tailgating is aggressive, dangerous and illegal. If a following vehicle gets too close behind you, increase the safety gap in front of your car to compensate and let it overtake as soon as you can

keeping calm

If you find yourself getting angry with other road users:

⊘ try and recognise how the isolated environment of your car is preventing you from reacting to other people as you would normally. In your daily life you probably meet all sorts of people, and even when they seem difficult you will make an effort to get along with them and create a pleasant atmosphere. Aim to do the same on the road

⊘ remember that if someone seems to be getting in your way, it's almost certain they're not doing it on purpose. Other people get distracted, or lose their way, or make a mistake – just as we do ourselves on occasion

⊘ don't get into stressful situations where you're more likely to lose control over your emotions. Plan your journey in advance and leave plenty of time so you don't find yourself running late and getting tense

⊘ recognise that getting upset over someone else's bad driving serves no useful purpose. You can't control how other people drive, so let them get on with it and concentrate on what you *can* control – your own driving. If you think someone is driving dangerously, let them get on their way and have their accident somewhere else, not near you

⊘ remind yourself that however important your appointment may be, it's not worth having a crash because you're rushing to get there on time.

communication

Communicating with other road users can help to defuse a tense situation. If you have done something to inconvenience another driver, consider holding up your hand, palm out and fingers together, to acknowledge you have made a mistake. When another driver gives way to you, always give a wave and a smile of acknowledgement. This sort of simple communication with other road users can make life on the road a lot more pleasant and unstressed.

Conversely, never use hand signals or your horn or lights to rebuke another road user. It will have no positive effect whatsoever, but it could annoy them and provoke them to retaliate, putting you and other road users at risk.

Don't get annoyed or frustrated if you are held up by a slow-driven vehicle. Wait until you reach a safe place before attempting to overtake

Politeness makes driving more pleasant for everyone. If someone does you a favour on the road, acknowledge it with a friendly wave

elderly drivers

Be patient with elderly drivers. They may no longer possess the sharp reactions of youth, but statistically they are still a lot safer on the road than young drivers. Accident rates for drivers aged 74 and over are lower than those of drivers aged 21 to 24, and less than half of those aged 17 to 21.

Don't blame an elderly driver who seems slow and hesitant behind the wheel. They may hate driving and share your wish that they weren't on the road, but for many older people without access to public transport driving is their only way of staying in touch with friends and family and getting to the shops.

learner drivers

It's hard to believe anyone could forget what it feels like to learn to drive, but as you'll discover there are other drivers who become sadly impatient with learners. Make a vow not to do this once you have passed your test. Give learners plenty of space to do something unpredictable, and don't hassle a learner who is holding you up – they may just get more nervous and take even longer to move out of your way.

Once you've passed your driving test, don't forget to make allowances for people who are still learning and who may be hesitant or slow

vulnerable road users

Never forget the fact that other road users such as pedestrians, horse riders, cyclists and motorcyclists are not cocooned in a shell of protective steel and need extra care and courtesy to ensure their safety. Pay particular attention to children who may act unpredictably and not follow the rules of the road. Remember that you, as an individual driving a car, have no more right to use the road than another individual riding a bicycle or a horse. Show them courtesy and be prepared to follow behind them, even if it means driving at a walking pace, rather than squeezing past where there is not enough room to overtake safely.

know the code

highway code rule 147

Be considerate Be careful of and considerate towards other road users, especially those requiring extra care.

You should:

➜ try to be understanding if other drivers cause problems; they may be inexperienced or not know the area well

➜ be patient; remember that anyone can make a mistake

➜ not allow yourself to become agitated or involved if someone is behaving badly on the road. This will only make the situation worse. Pull over, calm down and, when you feel relaxed, continue your journey

➜ slow down and hold back if a road user pulls out into your path at a junction. Allow them to get clear. Do not over-react by driving too close behind to intimidate them

➜ not throw anything out of a vehicle, for example, cigarette ends, cans, paper or carrier bags. This can endanger other road users, particularly motorcyclists and cyclists.

personal safety

If you adopt a responsible attitude towards your driving, minimise risk-taking, put safety first at all times and do not venture onto the road when tiredness or ill health reduce your alertness, or bad weather makes conditions treacherous, then you can dramatically reduce your chances of being involved in a road accident. But there are further measures you can take to ensure that if the worst does happen, you are protected as fully as possible.

car safety

Great progress has been made by car manufacturers in recent years to ensure that if you do have a crash your car will help to protect you from injury. When you buy a car, look for the following safety features:

- ❷ anti-lock brakes (ABS) which prevent the wheels locking up in an emergency stop, and allow you to steer and brake at the same time to avoid an obstacle
- ❷ air bags which inflate to cushion the body in a crash. Most new cars have driver and passenger airbags, but look also for side impact bags and curtain bags which protect the head
- ❷ active head restraints which are more effective than normal head restraints at preventing whiplash injuries if you are hit from behind
- ❷ traction control which prevents the wheels spinning in slippery conditions
- ❷ skid control which automatically cuts the power and activates the brakes on individual wheels if it senses a skid developing
- ❷ crash resistance. Check the model's Euro NCAP rating, a measure of how well it has performed under independent crash testing. Aim for a car which has been awarded four or five stars. Look at the car's rating in tests which simulate a collision with a pedestrian too – few manufacturers do as much as they could to minimise the risk to vulnerable road users in a collision.

belt up

The most important safety item in the car is the seatbelt. Always wear your seatbelt when driving, even if you're going just a few hundred yards down the road.

Check your posture so you're not sitting too close to the steering wheel, which could be dangerous if the airbag activates. Never put a rear-facing child seat on a passenger seat which has an active airbag. Make sure that your head restraint is properly adjusted (see p34).

lock up

Your car may be a tempting target for thieves even while you are driving it. They may try to open a door and reach in to grab a handbag or jacket while you are waiting at traffic lights. Make it a habit to keep the doors locked while you are driving. Some people don't like the feeling of being locked in a car; if you feel this way you should at least keep the doors locked while you are in town, and unlock them when you get out on the open road.

carjacking

Carjacking – when a thief hijacks your car while you are in it – is thankfully rare in this country. Be cautious if a driver gestures or flashes at you to stop on a deserted road, maybe pointing to a pretend fault on your car. Drive on till you get to a well-lit, busy garage, shopping area or a police station before stopping to check. The same applies if another vehicle runs into you for no apparent reason – if you have any doubts then drive on to the nearest safe place before pulling over. If you do get in a carjacking situation, on no account put up resistance. Let the assailant get into your car and move quietly away from it.

Airbags are an important safety feature fitted as standard equipment to many new cars

lone women drivers

There are times when all women driving on their own feel intimidated or uncomfortable about their safety, particularly if their car breaks down or when using dark, deserted car parks. Take the following steps to ensure your safety:

- ⊘ always carry a mobile phone. Nothing beats the reassurance of knowing that you can immediately call for help wherever you may be

- ⊘ join a breakdown recovery service so if you do break down somewhere you'd rather not linger, you can get help as soon as possible. Always tell the operator when you ring for assistance that you are a woman travelling alone – you will be given priority

- ⊘ if you break down on a motorway, remember that the hard shoulder is a very dangerous place and staying in your car is far more risky than getting clear of the carriageway. Wait on the embankment and only return to your car and lock the doors if you feel you are in personal danger. As soon as you feel safe to do so then get out of the car and continue waiting well away from the carriageway

- ⊘ when parking your car think about whether the car park will be dark or deserted by the time you return. If so, park near the exit, or find somewhere else which will be better lit or busier. Reverse into your parking space so you are able to drive straight out again without manoeuvring.

Carrying a mobile phone with you is a useful precaution in case of breakdown or accident

carrying children

All passengers must wear a seat belt or child restraint unless they are exempt for medical reasons. As the driver you are not responsible for adult passengers who choose to break the law by not wearing a seat belt (though you should insist they do: in a high-speed crash an unrestrained rear seat passenger can be catapulted forwards with such force that they crush anyone sitting in the front seat).

But where children under 14 are concerned you as the driver are legally responsible for seeing that they are properly restrained.

By law all children up to 1.35m (4ft 5in) tall or younger than 12 years old must use the appropriate child restraint. Limited exceptions apply to children aged 3 to 11 or up to 1.35m tall travelling in the rear seat. It is legal for these to use an adult seat belt instead of a child restraint:

- for short, essential but unexpected journeys where a restraint is not available
- where two occupied child restraints mean that a third restraint cannot be fitted.

Other safety factors to remember when carrying children are:

- choose the correct size and type of restraint for the child and get advice from the supplier on how to fit it properly

- never place a rear-facing child seat on the front passenger seat where an active airbag is fitted – if the bag inflates it could be fatal. In some cars the airbag can be deactivated to allow a child seat to be fitted, but the safest option is to put the child seat on the rear seat
- if child safety locks are fitted to the rear doors (preventing the door from being opened from the inside) ensure they are used whenever children are carried.

It is the driver's responsibility to ensure children under the age of 14 are properly restrained

it's the law	seatbelts, children and the law			
	OCCUPANT	FRONT SEAT	REAR SEAT	WHO IS RESPONSIBLE?
	Driver	must wear seat belt if fitted		driver
	Child aged under 3	child restraint must be used	child restraint must be used	driver
	Child aged 3 to 11 or up to 1.35m tall	child restraint must be used	child restraint must be used where seat belts are fitted (*see exceptions above)	driver
	Child aged 12 or 13 or over 1.35m tall	seat belt must be worn if available	seat belt must be worn if available	driver
	Passenger aged over 14	seat belt must be worn if available	seat belt must be worn if available	passenger

Cars rarely break down unless they have been poorly maintained or abused. Never ignore any faults which your car develops. Be alert for unusual noises or smells, and stop immediately to investigate. Keep a warning triangle and a fire extinguisher in the car for use in emergencies. Think about joining a breakdown service. Even if you are a competent home mechanic you will not want to try fixing your car on a busy road in bad weather, and the membership fee is worth paying for peace of mind alone.

safety first

If your car breaks down, your first priority is to ensure that it is not causing a hazard for other road users. Try to get it off the road if possible. If it is on the road, turn on the hazard warning lights, and keep the side lights on at night or in poor visibility.

Place a warning triangle on the road at least 45 metres (147 feet) behind your car on the same side of the road. If you have broken down on a bend or after the crest of a hill, place the triangle so it can be clearly seen by other drivers before they reach the bend or hill crest. On a very narrow road put the triangle on the verge or nearside footway.

Make sure your passengers get off the road to a place of safety. Never stand between your broken-down car and oncoming traffic, or stand where you might prevent other road users seeing your lights. Keep a high-visibility jacket in the boot and put it on so you can be more clearly seen.

Common causes of breakdowns include:

⊘ engine failure
if the engine cuts out while you are driving you will lose power assistance to the brakes and steering. This means you will need to use more force to steer the car, and will have to press the brake pedal harder to stop

⊘ tyre blow-out
if a tyre deflates while you are driving, grip the steering wheel firmly and allow the car to roll to a stop at the side of the road. Try to avoid using the brakes or steering harshly, which may cause you to lose control

⊘ puncture
only change a flat tyre if you can do so without putting yourself or others at risk – if not, call for professional assistance. Make sure the parking brake is on and chock the wheels. Also take care that the car is secure on its jack before removing the wheel, and double check that all nuts are properly tightened before driving off

⊘ overheating
if your engine overheats, stop and let it cool down before investigating further. Only when it is cool should you remove the filler cap and top up the coolant level if required

⊘ fire
reduce the risk of fire by carrying a fire extinguisher and always stopping and checking for the cause if you smell petrol fumes while driving. If your vehicle catches fire, immediately get the occupants out of the vehicle and to a safe place. Call the fire brigade. Do not try to extinguish a fire in the engine compartment, as opening the bonnet may make the fire flare. If it is safe then you may be able to direct a fire extinguisher through the small gap which opens up at the front of the bonnet when the bonnet catch is released.

Joining a breakdown service makes a lot of sense: it's easier and much safer to leave roadside repair and recovery to the professionals

motorway breakdowns

The motorway is a hazardous place to break down, so if your car develops a fault, move to the inside lane and try to carry on to the next exit or service station.

If you do have to stop on the motorway:

⊙ pull on to the hard shoulder and stop as far to the left as possible. Turn your front wheels to the left so if your car is hit by another vehicle it will not be pushed back onto the carriageway. Switch on your hazard warning lights and at night or in poor visibility keep your side lights on

⊙ if you aren't able to get your car to the hard shoulder, switch on your hazard warning lights and make certain it is safe before getting out of the car and making your way clear of the carriageway

⊙ if you are on a motorway with an Active Traffic Management scheme (see p122) do not stop on the hard shoulder, even if it is not being used as a running lane. Pull up instead in one of the emergency refuge areas which are situated alongside the hard shoulder at 500m intervals. Control centre operators are automatically alerted by CCTV when a vehicle enters an emergency rescue area

⊙ on the hard shoulder, exit the vehicle by the left-hand door and ensure your passengers do the same. Tell them to stay on the verge well away from the hard shoulder, and make sure that children are kept under control

⊙ leave any animals in the vehicle or, in an emergency, keep them under proper control on the verge

⊙ do not try to make even simple repairs such as changing a tyre

If you break down on the hard shoulder, keep well clear of the carriageway while waiting for assistance

Take special care if you break down where there are motorway roadworks being carried out

- do not place any warning device such as a warning triangle on the hard shoulder
- phone the emergency services. Use an emergency phone rather than your own mobile, as this allows the operator in the police (in some areas, the Highways Agency) control centre to pinpoint your location. The direction of the nearest emergency telephone is given on marker posts situated every 100 metres along the hard shoulder. Face the oncoming traffic while you are using the phone so you can see danger approaching. The operator will ask you for the number of the telephone you are using, details of yourself and your vehicle, and whether you belong to a motoring organisation. Tell the operator if you are a vulnerable motorist such as a woman travelling alone
- if you do decide to use your mobile phone to call for help, take note of the number on the nearest marker post as this can help to identify your location
- wait near your vehicle on the embankment away from the carriageway and hard shoulder
- if you feel at risk from another person, return to your vehicle by a left-hand door and lock all doors. Leave your vehicle again as soon as you feel safe to do so
- if you have a disability which prevents you from following the above advice, you should stay in your vehicle, switch on your hazard warning lights and either use a mobile phone to contact the emergency services or display a 'help' pennant
- when you rejoin the carriageway after a breakdown, build up speed on the hard shoulder before pulling out into a safe gap in the traffic
- if your car needs to be towed off the motorway, leave this job to a professional garage or breakdown service.

tunnels

A tunnel is a particularly hazardous place in which to break down or have an accident. Take extra care by observing all road signs and signals on the approach to a tunnel, and consider tuning in to a local radio station to listen for traffic warnings. Always switch on your dipped headlights in a tunnel, and if you are wearing sunglasses stop and remove them before you enter it.

Leave a generous separation distance from the vehicle in front, especially if you have to stop in a tunnel in congested traffic. Follow the instructions given on variable message signs.

In the event of a breakdown, put on your hazard warning lights and phone for help. If your car catches fire, try to keep driving until you are out of the tunnel before stopping. If this is not possible, switch on your hazard warning lights and try to put out the fire with your own extinguisher or one of those located in the tunnel. If you cannot put it out or in the case of a serious fire developing, make your way to the nearest emergency exit.

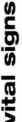

emergency telephone box on motorway (use the number to tell the operator the location of the box)

direction to nearest emergency telephone shown on marker post on motorway hard shoulder

tunnel ahead

direction to emergency pedestrian exit in tunnel

accidents

If you are involved in a road accident you have certain legal responsibilities. You should also try to gather as much information as possible for insurance purposes. Where you come across the scene of an accident involving other vehicles, you should stop to give assistance. It is useful to carry a first aid kit and take some training in how to use it in case you ever have to give emergency first aid to road casualties.

getting information

Even a minor accident may involve an insurance claim. You should gather as much information on the spot as you can. Draw a sketch map of the scene, and if you have a camera take some photographs. Make a note of:

- ⊖ the other driver's name, address and telephone number
- ⊖ whether the driver owns the other vehicle
- ⊖ the make, model and registration number of the other vehicle
- ⊖ details of the other driver's motor insurance
- ⊖ names and addresses of witnesses
- ⊖ road and weather conditions
- ⊖ what vehicles were doing at the time of the accident (such as whether their lights were on and if they were signalling)
- ⊖ what other people say to you
- ⊖ identification numbers of police officers attending the accident.

accident scenes

If other people have already stopped to give assistance, try not to let yourself be distracted by an accident scene. Where an incident has occurred on the other side of a motorway or dual carriageway, keep your attention on the road ahead as further accidents are often caused by drivers 'rubbernecking' at accidents instead of concentrating on their own driving.

If you need to stop to give assistance:

- ⊖ first stop and warn other traffic
- ⊖ switch on your hazard warning lights
- ⊖ make sure someone telephones for an ambulance if people are badly injured
- ⊖ get people who are not injured clear of the scene
- ⊖ place a warning triangle on the road at least 45 metres behind the crash scene
- ⊖ switch off all engines
- ⊖ make sure no one is smoking
- ⊖ do not put yourself at unnecessary risk.

If you are involved in a accident which causes damage or injury then you have a legal obligation to provide certain personal details (see below)

it's the law In an accident

If you are involved in an accident which causes damage or injury to any other person, vehicle, animal or property, you must by law:

- → stop
- → give your own and (if different) your vehicle owner's name and address, and the registration number of your vehicle, to anyone having reasonable grounds for requiring them
- → if you do not give your name and address at the time of the accident, report the accident to the police as soon as reasonably practicable, and in any case within 24 hours
- → if another person is injured and you do not produce your insurance certificate at the time of the accident to a police officer or to anyone having reasonable grounds to request it, you must report the accident to the police as soon as possible (and in any case within 24 hours), and produce your insurance certificate for the police within seven days.

If a vehicle catches fire, stand well clear and call for the fire brigade to deal with it

first aid

Carry a first aid kit in your car and take some training in how to use it so you are prepared if you ever have to help accident casualties.

At an accident scene do not move injured people out of their vehicles unless you have to do so to protect them from further danger (moving them could aggravate a back injury). Do not remove a motorcyclist's helmet unless it is essential to clear their airway as it could make their injury worse. If a casualty is unconscious, first check that they are still breathing (monitor their breathing for at least 10 seconds) before dealing with any heavy bleeding or burns.

⊙ resuscitation

If the casualty is not breathing you will need to begin the ABC of resuscitation: this means checking the Airway, Breathing and Circulation. Clear away any obstruction to the airway and loosen tight clothing. If breathing does not restart when the airway has been cleared, give mouth-to-mouth resuscitation. Lift the chin and tilt the head backwards. Pinch the casualty's nostrils and blow into the mouth (gently in the case of a child) until the chest rises. Repeat every four seconds until the casualty can breathe without assistance. If there is no pulse (circulation), start external chest compression. Press down firmly by about 4–5cm with the heel of your hand in the middle of the casualty's chest at a rate of 100 compressions per minute. Give two breaths after every 30 compressions.

⊙ recovery position

If a casualty is unconscious but breathing, putting them in the recovery position will maintain an open airway and ensure they do not swallow their tongue: place them on their side, supported by one leg and one arm, and open the airway (after checking that it is clear) by tilting the head and lifting the chin.

⊙ bleeding

Where there is heavy bleeding, apply firm hand pressure over the wound, preferably using some clean material. Don't press on any foreign body in the wound. Secure a pad with a bandage or length of cloth. Raise the limb or wound (if there are no fractures) to lessen the bleeding.

⊙ burns

Douse burns with cool liquid and continue to cool them for at least ten minutes. But do not put any creams on a burn and do not remove anything sticking to it.

⊙ shock

Casualties may be suffering from shock. Symptoms include sweating; rapid shallow breathing; clammy, grey skin and blue lips; faintness, nausea and dizzyness. Keep them warm and comfortable, give them constant reassurance and make sure they are not left alone. Do not give them anything to eat, drink or smoke. Stay at the scene until the emergency services arrive.

hazard warning plates

hazard information panel displayed by tanker carrying dangerous goods (in this case flammable liquid)

diamond symbols indicating other hazardous substances include:

toxic substance

oxidising substance

non-flammable compressed gas

radioactive substance

spontaneously combustible substance

corrosive substance

panel displayed by vehicle carrying dangerous goods in packages

dangerous goods

Learn to recognise the markings displayed on vehicles carrying hazardous goods. If an accident involves a vehicle containing dangerous goods, it is essential that all engines are switched off and no one smokes. Do not use a mobile phone nearby. Keep well clear of the vehicle and stay away from any liquids, dust or vapours. Call the emergency services and give as much information as possible about the labels and markings on the vehicle.

Keep at a safe distance if a tanker carrying a dangerous substance is involved in an accident

vital signs

temporary police warning signs at scene of accident or other danger

hospital with accident and emergency facilities

hospital without accident and emergency facilities

14 taking your test

There are two parts to the driving test. The first part is a theory test and the second a practical test. You cannot take your practical test until you have passed the theory test, and you must take your practical test within two years of passing the theory test. The theory test includes a multiple-choice examination, plus a separate hazard perception test based on video clips. The practical test involves driving for around 40 minutes in the presence of a driving examiner who will assess your driving. It includes an eyesight test, several set manoeuvres, an independent driving section, plus two questions about vehicle safety checks. The driving test is administered by the Driving Standards Agency (DSA) and you'll find useful information on applying for and taking your test on the website: www.direct.gov.uk/drivingtest.

theory test

The theory test consists of two elements. Firstly, there's a multiple-choice examination in which you have to answer correctly 43 out of 50 questions covering all aspects of driving on a touch-screen computer. Secondly, you have to identify the road hazards shown on 14 video clips by clicking a mouse button as soon as you see them.

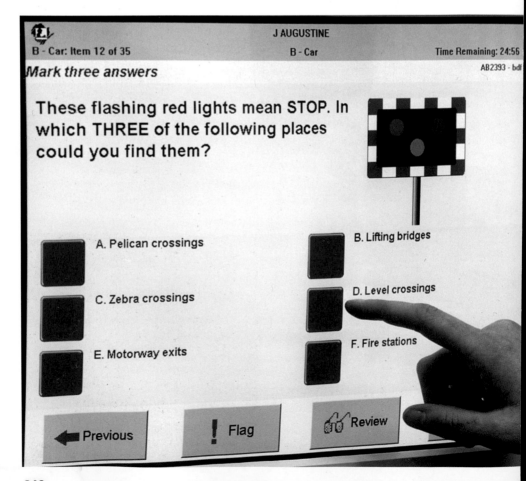

B - Car: Item 12 of 35   J AUGUSTINE   B - Car   Time Remaining: 24:56

AB2393 - bdf

Mark three answers

These flashing red lights mean STOP. In which THREE of the following places could you find them?

A. Pelican crossings

B. Lifting bridges

C. Zebra crossings

D. Level crossings

E. Motorway exits

F. Fire stations

Previous   ! Flag   Review

booking your test

You can book a theory test by postal application, telephone, or on-line. The cost of the theory test is currently £31.

Weekday, evening and saturday test sessions are available in addition to daytime appointments. If you need to cancel your theory test appointment, you must give at least three whole working days notice, or you forfeit your theory test fee. If you have hearing difficulties, dyslexia or light-sensitive epilepsy then let the DSA know at the time of making your booking and special arrangements will be made for you.

In Northern Ireland, driving tests are administered by the Driver and Vehicle Agency. The tests follow the same format.

what to take with you

At the test centre you will need to show both parts of your photocard driving licence. If you have one of the older style driving licences which doesn't include a photograph, you also need to take a passport with you. No other form of photographic ID will be accepted.

If you forget to bring the correct documents with you on the day, you won't be able to take your test and you will lose your fee.

Arrive in plenty of time for your theory test so that you don't feel rushed or stressed.

multiple-choice test

The theory test begins with a multiple-choice exam. To pass this you must answer correctly at least 43 out of 50 multiple-choice questions within the 57 minutes allowed (people with special needs can apply for additional time when they are booking their test).

Some questions will be presented as a case study. This shows a short scenario based on a real life situation that you could experience while driving. You will be asked five questions based on the scenario.

You select your answers by touching the button on the screen beside the answer that you want to select. You will be given the opportunity to practise doing this before starting the test.

If you think you have selected the wrong answer you can change it by touching the screen again. If you are unsure which answer is correct you can mark questions with a flag to help you go back to them. The system also prompts you to go back to questions you have not answered fully.

After the multiple-choice exam, you have a break of up to three minutes before taking the hazard perception test.

preparing for the multiple-choice test

The 50 questions in the multiple-choice test are selected from a bank of questions similar to those listed at the end of this book. Use these questions to practise taking the multiple-choice section of the theory test. If you are not sure of an answer, read the explanatory text alongside each question for more information, or refer to the relevant section of this book.

If you have read and made sure you thoroughly understand all the preceding chapters of this book, then you will know everything you need to answer any of the questions you may be asked in your test.

contact details

Driving Standards Agency (DSA)
Customer Enquiry Unit
PO Box 280
Newcastle-Upon-Tyne
NE99 1FP

telephone: 0300 200 1122
website: www.direct.gov.uk/drivingtest

Driver and Vehicle Agency (DVA) (Northern Ireland)
Customer Services, DVA, County Hall, Castlerock Rd, Coleraine BT51 3HS

telephone: 0845 601 4094
website: www.dvtani.gov.uk

hazard perception test

Before you sit the hazard perception test you will be shown a short tutorial video demonstrating how it works.

The test consists of 14 video clips, each about one minute long, showing driving situations involving other road users. You should press your mouse button as soon as you see a hazard which may require you to change speed or direction. The earlier you spot the hazard and respond, the higher the score you receive. The video will not stop or slow down when you respond but a red flag appears at the bottom of the screen each time you press the mouse button to show your response has been recorded. You can click the right or left button on the mouse to show you have identified the hazard.

There are a total of 15 scoreable hazards: 13 clips contain one scoreable hazard and one clip contains two of them. You can score up to five marks for each hazard depending on how quickly you identify it. Unlike the multiple-choice test, in this section you are not able to go back or change your response. You will not lose points for identifying non-scoring hazards.

It is not possible to pass the test by clicking the mouse button continuously: this will score zero points.

You must score at least 44 out of 75 points to pass the hazard perception test.

what is a hazard?

Imagine the video clip shows a car parked at the side of the road. It's a potential hazard, but at the moment it's not doing anything that will affect you. So if you clicked the mouse button at this point you wouldn't score anything (though you wouldn't lose any points either).

Then the car's right-hand indicator starts to flash. This means the driver is thinking of pulling out. This is now a developing hazard and you should click to show you have identified it.

preparing for the hazard perception test

The video clips you will see show real-life hazards of the sort you come across on the road every day. Whenever you are in a car, even as a passenger, test yourself by scanning the road ahead and identifying potential hazards. Read through this book carefully, paying special attention to Chapter 8 which deals with hazard perception, observation and anticipation. You may also find it useful to talk through some practice video sessions with your driving instructor.

pass or fail?

After completing both sections of the theory test you should receive your results, and feedback, within 30 minutes.

You must pass both the multiple-choice and hazard perception elements to pass your theory test. If you fail one element but pass the other, you still have to take the whole test over again.

If you have failed you can book another theory test straight away, but you must leave three clear working days before the date of your new test.

When you pass the theory test you will receive a pass certificate which is valid for two years. This means that if you don't pass your practical test within two years you will have to retake the theory test.

test tips

do
- prepare properly beforehand by studying and making sure you understand the answers to all the theory questions listed in the back of this book
- listen carefully to all the instructions you are given before and during the theory test

don't
- →
- →

video clip example 1

The hazard is the school crossing patrol with children ready to cross the road. You should click on the mouse button as soon as you realise that the patrol might walk into the road to stop traffic in front of you and let the children cross

video clip example 2

The hazard is the small child on a bicycle who cycles across the road. You should click on the mouse button as soon as you realise that the child might ride across the road, causing the motorcyclist in front of your car to brake

practical test

Taking the practical test isn't as daunting as you may think. You won't be asked to do anything you haven't already practised many times before with your instructor. But it's a fact that fewer than half of those who take the test pass it. Make sure you get as much practice as you can before booking your test, because taking the test before you're properly prepared will certainly result in a costly and confidence-denting failure.

booking your test

You can book your practical driving test by post, telephone, or on-line.

The cost of the practical test is currently £62 when taken on a weekday. There's usually a waiting time of about six weeks for a practical test. At test centres with longer waiting times, tests may be available at weekends and at early mornings and evenings during weekdays – in which case a higher test fee of £75 applies.

If you have hearing difficulties, dyslexia or any disability or restricted mobility which may affect your driving then you should let the DSA know at the time of booking.

If the date or time you are given for your driving test isn't suitable, or for any reason you need to postpone your test, you must give the DSA at least three working days notice (not counting the day of the test and day of notification) or you will lose your fee.

your test car

It is usually easiest to use your instructor's car on your test, even though you may have to pay a fee to do so. If you use your own car, you must ensure it is suitable for taking the test. If for whatever reason your car is not suitable you will not be permitted to take your test and will lose your fee.

If you do decide to use your own car, firstly you must make sure it is legally roadworthy and has a current MOT certificate, if applicable. There must be no warning lights, such as the airbag warning light, illuminated. It must be insured for you to drive and you will be asked to sign a declaration that your insurance is in order (you should contact your insurance company beforehand to tell them you will be taking a driving test in your car).

If you are planning to take your test in a hire car, you should check with the hire company that you are authorised to do so.

To be used for the test, a car must have:

- ◗ a valid tax disc
- ◗ L plates (or D plates, if taking your test in Wales) displayed front and rear but not interfering with the examiner's view
- ◗ a clear view to the rear other than by the exterior mirrors
- ◗ a clean, working front passenger seatbelt
- ◗ an integral head restraint fitted to the front passenger seat
- ◗ an additional interior rear-view mirror suitable for use by the examiner.
- ◗ a speedometer marked in mph
- ◗ a smoke-free environment.

If a dual accelerator is fitted it must be removed before the test. A car fitted with a temporary 'space-saver' spare wheel is not permitted.

Panel vans, and some convertible models such as the VW Beetle and Ford Ka cabriolets, are not allowed to be used for the test due to their restricted rear visibility.

If your car has been subject to a recall then it may be used only if you take proof that the vehicle has been checked and if necessary rectified. A number of vehicles have been subject to recall so check the DSA website for the full list of recalls to make sure your car is not affected.

For test use an extra rear-view mirror is required

what to take with you

When you arrive at the test centre you will need to show:

- ⮕ both parts of your photocard driving licence
- ⮕ your theory test pass certificate.

You should also bring your Driver's Record, if you have completed one. If you have one of the older style driving licences without a photograph, you must bring a passport too.

If you forget to bring the right documents with you on the day, your test will be cancelled and you will lose your fee.

coping with nerves

Of course you'll be nervous on your driving test – everyone is. Make sure on the day that you arrive for your test in good time to avoid any last minute panics. Get together all the documents you'll need the day before, and get an early night.

A reasonable degree of nervousness on your driving test isn't necessarily a bad thing as it sharpens up your senses and concentration. If it helps to ease the tension, you are welcome to have your instructor or a friend (over 16) accompany you, but they are not allowed to interfere in the test in any way. It is a good idea in any case to have your instructor along for the test as they will be able to give you some useful extra feedback about how you have performed.

test procedure

The driving test lasts around 40 minutes. It begins with an eyesight examination. You must be able to read the current style of numberplate from a distance of 20 metres. You can wear spectacles or contact lenses to do so, but if so you must keep them on when you are driving. The examiner will select a parked vehicle probably a little further away than 20 metres and ask you to read the numberplate. If you cannot read it, the examiner will measure the distance exactly and ask you to repeat the test. If you still cannot read it, you have failed and your driving test will go no further.

The practical test includes two safety check questions: for instance, you may be asked how you would check that the indicators are working (above) or that your head restraint is correctly adjusted (right)

safety check questions

At the start of the practical test, you are required to answer two questions about vehicle maintenance checks.

One of these is a 'tell me' question: you will be asked to tell the examiner how you would carry out a procedure, such as checking the engine oil.

The other is a 'show me' question: it requires you to show the examiner how you would carry out a safety check, such as inspecting the indicator lights to make sure they are working. You will not be asked to touch any hot engine parts, but you may be required to open the bonnet and indicate where you would check the various fluid levels.

The questions you may be asked are set out opposite – you will be asked a combination of one of the 'tell me' questions plus one of the 'show me' questions.

Your answers should refer specifically to your vehicle, so practise these maintenance checks on your driving test car and study its handbook before taking your test. If your car has electronic diagnostic systems which display information such as tyre pressures or oil level on the instrument panel, it is acceptable to refer to these in your answer.

If you fail to answer one or both of the safety check questions correctly it counts as one driving fault.

'tell me' questions

Q *tell me how you would check that the brakes are working before starting a journey*

A explain that when you operate the brake pedal the brakes should not feel spongy or slack. You would also test the brakes as you set off and check that they are working effectively and do not pull to one side.

Q *identify where the windscreen washer reservoir is and tell me how you would check the windscreen washer level*

A indicate the reservoir and explain where you would look to check the level of washer fluid in it.

Q *tell me how you would know if there was a problem with your anti-lock braking system*

A explain that the warning light should illuminate if there is a problem with the anti-lock braking system.

Q *tell me how you would check that the head lights and tail lights are working*

A explain you would operate the light switch (first turning on the ignition if necessary), and walk round the car checking the lights.

Q *tell me how you make sure your head restraint is correctly adjusted so it provides the best protection in the event of a crash*

A explain that the head restraint should be adjusted so the rigid part of the head restraint is at least as high as the eyes or top of the ears, and as close to the back of the head as is comfortable (not all head restraints are adjustable).

Q *tell me where you would find the information for the recommended tyre pressures for this car and how tyre pressures should be checked*

A explain that you would consult the manufacturer's handbook, use a reliable pressure gauge, check and adjust the pressures when the tyres are cold (not forgetting the spare tyre) and remember to refit the valve caps afterwards.

Q *tell me how you would check the tyres to ensure that they have sufficient tread depth and that their general condition is safe to use on the road*

A you would examine the tyres to check that there are no cuts or bulges, and that there is at least 1.6mm of tread depth across the central three-quarters of the width of the tyre and around the entire outer circumference.

'show me' questions

Q *show me how you would check that the power assisted steering is working before starting a journey*

A putting gentle pressure on the steering wheel and maintaining it while the engine is started should result in a slight but noticeable movement as the system begins to operate. Alternatively turning the steering wheel just after moving off will give an immediate indication that the power assistance is functioning. If the steering ever becomes heavy to use this indicates that the power assistance may not be working properly.

Q *show me how you would check that the horn is working (off road only)*

A press the horn button to sound the horn (turn on the ignition first if necessary).

Q *show me how you would check that the direction indicators are working*

A turn on the indicators or the hazard warning switch and walk round the car to check that all the indicators are functioning properly.

Q *show me how you would check that the brake lights are working on this car*

A press the brake pedal while looking at the reflection of the brake lights in a window or garage door (or ask someone else to check the lights while you hold down the pedal). You may need to switch the ignition on first.

Safety check questions require you to show how you would set the heater demisting controls (top), check the brake fluid level (above), and test the parking brake for excessive wear (right)

fault assessment

The examiner assesses faults according to three categories:

◯ dangerous faults

this is when a fault committed during the test has resulted in actual danger. Committing one dangerous fault results in test failure. A driving examiner who considers that a candidate is driving dangerously may stop the test on the spot

◯ serious faults

this is when a potentially dangerous incident occurs, or the candidate reveals a habitual driving fault. Committing one serious fault results in failure

◯ driving faults

these are less serious faults. Accumulating more than 15 driving faults results in failure. Don't panic if you think you have made one or two minor errors, as very few candidates fail through making too many driving faults.

if you pass

Congratulations! But don't be in too much of a rush to get behind the wheel on your own. You've just had a stressful hour and it is best to let your driving instructor drive you back from the test centre and wait till the euphoria has worn off before you drive on your own.

if you fail

Don't be too disheartened. If you failed your driving test first time that's no reason why you shouldn't go on to pass next time and become a good, safe driver. The most common reason why applicants fail is lack of preparation. Have you really clocked up enough hours on the road to feel completely at home in the car and at ease with basic techniques like moving off and changing gear? Have you driven in a wide enough variety of traffic situations and become familiar with the whole range of hazards you are likely to encounter during the test?

The examiner will give you a statement of failure showing all the faults you have made, plus a short debrief, running through the reasons why you failed. Go over these faults with your driving instructor and discuss what you need to do to address them.

If you fail your practical test you must wait at least ten working days before you can retake it.

It's best to keep the momentum going by booking another test date straight away, arranging more lessons and putting in as much practice as possible. Pay attention to the weak points revealed by your test, but don't concentrate only on the items where you failed, or you may find yourself getting out of practice in other areas.

after the test

Those few seconds as you wait for the examiner's verdict at the end of your test will be as nerve-racking as any in your life. Being told you've passed comes as a massive relief and opens a gateway to a fantastic range of new experiences and opportunities. But passing doesn't mean you should stop thinking about your driving. Your career as a driver is only just beginning, and for a good driver the learning never stops.

passing your test

If you pass and have a photocard driving licence issued after March 1 2004, your examiner will ask if you want your full licence issued to you automatically. If you do, the examiner will send your licence details electronically to the DVLA. You will then be given a pass certificate to prove you have passed your test and the DVLA will send you a full licence by post within three weeks.

If you have an older licence, you will be given a pass certificate which you must exchange for a full licence within two years. You will need to complete form D1 (available from the post office) and send it to the DVLA with the supporting documentation and the appropriate fee.

Pass Plus

Passing your driving test is an achievement to be proud of, but it is still only the first step to becoming a good driver. It means you have reached a basic level of driving competence, yet there are still many driving situations, such as driving on the motorway, that you have not experienced.

An excellent way to gain extra experience is to take the official Pass Plus course. You can do this within the first year of passing the practical driving test. Consisting of six special training sessions, including driving in all weathers, at night and on motorways, it not only takes you through a range of more advanced driving techniques, it also qualifies you for cheaper car insurance.

driving on your own

Your first drive alone in the car can be both exhilarating and stressful. Don't be too ambitious in your early journeys – you may tire quickly while driving. If you are still hesitant in some situations you may find it helps to fit P-plates, which indicate to others that you are a newly passed driver. But it is inevitable that when driving, as in other areas of life, you will encounter people who are rude, aggressive, impatient and bullying. Just concentrate on your own driving, and aim to let them get by without transferring their stress to you.

Beware of overconfidence in your first months and years of driving. It's a fact that this is the most dangerous time of your motoring life. As a new driver, you are more likely to have an accident in the first year after passing your test than at any other time in your motoring career.

Be particularly careful when you have passengers on board. Don't let them distract you or adversely influence your driving.

advanced driving

Too many drivers take little or no pride in their driving. They fail to concentrate, observe and anticipate properly what is happening on the road, and show little respect for other road users.

Don't become one of these bad drivers. Take your driving seriously and critically assess how you are performing when you drive. Take a regular look at the *Highway Code* to check you haven't forgotten anything or missed any revisions to the law. And if you get a chance to improve your driving, take it. Many employers provide defensive driving courses for staff who run a company car. These are a great idea and will help highlight any areas where your driving skills need attention.

Better still, think about taking an advanced driving test, such as is provided by the Institute of Advanced Motorists and RoSPA. Preparing for the advanced test gives you a chance to assess how your driving has progressed since you passed your driving test, and weed out any bad habits that may have crept in.

Taking an active interest in your driving has another advantage too – it turns it from a dull but necessary everyday task into a real source of interest, enjoyment and long-term satisfaction.

259

15 theory questions

To pass your theory test you will need to answer correctly 43 out of 50 questions on all aspects of driving. The following question bank shows examples of the types of question you will be asked. Test your knowledge by answering these questions and checking to see if you have answered correctly. If you don't understand one of the answers, refer to the accompanying explanatory text for extra information.

alertness

1.1 Mark one answer

Before you make a U-turn in the road, you should

- ☐ give an arm signal as well as using your indicators
- ☐ signal so that other drivers can slow down for you
- ☑ look over your shoulder for a final check select a
- ☐ select a higher gear than normal

If you want to make a U-turn, slow down and ensure that the road is clear in both directions. Make sure that the road is wide enough to carry out the manoeuvre safely.

1.2 Mark three answers

As you approach this bridge you should

- ☐ move into the middle of the road to get a better view
- ☑ slow down
- ☐ get over the bridge as quickly as possible
- ☑ consider using your horn
- ☐ find another route
- ☑ beware of pedestrians

This sign gives you a warning. The brow of the hill prevents you seeing oncoming traffic so you must be cautious. The bridge is narrow and there may not be enough room for you to pass an oncoming vehicle at this point. There is no footpath, so pedestrians may be walking in the road. Consider the hidden hazards and be ready to react if necessary.

1.3 Mark one answer

In which of these situations should you avoid overtaking?

- ☐ Just after a bend
- ☐ In a one-way street
- ☐ On a 30 mph road
- ☑ Approaching a dip in the road

As you begin to think about overtaking, ask yourself if it's really necessary. If you can't see well ahead stay back and wait for a safer place to pull out.

1.4 Mark one answer

This road marking warns

- ☐ drivers to use the hard shoulder
- ☐ overtaking drivers there is a bend to the left
- ☑ overtaking drivers to move back to the left
- ☐ drivers that it is safe to overtake

You should plan your overtaking to take into account any hazards ahead. In this picture the marking indicates that you are approaching a junction. You will not have time to overtake and move back into the left safely.

1.5 Mark one answer

Your mobile phone rings while you are travelling. You should

- ☐ stop immediately
- ☐ answer it immediately
- ☑ pull up in a suitable place
- ☐ pull up at the nearest kerb

The safest option is to switch off your mobile phone before you set off, and use a message service. Even hands-free systems are likely to distract your attention. Don't endanger other road users. If you need to make a call, pull up in a safe place when you can, you may need to go some distance before you can find one. It's illegal to use a hend-held mobile or similar device when driving or riding, except in a genuine emergency.

1.6   Mark one answer

Why are these yellow lines painted across the road?

☐ To help you choose the correct lane
☐ To help you keep the correct separation distance
☑ To make you aware of your speed
☐ To tell you the distance to the roundabout

These lines are often found on the approach to a roundabout or a dangerous junction. They give you extra warning to adjust your speed. Look well ahead and do this in good time.

1.7   Mark one answer

You are approaching traffic lights that have been on green for some time. You should

☐ accelerate hard
☐ maintain your speed
☑ be ready to stop
☐ brake hard

The longer traffic lights have been on green, the greater the chance of them changing. Always allow for this on approach and be prepared to stop.

1.8   Mark one answer

Which of the following should you do before stopping?

☐ Sound the horn
☑ Use the mirrors
☐ Select a higher gear
☐ Flash your headlights

Before pulling up check the mirrors to see what is happening behind you. Also assess what is ahead and make sure you give the correct signal if it helps other road users.

1.9   Mark one answer

When following a large vehicle you should keep well back because this

☐ allows you to corner more quickly
☐ helps the large vehicle to stop more easily
☑ allows the driver to see you in the mirrors
☐ helps you to keep out of the wind

If you're following a large vehicle but are so close to it that you can't see the exterior mirrors, the driver can't see you. Keeping well back will also allow you to see the road ahead by looking past either side of the large vehicle.

1.10   Mark one answer

When you see a hazard ahead you should use the mirrors. Why is this?

☐ Because you will need to accelerate out of danger
☑ To assess how your actions will affect following traffic
☐ Because you will need to brake sharply to a stop
☐ To check what is happening on the road ahead

You should be constantly scanning the road for clues about what is going to happen next. Check your mirrors regularly, particularly as soon as you spot a hazard. What is happening behind may affect your response to hazards ahead.

1.11   Mark one answer

You are waiting to turn right at the end of a road. Your view is obstructed by parked vehicles. What should you do?

☑ Stop and then move forward slowly and carefully for a proper view
☐ Move quickly to where you can see so you only block traffic from one direction
☐ Wait for a pedestrian to let you know when it is safe for you to emerge
☐ Turn your vehicle around immediately and find another junction to use

At junctions your view is often restricted by buildings, trees or parked cars. You need to be able to see in order to judge a safe gap. Edge forward slowly and keep looking all the time. Don't cause other road users to change speed or direction as you emerge.

1.12 Mark two answers

Objects hanging from your interior mirror may

- ☑ restrict your view
- ☐ improve your driving
- ☑ distract your attention
- ☐ help your concentration

Ensure that you can see clearly through the windscreen of your vehicle. Stickers or hanging objects could affect your field of vision or draw your eyes away from the road.

1.13 Mark four answers

Which of the following may cause loss of concentration on a long journey?

- ☑ Loud music
- ☑ Arguing with a passenger
- ☑ Using a mobile phone
- ☑ Putting in a cassette tape
- ☐ Stopping regularly to rest
- ☐ Pulling up to tune the radio

You should not allow yourself to be distracted when driving. You need to concentrate fully in order to be safe on the road. Loud music could mask other sounds, such as the audible warning of an emergency vehicle. Any distraction which causes you to take your hands off the steering wheel or your eyes off the road could be dangerous.

1.14 Mark two answers

On a long motorway journey boredom can cause you to feel sleepy. You should

- ☑ leave the motorway and find a safe place to stop
- ☐ keep looking around at the surrounding landscape
- ☐ drive faster to complete your journey sooner
- ☑ ensure a supply of fresh air into your vehicle
- ☐ stop on the hard shoulder for a rest

Plan your journey to include suitable rest stops. You should take all possible precautions against feeling sleepy while driving. Any lapse of concentration could have serious consequences.

1.15 Mark two answers

You are driving at dusk. You should switch your lights on

- ☑ even when street lights are not lit
- ☑ so others can see you
- ☐ only when others have done so
- ☐ only when street lights are lit

Your headlights and tail lights help others on the road to see you. It may be necessary to turn on your lights during the day if visibility is reduced, for example due to heavy rain. In these conditions the light might fade before the street lights are timed to switch on. Be seen to be safe.

1.16 Mark two answers

You are most likely to lose concentration when driving if you

- ☑ use a mobile phone
- ☑ listen to very loud music
- ☐ switch on the heated rear window
- ☐ look at the door mirrors

Distractions which cause you to take your hands off the steering wheel or your eyes off the road are potentially dangerous. You must be in full control of your vehicle at all times.

1.17 Mark four answers

Which FOUR are most likely to cause you to lose concentration while you are driving?

- ☑ Using a mobile phone
- ☑ Talking into a microphone
- ☑ Tuning your car radio
- ☑ Looking at a map
- ☐ Checking the mirrors
- ☐ Using the demisters

It's easy to be distracted. Planning your journey before you set off is important. A few sensible precautions are to tune your radio to stations in your area of travel, take planned breaks, and plan your route. Except for emergencies it is illegal to use a hand-held mobile phone while driving. Even using a hands-free kit can distract your attention.

1.18 Mark one answer

You should ONLY use a mobile phone when

☐ receiving a call
☑ suitably parked
☐ driving at less than 30 mph
☐ driving an automatic vehicle

It is illegal to use a hand-held mobile phone while driving, except in a genuine emergency. Even using hands-free kit can distract your attention. Park in a safe and convenient place before receiving or making a call or using text messaging. Then you will also be free to take notes or refer to papers.

1.19 Mark one answer

You are driving on a wet road. You have to stop your vehicle in an emergency. You should

☐ apply the handbrake and footbrake together
☑ keep both hands on the wheel
☐ select reverse gear
☐ give an arm signal

As you drive, look well ahead and all around so that you're ready for any hazards that might occur. There may be occasions when you have to stop in an emergency. React as soon as you can whilst keeping control of the vehicle.

1.20 Mark three answers

When you are moving off from behind a parked car you should

☑ look round before you move off
☑ use all the mirrors on the vehicle
☐ look round after moving off
☐ use the exterior mirrors only
☑ give a signal if necessary
☐ give a signal after moving off

Before moving off you should use all the mirrors to check if the road is clear. Look round to check the blind spots and give a signal if it is necessary to warn other road users of your intentions.

1.21 Mark one answer

You are travelling along this narrow country road. When passing the cyclist you should go

☐ slowly, sounding the horn as you pass
☐ quickly, leaving plenty of room
☑ slowly, leaving plenty of room
☐ quickly, sounding the horn as you pass

Look well ahead and only pull out if it is safe. You will need to use all of the road to pass the cyclist, so be extra-cautious. Look out for entrances to fields where tractors or other farm machinery could be waiting to pull out.

1.22 Mark one answer

Your vehicle is fitted with a hand-held telephone. To use the telephone you should

☐ reduce your speed
☑ find a safe place to stop
☐ steer the vehicle with one hand
☐ be particularly careful at junctions

Your attention should be on your driving at all times. Except in a genuine emergency never attempt to use a hand-held phone while on the move. It's illegal and very dangerous. Your eyes could wander from the road and at 60 mph your vehicle will travel about 27 metres (89 feet) every second.

1.23 Mark one answer

To answer a call on your mobile phone while travelling you should

☐ reduce your speed wherever you are
☑ stop in a proper and convenient place
☐ keep the call time to a minimum
☐ slow down and allow others to overtake

No phone call is important enough to risk endangering lives. It's better to switch your phone off completely when driving. If you must be contactable plan your route to include breaks so you can catch up on messages in safety. Always choose a safe and convenient place to take a break, such as a lay-by or service area.

1.24 Mark one answer

You lose your way on a busy road. What is the best action to take?

☐ Stop at traffic lights and ask pedestrians
☐ Shout to other drivers to ask them the way
☑ Turn into a side road, stop and check a map
☐ Check a map, and keep going with the traffic flow

It's easy to lose your way in an unfamiliar area. If you need to check a map or ask for directions, first find a safe place to stop.

1.25 Mark one answer

Windscreen pillars can obstruct your view. You should take particular care when

☐ driving on a motorway
☐ driving on a dual carriageway
☐ approaching a one-way street
☑ approaching bends and junctions

Windscreen pillars can obstruct your view, particularly at bends and junctions. Look out for other road users, particularly cyclists and pedestrians, as they can be hard to see.

1.26 Mark one answer

You cannot see clearly behind when reversing. What should you do?

☐ Open your window to look behind
☐ Open the door and look behind
☐ Look in the nearside mirror
☑ Ask someone to guide you

If you want to turn your car around try to find a place where you have good all-round vision. If this isn't possible and you're unable to see clearly, then get someone to guide you.

1.27 Mark one answer

What does the term 'blind spot' mean for a driver?

☐ An area covered by your right-hand mirror
☐ An area not covered by your headlights
☐ An area covered by your left-hand mirror
☑ An area not covered by your mirrors

Modern vehicles provide the driver with well-positioned mirrors which are essential to safe driving. However, they cannot see every angle of the scene behind and to the sides of the vehicle. This is why it is essential that you check over your shoulder, so that you are aware of any hazards not reflected in your mirrors.

1.28 Mark one answer

Your vehicle is fitted with a hands-free phone system. Using this equipment whilst driving

☐ is quite safe as long as you slow down
☑ could distract your attention from the road
☐ is recommended by The Highway Code
☐ could be very good for road safety

Using a hands-free system doesn't mean that you can safely drive and use a mobile phone. This type of mobile phone can still distract your attention from the road. As a driver, it is your responsibility to keep yourself and other road users safe at all times.

1.29 Mark one answer

Using a hands-free phone is likely to

☐ improve your safety
☐ increase your concentration
☐ reduce your view
☑ divert your attention

Unlike someone in the car with you, the person on the other end of the line is unable to see the traffic situations you are dealing with. They will not stop speaking to you even if you are approaching a hazardous situation. You need to be concentrating on your driving all of the time, but especially so when dealing with a hazard.

1.30 Mark one answer

What is the safest way to use a mobile phone in your vehicle?

☐ Use hands-free equipment
☑ Find a suitable place to stop
☐ Drive slowly on a quiet road
☐ Direct your call through the operator

It's illegal to use a hand-held mobile phone while driving, except in genuine emergencies. Even using hands-free kit is very likely to take your mind off your driving. If the use of a mobile causes you to drive in a careless or dangerous manner, you could be prosecuted for those offences. The penalties include an unlimited fine, disqualification and up to two years' imprisonment.

1.31 Mark one answer

Your mobile phone rings while you are on the motorway. Before answering you should

☐ reduce your speed to 30 mph
☐ pull up on the hard shoulder
☐ move into the left-hand lane
☑ stop in a safe place

When driving on motorways, you can't just pull up to answer your mobile phone. Do not stop on the hard shoulder or slip road. To avoid being distracted it's safer to switch it off when driving. If you need to be contacted plan your journey to include breaks at service areas so you can pick up any messages when you stop.

1.32 Mark one answer

You are turning right onto a dual carriageway. What should you do before emerging?

☐ Stop, apply the handbrake and then select a low gear
☐ Position your vehicle well to the left of the side road
☑ Check that the central reservation is wide enough for your vehicle
☐ Make sure that you leave enough room for a vehicle behind

Before emerging right onto a dual carriageway make sure that the central reserve is deep enough to protect your vehicle. If it's not, you should treat it as one road and check that it's clear in both directions before pulling out. Neglecting to do this could place part or all of your vehicle in the path of approaching traffic and cause a collision.

1.33 Mark one answer

You are waiting to emerge from a junction. The windscreen pillar is restricting your view. What should you be particularly aware of?

☐ Lorries
☐ Buses
☑ Motorcyclists
☐ Coaches

Windscreen pillars can completely block your view of pedestrians, motorcyclists and pedal cyclists. You should particularly watch out for these road users; don't just rely on a quick glance. Where possible make eye contact with them so you can be sure they have seen you too.

1.34 Mark one answer

When emerging from junctions, which is most likely to obstruct your view?

☑ Windscreen pillars
☐ Steering wheel
☐ Interior mirror
☐ Windscreen wipers

Windscreen pillars can block your view, particularly at junctions. Those road users most at risk of not being seen are cyclists, motorcyclists and pedestrians. Never rely on just a quick glance.

1.35   Mark one answer

Your vehicle is fitted with a navigation system. How should you avoid letting this distract you while driving?

☐ Keep going and input your destination into the system
☐ Keep going as the system will adjust to your route
☐ Stop immediately to view and use the system
☒ Stop in a safe place before using the system

Vehicle navigation systems can be useful when driving on unfamiliar routes. However, they can also distract you and cause you to lose control if you look at or adjust them while driving. Pull up in a convenient and safe place before adjusting them.

1.36   Mark one answer

You are driving on a motorway and want to use your mobile phone. What should you do?

☐ Try to find a safe place on the hard shoulder
☒ Leave the motorway and stop in a safe place
☐ Use the next exit and pull up on the slip road
☐ Move to the left lane and reduce your speed

Except in a genuine emergency you MUST NOT use your mobile phone when driving. If you need to use it leave the motorway and find a safe place to stop. Even a hands-free phone can distract your attention. Use your voicemail to receive calls. Driving requires all of your attention, all of the time.

1.37   Mark one answer

You must not use a hand-held phone while driving. Using a hands-free system

☐ is acceptable in a vehicle with power steering
☐ will significantly reduce your field of vision
☐ will affect your vehicle's electronic systems
☒ is still likely to distract your attention from the road

While driving your concentration is required all the time. Even using a hands-free kit can still distract your attention from the road. Any distraction, however brief, is potentially dangerous and could cause you to lose control. Except in a genuine emergency, it is an offence to use a hand-held phone while driving.

attitude

2.1
Mark one answer

At a pelican crossing the flashing amber light means you MUST

- ☐ stop and wait for the green light
- ☐ stop and wait for the red light
- ☐ give way to pedestrians waiting to cross
- ☑ give way to pedestrians already on the crossing

Pelican crossings are signal-controlled crossings operated by pedestrians. Pushbutton controls change the signals. Pelican crossings have no red-and-amber stage before green. Instead, they have a flashing amber light, which means you MUST give way to pedestrians already on the crossing, but if it is clear, you may continue.

2.2
Mark one answer

You should never wave people across at pedestrian crossings because

- ☑ there may be another vehicle coming
- ☐ they may not be looking
- ☐ it is safer for you to carry on
- ☐ they may not be ready to cross

If people are waiting to use a pedestrian crossing, slow down and be prepared to stop. Don't wave them across the road since another driver may, not have seen them, not have seen your signal and may not be able to stop safely.

2.3
Mark one answer

'Tailgating' means

- ☐ using the rear door of a hatchback car
- ☐ reversing into a parking space
- ☑ following another vehicle too closely
- ☐ driving with rear fog lights on

'Tailgating' is used to describe this dangerous practice, often seen in fast-moving traffic and on motorways. Following the vehicle in front too closely is dangerous because it
- restricts your view of the road ahead
- leaves you no safety margin if the vehicle in front slows down or stops suddenly.

2.4
Mark one answer

Following this vehicle too closely is unwise because

- ☐ your brakes will overheat
- ☐ your view ahead is increased
- ☐ your engine will overheat
- ☑ your view ahead is reduced

Staying back will increase your view of the road ahead. This will help you to see any hazards that might occur and allow you more time to react.

2.5
Mark one answer

You are following a vehicle on a wet road. You should leave a time gap of at least

- ☐ one second
- ☐ two seconds
- ☐ three seconds
- ☑ four seconds

Wet roads will reduce your tyres' grip on the road. The safe separation gap of at least two seconds in dry conditions should be doubled in wet weather.

2.6
Mark one answer

A long, heavily-laden lorry is taking a long time to overtake you. What should you do?

- ☐ Speed up
- ☑ Slow down
- ☐ Hold your speed
- ☐ Change direction

A long lorry with a heavy load will need more time to pass you than a car, especially on an uphill stretch of road. Slow down and allow the lorry to pass.

2.7 Mark three answers

Which of the following vehicles will use blue flashing beacons?

- ☐ Motorway maintenance
- ☑ Bomb disposal
- ☑ Blood transfusion
- ☑ Police patrol
- ☐ Breakdown recovery

When you see emergency vehicles with blue flashing beacons, move out of the way as soon as it is safe to do so.

2.8 Mark three answers

Which THREE of these emergency services might have blue flashing beacons?

- ☑ Coastguard
- ☑ Bomb disposal
- ☐ Gritting lorries
- ☐ Animal ambulances
- ☑ Mountain rescue
- ☐ Doctors' cars

When attending an emergency these vehicles will be travelling at speed. You should help their progress by pulling over and allowing them to pass. Do so safely. Don't stop suddenly or in a dangerous position.

2.9 Mark one answer

When being followed by an ambulance showing a flashing blue beacon you should

- ☑ pull over as soon as safely possible to let it pass
- ☐ accelerate hard to get away from it
- ☐ maintain your speed and course
- ☐ brake harshly and immediately stop in the road

Pull over in a place where the ambulance can pass safely. Check that there are no bollards or obstructions in the road that will prevent it from doing so.

2.10 Mark one answer

What type of emergency vehicle is fitted with a green flashing beacon?

- ☐ Fire engine
- ☐ Road gritter
- ☐ Ambulance
- ☑ Doctor's car

A green flashing beacon on a vehicle means the driver or passenger is a doctor on an emergency call. Give way to them if it's safe to do so. Be aware that the vehicle may be travelling quickly or may stop in a hurry.

2.11 Mark one answer

A flashing green beacon on a vehicle means

- ☐ police on non-urgent duties
- ☑ doctor on an emergency call
- ☐ road safety patrol operating
- ☐ gritting in progress

If you see a vehicle with a flashing green beacon approaching, allow it to pass when you can do so safely. Be aware that someone's life could depend on the driver making good progress through traffic.

2.12 Mark one answer

Diamond-shaped signs give instructions to

- ☑ tram drivers
- ☐ bus drivers
- ☐ lorry drivers
- ☐ taxi drivers

These signs only apply to trams. They are directed at tram drivers but you should know their meaning so that you're aware of the priorities and are able to anticipate the actions of the driver.

2.13 Mark one answer

On a road where trams operate, which of these vehicles will be most at risk from the tram rails?

- ☐ Cars
- ☑ Cycles
- ☐ Buses
- ☐ Lorries

The narrow wheels of a bicycle can become stuck in the tram rails, causing the cyclist to stop suddenly, wobble or even lose balance altogether. The tram lines are also slippery which could cause a cyclist to slide or fall off.

2.14 Mark one answer

What should you use your horn for?

☑ To alert others to your presence
☐ To allow you right of way
☐ To greet other road users
☐ To signal your annoyance

Your horn must not be used between 11.30 pm and 7 am in a built-up area or when you are stationary, unless a moving vehicle poses a danger. Its function is to alert other road users to your presence.

2.15 Mark one answer

You are in a one-way street and want to turn right. You should position yourself

☑ in the right-hand lane
☐ in the left-hand lane
☐ in either lane, depending on the traffic
☐ just left of the centre line

If you're travelling in a one-way street and wish to turn right you should take up a position in the right-hand lane. This will enable other road users not wishing to turn to proceed on the left. Indicate your intention and take up your position in good time.

2.16 Mark one answer

You wish to turn right ahead. Why should you take up the correct position in good time?

☐ To allow other drivers to pull out in front of you
☐ To give a better view into the road that you're joining
☑ To help other road users know what you intend to do
☐ To allow drivers to pass you on the right

If you wish to turn right into a side road take up your position in good time. Move to the centre of the road when it's safe to do so. This will allow vehicles to pass you on the left. Early planning will show other traffic what you intend to do.

2.17 Mark one answer

At which type of crossing are cyclists allowed to ride across with pedestrians?

☑ Toucan
☐ Puffin
☐ Pelican
☐ Zebra

A toucan crossing is designed to allow pedestrians and cyclists to cross at the same time. Look out for cyclists approaching the crossing at speed.

2.18 Mark one answer

You are travelling at the legal speed limit. A vehicle comes up quickly behind, flashing its headlights. You should

☐ accelerate to make a gap behind you
☐ touch the brakes sharply to show your brake lights
☐ maintain your speed to prevent the vehicle from overtaking
☑ allow the vehicle to overtake

Don't enforce the speed limit by blocking another vehicle's progress. This will only lead to the other driver becoming more frustrated. Allow the other vehicle to pass when you can do so safely.

2.19 Mark one answer

You should ONLY flash your headlights to other road users

☐ to show that you are giving way
☐ to show that you are about to turn
☐ to tell them that you have right of way
☑ to let them know that you are there

You should only flash your headlights to warn others of your presence. Don't use them to, greet others, show impatience or give priority to other road users. They could misunderstand your signal.

2.20 Mark one answer

You are approaching unmarked crossroads. How should you deal with this type of junction?

☐ Accelerate and keep to the middle
☐ Slow down and keep to the right
☐ Accelerate looking to the left
☑ Slow down and look both ways

Be extra-cautious, especially when your view is restricted by hedges, bushes, walls and large vehicles etc. In the summer months these junctions can become more difficult to deal with when growing foliage may obscure your view.

2.21 Mark one answer

You are approaching a pelican crossing. The amber light is flashing. You must

☑ give way to pedestrians who are crossing
☐ encourage pedestrians to cross
☐ not move until the green light appears
☐ stop even if the crossing is clear

While the pedestrians are crossing don't encourage them to cross by waving or flashing your headlights: other road users may misunderstand your signal. Don't harass them by creeping forward or revving your engine.

2.22 Mark one answer

The conditions are good and dry. You could use the 'two-second rule'

☐ before restarting the engine after it has stalled
☑ to keep a safe gap from the vehicle in front
☐ before using the 'Mirror-Signal-Manoeuvre' routine
☐ when emerging on wet roads

To measure this, choose a fixed reference point such as a bridge, sign or tree. When the vehicle ahead passes the object, say to yourself 'Only a fool breaks the two second rule.' If you reach the object before you finish saying this, you're TOO CLOSE.

2.23 Mark one answer

At a puffin crossing, which colour follows the green signal?

☐ Steady red
☐ Flashing amber
☑ Steady amber
☐ Flashing green

Puffin crossings have infra-red sensors which detect when pedestrians are crossing and hold the red traffic signal until the crossing is clear. The use of a sensor means there is no flashing amber phase as there is with a pelican crossing.

2.24 Mark one answer

You are in a line of traffic. The driver behind you is following very closely. What action should you take?

☐ Ignore the following driver and continue to travel within the speed limit
☑ Slow down, gradually increasing the gap between you and the vehicle in front
☐ Signal left and wave the following driver past
☐ Move over to a position just left of the centre line of the road

It can be worrying to see that the car behind is following you too closely. Give yourself a greater safety margin by easing back from the vehicle in front.

2.25 Mark one answer

A vehicle has a flashing green beacon. What does this mean?

☑ A doctor is answering an emergency call
☐ The vehicle is slow-moving
☐ It is a motorway police patrol vehicle
☐ The vehicle is carrying hazardous chemicals

A doctor attending an emergency may show a green flashing beacon on their vehicle. Give way to them when you can do so safely as they will need to reach their destination quickly. Be aware that they might pull over suddenly.

2.26 Mark one answer

A bus has stopped at a bus stop ahead of you. Its right-hand indicator is flashing. You should

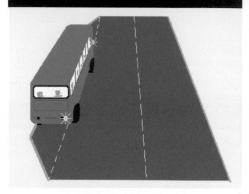

☐ flash your headlights and slow down
☑ slow down and give way if it is safe to do so
☐ sound your horn and keep going
☐ slow down and then sound your horn

Give way to buses whenever you can do so safely, especially when they signal to pull away from bus stops. Look out for people leaving the bus and crossing the road.

2.27 Mark one answer

You are driving on a clear night. There is a steady stream of oncoming traffic. The national speed limit applies. Which lights should you use?

☐ Full beam headlights
☐ Sidelights
☑ Dipped headlights
☐ Fog lights

Use the full beam headlights only when you can be sure that you won't dazzle other road users.

2.28 Mark one answer

You are driving behind a large goods vehicle. It signals left but steers to the right. You should

☑ slow down and let the vehicle turn
☐ drive on, keeping to the left
☐ overtake on the right of it
☐ hold your speed and sound your horn

Large, long vehicles need extra room when making turns at junctions. They may move out to the right in order to make a left turn. Keep well back and don't attempt to pass on the left.

2.29 Mark one answer

You are driving along this road. The red van cuts in close in front of you. What should you do?

☐ Accelerate to get closer to the red van
☐ Give a long blast on the horn
☒ Drop back to leave the correct separation distance
☐ Flash your headlights several times

There are times when other drivers make incorrect or ill-judged decisions. Be tolerant and try not to retaliate or react aggressively. Always consider the safety of other road users, your passengers and yourself.

2.30 Mark one answer

You are waiting in a traffic queue at night. To avoid dazzling following drivers you should

☒ apply the handbrake only
☐ apply the footbrake only
☐ switch off your headlights
☐ use both the handbrake and footbrake

You should consider drivers behind as brake lights can dazzle. However, if you are driving in fog it's safer to keep your foot on the footbrake. In this case it will give the vehicle behind extra warning of your presence.

2.31 Mark one answer

You are driving in traffic at the speed limit for the road. The driver behind is trying to overtake. You should

☐ move closer to the car ahead, so the driver behind has no room to overtake
☐ wave the driver behind to overtake when it is safe
☒ keep a steady course and allow the driver behind to overtake
☐ accelerate to get away from the driver behind

Keep a steady course to give the driver behind an opportunity to overtake safely. If necessary, slow down. Reacting incorrectly to another driver's impatience can lead to danger.

2.32 Mark one answer

A bus lane on your left shows no times of operation. This means it is

☐ not in operation at all
☐ only in operation at peak times
☒ in operation 24 hours a day
☐ only in operation in daylight hours

Don't drive or park in a bus lane when it's in operation. This can cause disruption to traffic and delays to public transport.

2.33 Mark two answers

You are driving along a country road. A horse and rider are approaching. What should you do?

☐ Increase your speed
☐ Sound your horn
☐ Flash your headlights
☒ Drive slowly past
☒ Give plenty of room
☐ Rev your engine

It's important that you reduce your speed. Passing too closely at speed could startle the horse and unseat the rider.

2.34 Mark one answer

A person herding sheep asks you to stop. You should

☐ ignore them as they have no authority
☒ stop and switch off your engine
☐ continue on but drive slowly
☐ try and get past quickly

Allow the sheep to clear the road before you proceed. Animals are unpredictable and startle easily; they could turn and run into your path or into the path of another moving vehicle.

2.35 Mark one answer

When overtaking a horse and rider you should

☐ sound your horn as a warning
☐ go past as quickly as possible
☐ flash your headlights as a warning
☒ go past slowly and carefully

Horses can become startled by the sound of a car engine or the rush of air caused by passing too closely. Keep well back and only pass when it is safe; leave them plenty of room. You may have to use the other side of the road to go past: if you do, first make sure there is no oncoming traffic.

2.36 Mark one answer

You are approaching a zebra crossing. Pedestrians are waiting to cross. You should

☐ give way to the elderly and infirm only
☒ slow down and prepare to stop
☐ use your headlights to indicate they can cross
☐ wave at them to cross the road

Look out on the approach especially for children and older pedestrians. They may walk across without looking. Zebra crossings have flashing amber beacons on both sides of the road, black and white stripes on the crossing and white zigzag markings on both sides of the crossing. Where you can see pedestrians waiting to cross, slow down and prepare to stop.

2.37 Mark one answer

A vehicle pulls out in front of you at a junction. What should you do?

☐ Swerve past it and sound your horn
☒ Flash your headlights and drive up close behind
☐ Slow down and be ready to stop
☐ Accelerate past it immediately

Try to be ready for the unexpected. Plan ahead and learn to anticipate hazards. You'll then give yourself more time to react to any problems that might occur. Be tolerant of the behaviour of other road users who don't behave correctly.

2.38 Mark one answer

You stop for pedestrians waiting to cross at a zebra crossing. They do not start to cross. What should you do?

☒ Be patient and wait
☐ Sound your horn
☐ Carry on
☐ Wave them to cross

If you stop for pedestrians and they don't start to cross don't wave them across or sound your horn. This could be dangerous if another vehicle is approaching which hasn't seen or heard your signal.

2.39 Mark one answer

You are following this lorry. You should keep well back from it to

☒ give you a good view of the road ahead
☐ stop following traffic from rushing through the junction
☐ prevent traffic behind you from overtaking
☐ allow you to hurry through the traffic lights if they change

By keeping well back you will increase your width of vision around the rear of the lorry. This will allow you to see further down the road and be prepared for any hazards.

2.40 Mark one answer

You are approaching a red light at a puffin crossing. Pedestrians are on the crossing. The red light will stay on until

☐ you start to edge forward on to the crossing
☒ the pedestrians have reached a safe position
☐ the pedestrians are clear of the front of your vehicle
☐ a driver from the opposite direction reaches the crossing

The electronic device will automatically detect that the pedestrians have reached a safe position. Don't proceed until the green light shows it is safe for vehicles to do so.

2.41 Mark one answer

Which instrument panel warning light would show that headlights are on full beam?

□

□

□

You should be aware of where all the warning lights and visual aids are on the vehicle you are driving. If you are driving a vehicle for the first time you should take time to check all the controls.

2.42 Mark one answer

At puffin crossings, which light will not show to a driver?

- ☑ Flashing amber
- □ Red
- □ steady amber
- □ green

A flashing amber light is shown at pelican crossings, but puffin crossings are different. They are controlled electronically and automatically detect when pedestrians are on the crossing. The phase is shortened or lengthened according to the position of the pedestrians.

2.43 Mark one answer

You should leave at least a two-second gap between your vehicle and the one in front when conditions are

- □ wet
- ☑ good
- □ damp
- □ foggy

In good, dry conditions an alert driver who's driving a vehicle with tyres and brakes in good condition, needs to keep a distance of at least two seconds from the car in front.

2.44 Mark one answer

You are driving at night on an unlit road behind another vehicle. You should

- □ flash your headlights
- ☑ use dipped beam headlights
- □ switch off your headlights
- □ use full beam headlights

If you follow another vehicle with your headlights on full beam they could dazzle the driver. Leave a safe distance and ensure that the light from your dipped beam falls short of the vehicle in front.

2.45 Mark one answer

You are driving a slow-moving vehicle on a narrow winding road. You should

- □ keep well out to stop vehicles overtaking dangerously
- □ wave following vehicles past you if you think they can overtake quickly
- ☑ pull in safely when you can, to let following vehicles overtake
- □ give a left signal when it is safe for vehicles to overtake you

Try not to hold up a queue of traffic. Other road users may become impatient and this could lead to reckless actions. If you're driving a slow-moving vehicle and the road is narrow, look for a safe place to pull in. DON'T wave other traffic past since this could be dangerous if you or they haven't seen an oncoming vehicle.

2.46 Mark two answers

You have a loose filler cap on your diesel fuel tank. This will

- ☑ waste fuel and money
- ☑ make roads slippery for other road users
- □ improve your vehicle's fuel consumption
- □ increase the level of exhaust emissions

Diesel fuel is especially slippery if spilled on a wet road. At the end of a dry spell of weather you should be aware that the road surfaces may have a high level of diesel spillage that hasn't been washed away by rain.

2.47   Mark one answer

To avoid spillage after refuelling, you should make sure that

☐ your tank is only three quarters full
☐ you have used a locking filler cap
☐ you check your fuel gauge is working
☑ your filler cap is securely fastened

When learning to drive it is a good idea to practise filling your car with fuel. Ask your instructor if you can use a petrol station and fill the fuel tank yourself. You need to know where the filler cap is located on the car you are driving in order to park on the correct side of the pump. Take care not to overfill the tank or spill fuel. Make sure you secure the filler cap as soon as you have replaced the fuel nozzle.

2.48   Mark one answer

If your vehicle uses diesel fuel, take extra care when refuelling. Diesel fuel when spilt is

☐ sticky
☐ odourless
☐ clear
☑ slippery

If you are using diesel, or are at a pump which has a diesel facility, be aware that there may be spilt fuel on the ground. Fuel contamination on the soles of your shoes may cause them to slip when using the foot pedals.

2.49   Mark one answer

What style of driving causes increased risk to everyone?

☐ Considerate
☐ Defensive
☑ Competitive
☐ Responsible

Competitive driving increases the risks to everyone and is the opposite of responsible, considerate and defensive driving. Defensive driving is about questioning the actions of other road users and being prepared for the unexpected. Don't be taken by surprise.

2.50   Mark one answer

Young, inexperienced and newly qualified drivers can often be involved in crashes. This is due to

☐ being too cautious at junctions
☐ driving in the middle of their lane
☑ showing off and being competitive
☐ staying within the speed limit

Newly qualified, and particularly young drivers, are more vulnerable in the first year after passing the test. Inexperience plays a part in this but it's essential to have the correct attitude. Be responsible and always show courtesy and consideration to other road users.

Safety and your vehicle

3.1 Mark two answers

Which TWO are badly affected if the tyres are under-inflated?

- ☑ Braking
- ☑ Steering
- ☐ Changing gear
- ☐ Parking

Your tyres are your only contact with the road so it is very important to ensure that they are free from defects, have sufficient tread depth and are correctly inflated. Correct tyre pressures help reduce the risk of skidding and provide a safer and more comfortable drive or ride.

3.2 Mark one answer

You must NOT sound your horn

- ☐ between 10 pm and 6 am in a built-up area
- ☐ at any time in a built-up area
- ☑ between 11.30 pm and 7 am in a built-up area
- ☐ between 11.30 pm and 6 am on any road

Vehicles can be noisy. Every effort must be made to prevent excessive noise, especially in built up areas at night. Don't
- rev the engine
- sound the horn unnecessarily.

It is illegal to sound your horn in a built-up area between 11.30 pm and 7 am, except when another vehicle poses a danger.

3.3 Mark three answers

The pictured vehicle is 'environmentally friendly' because it

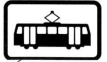

- ☑ reduces noise pollution
- ☐ uses diesel fuel
- ☑ uses electricity
- ☐ uses unleaded fuel
- ☐ reduces parking spaces
- ☑ reduces town traffic

Trams are powered by electricity and therefore do not emit exhaust fumes. They are also much quieter than petrol or diesel engined vehicles and can carry a large number of passengers.

3.4 Mark one answer

Supertrams or Light Rapid Transit (LRT) systems are environmentally friendly because

- ☐ they use diesel power
- ☐ they use quieter roads
- ☑ they use electric power
- ☐ they do not operate during rush hour

This means that they do not emit toxic fumes, which add to city pollution problems. They are also a lot quieter and smoother to ride on.

3.5 Mark one answer

'Red routes' in major cities have been introduced to

- ☐ raise the speed limits
- ☑ help the traffic flow
- ☐ provide better parking
- ☐ allow lorries to load more freely

Traffic jams today are often caused by the volume of traffic. However, inconsiderate parking can lead to the closure of an inside lane or traffic having to wait for oncoming vehicles. Driving slowly in traffic increases fuel consumption and causes a build-up of exhaust fumes.

3.6 Mark one answer

Road humps, chicanes, and narrowings are

- ☐ always at major road works
- ☐ used to increase traffic speed
- ☐ at toll-bridge approaches only
- ☑ traffic calming measures

Traffic calming measures help keep vehicle speeds low in congested areas where there are pedestrians and children. A pedestrian is much more likely to survive a collision with a vehicle travelling at 20 mph than at 40 mph.

3.7 Mark one answer

The purpose of a catalytic converter is to reduce

☐ fuel consumption
☐ the risk of fire
☐ toxic exhaust gases
☐ engine wear

Catalytic converters are designed to reduce a large percentage of toxic emissions. They work more efficiently when the engine has reached its normal working temperature.

3.8 Mark one answer

Catalytic converters are fitted to make the

☐ engine produce more power
☐ exhaust system easier to replace
☐ engine run quietly
☐ exhaust fumes cleaner

Harmful gases in the exhaust system pollute the atmosphere. These gases are reduced by up to 90% if a catalytic converter is fitted. Cleaner air benefits everyone, especially people who live or work near congested roads.

3.9 Mark one answer

It is essential that tyre pressures are checked regularly. When should this be done?

☐ After any lengthy journey
☐ After travelling at high speed
☐ When tyres are hot
☐ When tyres are cold

When you check the tyre pressures do so when the tyres are cold. This will give you a more accurate reading. The heat generated from a long journey will raise the pressure inside the tyre.

3.10 Mark one answer

When should you NOT use your horn in a built-up area?

☐ Between 8 pm and 8 am
☐ Between 9 pm and dawn
☐ Between dusk and 8 am
☐ Between 11.30 pm and 7 am

By law you must not sound your horn in a built-up area between 11.30 pm and 7.00 am. The exception to this is when another road user poses a danger.

3.11 Mark one answer

You will use more fuel if your tyres are

☐ under-inflated
☐ of different makes
☐ over-inflated
☐ new and hardly used

Check your tyre pressures frequently – normally once a week. If pressures are lower than those recommended by the manufacturer, there will be more 'rolling resistance'. The engine will have to work harder to overcome this, leading to increased fuel consumption.

3.12 Mark two answers

How should you dispose of a used battery?

☐ Take it to a local authority site
☐ Put it in the dustbin
☐ Break it up into pieces
☐ Leave it on waste land
☐ Take it to a garage
☐ Burn it on a fire

Batteries contain acid which is hazardous and must be disposed of safely.

3.13 Mark one answer

What is most likely to cause high fuel consumption?

☐ Poor steering control
☐ Accelerating around bends
☐ Staying in high gears
☐ Harsh braking and accelerating

Accelerating and braking gently and smoothly will help to save fuel, reduce wear on your vehicle and is better for the environment.

3.14 Mark one answer

The fluid level in your battery is low. What should you top it up with?

☐ Battery acid
☐ Distilled water
☐ Engine oil
☐ Engine coolant

Some modern batteries are maintenance-free. Check your vehicle handbook and, if necessary, make sure that the plates in each battery cell are covered.

3.15 Mark one answer

You are parked on the road at night. Where must you use parking lights?

☐ Where there are continuous white lines in the middle of the road
☐ Where the speed limit exceeds 30 mph
☐ Where you are facing oncoming traffic
☐ Where you are near a bus stop

When parking at night, park in the direction of the traffic. This will enable other road users to see the reflectors on the rear of your vehicle. Use your parking lights if the speed limit is over 30 mph.

3.16 Mark three answers

Motor vehicles can harm the environment. This has resulted in

☐ air pollution
☐ damage to buildings
☐ less risk to health
☐ improved public transport
☐ less use of electrical vehicles
☐ using up of natural resources

Exhaust emissions are harmful to health. Together with vibration from heavy traffic this can result in damage to buildings. Most petrol and diesel fuels come from a finite and non-renewable source. Anything you can do to reduce your use of these fuels will help the environment.

3.17 Mark three answers

Excessive or uneven tyre wear can be caused by faults in which THREE of the following?

☐ The gearbox
☐ The braking system
☐ The accelerator
☐ The exhaust system
☐ Wheel alignment
☐ The suspension

Regular servicing will help to detect faults at an early stage and this will avoid the risk of minor faults becoming serious or even dangerous.

3.18 Mark one answer

You need to top up your battery. What level should you fill to?

☐ The top of the battery
☐ Half-way up the battery
☐ Just below the cell plates
☐ Just above the cell plates

Top up the battery with distilled water and make sure each cell plate is covered.

3.19 Mark one answer

You are parking on a two-way road at night. The speed limit is 40 mph. You should park on the

☐ left with parking lights on
☐ left with no lights on
☐ right with parking lights on
☐ right with dipped headlights on

At night all vehicles must display parking lights when parked on a road with a speed limit greater than 30 mph. They should be close to the kerb, facing in the direction of the traffic flow and not within a distance as specified in *The Highway Code*.

3.20 Mark one answer

Before starting a journey it is wise to plan your route. How can you do this?

☐ Look at a map
☐ Contact your local garage
☐ Look in your vehicle handbook
☐ Check your vehicle registration document

Planning your journey before you set out can help to make it much easier, more pleasant and may help to ease traffic congestion. Look at a map to help you to do this. You may need different scale maps depending on where and how far you're going. Printing or writing out the route can also help.

3.21 Mark one answer   NI EXEMPT

It can help to plan your route before starting a journey. You can do this by contacting

☐ your local filling station
☐ a motoring organisation
☐ the Driver Vehicle Licensing Agency
☐ your vehicle manufacturer

Most motoring organisations will give you a detailed plan of your trip showing directions and distance. Some will also include advice on rest and fuel stops. The Highways Agency website will also give you information on roadworks and incidents and gives expected delay times.

3.22   Mark one answer

How can you plan your route before starting a long journey?

☐ Check your vehicle's workshop manual
☐ Ask your local garage
☐ Use a route planner on the internet
☐ Consult your travel agents

Various route planners are available on the internet. Most of them give you various options allowing you to choose the most direct, quickest or scenic route. They can also include rest and fuel stops and distances. Print them off and take them with you.

3.23   Mark one answer

Planning your route before setting out can be helpful. How can you do this?

☐ Look in a motoring magazine
☐ Only visit places you know
☐ Try to travel at busy times
☐ Print or write down the route

Print or write down your route before setting out. Some places are not well signed so using place names and road numbers may help you avoid problems en route. Try to get an idea of how far you're going before you leave. You can also use it to re-check the next stage at each rest stop.

3.24   Mark one answer

Why is it a good idea to plan your journey to avoid busy times?

☐ You will have an easier journey
☐ You will have a more stressful journey
☐ Your journey time will be longer
☐ It will cause more traffic congestion

No one likes to spend time in traffic queues. Try to avoid busy times related to school or work travel. As well as moving vehicles you should also consider congestion caused by parked cars, buses and coaches around schools.

3.25   Mark one answer

Planning your journey to avoid busy times has a number of advantages. One of these is

☐ your journey will take longer
☐ you will have a more pleasant journey
☐ you will cause more pollution
☐ your stress level will be greater

Having a pleasant journey can have safety benefits. You will be less tired and stressed and this will allow you to concentrate more on your driving or riding.

3.26   Mark one answer

It is a good idea to plan your journey to avoid busy times. This is because

☐ your vehicle will use more fuel
☐ you will see less road works
☐ it will help to ease congestion
☐ you will travel a much shorter distance

Avoiding busy times means that you are not adding needlessly to traffic congestion. Other advantages are that you will use less fuel and feel less stressed.

3.27   Mark one answer

By avoiding busy times when travelling

☐ you are more likely to be held up
☐ your journey time will be longer
☐ you will travel a much shorter distance
☐ you are less likely to be delayed

If possible, avoid the early morning and, late afternoon and early evening 'rush hour'. Doing this should allow you to travel in a more relaxed frame of mind, concentrate solely on what you're doing and arrive at your destination feeling less stressed.

3.28   Mark one answer

It can help to plan your route before starting a journey. Why should you also plan an alternative route?

☐ Your original route may be blocked
☐ Your maps may have different scales
☐ You may find you have to pay a congestion charge
☐ Because you may get held up by a tractor

It can be frustrating and worrying to find your planned route is blocked by roadworks or diversions. If you have planned an alternative you will feel less stressed and more able to concentrate fully on your driving or riding. If your original route is mostly using non-motorway roads it's a good idea to plan an alternative using non-motorway roads. Always carry a map with you just in case you need to refer to it.

3.29 Mark one answer

As well as planning your route before starting a journey, you should also plan an alternative route. Why is this?

☐ To let another driver overtake
☐ Your first route may be blocked
☐ To avoid a railway level crossing
☐ In case you have to avoid emergency vehicles

It's a good idea to plan an alternative route in case your original route is blocked for any reason. You're less likely to feel worried and stressed if you've got an alternative in mind. This will enable you to concentrate fully on your driving or riding. Always carry a map that covers the area you will travel in.

3.30 Mark one answer

You are making an appointment and will have to travel a long distance. You should

☐ allow plenty of time for your journey
☐ plan to go at busy times
☐ avoid all national speed limit roads
☐ prevent other drivers from overtaking

Always allow plenty of time for your journey in case of unforeseen problems. Anything can happen, punctures, breakdowns, road closures, diversions etc. You will feel less stressed and less inclined to take risks if you are not 'pushed for time'.

3.31 Mark one answer

Rapid acceleration and heavy braking can lead to

☐ reduced pollution
☐ increased fuel consumption
☐ reduced exhaust emissions
☐ increased road safety

Using the controls smoothly can reduce fuel consumption by about 15% as well as reducing wear and tear on your vehicle. Plan ahead and anticipate changes of speed well in advance. This will reduce the need to accelerate rapidly or brake sharply.

3.32 Mark one answer

What percentage of all emissions does road transport account for?

☐ 10%
☐ 20%
☐ 30%
☐ 40%

Transport is an essential part of modern life but it does have environmental effects. In heavily populated areas traffic is the biggest source of air pollution. Eco-safe driving and riding will reduce emissions and can make a surprising difference to local air quality.

3.33 Mark one answer

Which of these, if allowed to get low, could cause you to crash?

☐ Anti-freeze level
☐ Brake fluid level
☐ Battery water level
☐ Radiator coolant level

You should carry out frequent checks on all fluid levels but particularly brake fluid. As the brake pads or shoes wear down the brake fluid level will drop. If it drops below the minimum mark on the fluid reservoir, air could enter the hydraulic system and lead to a loss of braking efficiency or complete brake failure.

3.34 Mark one answer

New petrol-engined cars must be fitted with catalytic converters. The reason for this is to

☐ control exhaust noise levels
☐ prolong the life of the exhaust system
☐ allow the exhaust system to be recycled
☐ reduce harmful exhaust emissions

We should all be concerned about the effect traffic has on our environment. Fumes from vehicles are polluting the air around us. Catalytic converters act like a filter, removing some of the toxic waste from exhaust gases.

3.35 Mark one answer

What can cause heavy steering?

☐ Driving on ice
☐ Badly worn brakes
☐ Over-inflated tyres
☐ Under-inflated tyres

If your tyre pressures are low this will increase the drag on the road surface and make the steering feel heavy. Your vehicle will also use more fuel. Incorrectly inflated tyres can affect the braking, cornering and handling of your vehicle to a dangerous level.

3.36 Mark two answers

Driving with under-inflated tyres can affect

☐ engine temperature
☐ fuel consumption
☐ braking
☐ oil pressure

Keeping your vehicle's tyres correctly inflated is a legal requirement. Driving with correctly inflated tyres will use less fuel and your vehicle will brake more safely.

3.37 Mark two answers

Excessive or uneven tyre wear can be caused by faults in the

☐ gearbox
☐ braking system
☐ suspension
☐ exhaust system

Uneven wear on your tyres can be caused by the condition of your vehicle. Having it serviced regularly will ensure that the brakes, steering and wheel alignment are maintained in good order.

3.38 Mark one answer

The main cause of brake fade is

☐ the brakes overheating
☐ air in the brake fluid
☐ oil on the brakes
☐ the brakes out of adjustment

If your vehicle is fitted with drum brakes they can get hot and lose efficiency. This happens when they're used continually, such as on a long, steep, downhill stretch of road. Using a lower gear will assist the braking and help prevent the vehicle gaining momentum.

3.39 Mark one answer

Your anti-lock brakes warning light stays on. You should

☐ check the brake fluid level
☐ check the footbrake free play
☐ check that the handbrake is released
☐ have the brakes checked immediately

Consult the vehicle handbook or garage before driving the vehicle. Only drive to a garage if it is safe to do so. If you're not sure get expert help.

3.40 Mark one answer

While driving, this warning light on your dashboard comes on. It means

☐ a fault in the braking system
☐ the engine oil is low
☐ a rear light has failed
☐ your seat belt is not fastened

Don't ignore this warning light. A fault in your braking system could have dangerous consequences.

3.41 Mark one answer

It is important to wear suitable shoes when you are driving. Why is this?

☐ To prevent wear on the pedals
☐ To maintain control of the pedals
☐ To enable you to adjust your seat
☐ To enable you to walk for assistance if you break down

When you're going to drive, ensure that you're wearing suitable clothing. Comfortable shoes will ensure that you have proper control of the foot pedals.

3.42 Mark one answer

What will reduce the risk of neck injury resulting from a collision?

☐ An air-sprung seat
☐ Anti-lock brakes
☐ A collapsible steering wheel
☐ A properly adjusted head restraint

If you're involved in a collision, head restraints will reduce the risk of neck injury. They must be properly adjusted. Make sure they aren't positioned too low, in a crash this could cause damage to the neck.

Safety and your vehicle

3.43 Mark one answer

You are testing your suspension. You notice that your vehicle keeps bouncing when you press down on the front wing. What does this mean?

☐ Worn tyres
☐ Tyres under-inflated
☐ Steering wheel not located centrally
☐ Worn shock absorbers

If you find that your vehicle bounces as you drive around a corner or bend in the road, the shock absorbers might be worn. Press down on the front wing and, if the vehicle continues to bounce, take it to be checked by a qualified mechanic.

3.44 Mark one answer

A roof rack fitted to your car will

☐ reduce fuel consumption
☐ improve the road handling
☐ make your car go faster
☐ increase fuel consumption

If you are carrying anything on a roof rack, make sure that any cover is securely fitted and does not flap about while driving. Aerodynamically designed roof boxes are available which reduce wind resistance and, in turn, fuel consumption.

3.45 Mark one answer

It is illegal to drive with tyres that

☐ have been bought second-hand
☐ have a large deep cut in the side wall
☐ are of different makes
☐ are of different tread patterns

When checking your tyres for cuts and bulges in the side walls, don't forget the inner walls (ie those facing each other under the vehicle).

3.46 Mark one answer

The legal minimum depth of tread for car tyres over three quarters of the breadth is

☐ 1 mm
☐ 1.6 mm
☐ 2.5 mm
☐ 4 mm

Tyres must have sufficient depth of tread to give them a good grip on the road surface. The legal minimum for cars is 1.6 mm. This depth should be across the central three quarters of the breadth of the tyre and around the entire circumference.

3.47 Mark one answer

You are carrying two 13-year-old children and their parents in your car. Who is responsible for seeing that the children wear seat belts?

☐ The children's parents
☐ You, the driver
☐ The front-seat passenger
☐ The children

Seat belts save lives and reduce the risk of injury. If you are carrying passengers under 14 years of age it's your responsibility as the driver to ensure that their seat belts are fastened or they are seated in an approved child restraint.

3.48 Mark one answer

When a roof rack is not in use it should be removed. Why is this?

☐ It will affect the suspension
☐ It is illegal
☐ It will affect your braking
☐ It will waste fuel

We are all responsible for the environment we live in. If each driver takes responsibility for conserving fuel, together it will make a difference.

3.49 Mark three answers

How can you, as a driver, help the environment?

☐ By reducing your speed
☐ By gentle acceleration
☐ By using leaded fuel
☐ By driving faster
☐ By harsh acceleration
☐ By servicing your vehicle properly

Rapid acceleration and heavy braking lead to greater fuel consumption. They also increase wear and tear on your vehicle. Having your vehicle regularly serviced means your engine will maintain its efficiency, produce cleaner emissions and lengthen its life.

3.50 Mark three answers

To help the environment, you can avoid wasting fuel by

☐ having your vehicle properly serviced
☐ making sure your tyres are correctly inflated
☐ not over-revving in the lower gears
☐ driving at higher speeds where possible
☐ keeping an empty roof rack properly fitted
☐ servicing your vehicle less regularly

If you don't have your vehicle serviced regularly, the engine will not burn all the fuel efficiently. This will cause excess gases to be discharged into the atmosphere.

3.51 Mark three answers

To reduce the volume of traffic on the roads you could

☐ use public transport more often
☐ share a car when possible
☐ walk or cycle on short journeys
☐ travel by car at all times
☐ use a car with a smaller engine
☐ drive in a bus lane

Walking or cycling are good ways to get exercise. Using public transport also gives the opportunity for exercise if you walk to the railway station or bus stop. Leave the car at home whenever you can.

3.52 Mark three answers

Which THREE of the following are most likely to waste fuel?

☐ Reducing your speed
☐ Carrying unnecessary weight
☐ Using the wrong grade of fuel
☐ Under-inflated tyres
☐ Using different brands of fuel
☐ A fitted, empty roof rack

Wasting fuel costs you money and also causes unnecessary pollution. Ensuring your tyres are correctly inflated, avoiding carrying unnecessary weight, and removing a roof rack that is not in use, will all help to reduce your fuel consumption.

3.53 Mark three answers

Which THREE things can you, as a road user, do to help the environment?

☐ Cycle when possible
☐ Drive on under-inflated tyres
☐ Use the choke for as long as possible on a cold engine
☐ Have your vehicle properly tuned and serviced
☐ Watch the traffic and plan ahead
☐ Brake as late as possible without skidding

Although the car is a convenient form of transport it can also cause damage to health and the environment, especially when used on short journeys. Before you travel consider other types of transport. Walking and cycling are better for your health and public transport can be quicker, more convenient and less stressful than driving.

3.54 Mark one answer

To help protect the environment you should NOT

☐ remove your roof rack when unloaded
☐ use your car for very short journeys
☐ walk, cycle, or use public transport
☐ empty the boot of unnecessary weight

Try not to use your car as a matter of routine. For shorter journeys, consider walking or cycling instead – this is much better for both you and the environment.

3.55 Mark three answers

Which THREE does the law require you to keep in good condition?

☐ Gears
☐ Transmission
☐ Headlights
☐ Windscreen
☐ Seat belts

Other things to check include lights, get someone to help you check the brake lights and indicators. Battery, a lot of these are now maintenance-free. Steering, check for play in the steering. Oil, water and suspension also need checking. Always check that the speedometer is working once you've moved off.

3.56 Mark one answer

Driving at 70 mph uses more fuel than driving at 50 mph by up to

☐ 10%
☐ 30%
☐ 75%
☐ 100%

Your vehicle will use less fuel if you avoid heavy acceleration. The higher the engine revs, the more fuel you will use. Using the same gear, a vehicle travelling at 70mph will use up to 30% more fuel to cover the same distance, than at 50mph. However, don't travel so slowly that you inconvenience or endanger other road users.

3.57 Mark one answer

Your vehicle pulls to one side when braking. You should

☐ change the tyres around
☐ consult your garage as soon as possible
☐ pump the pedal when braking
☐ use your handbrake at the same time

The brakes on your vehicle must be effective and properly adjusted. If your vehicle pulls to one side when braking, take it to be checked by a qualified mechanic. Don't take risks.

3.58　Mark one answer
Unbalanced wheels on a car may cause

☐ the steering to pull to one side
☐ the steering to vibrate
☐ the brakes to fail
☐ the tyres to deflate

If your wheels are out of balance it will cause the steering to vibrate at certain speeds. It is not a fault that will rectify itself. You will have to take your vehicle to a garage or tyre fitting firm as this is specialist work.

3.59　Mark two answers
Turning the steering wheel while your car is stationary can cause damage to the

☐ gearbox
☐ engine
☐ brakes
☐ steering
☐ tyres

Turning the steering wheel when the car is not moving can cause unnecessary wear to the tyres and steering mechanism. This is known as 'dry' steering.

3.60　Mark one answer
You have to leave valuables in your car. It would be safer to

☐ put them in a carrier bag
☐ park near a school entrance
☐ lock them out of sight
☐ park near a bus stop

If you have to leave valuables in your car, always lock them out of sight. If you can see them, so can a thief.

3.61　Mark one answer
How could you deter theft from your car when leaving it unattended?

☐ Leave valuables in a carrier bag
☐ Lock valuables out of sight
☐ Put valuables on the seats
☐ Leave valuables on the floor

If you can see valuables in your car so can a thief. If you can't take them with you lock them out of sight or you risk losing them, as well as having your car damaged.

3.62　Mark one answer
Which of the following may help to deter a thief from stealing your car?

☐ Always keeping the headlights on
☐ Fitting reflective glass windows
☐ Always keeping the interior light on
☐ Etching the car number on the windows

Having your car registration number etched on all your windows is a cheap and effective way to deter professional car thieves.

3.63　Mark one answer
Which of the following should not be kept in your vehicle?

☐ A first aid kit
☐ A road atlas
☐ The tax disc
☐ The vehicle documents

Never leave the vehicle's documents inside it. They would help a thief dispose of the vehicle more easily.

3.64　Mark one answer
What should you do when leaving your vehicle?

☐ Put valuable documents under the seats
☐ Remove all valuables
☐ Cover valuables with a blanket
☐ Leave the interior light on

When leaving your vehicle unattended it is best to take valuables with you. If you can't, then lock them out of sight in the boot. If you can see valuables in your car, so can a thief.

3.65　Mark one answer
Which of these is most likely to deter the theft of your vehicle?

☐ An Immobiliser
☐ Tinted windows
☐ Locking wheel nuts
☐ A sun screen

An immobiliser makes it more difficult for your vehicle to be driven off by a thief. It is a particular deterrent to opportunist thieves.

3.66 Mark one answer

When parking and leaving your car you should

☐ park under a shady tree
☐ remove the tax disc
☐ park in a quiet road
☐ engage the steering lock

When you leave your car always engage the steering lock. This increases the security of your vehicle, as the ignition key is needed to release the steering lock.

3.67 Mark one answer

When leaving your vehicle parked and unattended you should

☐ park near a busy junction
☐ park in a housing estate
☐ remove the key and lock it
☐ leave the left indicator on

An unlocked car is an open invitation to thieves. Leaving the keys in the ignition not only makes your car easy to steal, it could also invalidate your insurance.

3.68 Mark two answers

Which TWO of the following will improve fuel consumption?

☐ Reducing your road speed
☐ Planning well ahead
☐ Late and harsh braking
☐ Driving in lower gears
☐ Short journeys with a cold engine
☐ Rapid acceleration

Harsh braking, constant gear changes and harsh acceleration increase fuel consumption. An engine uses less fuel when travelling at a constant low speed. You need to look well ahead so you are able to anticipate hazards early. Easing off the accelerator and timing your approach, at junctions, for example, could actually improve the fuel consumption of your vehicle.

3.69 Mark one answer

You service your own vehicle. How should you get rid of the old engine oil?

☐ Take it to a local authority site
☐ Pour it down a drain
☐ Tip it into a hole in the ground
☐ Put it into your dustbin

It is illegal to pour engine oil down any drain. Oil is a pollutant and harmful to wildlife. Dispose of it safely at an authorised site.

3.70 Mark one answer

Why do MOT tests include a strict exhaust emission test?

☐ To recover the cost of expensive garage equipment
☐ To help protect the environment against pollution
☐ To discover which fuel supplier is used the most
☐ To make sure diesel and petrol engines emit the same fumes

Emission tests are carried out to ensure your vehicle's engine is operating efficiently. This ensures the pollution produced by the engine is kept to a minimum. If your vehicle is not serviced regularly, it may fail the annual MOT test.

3.71 Mark three answers

To reduce the damage your vehicle causes to the environment you should

☐ use narrow side streets
☐ avoid harsh acceleration
☐ brake in good time
☐ anticipate well ahead
☐ use busy routes

By looking well ahead and recognising hazards early you can avoid last-minute harsh braking. Watch the traffic flow and look well ahead for potential hazards so you can control your speed accordingly. Avoid over-revving the engine and accelerating harshly as this increases wear to the engine and uses more fuel.

3.72 Mark one answer

Your vehicle has a catalytic converter. Its purpose is to reduce

☐ exhaust noise
☐ fuel consumption
☐ exhaust emissions
☐ engine noise

Catalytic converters reduce the harmful gases given out by the engine. The gases are changed by a chemical process as they pass through a special filter.

3.73 Mark two answers

A properly serviced vehicle will give

☐ lower insurance premiums
☐ you a refund on your road tax
☐ better fuel economy
☐ cleaner exhaust emissions

When you purchase your vehicle, check at what intervals you should have it serviced. This can vary depending on model and manufacturer. Use the service manual and keep it up to date. The cost of a service may well be less than the cost of running a poorly maintained vehicle.

3.74 Mark one answer

You enter a road where there are road humps. What should you do?

☐ Maintain a reduced speed throughout
☐ Accelerate quickly between each one
☐ Always keep to the maximum legal speed
☐ Drive slowly at school times only

The humps are there for a reason – to reduce the speed of the traffic. Don't accelerate harshly between them as this means you will only have to brake harshly to negotiate the next hump. Harsh braking and accelerating uses more fuel.

3.75 Mark one answer

When should you especially check the engine oil level?

☐ Before a long journey
☐ When the engine is hot
☐ Early in the morning
☐ Every 6000 miles

During long journeys an engine can use more oil than on shorter trips. Insufficient oil is potentially dangerous: it can lead to excessive wear and expensive repairs. Most cars have a dipstick to allow the oil level to be checked. If not, you should refer to the vehicle's handbook. Also make checks on
- fuel
- water
- tyres.

3.76 Mark one answer

You are having difficulty finding a parking space in a busy town. You can see there is space on the zigzag lines of a zebra crossing. Can you park there?

☐ No, unless you stay with your car
☐ Yes, in order to drop off a passenger
☐ Yes, if you do not block people from crossing
☐ No, not in any circumstances

It's an offence to park there. You will be causing an obstruction by obscuring the view of both pedestrians and drivers.

3.77 Mark one answer

When leaving your car unattended for a few minutes you should

☐ leave the engine running
☐ switch the engine off but leave the key in
☐ lock it and remove the key
☐ park near a traffic warden

Always switch off the engine, remove the key and lock your car, even if you are only leaving it for a few minutes.

3.78 Mark one answer

When parking and leaving your car for a few minutes you should

☐ leave it unlocked
☐ lock it and remove the key
☐ leave the hazard warning lights on
☐ leave the interior light on

Always remove the key and lock your car even if you only leave it for a few minutes.

3.79 Mark one answer

When leaving your vehicle where should you park if possible?

☐ Opposite a traffic island
☐ In a secure car park
☐ On a bend
☐ At or near a taxi rank

Whenever possible leave your car in a secure car park. This will help stop thieves.

3.80 Mark three answers

In which THREE places would parking your vehicle cause danger or obstruction to other road users?

☐ In front of a property entrance
☐ At or near a bus stop
☐ On your driveway
☐ In a marked parking space
☐ On the approach to a level crossing

Don't park your vehicle where parking restrictions apply. Think carefully before you slow down and stop. Look at road markings and signs to ensure that you aren't parking illegally.

3.81 Mark three answers

In which THREE places would parking cause an obstruction to others?

☐ Near the brow of a hill
☐ In a lay-by
☐ Where the kerb is raised
☐ Where the kerb has been lowered for wheelchairs
☐ At or near a bus stop

Think about the effect your parking will have on other road users. Don't forget that not all vehicles are the size of a car. Large vehicles will need more room to pass and might need more time too.

Parking out of the view of traffic, such as before the brow of a hill, causes unnecessary risks. Think before you park.

3.82 Mark one answer

You are away from home and have to park your vehicle overnight. Where should you leave it?

☐ Opposite another parked vehicle
☐ In a quiet road
☐ Opposite a traffic island
☐ In a secure car park

When leaving your vehicle unattended, use a secure car park whenever possible.

3.83 Mark one answer

The most important reason for having a properly adjusted head restraint is to

☐ make you more comfortable
☐ help you to avoid neck injury
☐ help you to relax
☐ help you to maintain your driving position

The restraint should be adjusted so that it gives maximum protection to the head and neck. This will help in the event of a rear end collision.

3.84 Mark two answers

As a driver you can cause more damage to the environment by

☐ choosing a fuel-efficient vehicle
☐ making a lot of short journeys
☐ driving in as high a gear as possible
☐ accelerating as quickly as possible
☐ having your vehicle regularly serviced

For short journeys it may be quicker to walk, or cycle, which is far better for your health. Time spent stationary in traffic with the engine running is damaging to health, the environment and expensive in fuel costs.

3.85 Mark one answer

As a driver, you can help reduce pollution levels in town centres by

☐ driving more quickly
☐ over-revving in a low gear
☐ walking or cycling
☐ driving short journeys

Using a vehicle for short journeys means the engine does not have time to reach its normal running temperature. When an engine is running below its normal running temperature it produces increased amounts of pollution. Walking and cycling do not create pollution and have health benefits as well.

3.86 Mark one answer

How can you reduce the chances of your car being broken into when leaving it unattended?

☐ Take all valuables with you
☐ Park near a taxi rank
☐ Place any valuables on the floor
☐ Park near a fire station

When leaving your car take all valuables with you if you can, otherwise lock them out of sight.

3.87 Mark one answer

How can you help to prevent your car radio being stolen?

☐ Park in an unlit area
☐ Hide the radio with a blanket
☐ Park near a busy junction
☐ Install a security-coded radio

A security-coded radio can deter thieves as it is likely to be of little use when removed from the vehicle.

3.88 Mark one answer

You are parking your car. You have some valuables which you are unable to take with you. What should you do?

☐ Park near a police station
☐ Put them under the driver's seat
☐ Lock them out of sight
☐ Park in an unlit side road

Your vehicle is like a shop window for thieves. Either remove all valuables or lock them out of sight.

3.89 Mark one answer

Wherever possible, which one of the following should you do when parking at night?

☐ Park in a quiet car park
☐ Park in a well-lit area
☐ Park facing against the flow of traffic
☐ Park next to a busy junction

If you are away from home, try to avoid leaving your vehicle unattended in poorly-lit areas. If possible park in a secure, well-lit car park.

3.90 Mark one answer

How can you lessen the risk of your vehicle being broken into at night?

☐ Leave it in a well-lit area
☐ Park in a quiet side road
☐ Don't engage the steering lock
☐ Park in a poorly-lit area

Having your vehicle broken into or stolen can be very distressing and inconvenient. Avoid leaving your vehicle unattended in poorly-lit areas.

3.91 Mark one answer

To help keep your car secure you could join a

☐ vehicle breakdown organisation
☐ vehicle watch scheme
☐ advanced driver's scheme
☐ car maintenance class

The vehicle watch scheme helps reduce the risk of having your car stolen. By displaying high visibility vehicle watch stickers in your car you are inviting the police to stop your vehicle if seen in use between midnight and 5 am.

3.92 Mark one answer

On a vehicle, where would you find a catalytic converter?

☐ In the fuel tank
☐ In the air filter
☐ On the cooling system
☐ On the exhaust system

Although carbon dioxide is still produced, a catalytic converter reduces the toxic and polluting gases by up to 90%. Unleaded fuel must be used in vehicles fitted with a catalytic converter.

3.93 Mark one answer

When leaving your car to help keep it secure you should

☐ leave the hazard warning lights on
☐ lock it and remove the key
☐ park on a one-way street
☐ park in a residential area

To help keep your car secure when you leave it, you should always remove the key from the ignition, lock it and take the key with you. Don't make it easy for thieves.

3.94 Mark one answer

You will find that driving smoothly can

☐ reduce journey times by about 15%
☐ increase fuel consumption by about 15%
☐ reduce fuel consumption by about 15%
☐ increase journey times by about 15%

Not only will you save about 15% of your fuel by driving smoothly, but you will also reduce the amount of wear and tear on your vehicle as well as reducing pollution. You will also feel more relaxed and have a more pleasant journey.

3.95 Mark one answer

You can save fuel when conditions allow by

☐ using lower gears as often as possible
☐ accelerating sharply in each gear
☐ using each gear in turn
☐ missing out some gears

Missing out intermediate gears when appropriate, helps to reduce the amount of time spent accelerating and decelerating – the time when your vehicle uses most fuel.

3.96 Mark one answer

How can driving in an Eco-safe manner help protect the environment?

☐ Through the legal enforcement of speed regulations
☐ By increasing the number of cars on the road
☐ Through increased fuel bills
☐ By reducing exhaust emissions

Eco-safe driving is all about becoming a more environmentally-friendly driver. This will make your journeys more comfortable as well as considerably reducing your fuel bills and reducing emissions that can damage the environment.

3.97 Mark one answer
What does Eco-safe driving achieve?

☐ Increased fuel consumption
☐ Improved road safety
☐ Damage to the environment
☐ Increased exhaust emissions

The emphasis is on hazard awareness and planning ahead. By looking well ahead you will have plenty of time to deal with hazards safely and won't need to brake sharply. This will also reduce damage to the environment.

3.98 Mark one answer
How can missing out some gear changes save fuel?

☐ By reducing the amount of time you are accelerating
☐ Because there is less need to use the footbrake
☐ By controlling the amount of steering
☐ Because coasting is kept to a minimum

Missing out some gears helps to reduce the amount of time you are accelerating and this saves fuel. You don't always need to change up or down through each gear. As you accelerate between each gear more fuel is injected into the engine than if you had maintained constant acceleration. Fewer gear changes means less fuel used.

3.99 Mark one answer
Missing out some gears saves fuel by reducing the amount of time you spend

☐ braking
☐ coasting
☐ steering
☐ accelerating

It is not always necessary to change up or down through each gear. Missing out intermediate gears helps to reduce the amount of time you are accelerating. Because fuel consumption is at its highest when accelerating this can save fuel.

3.100 Mark one answer
You are checking your trailer tyres. What is the legal minimum tread depth over the central three quarters of its breadth?

☐ 1 mm
☐ 1.6 mm
☐ 2 mm
☐ 2.6 mm

Trailers and caravans may be left in storage over the winter months and tyres can deteriorate. It's important to check their tread depth and also the pressures and general condition. The legal tread depth applies to the central three quarters of its breadth over its entire circumference.

3.101 Mark one answer
Fuel consumption is at its highest when you are

☐ braking
☐ coasting
☐ accelerating
☐ steering

Always try to use the accelerator smoothly. Taking your foot off the accelerator allows the momentum of the car to take you forward, especially when going downhill. This can save a considerable amount of fuel without any loss of control over the vehicle.

3.102 Mark one answer
Car passengers MUST wear a seat belt/restraint if one is available, unless they are

☐ under 14 years old
☐ under 1.5 metres (5 feet) in height
☐ sitting in the rear seat
☐ exempt for medical reasons

If you have adult passengers it is their responsibility to wear a seat belt, but you should still remind them to use them as they get in the car. It is your responsibility to ensure that all children in your car are secured with an appropriate restraint.

3.103 Mark one answer
Car passengers MUST wear a seat belt if one is available, unless they are

☐ in a vehicle fitted with air bags
☐ travelling within a congestion charging zone
☐ sitting in the rear seat
☐ exempt for medical reasons

When adult passengers are travelling in a vehicle, it is their own responsibility to wear a seat belt. However, you should still remind them to use a seat belt.

3.104 Mark one answer

You are driving the children of a friend home from school. They are both under 14 years old. Who is responsible for making sure they wear a seat belt or approved child restraint where required?

☐ An adult passenger
☐ The children
☐ You, the driver
☐ Your friend

Passengers should always be secured and safe. Children should be encouraged to fasten their seat belts or approved restraints themselves from an early age so that it becomes a matter of routine. As the driver you must check that they are fastened securely. It's your responsibility.

3.105 Mark one answer

You have too much oil in your engine. What could this cause?

☐ Low oil pressure
☐ Engine overheating
☐ Chain wear
☐ Oil leaks

Too much oil in the engine will create excess pressure and could damage engine seals and cause oil leaks. Any excess oil should be drained off.

3.106 Mark one answer

You are carrying a 5-year-old child in the back seat of your car. They are under 1.35 metres (4 feet 5 inches). A correct child restraint is NOT available. They MUST

☐ sit behind the passenger seat
☐ use an adult seat belt
☐ share a belt with an adult
☐ sit between two other children

Usually a correct child restraint MUST be used. In a few exceptional cases if one is not available an adult seat belt MUST be used. In a collision unrestrained objects and people can cause serious injury or even death.

3.107 Mark one answer

You are carrying a child using a rear-facing baby seat. You want to put it on the front passenger seat. What MUST you do before setting off?

☐ Deactivate all front and rear airbags
☐ Make sure any front passenger airbag is deactivated
☐ Make sure all the child safety locks are off
☐ Recline the front passenger seat

You MUST deactivate any frontal passenger airbag when using a rear-facing baby seat in a front passenger seat. It is ILLEGAL if you don't. If activated in a crash it could cause serious injury or death. Ensure you follow the manufacturer's instructions. In some cars this is now done automatically.

3.108 Mark one answer

You are carrying an 11-year-old child in the back seat of your car. They are under 1.35 metres (4 feet 5 inches) in height. You MUST make sure that

☐ they sit between two belted people
☐ they can fasten their own seat belt
☐ a suitable child restraint is available
☐ they can see clearly out of the front window

It is your responsibility as a driver to ensure that children are secure and safe in your vehicle. Make sure you are familiar with the rules. In a few very exceptional cases when a child restraint is not available, an adult seat belt MUST be used. Child restraints and seat belts save lives!

3.109 Mark one answer

You are parked at the side of the road. You will be waiting for some time for a passenger. What should you do?

☐ Switch off the engine
☐ Apply the steering lock
☐ Switch off the radio
☐ Use your headlights

If your vehicle is stationary and is likely to remain so for some time, switch off the engine. We should all try to reduce global warming and pollution.

3.110   Mark one answer

You are using a rear-facing baby seat. You want to put it on the front passenger seat which is protected by a frontal airbag. What MUST you do before setting off?

☐ Deactivate the airbag
☐ Turn the seat to face sideways
☐ Ask a passenger to hold the baby
☐ Put the child in an adult seat belt

If the airbag activates near a baby seat, it could cause serious injury or even death to the child. It is illegal to fit a rear-facing baby seat into a passenger seat protected by an active frontal airbag. You MUST secure it in a different seat or deactivate the relevant airbag. Follow the manufacturer's advice when fitting a baby seat.

3.111   Mark one answer

You are carrying a five-year-old child in the back seat of your car. They are under 1.35 metres (4 feet 5 inches) in height. They MUST use an adult seat belt ONLY if

☐ a correct child restraint is not available
☐ it is a lap type belt
☐ they sit between two adults
☐ it can be shared with another adult

You should make all efforts to ensure a correct child restraint is used, with very few exceptions. If in specific circumstances one is not available, then an adult seat belt MUST be used. Unrestrained objects, including people, can be thrown violently around in a collision, and may cause serious injury or even death!

3.112   Mark one answer

You are leaving your vehicle parked on a road unattended. When may you leave the engine running?

☐ If you will be parking for less than five minutes
☐ If the battery keeps going flat
☐ When parked in a 20 mph zone
☐ Never if you are away from the vehicle

When you leave your vehicle parked on a road, switch off the engine and secure the vehicle. Make sure there aren't any valuables visible, shut all the windows, lock the vehicle, set the alarm if it has one and use an anti-theft device such as a steering wheel lock.

Safety margins

4.1 Mark one answer
Braking distances on ice can be

☐ twice the normal distance
☐ five times the normal distance
☐ seven times the normal distance
☐ ten times the normal distance

In icy and snowy weather, your stopping distance will increase by up to ten times compared to good, dry conditions.
　Take extra care when braking, accelerating and steering, to cut down the risk of skidding.

4.2 Mark one answer
Freezing conditions will affect the distance it takes you to come to a stop. You should expect stopping distances to increase by up to

☐ two times
☐ three times
☐ five times
☐ ten times

Your tyre grip is greatly reduced on icy roads and you need to allow up to ten times the normal stopping distance.

4.3 Mark one answer
In windy conditions you need to take extra care when

☐ using the brakes
☐ making a hill start
☐ turning into a narrow road
☐ passing pedal cyclists

You should always give cyclists plenty of room when overtaking. When it's windy, a sudden gust could blow them off course.

4.4 Mark one answer
When approaching a right-hand bend you should keep well to the left. Why is this?

☐ To improve your view of the road
☐ To overcome the effect of the road's slope
☐ To let faster traffic from behind overtake
☐ To be positioned safely if you skid

Doing this will give you an earlier view around the bend and enable you to see any hazards sooner.
　It also reduces the risk of collision with an oncoming vehicle that may have drifted over the centre line while taking the bend.

4.5 Mark one answer
You have just gone through deep water. To dry off the brakes you should

☐ accelerate and keep to a high speed for a short time
☐ go slowly while gently applying the brakes
☐ avoid using the brakes at all for a few miles
☐ stop for at least an hour to allow them time to dry

Water on the brakes will act as a lubricant, causing them to work less efficiently. Using the brakes lightly as you go along will dry them out.

4.6 Mark two answers
In very hot weather the road surface can become soft. Which TWO of the following will be most affected?

☐ The suspension
☐ The grip of the tyres
☐ The braking
☐ The exhaust

Only a small part of your tyres is in contact with the road. This is why you must consider the surface on which you're travelling, and alter your speed to suit the road conditions.

4.7 Mark one answer

Where are you most likely to be affected by a side wind?

☐ On a narrow country lane
☐ On an open stretch of road
☐ On a busy stretch of road
☐ On a long, straight road

In windy conditions, care must be taken on exposed roads. A strong gust of wind can blow you off course. Watch out for other road users who are particularly likely to be affected, such as cyclists, motorcyclists, high-sided lorries and vehicles towing trailers.

4.8 Mark one answer

In good conditions, what is the typical stopping distance at 70 mph?

☐ 53 metres (175 feet)
☐ 60 metres (197 feet)
☐ 73 metres (240 feet)
☐ 96 metres (315 feet)

Note that this is the typical stopping distance. It will take at least this distance to think, brake and stop in good conditions. In poor conditions it will take much longer.

4.9 Mark one answer

What is the shortest overall stopping distance on a dry road at 60 mph?

☐ 53 metres (175 feet)
☐ 58 metres (190 feet)
☐ 73 metres (240 feet)
☐ 96 metres (315 feet)

This distance is the equivalent of 18 car lengths. Try pacing out 73 metres and then look back. It's probably further than you think.

4.10 Mark one answer

You are following a vehicle at a safe distance on a wet road. Another driver overtakes you and pulls into the gap you have left. What should you do?

☐ Flash your headlights as a warning
☐ Try to overtake safely as soon as you can
☐ Drop back to regain a safe distance
☐ Stay close to the other vehicle until it moves on

Wet weather will affect the time it takes for you to stop and can affect your control. Your speed should allow you to stop safely and in good time. If another vehicle pulls into the gap you've left, ease back until you've regained your stopping distance.

4.11 Mark one answer

You are travelling at 50 mph on a good, dry road. What is your typical overall stopping distance?

☐ 36 metres (118 feet)
☐ 53 metres (175 feet)
☐ 75 metres (245 feet)
☐ 96 metres (315 feet)

Even in good conditions it will usually take you further than you think to stop. Don't just learn the figures, make sure you understand how far the distance is.

4.12 Mark one answer

You are on a good, dry, road surface. Your brakes and tyres are good. What is the typical overall stopping distance at 40 mph?

☐ 23 metres (75 feet)
☐ 36 metres (118 feet)
☐ 53 metres (175 feet)
☐ 96 metres (315 feet)

Stopping distances are affected by a number of variable factors. These include the type, model and condition of your vehicle, road and weather conditions, and your reaction time. Look well ahead for hazards and leave enough space between you and the vehicle in front. This should allow you to pull up safely if you have to, without braking sharply.

4.13 Mark one answer

What should you do when overtaking a motorcyclist in strong winds?

☐ Pass close
☐ Pass quickly
☐ Pass wide
☐ Pass immediately

In strong winds riders of two-wheeled vehicles are particularly vulnerable. When you overtake them allow plenty of room. Always check to the left as you pass.

4.14 Mark one answer

You are overtaking a motorcyclist in strong winds? What should you do?

☐ Allow extra room
☐ Give a thank you wave
☐ Move back early
☐ Sound your horn

It is easy for motorcyclists to be blown off course. Always give them plenty of room if you decide to overtake, especially in strong winds. Decide whether you need to overtake at all. Always check to the left as you pass.

4.15 Mark one answer

Overall stopping distance is made up of thinking and braking distance. You are on a good, dry road surface with good brakes and tyres. What is the typical BRAKING distance from 50 mph?

☐ 14 metres (46 feet)
☐ 24 metres (80 feet)
☐ 38 metres (125 feet)
☐ 55 metres (180 feet)

Be aware this is just the braking distance. You need to add the thinking distance to this to give the OVERALL STOPPING DISTANCE. At 50 mph the typical thinking distance will be 15 metres (50 feet), plus a braking distance of 38 metres (125 feet), giving an overall stopping distance of 53 metres (175 feet). The distance could be greater than this depending on your attention and response to any hazards. These figures are a general guide.

4.16 Mark one answer

In heavy motorway traffic the vehicle behind you is following too closely. How can you lower the risk of a collision?

☐ Increase your distance from the vehicle in front
☐ Operate the brakes sharply
☐ Switch on your hazard lights
☐ Move onto the hard shoulder and stop

On busy roads traffic may still travel at high speeds despite being close together. Don't follow too closely to the vehicle in front. If a driver behind seems to be 'pushing' you, gradually increase your distance from the vehicle in front by slowing down gently. This will give you more space in front if you have to brake, and lessen the risk of a collision involving several vehicles.

4.17 Mark one answer

You are following other vehicles in fog. You have your lights on. What else can you do to reduce the chances of being in a collision?

☐ Keep close to the vehicle in front
☐ Use your main beam instead of dipped headlights
☐ Keep up with the faster vehicles
☐ Reduce your speed and increase the gap in front

When it's foggy use dipped headlights. This will help you see and be seen by other road users. If visibility is seriously reduced consider using front and rear fog lights. Keep a sensible speed and don't follow the vehicle in front too closely. If the road is wet and slippery you'll need to allow twice the normal stopping distance.

4.18 Mark three answers

To avoid a collision when entering a contraflow system, you should

☐ reduce speed in good time
☐ switch lanes at any time to make progress
☐ choose an appropriate lane in good time
☐ keep the correct separation distance
☐ increase speed to pass through quickly
☐ follow other motorists closely to avoid long queues

In a contraflow system you will be travelling close to oncoming traffic and sometimes in narrow lanes. You should obey the temporary speed limit signs, get into the correct lane at the proper time and keep a safe separation distance from the vehicle ahead. When traffic is at a very low speed, merging in turn is recommended if it's safe and appropriate.

4.19 Mark one answer

What is the most common cause of skidding?

☐ Worn tyres
☐ Driver error
☐ Other vehicles
☐ Pedestrians

A skid happens when the driver changes the speed or direction of their vehicle so suddenly that the tyres can't keep their grip on the road.

Remember that the risk of skidding on wet or icy roads is much greater than in dry conditions.

4.20 Mark one answer
You are driving on an icy road. How can you avoid wheelspin?

☐ Drive at a slow speed in as high a gear as possible
☐ Use the handbrake if the wheels start to slip
☐ Brake gently and repeatedly
☐ Drive in a low gear at all times

If you're travelling on an icy road extra caution will be required to avoid loss of control. Keeping your speed down and using the highest gear possible will reduce the risk of the tyres losing their grip on this slippery surface.

4.21 Mark one answer
Skidding is mainly caused by

☐ the weather
☐ the driver
☐ the vehicle
☐ the road

You should always consider the conditions and drive accordingly.

4.22 Mark two answers
You are driving in freezing conditions. What should you do when approaching a sharp bend?

☐ Slow down before you reach the bend
☐ Gently apply your handbrake
☐ Firmly use your footbrake
☐ Coast into the bend
☐ Avoid sudden steering movements

Harsh use of the accelerator, brakes or steering are likely to lead to skidding, especially on slippery surfaces. Avoid steering and braking at the same time.
  In icy conditions it's very important that you constantly assess what's ahead, so that you can take appropriate action in plenty of time.

4.23 Mark one answer
You are turning left on a slippery road. The back of your vehicle slides to the right. You should

☐ brake firmly and not turn the steering wheel
☐ steer carefully to the left
☐ steer carefully to the right
☐ brake firmly and steer to the left

Steer into the skid but be careful not to overcorrect with too much steering. Too much movement may lead to a skid in the opposite direction. Skids don't just happen, they are caused. The three important factors in order are, the driver, the vehicle and the road conditions.

4.24 Mark four answers
Before starting a journey in freezing weather you should clear ice and snow from your vehicle's

☐ aerial
☐ windows
☐ bumper
☐ lights
☐ mirrors
☐ number plates

Don't travel unless you have no choice. Making unnecessary journeys in bad weather can increase the risk of having a collision. It's important that you can see and be seen. Make sure any snow or ice is cleared from lights, mirrors, number plates and windows.

4.25 Mark one answer
You are trying to move off on snow. You should use

☐ the lowest gear you can
☐ the highest gear you can
☐ a high engine speed
☐ the handbrake and footbrake together

If you attempt to move off in a low gear, such as first, the engine will rev at a higher speed. This could cause the wheels to spin and dig further into the snow.

4.26 Mark one answer
When driving in falling snow you should

☐ brake firmly and quickly
☐ be ready to steer sharply
☐ use sidelights only
☐ brake gently in plenty of time

Braking on snow can be extremely dangerous. Be gentle with both the accelerator and brake to prevent wheelspin.

4.27 Mark one answer
The MAIN benefit of having four-wheel drive is to improve

☐ road holding
☐ fuel consumption
☐ stopping distances
☐ passenger comfort

By driving all four wheels there is improved grip, but this does not replace the skills you need to drive safely. The extra grip helps road holding when travelling on slippery or uneven roads.

4.28 Mark one answer

You are about to go down a steep hill. To control the speed of your vehicle you should

☐ select a high gear and use the brakes carefully
☐ select a high gear and use the brakes firmly
☐ select a low gear and use the brakes carefully
☐ select a low gear and avoid using the brakes

When going down a steep hill your vehicle will speed up. This will make it more difficult for you to stop. Select a lower gear to give you more engine braking and control. Use this in combination with careful use of the brakes.

4.29 Mark two answers

You wish to park facing DOWNHILL. Which TWO of the following should you do?

☐ Turn the steering wheel towards the kerb
☐ Park close to the bumper of another car
☐ Park with two wheels on the kerb
☐ Put the handbrake on firmly
☐ Turn the steering wheel away from the kerb

Turning the wheels towards the kerb will allow it to act as a chock, preventing any forward movement of the vehicle. It will also help to leave it in gear, or select Park if you have an automatic.

4.30 Mark one answer

You are driving in a built-up area. You approach a speed hump. You should

☐ move across to the left-hand side of the road
☐ wait for any pedestrians to cross
☐ slow your vehicle right down
☐ stop and check both pavements

Many towns have speed humps to slow down traffic. Slow down when driving over them. If you go too fast they may affect your steering and suspension, causing you to lose control or even damaging it. Be aware of pedestrians in these areas.

4.31 Mark one answer

You are on a long, downhill slope. What should you do to help control the speed of your vehicle?

☐ Select neutral
☐ Select a lower gear
☐ Grip the handbrake firmly
☐ Apply the parking brake gently

Selecting a low gear when travelling downhill will help you to control your speed.
 The engine will assist the brakes and help prevent your vehicle gathering speed.

4.32 Mark one answer

Anti-lock brakes prevent wheels from locking. This means the tyres are less likely to

☐ aquaplane
☐ skid
☐ puncture
☐ wear

If an anti-lock braking system is fitted it activates automatically when maximum braking pressure is applied or when it senses that the wheels are about to lock. It prevents the wheels from locking so you can continue to steer the vehicle during braking. It does not remove the need for good driving practices such as anticipation and correct speed for the conditions.

4.33 Mark one answer

Anti-lock brakes reduce the chances of a skid occurring particularly when

☐ driving down steep hills
☐ braking during normal driving
☐ braking in an emergency
☐ driving on good road surfaces

The anti-lock braking system will operate when the brakes have been applied harshly.
 It will reduce the chances of your car skidding, but it is not a miracle cure for careless driving.

4.34 Mark one answer
Vehicles fitted with anti-lock brakes

☐ are impossible to skid
☐ can be steered while you are braking
☐ accelerate much faster
☐ are not fitted with a handbrake

Preventing the wheels from locking means that the vehicle's steering and stability can be maintained, leading to safer stopping.

However, you must ensure that the engine does not stall, as this could disable the power steering. Look in your vehicle handbook for the correct method when stopping in an emergency.

4.35 Mark two answers
Anti-lock brakes may not work as effectively if the road surface is

☐ dry
☐ loose
☐ wet
☐ good
☐ firm

Poor contact with the road surface could cause one or more of the tyres to lose grip on the road. This is more likely to happen when braking in poor weather conditions, when the road surface is uneven or has loose chippings.

4.36 Mark one answer
Anti-lock brakes are of most use when you are

☐ braking gently
☐ driving on worn tyres
☐ braking excessively
☐ driving normally

Anti-lock brakes will not be required when braking normally. Looking well down the road and anticipating possible hazards could prevent you having to brake late and harshly. Knowing that you have anti-lock brakes is not an excuse to drive in a careless or reckless way.

4.37 Mark one answer
Driving a vehicle fitted with anti-lock brakes allows you to

☐ brake harder because it is impossible to skid
☐ drive at higher speeds
☐ steer and brake at the same time
☐ pay less attention to the road ahead

When stopping in an emergency anti-lock brakes will help you continue to steer when braking. In poor weather conditions this may be less effective. You need to depress the clutch pedal to prevent the car stalling as most power steering systems use an engine-driven pump and will only operate when the engine is running. Look in your vehicle handbook for the correct method when stopping in an emergency.

4.38 Mark one answer
Anti-lock brakes can greatly assist with

☐ a higher cruising speed
☐ steering control when braking
☐ control when accelerating
☐ motorway driving

If the wheels of your vehicle lock they will not grip the road and you will lose steering control. In good conditions the anti-lock system will prevent the wheels locking and allow you to retain steering control.

4.39 Mark one answer
You are driving a vehicle fitted with anti-lock brakes. You need to stop in an emergency. You should apply the footbrake

☐ slowly and gently
☐ slowly but firmly
☐ rapidly and gently
☐ rapidly and firmly

Look well ahead down the road as you drive and give yourself time and space to react safely to any hazards. You may have to stop in an emergency due to a misjudgement by another driver or a hazard arising suddenly such as a child running out into the road. In this case, if your vehicle has anti-lock brakes, you should apply the brakes immediately and keep them firmly applied until you stop.

4.40 Mark two answers

Your vehicle has anti-lock brakes, but they may not always prevent skidding. This is most likely to happen when driving

- ☐ in foggy conditions
- ☐ on surface water
- ☐ on loose road surfaces
- ☐ on dry tarmac
- ☐ at night on unlit roads

In very wet weather water can build up between the tyre and the road surface. As a result your vehicle actually rides on a thin film of water and your tyres will not grip the road. Gravel or shingle surfaces also offer less grip and can present problems when braking. An anti-lock braking system may be ineffective in these conditions.

4.41 Mark one answer

You are driving along a country road. You see this sign. AFTER dealing safely with the hazard you should always

- ☐ check your tyre pressures
- ☐ switch on your hazard warning lights
- ☐ accelerate briskly
- ☐ test your brakes

Deep water can affect your brakes, so you should check that they're working properly before you build up speed again. Before you do this, remember to check your mirrors and consider what's behind you.

4.42 Mark one answer

You are driving in heavy rain. Your steering suddenly becomes very light. You should

- ☐ steer towards the side of the road
- ☐ apply gentle acceleration
- ☐ brake firmly to reduce speed
- ☐ ease off the accelerator

If the steering becomes light in these conditions it is probably due to a film of water that has built up between your tyres and the road surface. Easing off the accelerator should allow your tyres to displace the film of water and they should then regain their grip on the road.

4.43 Mark one answer

The roads are icy. You should drive slowly

- ☐ in the highest gear possible
- ☐ in the lowest gear possible
- ☐ with the handbrake partly on
- ☐ with your left foot on the brake

Driving at a slow speed in a high gear will reduce the likelihood of wheel-spin and help your vehicle maintain the best possible grip.

4.44 Mark one answer

You are driving along a wet road. How can you tell if your vehicle is aquaplaning?

- ☐ The engine will stall
- ☐ The engine noise will increase
- ☐ The steering will feel very heavy
- ☐ The steering will feel very light

If you drive at speed in very wet conditions your steering may suddenly feel 'light'. This means that the tyres have lifted off the surface of the road and are skating on the surface of the water. This is known as aquaplaning. Reduce speed by easing off the accelerator, but don't brake until your steering returns to normal.

4.45 Mark two answers

How can you tell if you are driving on ice?

- ☐ The tyres make a rumbling noise
- ☐ The tyres make hardly any noise
- ☐ The steering becomes heavier
- ☐ The steering becomes lighter

Drive extremely carefully when the roads are icy. When travelling on ice, tyres make virtually no noise and the steering feels unresponsive.

In icy conditions, avoid harsh braking, acceleration and steering.

4.46 Mark one answer

You are driving along a wet road. How can you tell if your vehicle's tyres are losing their grip on the surface?

- ☐ The engine will stall
- ☐ The steering will feel very heavy
- ☐ The engine noise will increase
- ☐ The steering will feel very light

If you drive at speed in very wet conditions your steering may suddenly feel lighter than usual. This means that the tyres have lifted off the surface of the road and are skating on the surface of the water. This is known as aquaplaning. Reduce speed but don't brake until your steering returns to a normal feel.

4.47 Mark one answer

Your overall stopping distance will be much longer when driving

☐ in the rain
☐ in fog
☐ at night
☐ in strong winds

Extra care should be taken in wet weather as, on wet roads, your stopping distance could be double that necessary for dry conditions.

4.48 Mark one answer

You have driven through a flood. What is the first thing you should do?

☐ Stop and check the tyres
☐ Stop and dry the brakes
☐ Check your exhaust
☐ Test your brakes

Before you test your brakes you must check for following traffic. If it is safe, gently apply the brakes to clear any water that may be covering the braking surfaces.

4.49 Mark one answer

You are on a fast, open road in good conditions. For safety, the distance between you and the vehicle in front should be

☐ a two-second time gap
☐ one car length
☐ 2 metres (6 feet 6 inches)
☐ two car lengths

One useful method of checking that you've allowed enough room between you and the vehicle in front is the two-second rule.

To check for a two-second time gap, choose a stationary object ahead, such as a bridge or road sign. When the car in front passes the object say 'Only a fool breaks the two-second rule'. If you reach the object before you finish saying it you're too close.

4.50 Mark one answer

How can you use your vehicle's engine as a brake?

☐ By changing to a lower gear
☐ By selecting reverse gear
☐ By changing to a higher gear
☐ By selecting neutral gear

When driving on downhill stretches of road selecting a lower gear gives increased engine braking. This will prevent excess use of the brakes, which become less effective if they overheat.

4.51 Mark one answer

Anti-lock brakes are most effective when you

☐ keep pumping the foot brake to prevent skidding
☐ brake normally, but grip the steering wheel tightly
☐ brake promptly and firmly until you have slowed down
☐ apply the handbrake to reduce the stopping distance

Releasing the brake before you have slowed right down will disable the system.

If you have to brake in an emergency ensure that you keep your foot firmly on the brake pedal until the vehicle has stopped.

4.52 Mark one answer

Your car is fitted with anti-lock brakes. You need to stop in an emergency. You should

☐ brake normally and avoid turning the steering wheel
☐ press the brake pedal promptly and firmly until you have stopped
☐ keep pushing and releasing the foot brake quickly to prevent skidding
☐ apply the handbrake to reduce the stopping distance

Keep pressure on the brake pedal until you have come to a stop. The anti-lock mechanism will activate automatically if it senses the wheels are about to lock.

4.53 Mark one answer
When would an anti-lock braking system start to work?

☐ After the parking brake has been applied
☐ Whenever pressure on the brake pedal is applied
☐ Just as the wheels are about to lock
☐ When the normal braking system fails to operate

The anti-lock braking system has sensors that detect when the wheels are about to lock. It releases the brakes momentarily to allow the wheels to revolve and grip, then automatically reapplies them. This cycle is repeated several times a second to maximise braking performance.

4.54 Mark one answer
Anti-lock brakes will take effect when

☐ you do not brake quickly enough
☐ maximum brake pressure has been applied
☐ you have not seen a hazard ahead
☐ speeding on slippery road surfaces

If your car is fitted with anti-lock brakes they will take effect when you use them very firmly in an emergency. The system will only activate when it senses the wheels are about to lock.

4.55 Mark one answer
You are on a wet motorway with surface spray. You should use

☐ hazard flashers
☐ dipped headlights
☐ rear fog lights
☐ sidelights

When surface spray reduces visibility switch on your dipped headlights. This will help other road users to see you.

4.56 Mark one answer
Your vehicle is fitted with anti-lock brakes. To stop quickly in an emergency you should

☐ brake firmly and pump the brake pedal on and off
☐ brake rapidly and firmly without releasing the brake pedal
☐ brake gently and pump the brake pedal on and off
☐ brake rapidly once, and immediately release the brake pedal

Once you have applied the brake keep your foot firmly on the pedal. Releasing the brake and reapplying it will disable the anti-lock brake system.

4.57 Mark one answer
Travelling for long distances in neutral (known as coasting)

☐ improves the driver's control
☐ makes steering easier
☐ reduces the driver's control
☐ uses more fuel

Coasting, is the term used when the clutch is held down, or the gear lever is in neutral, and the vehicle is allowed to freewheel.
This reduces the driver's control of the vehicle. When you coast, the engine can't drive the wheels to pull you through a corner. Coasting also removes the assistance of engine braking that helps to slow the car.

4.58 Mark one answer
How can you tell when you are driving over black ice?

☐ It is easier to brake
☐ The noise from your tyres sounds louder
☐ You will see tyre tracks on the road
☐ Your steering feels light

Sometimes you may not be able to see that the road is icy. Black ice makes a road look damp. The signs that you're travelling on black ice can be that
• the steering feels light
• the noise from your tyres suddenly goes quiet.

4.59 Mark three answers
When driving in fog, which THREE of these are correct?

☐ Use dipped headlights
☐ Position close to the centre line
☐ Allow more time for your journey
☐ Keep close to the car in front
☐ Slow down
☐ Use side lights only

Don't venture out if your journey is not necessary. If you have to travel and someone is expecting you at the other end, let them know that you will be taking longer than usual for your journey. This will stop them worrying if you don't turn up on time and will also take the pressure off you, so you don't feel you have to rush.

5.1 Mark two answers

Where would you expect to see these markers?

☐ On a motorway sign
☐ At the entrance to a narrow bridge
☐ On a large goods vehicle
☐ On a builder's skip placed on the road

These markers must be fitted to vehicles over 13 metres long, large goods vehicles, and rubbish skips placed in the road. They are reflective to make them easier to see in the dark.

5.2 Mark one answer

What is the main hazard shown in this picture?

☐ Vehicles turning right
☐ Vehicles doing U-turns
☐ The cyclist crossing the road
☐ Parked cars around the corner

Look at the picture carefully and try to imagine you're there. The cyclist in this picture appears to be trying to cross the road. You must be able to deal with the unexpected, especially when you're approaching a hazardous junction. Look well ahead to give yourself time to deal with any hazards.

5.3 Mark one answer

Which road user has caused a hazard?

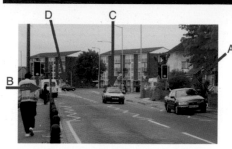

☐ The parked car (arrowed A)
☐ The pedestrian waiting to cross (arrowed B)
☐ The moving car (arrowed C)
☐ The car turning (arrowed D)

The car arrowed A is parked within the area marked by zigzag lines at the pedestrian crossing. Parking here is illegal. It also
• blocks the view for pedestrians wishing to cross the road
• restricts the view of the crossing for approaching traffic.

5.4 Mark one answer

What should the driver of the car approaching the crossing do?

☐ Continue at the same speed
☐ Sound the horn
☐ Drive through quickly
☐ Slow down and get ready to stop

Look well ahead to see if any hazards are developing. This will give you more time to deal with them in the correct way. The man in the picture is clearly intending to cross the road. You should be travelling at a speed that allows you to check your mirror, slow down and stop in good time. You shouldn't have to brake harshly.

5.5   Mark three answers

What THREE things should the driver of the grey car (arrowed) be especially aware of?

- ☐ Pedestrians stepping out between cars
- ☐ Other cars behind the grey car
- ☐ Doors opening on parked cars
- ☐ The bumpy road surface
- ☐ Cars leaving parking spaces
- ☐ Empty parking spaces

You need to be aware that other road users may not have seen you. Always be on the lookout for hazards that may develop suddenly and need you to take avoiding action.

5.6   Mark one answer

You see this sign ahead. You should expect the road to

- ☐ go steeply uphill
- ☐ go steeply downhill
- ☐ bend sharply to the left
- ☐ bend sharply to the right

Adjust your speed in good time and select the correct gear for your speed. Going too fast into the bend could cause you to lose control.

Braking late and harshly while changing direction reduces your vehicle's grip on the road, and is likely to cause a skid.

5.7   Mark one answer

You are approaching this cyclist. You should

- ☐ overtake before the cyclist gets to the junction
- ☐ flash your headlights at the cyclist
- ☐ slow down and allow the cyclist to turn
- ☐ overtake the cyclist on the left-hand side

Keep well back and allow the cyclist room to take up the correct position for the turn.

Don't get too close behind or try to squeeze past.

5.8   Mark one answer

Why must you take extra care when turning right at this junction?

- ☐ Road surface is poor
- ☐ Footpaths are narrow
- ☐ Road markings are faint
- ☐ There is reduced visibility

You may have to pull forward slowly until you can see up and down the road. Be aware that the traffic approaching the junction can't see you either. If you don't know that it's clear, don't go.

5.9   Mark one answer

When approaching this bridge you should give way to

☐ bicycles
☐ buses
☐ motorcycles
☐ cars

A double-deck bus or high-sided lorry will have to take up a position in the centre of the road so that it can clear the bridge. There is normally a sign to indicate this.

Look well down the road, through the bridge and be aware you may have to stop and give way to an oncoming large vehicle.

5.10   Mark one answer

What type of vehicle could you expect to meet in the middle of the road?

☐ Lorry

☐ Bicycle
☐ Car
☐ Motorcycle

The highest point of the bridge is in the centre so a large vehicle might have to move to the centre of the road to allow it enough room to pass under the bridge.

5.11   Mark one answer

At this blind junction you must stop

☐ behind the line, then edge forward to see clearly
☐ beyond the line at a point where you can see clearly
☐ only if there is traffic on the main road
☐ only if you are turning to the right

The 'stop' sign has been put here because there is a poor view into the main road. You must stop because it will not be possible to assess the situation on the move, however slowly you are travelling.

5.12   Mark one answer

A driver pulls out of a side road in front of you. You have to brake hard. You should

☐ ignore the error and stay calm
☐ flash your lights to show your annoyance
☐ sound your horn to show your annoyance
☐ overtake as soon as possible

Where there are a number of side roads, be alert. Be especially careful if there are a lot of parked vehicles because they can make it more difficult for drivers emerging to see you. Try to be tolerant if a vehicle does emerge and you have to brake quickly. Don't react aggressively.

5.13   Mark one answer

An elderly person's driving ability could be affected because they may be unable to

☐ obtain car insurance
☐ understand road signs
☐ react very quickly
☐ give signals correctly

Be tolerant of older drivers. Poor eyesight and hearing could affect the speed with which they react to a hazard and may cause them to be hesitant.

5.14 Mark one answer

You have just passed these warning lights. What hazard would you expect to see next?

☐ A level crossing with no barrier
☐ An ambulance station
☐ A school crossing patrol
☐ An opening bridge

These lights warn that children may be crossing the road to a nearby school. Slow down so that you're ready to stop if necessary.

5.15 Mark one answer

You are planning a long journey. Do you need to plan rest stops?

☐ Yes, you should plan to stop every half an hour
☐ Yes, regular stops help concentration
☐ No, you will be less tired if you get there as soon as possible
☐ No, only fuel stops will be needed

Try to plan your journey so that you can take rest stops. It's recommended that you take a break of at least 15 minutes after every two hours of driving. This should help to maintain your concentration.

5.16 Mark one answer

A driver does something that upsets you. You should

☐ try not to react
☐ let them know how you feel
☐ flash your headlights several times
☐ sound your horn

There are times when other road users make a misjudgement or mistake. When this happens try not to get annoyed and don't react by showing anger. Sounding your horn, flashing your headlights or shouting won't help the situation. Good anticipation will help to prevent these incidents becoming collisions.

5.17 Mark one answer

The red lights are flashing. What should you do when approaching this level crossing?

☐ Go through quickly
☐ Go through carefully
☐ Stop before the barrier
☐ Switch on hazard warning lights

At level crossings the red lights flash before and when the barrier is down. At most crossings an amber light will precede the red lights. You must stop behind the white line unless you have already crossed it when the amber light comes on. NEVER zigzag around half-barriers.

5.18 Mark one answer

You are approaching crossroads. The traffic lights have failed. What should you do?

☐ Brake and stop only for large vehicles
☐ Brake sharply to a stop before looking
☐ Be prepared to brake sharply to a stop
☐ Be prepared to stop for any traffic

When approaching a junction where the traffic lights have failed, you should proceed with caution. Treat the situation as an unmarked junction and be prepared to stop.

5.19 Mark one answer

What should the driver of the red car (arrowed) do?

☐ Wave the pedestrians who are waiting to cross
☐ Wait for the pedestrian in the road to cross
☐ Quickly drive behind the pedestrian in the road
☐ Tell the pedestrian in the road she should not have crossed

Some people might take longer to cross the road. They may be older or have a disability. Be patient and don't hurry them by showing your impatience. They might have poor eyesight or not be able to hear traffic approaching. If pedestrians are standing at the side of the road, don't signal or wave them to cross. Other road users may not have seen your signal and this could lead the pedestrians into a hazardous situation.

5.20 Mark one answer

You are following a slower-moving vehicle on a narrow country road. There is a junction just ahead on the right. What should you do?

☐ Overtake after checking your mirrors and signalling
☐ Stay behind until you are past the junction
☐ Accelerate quickly to pass before the junction
☐ Slow down and prepare to overtake on the left

You should never overtake as you approach a junction. If a vehicle emerged from the junction while you were overtaking, a dangerous situation could develop very quickly.

5.21 Mark one answer

What should you do as you approach this overhead bridge?

☐ Move out to the centre of the road before going through
☐ Find another route, this is only for high vehicles
☐ Be prepared to give way to large vehicles in the middle of the road
☐ Move across to the right-hand side before going through

Oncoming large vehicles may need to move to the middle of the road so that they can pass safely under the bridge. There will not be enough room for you to continue and you should be ready to stop and wait.

5.22 Mark one answer

Why are mirrors often slightly curved (convex)?

☐ They give a wider field of vision
☐ They totally cover blind spots
☐ They make it easier to judge the speed of following traffic
☐ They make following traffic look bigger

Although a convex mirror gives a wide view of the scene behind, you should be aware that it will not show you everything behind or to the side of the vehicle. Before you move off you will need to check over your shoulder to look for anything not visible in the mirrors.

5.23 Mark one answer

You see this sign on the rear of a slowmoving lorry that you want to pass. It is travelling in the middle lane of a three-lane motorway. You should

☐ cautiously approach the lorry then pass on either side
☐ follow the lorry until you can leave the motorway
☐ wait on the hard shoulder until the lorry has stopped
☐ approach with care and keep to the left of the lorry

This sign is found on slow-moving or stationary works vehicles. If you wish to overtake, do so on the left, as indicated.

Be aware that there might be workmen in the area.

5.24 Mark one answer

You think the driver of the vehicle in front has forgotten to cancel their right indicator. You should

☐ flash your lights to alert the driver
☐ sound your horn before overtaking
☐ overtake on the left if there is room
☐ stay behind and not overtake

The driver may be unsure of the location of a junction and turn suddenly. Be cautious and don't attempt to overtake.

5.25 Mark one answer

What is the main hazard the driver of the red car (arrowed) should be aware of?

☐ Glare from the sun may affect the driver's vision
☐ The black car may stop suddenly
☐ The bus may move out into the road
☐ Oncoming vehicles will assume the driver is turning right

If you can do so safely give way to buses signalling to move off at bus stops. Try to anticipate the actions of other road users around you. The driver of the red car should be prepared for the bus pulling out.

As you approach a bus stop look to see how many passengers are waiting to board. If the last one has just got on, the bus is likely to move off.

5.26 Mark one answer

This yellow sign on a vehicle indicates this is

☐ a broken-down vehicle
☐ a school bus
☐ an ice cream van
☐ a private ambulance

Buses which carry children to and from school may stop at places other than scheduled bus stops. Be aware that they might pull over at any time to allow children to get on or off. This will normally be when traffic is heavy during rush hour.

5.27 Mark two answers

What TWO main hazards should you be aware of when going along this street?

☐ Glare from the sun
☐ Car doors opening suddenly
☐ Lack of road markings
☐ The headlights on parked cars being switched on
☐ Large goods vehicles
☐ Children running out from between vehicles

On roads where there are many parked vehicles you should take extra care. You might not be able to see children between parked cars and they may run out into the road without looking.

People may open car doors without realising the hazard this can create. You will also need to look well down the road for oncoming traffic.

5.28 Mark one answer

What is the main hazard you should be aware of when following this cyclist?

☐ The cyclist may move to the left and dismount
☐ The cyclist may swerve out into the road
☐ The contents of the cyclist's carrier may fall onto the road
☐ The cyclist may wish to turn right at the end of the road

When following a cyclist be aware that they have to deal with the hazards around them.

They may wobble or swerve to avoid a pothole in the road or see a potential hazard and change direction suddenly. Don't follow them too closely or rev your engine impatiently.

5.29 Mark one answer

A driver's behaviour has upset you. It may help if you

☐ stop and take a break
☐ shout abusive language
☐ gesture to them with your hand
☐ follow their car, flashing your headlights

Tiredness may make you more irritable than you would be normally. You might react differently to situations because of it. If you feel yourself becoming tense, take a break.

5.30 Mark one answer

In areas where there are 'traffic calming' measures you should

☐ travel at a reduced speed
☐ always travel at the speed limit
☐ position in the centre of the road
☐ only slow down if pedestrians are near

Traffic calming measures such as road humps, chicanes and narrowings are intended to slow you down. Maintain a reduced speed until you reach the end of these features. They are there to protect pedestrians. Kill your speed!

5.31 Mark two answers

When approaching this hazard why should you slow down?

☐ Because of the bend
☐ Because it's hard to see to the right
☐ Because of approaching traffic
☐ Because of animals crossing
☐ Because of the level crossing

There are two hazards clearly signed in this picture. You should be preparing for the bend by slowing down and selecting the correct gear. You might also have to stop at the level crossing, so be alert and be prepared to stop if necessary.

5.32 Mark one answer

Why are place names painted on the road surface?

☐ To restrict the flow of traffic
☐ To warn you of oncoming traffic
☐ To enable you to change lanes early
☐ To prevent you changing lanes

The names of towns and cities may be painted on the road at busy junctions and complex road systems. Their purpose is to let you move into the correct lane in good time, allowing traffic to flow more freely.

5.33 Mark one answer

Some two-way roads are divided into three lanes. Why are these particularly dangerous?

☐ Traffic in both directions can use the middle lane to overtake
☐ Traffic can travel faster in poor weather conditions
☐ Traffic can overtake on the left
☐ Traffic uses the middle lane for emergencies only

If you intend to overtake you must consider that approaching traffic could be planning the same manoeuvre. When you have considered the situation and have decided it is safe, indicate your intentions early. This will show the approaching traffic that you intend to pull out.

5.34 Mark one answer

You are on a dual carriageway. Ahead you see a vehicle with an amber flashing light. What could this be?

☐ An ambulance
☐ A fire engine
☐ A doctor on call
☐ A disabled person's vehicle

An amber flashing light on a vehicle indicates that it is slow-moving. Battery powered vehicles used by disabled people are limited to 8 mph. It's not advisable for them to be used on dual carriageways where the speed limit exceeds 50 mph. If they are then an amber flashing light must be used.

5.35 Mark one answer

What does this signal from a police officer mean to oncoming traffic?

☐ Go ahead
☐ Stop
☐ Turn left
☐ Turn right

Police officers may need to direct traffic, for example, at a junction where the traffic lights have broken down. Check your copy of *The Highway Code* for the signals that they use.

5.36 Mark two answers

Why should you be especially cautious when going past this stationary bus?

☐ There is traffic approaching in the distance
☐ The driver may open the door
☐ It may suddenly move off
☐ People may cross the road in front of it
☐ There are bicycles parked on the pavement

A stationary bus at a bus stop can hide pedestrians just in front of it who might be about to cross the road. Only go past at a speed that will enable you to stop safely if you need to.

5.37 Mark three answers

Overtaking is a major cause of collisions. In which THREE of these situations should you NOT overtake?

☐ If you are turning left shortly afterwards
☐ When you are in a one-way street
☐ When you are approaching a junction
☐ If you are travelling up a long hill
☐ When your view ahead is blocked

You should not overtake unless it is really necessary. Arriving safely is more important than taking risks. Also look out for road signs and markings that show it is illegal or would be unsafe to overtake. In many cases overtaking is unlikely to significantly improve journey times.

5.38 Mark three answers

Which THREE result from drinking alcohol?

☐ Less control
☐ A false sense of confidence
☐ Faster reactions
☐ Poor judgement of speed
☐ Greater awareness of danger

You must understand the serious dangers of mixing alcohol with driving or riding.
 Alcohol will severely reduce your ability to drive or ride safely. Just one drink could put you over the limit. Don't risk people's lives – DON'T DRINK AND DRIVE OR RIDE!

5.39 Mark one answer

What does the solid white line at the side of the road indicate?

☐ Traffic lights ahead
☐ Edge of the carriageway
☐ Footpath on the left
☐ Cycle path

The continuous white line shows the edge of the carriageway. It can be especially useful when visibility is restricted, for example at night or in bad weather. It is discontinued where it crosses junctions, lay-bys etc.

5.40 Mark one answer

You are driving towards this level crossing. What would be the first warning of an approaching train?

☐ Both half barriers down
☐ A steady amber light
☐ One half barrier down
☐ Twin flashing red lights

The steady amber light will be followed by twin flashing red lights that mean you must stop. An alarm will also sound to alert you to the fact that a train is approaching.

5.41 Mark one answer

You are behind this cyclist. When the traffic lights change, what should you do?

☐ Try to move off before the cyclist
☐ Allow the cyclist time and room
☐ Turn right but give the cyclist room
☐ Tap your horn and drive through first

Hold back and allow the cyclist to move off. In some towns, junctions have special areas marked across the front of the traffic lane. These allow cyclists to wait for the lights to change and move off ahead of other traffic.

5.42 Mark one answer

While driving, you see this sign ahead. You should

- ☐ stop at the sign
- ☐ slow, but continue around the bend
- ☐ slow to a crawl and continue
- ☐ stop and look for open farm gates

Drive around the bend at a steady speed in the correct gear. Be aware that you might have to stop for approaching trains.

5.43 Mark one answer

When the traffic lights change to green the white car should

- ☐ wait for the cyclist to pull away
- ☐ move off quickly and turn in front of the cyclist
- ☐ move close up to the cyclist to beat the lights
- ☐ sound the horn to warn the cyclist

If you are waiting at traffic lights, check all around you before you move away, as cyclists often filter through waiting traffic.

Allow the cyclist to move off safely.

5.44 Mark one answer

You intend to turn left at the traffic lights. Just before turning you should

- ☐ check your right mirror
- ☐ move close up to the white car
- ☐ straddle the lanes
- ☐ check for bicycles on your left

Check your nearside for cyclists before moving away. This is especially important if you have been in a stationary queue of traffic and are about to move off, as cyclists often try to filter past on the nearside of stationary vehicles.

5.45 Mark one answer

You should reduce your speed when driving along this road because

- ☐ there is a staggered junction ahead
- ☐ there is a low bridge ahead
- ☐ there is a change in the road surface
- ☐ the road ahead narrows

Traffic could be turning off ahead of you, to the left or right.

Vehicles turning left will be slowing down before the junction and any vehicles turning right may have to stop to allow oncoming traffic to clear. Be prepared for this as you might have to slow down or stop behind them.

5.46   Mark one answer

You are driving at 60 mph. As you approach this hazard you should

☐ maintain your speed
☐ reduce your speed
☐ take the next right turn
☐ take the next left turn

There could be stationary traffic ahead, waiting to turn right. Other traffic could be emerging and it may take time for them to gather speed.

5.47   Mark one answer

What might you expect to happen in this situation?

☐ Traffic will move into the right-hand lane
☐ Traffic speed will increase
☐ Traffic will move into the left-hand lane
☐ Traffic will not need to change position

Be courteous and allow the traffic to merge into the left-hand lane.

5.48   Mark one answer

You are driving on a road with several lanes. You see these signs above the lanes. What do they mean?

☐ The two right lanes are open
☐ The two left lanes are open
☐ Traffic in the left lanes should stop
☐ Traffic in the right lanes should stop

If you see a red cross above your lane it means that there is an obstruction ahead.
    You will have to move into one of the lanes which is showing the green light. If all the lanes are showing a red cross, then you must stop.

5.49   Mark one answer

You are invited to a pub lunch. You know that you will have to drive in the evening. What is your best course of action?

☐ Avoid mixing your alcoholic drinks
☐ Not drink any alcohol at all
☐ Have some milk before drinking alcohol
☐ Eat a hot meal with your alcoholic drinks

Alcohol will stay in the body for several hours and may make you unfit to drive later in the day. Drinking during the day will also affect your performance at work or study.

5.50   Mark one answer

You have been convicted of driving whilst unfit through drink or drugs. You will find this is likely to cause the cost of one of the following to rise considerably. Which one?

☐ Road fund licence
☐ Insurance premiums
☐ Vehicle test certificate
☐ Driving licence

You have shown that you are a risk to yourself and others on the road. For this reason insurance companies may charge you a higher premium.

5.51 Mark one answer

What advice should you give to a driver who has had a few alcoholic drinks at a party?

☐ Have a strong cup of coffee and then drive home
☐ Drive home carefully and slowly
☐ Go home by public transport
☐ Wait a short while and then drive home

Drinking black coffee or waiting a few hours won't make any difference. Alcohol takes time to leave the body.
A driver who has been drinking should go home by public transport or taxi. They might even be unfit to drive the following morning.

5.52 Mark one answer

You have been taking medicine for a few days which made you feel drowsy. Today you feel better but still need to take the medicine. You should only drive

☐ if your journey is necessary
☐ at night on quiet roads
☐ if someone goes with you
☐ after checking with your doctor

Take care – it's not worth taking risks.
Always check with your doctor to be really sure. You may not feel drowsy now, but the medicine could have an effect on you later in the day.

5.53 Mark one answer

You are about to return home from holiday when you become ill. A doctor prescribes drugs which are likely to affect your driving. You should

☐ drive only if someone is with you
☐ avoid driving on motorways
☐ not drive yourself
☐ never drive at more than 30 mph

Find another way to get home even if this proves to be very inconvenient. You must not put other road users, your passengers or yourself at risk.

5.54 Mark two answers

During periods of illness your ability to drive may be impaired. You MUST

☐ see your doctor each time before you drive
☐ only take smaller doses of any medicines
☐ be medically fit to drive
☐ not drive after taking certain medicines
☐ take all your medicines with you when you drive

Be responsible and only drive if you are fit to do so. Some medication can affect your concentration and judgement when dealing with hazards. It may also cause you to become drowsy or even fall asleep. Driving while taking such medication is highly dangerous.

5.55 Mark two answers

You feel drowsy when driving. You should

☐ stop and rest as soon as possible
☐ turn the heater up to keep you warm and comfortable
☐ make sure you have a good supply of fresh air
☐ continue with your journey but drive more slowly
☐ close the car windows to help you concentrate

You will be putting other road users at risk if you continue to drive when drowsy. Pull over and stop in a safe place. If you are driving a long distance, think about finding some accommodation so you can get some sleep before continuing your journey.

5.56 Mark two answers

You are driving along a motorway and become tired. You should

☐ stop at the next service area and rest
☐ leave the motorway at the next exit and rest
☐ increase your speed and turn up the radio volume
☐ close all your windows and set heating to warm
☐ pull up on the hard shoulder and change drivers

If you have planned your journey properly, to include rest stops, you should arrive at your destination in good time.

5.57 Mark one answer

You are taking drugs that are likely to affect your driving. What should you do?

☐ Seek medical advice before driving
☐ Limit your driving to essential journeys
☐ Only drive if accompanied by a full licence-holder
☐ Drive only for short distances

Check with your doctor or pharmacist if you think that the drugs you're taking are likely to make you feel drowsy or impair your judgement.

5.58 Mark one answer

You are about to drive home. You feel very tired and have a severe headache. You should

☐ wait until you are fit and well before driving
☐ drive home, but take a tablet for headaches
☐ drive home if you can stay awake for the journey
☐ wait for a short time, then drive home slowly

All your concentration should be on your driving. Any pain you feel will distract you and you should avoid driving when drowsy. The safest course of action is to wait until you have rested and feel better.

5.59 Mark one answer

If you are feeling tired it is best to stop as soon as you can. Until then you should

☐ increase your speed to find a stopping place quickly
☐ ensure a supply of fresh air
☐ gently tap the steering wheel
☐ keep changing speed to improve concentration

If you're going on a long journey plan your route before you leave. This will help you to be decisive at intersections and junctions, plan rest stops and have an idea of how long the journey will take.
   Make sure your vehicle is well-ventilated to stop you becoming drowsy. You need to maintain concentration so that your judgement is not impaired.

5.60 Mark three answers

Driving long distances can be tiring. You can prevent this by

☐ stopping every so often for a walk
☐ opening a window for some fresh air
☐ ensuring plenty of refreshment breaks
☐ completing the journey without stopping
☐ eating a large meal before driving

Long-distance driving can be boring. This, coupled with a stuffy, warm vehicle, can make you feel tired. Make sure you take rest breaks to keep yourself awake and alert. Stop in a safe place before you get to the stage of fighting sleep.

5.61 Mark one answer

You go to a social event and need to drive a short time after. What precaution should you take?

☐ Avoid drinking alcohol on an empty stomach
☐ Drink plenty of coffee after drinking alcohol
☐ Avoid drinking alcohol completely
☐ Drink plenty of milk before drinking alcohol

This is always going to be the safest option. Just one drink could put you over the limit and dangerously impair your judgement and reactions.

5.62 Mark one answer

You take some cough medicine given to you by a friend. What should you do before driving?

☐ Ask your friend if taking the medicine affected their driving
☐ Drink some strong coffee one hour before driving
☐ Check the label to see if the medicine will affect your driving
☐ Drive a short distance to see if the medicine is affecting your driving

Never drive if you have taken drugs, without first checking what the side effects might be. They might affect your judgement and perception, and therefore endanger lives.

5.63 Mark one answer

You take the wrong route and find you are on a one-way street. You should

☐ reverse out of the road
☐ turn round in a side road
☐ continue to the end of the road
☐ reverse into a driveway

Never reverse or turn your vehicle around in a one-way street. This is highly dangerous. Carry on and find another route, checking the direction signs as you drive. If you need to check a map, first stop in a safe place.

5.64   Mark three answers

Which THREE are likely to make you lose concentration while driving?

☐ Looking at road maps
☐ Listening to loud music
☐ Using your windscreen washers
☐ Looking in your wing mirror
☐ Using a mobile phone

Looking at road maps while driving is very dangerous. If you aren't sure of your route stop in a safe place and check the map.

You must not allow anything to take your attention away from the road. If you need to use a mobile phone, stop in a safe place before doing so.

5.65   Mark one answer

You are driving along this road. The driver on the left is reversing from a driveway. You should

☐ move to the opposite side of the road
☐ drive through as you have priority
☐ sound your horn and be prepared to stop
☐ speed up and drive through quickly

White lights at the rear of a car show that it is about to reverse. Sound your horn to warn of your presence and reduce your speed as a precaution.

5.66   Mark one answer

You have been involved in an argument before starting your journey. This has made you feel angry. You should

☐ start to drive, but open a window
☐ drive slower than normal and turn your radio on
☐ have an alcoholic drink to help you relax before driving
☐ calm down before you start to drive

If you are feeling upset or angry you should wait until you have calmed down before setting out on a journey.

5.67   Mark one answer

You start to feel tired while driving. What should you do?

☐ Increase your speed slightly
☐ Decrease your speed slightly
☐ Find a less busy route
☐ Pull over at a safe place to rest

If you start to feel tired, stop at a safe place for a rest break.

Every year many fatal incidents are caused by drivers falling asleep at the wheel.

5.68   Mark one answer

You are driving on this dual carriageway. Why may you need to slow down?

☐ There is a broken white line in the centre
☐ There are solid white lines either side
☐ There are roadworks ahead of you
☐ There are no footpaths

Look well ahead and read any road signs as you drive. They are there to inform you of what is ahead. In this case you may need to slow right down and change direction.

Make sure you can take whatever action is necessary in plenty of time. Check your mirrors so you know what is happening around you before you change speed or direction.

5.69 Mark one answer

You have just been overtaken by this motorcyclist who is cutting in sharply. You should

☐ sound the horn
☐ brake firmly
☐ keep a safe gap
☐ flash your lights

If another vehicle cuts in too sharply, ease off the accelerator and drop back to allow a safe separation distance. Try not to overreact by braking sharply or swerving, as you could lose control. If vehicles behind you are too close or unprepared, it could lead to a crash.

5.70 Mark one answer

You are about to drive home. You cannot find the glasses you need to wear. You should

☐ drive home slowly, keeping to quiet roads
☐ borrow a friend's glasses and use those
☐ drive home at night, so that the lights will help you
☐ find a way of getting home without driving

Don't be tempted to drive if you've lost or forgotten your glasses. You must be able to see clearly when driving.

5.71 Mark three answers

Which THREE of these are likely effects of drinking alcohol?

☐ Reduced co-ordination
☐ Increased confidence
☐ Poor judgement
☐ Increased concentration
☐ Faster reactions
☐ Colour blindness

Alcohol can increase confidence to a point where a driver's behaviour might become 'out of character'. Someone who normally behaves sensibly suddenly takes risks and enjoys it. Never let yourself or your friends get into this situation.

5.72 Mark one answer

How does alcohol affect you?

☐ It speeds up your reactions
☐ It increases your awareness
☐ It improves your co-ordination
☐ It reduces your concentration

Concentration and good judgement are needed at all times to be a good, safe driver. Don't put yourself or others at risk by drinking and driving.

5.73 Mark one answer

Your doctor has given you a course of medicine. Why should you ask how it will affect you?

☐ Drugs make you a better driver by quickening your reactions
☐ You will have to let your insurance company know about the medicine
☐ Some types of medicine can cause your reactions to slow down
☐ The medicine you take may affect your hearing

Always check the label of any medication container. The contents might affect your driving. If you aren't sure, ask your doctor or pharmacist.

5.74 Mark one answer

You are on a motorway. You feel tired. You should

☐ carry on but go slowly
☐ leave the motorway at the next exit
☐ complete your journey as quickly as possible
☐ stop on the hard shoulder

If you do feel tired and there's no service station for many miles, leave the motorway at the next exit. Find a road off the motorway where you can pull up and stop safely.

5.75 Mark one answer

You find that you need glasses to read vehicle number plates at the required distance. When MUST you wear them?

☐ Only in bad weather conditions
☐ At all times when driving
☐ Only when you think it necessary
☐ Only in bad light or at night time

Have your eyesight tested before you start your practical training. Then, throughout your driving life, have checks periodically to ensure that your eyes haven't deteriorated.

5.76 Mark two answers

Which TWO things would help to keep you alert during a long journey?

☐ Finishing your journey as fast as you can
☐ Keeping off the motorways and using country roads
☐ Making sure that you get plenty of fresh air
☐ Making regular stops for refreshments

Make sure that the vehicle you're driving is well ventilated. A warm, stuffy atmosphere will make you feel drowsy. Open a window and turn down the heating.

5.77 Mark one answer

Which of the following types of glasses should NOT be worn when driving at night?

☐ Half-moon
☐ Round
☐ Bi-focal
☐ Tinted

If you are driving at night or in poor visibility, tinted lenses will reduce the efficiency of your vision, by reducing the amount of available light reaching your eyes.

5.78 Mark three answers

Drinking any amount of alcohol is likely to

☐ slow down your reactions to hazards
☐ increase the speed of your reactions
☐ worsen your judgement of speed
☐ improve your awareness of danger
☐ give a false sense of confidence

If you are going to drive it's always the safest option not to drink at all. Don't be tempted – it's not worth it.

5.79 Mark three answers

What else can seriously affect your concentration, other than alcoholic drinks?

☐ Drugs
☐ Tiredness
☐ Tinted windows
☐ Contact lenses
☐ Loud music

Even a slight distraction can allow your concentration to drift. Maintain full concentration at all times so you stay in full control of your vehicle.

5.80 Mark one answer

As a driver you find that your eyesight has become very poor. Your optician says they cannot help you. The law says that you should tell

☐ the licensing authority
☐ your own doctor
☐ the local police station
☐ another optician

This will have a serious effect on your judgement and concentration. If you cannot meet the eyesight requirements you must tell DVLA (or DVA in Northern Ireland).

5.81 Mark one answer

When should you use hazard warning lights?

☐ When you are double-parked on a two way road
☐ When your direction indicators are not working
☐ When warning oncoming traffic that you intend to stop
☐ When your vehicle has broken down and is causing an obstruction

Hazard warning lights are an important safety feature and should be used if you have broken down and are causing an obstruction. Don't use them as an excuse to park illegally such as when using a cash machine or post box. You may also use them on motorways to warn traffic behind you of danger ahead.

5.82 Mark one answer

You want to turn left at this junction. The view of the main road is restricted. What should you do?

☐ Stay well back and wait to see if something comes
☐ Build up your speed so that you can emerge quickly
☐ Stop and apply the handbrake even if the road is clear
☐ Approach slowly and edge out until you can see more clearly

You should slow right down, and stop if necessary, at any junction where the view is restricted. Edge forward until you can see properly. Only then can you decide if it is safe to go.

5.83 Mark one answer

When may you use hazard warning lights?

☐ To park alongside another car
☐ To park on double yellow lines
☐ When you are being towed
☐ When you have broken down

Hazard warning lights may be used to warn other road users when you have broken down and are causing an obstruction, or are on a motorway and want to warn following traffic of a hazard ahead. Don't use them when being towed or when parking illegally.

5.84 Mark one answer

Hazard warning lights should be used when vehicles are

☐ broken down and causing an obstruction
☐ faulty and moving slowly
☐ being towed along a road
☐ reversing into a side road

Don't use hazard lights as an excuse for illegal parking. If you do use them, don't forget to switch them off when you move away. There must be a warning light on the control panel to show when the hazard lights are in operation.

5.85 Mark one answer

When driving a car fitted with automatic transmission what would you use 'kick down' for?

☐ Cruise control
☐ Quick acceleration
☐ Slow braking
☐ Fuel economy

'Kick down' selects a lower gear, enabling the vehicle to accelerate faster.

5.86 Mark two answers

You are driving along this motorway. It is raining. When following this lorry you should

☐ allow at least a two-second gap
☐ move left and drive on the hard shoulder
☐ allow at least a four-second gap
☐ be aware of spray reducing your vision
☐ move right and stay in the right-hand lane

The usual two second time gap will increase to four seconds when the roads are wet. If you stay well back you will

• be able to see past the vehicle
• be out of the spray thrown up by the lorry's tyres
• give yourself more time to stop if the need arises
• increase your chances of being seen by the lorry driver.

5.87 Mark one answer

You are driving towards this left-hand bend. What dangers should you be aware of?

☐ A vehicle overtaking you
☐ No white lines in the centre of the road
☐ No sign to warn you of the bend
☐ Pedestrians walking towards you

Pedestrians walking on a road with no pavement should walk against the direction of the traffic. You can't see around this bend: there may be hidden dangers.

Always keep this in mind so you give yourself time to react if a hazard does arise.

5.88 Mark two answers

The traffic ahead of you in the left-hand lane is slowing. You should

☐ be wary of cars on your right cutting in
☐ accelerate past the vehicles in the left-hand lane
☐ pull up on the left-hand verge
☐ move across and continue in the right-hand lane
☐ slow down, keeping a safe separation distance

Allow the traffic to merge into the nearside lane. Leave enough room so that your separation distance is not reduced drastically if a vehicle pulls in ahead of you.

5.89 Mark two answers

As a provisional licence holder, you must not drive a motor car

☐ at more than 40 mph
☐ on your own
☐ on the motorway
☐ under the age of 18 years at night
☐ with passengers in the rear seats

When you have passed your practical test you will be able to drive on a motorway. It is recommended that you have instruction on motorway driving before you venture out on your own. Ask your instructor about this.

5.90 Mark two answers

You are not sure if your cough medicine will affect you. What TWO things should you do?

☐ Ask your doctor
☐ Check the medicine label
☐ Drive if you feel alright
☐ Ask a friend or relative for advice

If you're taking medicine or drugs prescribed by your doctor, check to ensure that they won't make you drowsy. If you forget to ask at the time of your visit to the surgery, check with your pharmacist.

Some over-the-counter medication can also cause drowsiness. Read the label and don't drive if you are affected.

5.91 Mark one answer

For which of these may you use hazard warning lights?

☐ When driving on a motorway to warn traffic behind of a hazard ahead
☐ When you are double-parked on a two-way road
☐ When your direction indicators are not working
☐ When warning oncoming traffic that you intend to stop

Hazard warning lights are an important safety feature. Use them when driving on a motorway to warn traffic behind you of danger ahead.

You should also use them if your vehicle has broken down and is causing an obstruction.

5.92 Mark one answer

You are waiting to emerge at a junction. Your view is restricted by parked vehicles. What can help you to see traffic on the road you are joining?

☐ Looking for traffic behind you
☐ Reflections of traffic in shop windows
☐ Making eye contact with other road users
☐ Checking for traffic in your interior mirror

When your view is restricted into the new road you must still be completely sure it is safe to emerge. Try to look for traffic through the windows of the parked cars or the reflections in shop windows. Keep looking in all directions as you slowly edge forwards until you can see it is safe.

5.93 Mark one answer

After passing your driving test, you suffer from ill health. This affects your driving. You MUST

☐ inform your local police station
☐ avoid using motorways
☐ always drive accompanied
☐ inform the licensing authority

The licensing authority won't automatically take away your licence without investigation. For advice, contact the Driver and Vehicle Licensing Agency (or DVA in Northern Ireland).

5.94   Mark one answer

Why should the junction on the left be kept clear?

☐ To allow vehicles to enter and emerge
☐ To allow the bus to reverse
☐ To allow vehicles to make a U-turn
☐ To allow vehicles to park

You should always try to keep junctions clear. If you are in queueing traffic make sure that when you stop you leave enough space for traffic to flow in and out of the junction.

5.95   Mark one answer

Your motorway journey seems boring and you feel drowsy. What should you do?

☐ Stop on the hard shoulder for a sleep
☐ Open a window and stop as soon as it's safe and legal
☐ Speed up to arrive at your destination sooner
☐ Slow down and let other drivers overtake

Never stop on the hard shoulder to rest. If there is no service station for several miles, leave the motorway at the next exit and find somewhere safe and legal to pull over.

5.96   Mark one answer

You are driving on a motorway. The traffic ahead is braking sharply because of an incident. How could you warn traffic behind you?

☐ Briefly use the hazard warning lights
☐ Switch on the hazard warning lights continuously
☐ Briefly use the rear fog lights
☐ Switch on the headlights continuously

The only time you are permitted to use your hazard warning lights while moving is if you are on a motorway or dual carriageway and you need to warn other road users, particularly those behind, of a hazard or obstruction ahead. Only use them long enough to ensure your warning has been seen.

Vulnerable road users

6.1   Mark one answer

Which sign means that there may be people walking along the road?

Always check the road signs. Triangular signs are warning signs and they'll keep you informed of hazards ahead and help you to anticipate any problems. There are a number of different signs showing pedestrians. Learn the meaning of each one.

6.2   Mark one answer

You are turning left at a junction. Pedestrians have started to cross the road. You should

☐ go on, giving them plenty of room
☐ stop and wave at them to cross
☐ blow your horn and proceed
☐ give way to them

If you're turning into a side road, pedestrians already crossing the road have priority and you should give way to them.

Don't wave them across the road, sound your horn, flash your lights or give any other misleading signal. Other road users may misinterpret your signal and this may lead the pedestrians into a dangerous situation. If a pedestrian is slow or indecisive be patient and wait. Don't hurry them across by revving your engine.

6.3   Mark one answer

You are turning left from a main road into a side road. People are already crossing the road into which you are turning. You should

☐ continue, as it is your right of way
☐ signal to them to continue crossing
☐ wait and allow them to cross
☐ sound your horn to warn them of your presence

Always check the road into which you are turning. Approaching at the correct speed will allow you enough time to observe and react.

Give way to any pedestrians already crossing the road.

6.4   Mark one answer

You are at a road junction, turning into a minor road. There are pedestrians crossing the minor road. You should

☐ stop and wave the pedestrians across
☐ sound your horn to let the pedestrians know that you are there
☐ give way to the pedestrians who are already crossing
☐ carry on; the pedestrians should give way to you

Always look into the road into which you are turning. If there are pedestrians crossing, give way to them, but don't wave or signal to them to cross. Signal your intention to turn as you approach.

6.5 Mark one answer

You are turning left into a side road. What hazards should you be especially aware of?

☐ One way street
☐ Pedestrians
☐ Traffic congestion
☐ Parked vehicles

Make sure that you have reduced your speed and are in the correct gear for the turn. Look into the road before you turn and always give way to any pedestrians who are crossing.

6.6 Mark one answer

You intend to turn right into a side road. Just before turning you should check for motorcyclists who might be

☐ overtaking on your left
☐ following you closely
☐ emerging from the side road
☐ overtaking on your right

Never attempt to change direction to the right without first checking your right-hand mirror. A motorcyclist might not have seen your signal and could be hidden by the car behind you. This action should become a matter of routine.

6.7 Mark one answer

A toucan crossing is different from other crossings because

☐ moped riders can use it
☐ it is controlled by a traffic warden
☐ it is controlled by two flashing lights
☐ cyclists can use it

Toucan crossings are shared by pedestrians and cyclists and they are shown the green light together. Cyclists are permitted to cycle across.
   The signals are push-button operated and there is no flashing amber phase.

6.8 Mark one answer

How will a school crossing patrol signal you to stop?

☐ By pointing to children on the opposite pavement
☐ By displaying a red light
☐ By displaying a stop sign
☐ By giving you an arm signal

If a school crossing patrol steps out into the road with a stop sign you must stop. Don't wave anyone across the road and don't get impatient or rev your engine.

6.9 Mark one answer

Where would you see this sign?

☐ In the window of a car taking children to school
☐ At the side of the road
☐ At playground areas
☐ On the rear of a school bus or coach

Vehicles that are used to carry children to and from school will be travelling at busy times of the day. If you're following a vehicle with this sign be prepared for it to make frequent stops. It might pick up or set down passengers in places other than normal bus stops.

6.10 Mark one answer

Which sign tells you that pedestrians may be walking in the road as there is no pavement?

☐   ☐

☐   ☐

Give pedestrians who are walking at the side of the road plenty of room when you pass them. They may turn around when they hear your engine and unintentionally step into the path of your vehicle.

6.11 Mark one answer

What does this sign mean?

☐ No route for pedestrians and cyclists
☐ A route for pedestrians only
☐ A route for cyclists only
☐ A route for pedestrians and cyclists

This sign shows a shared route for pedestrians and cyclists: when it ends, the cyclists will be rejoining the main road.

6.12 Mark one answer

You see a pedestrian with a white stick and red band. This means that the person is

☐ physically disabled
☐ deaf only
☐ blind only
☐ deaf and blind

If someone is deaf as well as blind, they may be carrying a white stick with a red reflective band. You can't see if a pedestrian is deaf. Don't assume everyone can hear you approaching.

6.13 Mark one answer

What action would you take when elderly people are crossing the road?

☐ Wave them across so they know that you have seen them
☐ Be patient and allow them to cross in their own time
☐ Rev the engine to let them know that you are waiting
☐ Tap the horn in case they are hard of hearing

Be aware that older people might take a long time to cross the road. They might also be hard of hearing and not hear you approaching. Don't hurry older people across the road by getting too close to them or revving your engine.

6.14 Mark one answer

You see two elderly pedestrians about to cross the road ahead. You should

☐ expect them to wait for you to pass
☐ speed up to get past them quickly
☐ stop and wave them across the road
☐ be careful, they may misjudge your speed

Older people may have impaired hearing, vision, concentration and judgement. They may also walk slowly and so could take a long time to cross the road.

6.15 Mark one answer

You are coming up to a roundabout. A cyclist is signalling to turn right. What should you do?

☐ Overtake on the right
☐ Give a horn warning
☐ Signal the cyclist to move across
☐ Give the cyclist plenty of room

If you're following a cyclist who's signalling to turn right at a roundabout leave plenty of room. Give them space and time to get into the correct lane.

6.16 Mark two answers

Which TWO should you allow extra room when overtaking?

☐ Motorcycles
☐ Tractors
☐ Bicycles
☐ Road-sweeping vehicles

Don't pass riders too closely as this may cause them to lose balance. Always leave as much room as you would for a car, and don't cut in.

6.17 Mark one answer

Why should you look particularly for motorcyclists and cyclists at junctions?

☐ They may want to turn into the side road
☐ They may slow down to let you turn
☐ They are harder to see
☐ They might not see you turn

Cyclists and motorcyclists are smaller than other vehicles and so are more difficult to see. They can easily become hidden from your view by cars parked near a junction.

6.18 Mark one answer

You are waiting to come out of a side road. Why should you watch carefully for motorcycles?

☐ Motorcycles are usually faster than cars
☐ Police patrols often use motorcycles
☐ Motorcycles are small and hard to see
☐ Motorcycles have right of way

If you're waiting to emerge from a side road watch out for motorcycles: they're small and can be difficult to see. Be especially careful if there are parked vehicles restricting your view, there might be a motorcycle approaching.

IF YOU DON'T KNOW, DON'T GO.

6.19 Mark one answer

In daylight, an approaching motorcyclist is using a dipped headlight. Why?

☐ So that the rider can be seen more easily
☐ To stop the battery overcharging
☐ To improve the rider's vision
☐ The rider is inviting you to proceed

A motorcycle can be lost from sight behind another vehicle. The use of the headlight helps to make it more conspicuous and therefore more easily seen.

6.20 Mark one answer

Motorcyclists should wear bright clothing mainly because

☐ they must do so by law
☐ it helps keep them cool in summer
☐ the colours are popular
☐ drivers often do not see them

Motorcycles are small vehicles and can be difficult to see. If the rider wears bright clothing it can make it easier for other road users to see them approaching, especially at junctions.

6.21 Mark one answer

There is a slow-moving motorcyclist ahead of you. You are unsure what the rider is going to do. You should

☐ pass on the left
☐ pass on the right
☐ stay behind
☐ move closer

If a motorcyclist is travelling slowly it may be that they are looking for a turning or entrance. Be patient and stay behind them in case they need to make a sudden change of direction.

6.22 Mark one answer

Motorcyclists will often look round over their right shoulder just before turning right. This is because

☐ they need to listen for following traffic
☐ motorcycles do not have mirrors
☐ looking around helps them balance as they turn
☐ they need to check for traffic in their blind area

If you see a motorcyclist take a quick glance over their shoulder, this could mean they are about to change direction.

Recognising a clue like this helps you to be prepared and take appropriate action, making you safer on the road.

6.23 Mark three answers

At road junctions which of the following are most vulnerable?

☐ Cyclists
☐ Motorcyclists
☐ Pedestrians
☐ Car drivers
☐ Lorry drivers

Pedestrians and riders on two wheels can be harder to see than other road users.

Make sure you keep a look-out for them, especially at junctions. Good effective observation, coupled with appropriate action, can save lives.

6.24 Mark one answer

Motorcyclists are particularly vulnerable

☐ when moving off
☐ on dual carriageways
☐ when approaching junctions
☐ on motorways

Another road user failing to see a motorcyclist is a major cause of collisions at junctions. Wherever streams of traffic join or cross there's the potential for this type of incident to occur.

6.25 Mark two answers

You are approaching a roundabout. There are horses just ahead of you. You should

☐ be prepared to stop
☐ treat them like any other vehicle
☐ give them plenty of room
☐ accelerate past as quickly as possible
☐ sound your horn as a warning

Horse riders often keep to the outside of the roundabout even if they are turning right. Give them plenty of room and remember that they may have to cross lanes of traffic.

6.26 Mark one answer

As you approach a pelican crossing the lights change to green. Elderly people are halfway across. You should

☐ wave them to cross as quickly as they can
☐ rev your engine to make them hurry
☐ flash your lights in case they have not heard you
☐ wait because they will take longer to cross

Even if the lights turn to green, wait for them to clear the crossing. Allow them to cross the road in their own time, and don't try to hurry them by revving your engine.

6.27 Mark one answer

There are flashing amber lights under a school warning sign. What action should you take?

☐ Reduce speed until you are clear of the area
☐ Keep up your speed and sound the horn
☐ Increase your speed to clear the area quickly
☐ Wait at the lights until they change to green

The flashing amber lights are switched on to warn you that children may be crossing near a school. Slow down and take extra care as you may have to stop.

6.28 Mark one answer

These road markings must be kept clear to allow

Ⓜ SCHOOL KEEP CLEAR Ⓜ

☐ school children to be dropped off
☐ for teachers to park
☐ school children to be picked up
☐ a clear view of the crossing area

The markings are there to show that the area must be kept clear to allow an unrestricted view for
• approaching drivers and riders
• children wanting to cross the road.

6.29 Mark one answer

Where would you see this sign?

☐ Near a school crossing
☐ At a playground entrance
☐ On a school bus
☐ At a 'pedestrians only' area

Watch out for children crossing the road from the other side of the bus.

6.30 Mark one answer

You are following two cyclists. They approach a roundabout in the left-hand lane. In which direction should you expect the cyclists to go?

☐ Left
☐ Right
☐ Any direction
☐ Straight ahead

Cyclists approaching a roundabout in the left-hand lane may be turning right but may not have been able to get into the correct lane due to the heavy traffic. They may also feel safer keeping to the left all the way round the roundabout. Be aware of them and give them plenty of room.

6.31 Mark one answer

You are travelling behind a moped. You want to turn left just ahead. You should

☐ overtake the moped before the junction
☐ pull alongside the moped and stay level until just before the junction
☐ sound your horn as a warning and pull in front of the moped
☐ stay behind until the moped has passed the junction

Passing the moped and turning into the junction could mean that you cut across the front of the rider. This might force them to slow down, stop or even lose control.
   Slow down and stay behind the moped until it has passed the junction and you can then turn safely.

6.32 Mark one answer

You see a horse rider as you approach a roundabout. They are signalling right but keeping well to the left. You should

☐ proceed as normal
☐ keep close to them
☐ cut in front of them
☐ stay well back

Allow the horse rider to enter and exit the roundabout in their own time. They may feel safer keeping to the left all the way around the roundabout. Don't get up close behind or alongside them. This is very likely to upset the horse and create a dangerous situation.

6.33 Mark one answer

How would you react to drivers who appear to be inexperienced?

☐ Sound your horn to warn them of your presence
☐ Be patient and prepare for them to react more slowly
☐ Flash your headlights to indicate that it is safe for them to proceed
☐ Overtake them as soon as possible

Learners might not have confidence when they first start to drive. Allow them plenty of room and don't react adversely to their hesitation. We all learn from experience, but new drivers will have had less practice in dealing with all the situations that might occur.

6.34 Mark one answer

You are following a learner driver who stalls at a junction. You should

☐ be patient as you expect them to make mistakes
☐ stay very close behind and flash your headlights
☐ start to rev your engine if they take too long to restart
☐ immediately steer around them and drive on

Learning is a process of practice and experience. Try to understand this and tolerate those who are at the beginning of this process.

6.35 Mark one answer

You are on a country road. What should you expect to see coming towards you on YOUR side of the road?

☐ Motorcycles
☐ Bicycles
☐ Pedestrians
☐ Horse riders

On a quiet country road always be aware that there may be a hazard just around the next bend, such as a slow-moving vehicle or pedestrians. Pedestrians are advised to walk on the right-hand side of the road if there is no pavement, so they may be walking towards you on your side of the road.

6.36 Mark one answer

You are turning left into a side road. Pedestrians are crossing the road near the junction. You must

☐ wave them on
☐ sound your horn
☐ switch on your hazard lights
☐ wait for them to cross

Check that it's clear before you turn into a junction. If there are pedestrians crossing they have priority, so let them cross in their own time.

6.37 Mark one answer

You are following a car driven by an elderly driver. You should

☐ expect the driver to drive badly
☐ flash your lights and overtake
☐ be aware that the driver's reactions may not be as fast as yours
☐ stay very close behind but be careful

You must show consideration to other road users. The reactions of older drivers may be slower and they might need more time to deal with a situation. Be tolerant and don't lose patience or show your annoyance.

6.38 Mark one answer

You are following a cyclist. You wish to turn left just ahead. You should

☐ overtake the cyclist before the junction
☐ pull alongside the cyclist and stay level until after the junction
☐ hold back until the cyclist has passed the junction
☐ go around the cyclist on the junction

Make allowances for cyclists. Allow them plenty of room. Don't try to overtake and then immediately turn left. Be patient and stay behind them until they have passed the junction.

6.39 Mark one answer

A horse rider is in the left-hand lane approaching a roundabout. You should expect the rider to

☐ go in any direction
☐ turn right
☐ turn left
☐ go ahead

Horses and their riders will move more slowly than other road users. They might not have time to cut across heavy traffic to take up positions in the offside lane. For this reason a horse and rider may approach a roundabout in the left-hand lane, even though they're turning right.

6.40 Mark one answer

Powered vehicles used by disabled people are small and hard to see. How do they give early warning when on a dual carriageway?

☐ They will have a flashing red light
☐ They will have a flashing green light
☐ They will have a flashing blue light
☐ They will have a flashing amber light

Powered vehicles used by disabled people are small, low, hard to see and travel very slowly. On a dual carriageway a flashing amber light will warn other road users.

6.41 Mark one answer

You should never attempt to overtake a cyclist

☐ just before you turn left
☐ on a left hand bend
☐ on a one-way street
☐ on a dual carriageway

If you want to turn left and there's a cyclist in front of you, hold back. Wait until the cyclist has passed the junction and then turn left behind them.

6.42 Mark one answer

Ahead of you there is a moving vehicle with a flashing amber beacon. This means it is

☐ slow moving
☐ broken down
☐ a doctor's car
☐ a school crossing patrol

As you approach the vehicle, assess the situation. Due to its slow progress you will need to judge whether it is safe to overtake.

6.43 Mark one answer

What does this sign mean?

☐ Contraflow pedal cycle lane
☐ With-flow pedal cycle lane
☐ Pedal cycles and buses only
☐ No pedal cycles or buses

The picture of a cycle will also usually be painted on the road, sometimes with a different coloured surface. Leave these clear for cyclists and don't pass too closely when you overtake.

6.44 Mark one answer

You notice horse riders in front. What should you do FIRST?

☐ Pull out to the middle of the road
☐ Slow down and be ready to stop
☐ Accelerate around them
☐ Signal right

Be particularly careful when approaching horse riders – slow down and be prepared to stop. Always pass wide and slowly and look out for signals given by horse riders.

Horses are unpredictable: always treat them as potential hazards and take great care when passing them.

6.45 Mark one answer

You must not stop on these road markings because you may obstruct

W-SCHOOL KEEP CLEAR -W

☐ children's view of the crossing area
☐ teachers' access to the school
☐ delivery vehicles' access to the school
☐ emergency vehicles' access to the school

These markings are found on the road outside schools. DO NOT stop (even to set down or pick up children) or park on them.

The markings are to make sure that drivers, riders, children and other pedestrians have a clear view.

6.46 Mark one answer

The left-hand pavement is closed due to street repairs. What should you do?

☐ Watch out for pedestrians walking in the road
☐ Use your right-hand mirror more often
☐ Speed up to get past the roadworks quicker
☐ Position close to the left-hand kerb

Where street repairs have closed off pavements, proceed carefully and slowly as pedestrians might have to walk in the road.

6.47 Mark one answer

You are following a motorcyclist on an uneven road. You should

☐ allow less room so you can be seen in their mirrors
☐ overtake immediately
☐ allow extra room in case they swerve to avoid potholes
☐ allow the same room as normal because road surfaces do not affect motorcyclists

Potholes and bumps in the road can unbalance a motorcyclist. For this reason the rider might swerve to avoid an uneven road surface. Watch out at places where this is likely to occur.

6.48 Mark one answer

What does this sign tell you?

☐ No cycling
☐ Cycle route ahead
☐ Cycle parking only
☐ End of cycle route

With people's concern today for the environment, cycle routes are being created in our towns and cities. These are usually defined by road markings and signs.

Respect the presence of cyclists on the road and give them plenty of room if you need to pass.

6.49 Mark one answer

You are approaching this roundabout and see the cyclist signal right. Why is the cyclist keeping to the left?

☐ It is a quicker route for the cyclist
☐ The cyclist is going to turn left instead
☐ The cyclist thinks *The Highway Code* does not apply to bicycles
☐ The cyclist is slower and more vulnerable

Cycling in today's heavy traffic can be hazardous. Some cyclists may not feel happy about crossing the path of traffic to take up a position in an outside lane. Be aware of this and understand that, although in the left-hand lane, the cyclist might be turning right.

6.50 Mark one answer

You are approaching this crossing. You should

☐ prepare to slow down and stop
☐ stop and wave the pedestrians across
☐ speed up and pass by quickly
☐ continue unless the pedestrians step out

Be courteous and prepare to stop. Do not wave people across as this could be dangerous if another vehicle is approaching the crossing.

6.51 Mark one answer

You see a pedestrian with a dog. The dog has a yellow or burgundy coat. This especially warns you that the pedestrian is

☐ elderly
☐ dog training
☐ colour blind
☐ deaf

Take extra care as the pedestrian may not be aware of vehicles approaching.

6.52 Mark one answer

At toucan crossings

☐ you only stop if someone is waiting to cross
☐ cyclists are not permitted
☐ there is a continuously flashing amber beacon
☐ pedestrians and cyclists may cross

There are some crossings where cycle routes lead the cyclists to cross at the same place as pedestrians. These are called toucan crossings. Always look out for cyclists, as they're likely to be approaching faster than pedestrians.

6.53 Mark one answer

Some junctions controlled by traffic lights have a marked area between two stop lines. What is this for?

☐ To allow taxis to position in front of other traffic
☐ To allow people with disabilities to cross the road
☐ To allow cyclists and pedestrians to cross the road together
☐ To allow cyclists to position in front of other traffic

These are known as advanced stop lines. When the lights are red (or about to become red) you should stop at the first white line. However, if you have crossed that line as the lights change you must stop at the second line even if it means you are in the area reserved for cyclists.

6.54 Mark one answer

At some traffic lights there are advance stop lines and a marked area. What are these for?

☐ To allow cyclists to position in front of other traffic
☐ To let pedestrians cross when the lights change
☐ To prevent traffic from jumping the lights
☐ To let passengers get off a bus which is queueing

You should always stop at the first white line. Avoid going into the marked area which is reserved for cyclists only. However, if you have crossed the first white line at the time the signal changes to red you must stop at the second line even if you are in the marked area.

6.55 Mark one answer

When you are overtaking a cyclist you should leave as much room as you would give to a car. What is the main reason for this?

☐ The cyclist might speed up
☐ The cyclist might get off the bike
☐ The cyclist might swerve
☐ The cyclist might have to make a left turn

Before overtaking assess the situation.

Look well ahead to see if the cyclist will need to change direction. Be especially aware of the cyclist approaching parked vehicles as they will need to alter course.

Do not pass too closely or cut in sharply.

6.56 Mark three answers

Which THREE should you do when passing sheep on a road?

☐ Allow plenty of room
☐ Go very slowly
☐ Pass quickly but quietly
☐ Be ready to stop
☐ Briefly sound your horn

Slow down and be ready to stop if you see animals in the road ahead. Animals are easily frightened by noise and vehicles passing too close to them. Stop if signalled to do so by the person in charge.

6.57 Mark one answer

At night you see a pedestrian wearing reflective clothing and carrying a bright red light. What does this mean?

☐ You are approaching roadworks
☐ You are approaching an organised walk
☐ You are approaching a slow-moving vehicle
☐ You are approaching a traffic danger spot

The people on the walk should be keeping to the left, but don't assume this. Pass slowly, make sure you have time to do so safely. Be aware that the pedestrians have their backs to you and may not know that you're there.

6.58 Mark one answer

You have just passed your test. How can you reduce your risk of being involved in a collision?

☐ By always staying close to the vehicle in front
☐ By never going over 40 mph
☐ By staying only in the left-hand lane on all roads
☐ By taking further training

New drivers and riders are often involved in a collision or incident early in their driving career. Due to a lack of experience they may not react to hazards as quickly as more experienced road users. Approved training courses are offered by driver and rider training schools. The Pass Plus scheme has been created by DSA for new drivers who would like to improve their basic skills and safely widen their driving experience.

6.59 Mark one answer

You want to reverse into a side road. You are not sure that the area behind your car is clear. What should you do?

☐ Look through the rear window only
☐ Get out and check
☐ Check the mirrors only
☐ Carry on, assuming it is clear

If you cannot be sure whether there is anything behind you, it is always safest to check before reversing. There may be a small child or a low obstruction close behind your car. The shape and size of your vehicle can restrict visibility.

6.60 Mark one answer

You are about to reverse into a side road. A pedestrian wishes to cross behind you. You should

☐ wave to the pedestrian to stop
☐ give way to the pedestrian
☐ wave to the pedestrian to cross
☐ reverse before the pedestrian starts to cross

If you need to reverse into a side road try to find a place that's free from traffic and pedestrians. Look all around before and during the manoeuvre. Stop and give way to any pedestrians who want to cross behind you. Avoid waving them across, sounding the horn, flashing your lights or giving any misleading signals that could lead them into a dangerous situation.

6.61　Mark one answer

Who is especially in danger of not being seen as you reverse your car?

☐ Motorcyclists
☐ Car drivers
☐ Cyclists
☐ Children

As you look through the rear of your vehicle you may not be able to see a small child.

Be aware of this before you reverse. If there are children about, get out and check if it is clear before reversing.

6.62　Mark one answer

You are reversing around a corner when you notice a pedestrian walking behind you. What should you do?

☐ Slow down and wave the pedestrian across
☐ Continue reversing and steer round the pedestrian
☐ Stop and give way
☐ Continue reversing and sound your horn

Wait until the pedestrian has passed, then look around again before you start to reverse. Don't forget that you may not be able to see a small child directly behind your vehicle. Be aware of the possibility of hidden dangers.

6.63　Mark one answer

You want to turn right from a junction but your view is restricted by parked vehicles. What should you do?

☐ Move out quickly, but be prepared to stop
☐ Sound your horn and pull out if there is no reply
☐ Stop, then move slowly forward until you have a clear view
☐ Stop, get out and look along the main road to check

If you want to turn right from a junction and your view is restricted, STOP. Ease forward until you can see – there might be something approaching.

IF YOU DON'T KNOW, DON'T GO.

6.64　Mark one answer

You are at the front of a queue of traffic waiting to turn right into a side road. Why is it important to check your right mirror just before turning?

☐ To look for pedestrians about to cross
☐ To check for overtaking vehicles
☐ To make sure the side road is clear
☐ To check for emerging traffic

There could be a motorcyclist riding along the outside of the queue. Always check your mirror before turning as situations behind you can change in the time you have been waiting to turn.

6.65　Mark one answer

What must a driver do at a pelican crossing when the amber light is flashing?

☐ Signal the pedestrian to cross
☐ Always wait for the green light before proceeding
☐ Give way to any pedestrians on the crossing
☐ Wait for the red-and-amber light before proceeding

The flashing amber light allows pedestrians already on the crossing to get to the other side before a green light shows to the traffic. Be aware that some pedestrians, such as elderly people and young children, need longer to cross. Let them do this at their own pace.

6.66　Mark two answers

You have stopped at a pelican crossing. A disabled person is crossing slowly in front of you. The lights have now changed to green. You should

☐ allow the person to cross
☐ drive in front of the person
☐ drive behind the person
☐ sound your horn
☐ be patient
☐ edge forward slowly

At a pelican crossing the green light means you may proceed as long as the crossing is clear. If someone hasn't finished crossing, be patient and wait for them.

6.67 Mark one answer

You are driving past a line of parked cars. You notice a ball bouncing out into the road ahead. What should you do?

☐ Continue driving at the same speed and sound your horn
☐ Continue driving at the same speed and flash your headlights
☐ Slow down and be prepared to stop for children
☐ Stop and wave the children across to fetch their ball

Beware of children playing in the street and running out into the road. If a ball bounces out from the pavement, slow down and stop. Don't encourage anyone to retrieve it. Other road users may not see your signal and you might lead a child into a dangerous situation.

6.68 Mark one answer

You want to turn right from a main road into a side road. Just before turning you should

☐ cancel your right-turn signal
☐ select first gear
☐ check for traffic overtaking on your right
☐ stop and set the handbrake

Motorcyclists often overtake queues of vehicles. Make one last check in your mirror and your blind spot to avoid turning across their path.

6.69 Mark one answer

You are driving in slow-moving queues of traffic. Just before changing lane you should

☐ sound the horn
☐ look for motorcyclists filtering through the traffic
☐ give a 'slowing down' arm signal
☐ change down to first gear

In this situation motorcyclists could be passing you on either side. Always check before you change lanes or change direction.

6.70 Mark one answer

You are driving in town. There is a bus at the bus stop on the other side of the road. Why should you be careful?

☐ The bus may have broken down
☐ Pedestrians may come from behind the bus
☐ The bus may move off suddenly
☐ The bus may remain stationary

If you see a bus ahead watch out for pedestrians. They may not be able to see you if they're crossing from behind the bus.

6.71 Mark one answer

How should you overtake horse riders?

☐ Drive up close and overtake as soon as possible
☐ Speed is not important but allow plenty of room
☐ Use your horn just once to warn them
☐ Drive slowly and leave plenty of room

When you're on country roads be aware of particular dangers. Be prepared for farm animals, horses, pedestrians, farm vehicles and wild animals. Always be prepared to slow down or stop.

6.72 Mark one answer

You are driving on a main road. You intend to turn right into a side road. Just before turning you should

☐ adjust your interior mirror
☐ flash your headlamps
☐ steer over to the left
☐ check for traffic overtaking on your right

A last check in the offside mirror and blind spot will allow you sight of any cyclist or motorcyclist overtaking as you wait to turn.

6.73 Mark one answer

Why should you allow extra room when overtaking a motorcyclist on a windy day?

☐ The rider may turn off suddenly to get out of the wind
☐ The rider may be blown across in front of you
☐ The rider may stop suddenly
☐ The rider may be travelling faster than normal

If you're driving in high winds, be aware that the conditions might force a motorcyclist or cyclist to swerve or wobble.

Take this into consideration if you're following or wish to overtake a two-wheeled vehicle.

6.74 Mark one answer

Where in particular should you look out for motorcyclists?

☐ In a filling station
☐ At a road junction
☐ Near a service area
☐ When entering a car park

Always look out for motorcyclists, and cyclists, particularly at junctions. They are smaller and usually more difficult to see than other vehicles.

6.75 Mark one answer

Where should you take particular care to look out for motorcyclists and cyclists?

☐ On dual carriageways
☐ At junctions
☐ At zebra crossings
☐ On one-way streets

Motorcyclists and cyclists are often more difficult to see on the road. This is especially the case at junctions. You may not be able to see a motorcyclist approaching a junction if your view is blocked by other traffic. A motorcycle may be travelling as fast as a car, sometimes faster. Make sure that you judge speeds correctly before you emerge.

6.76 Mark one answer

The road outside this school is marked with yellow zigzag lines. What do these lines mean?

☐ You may park on the lines when dropping off schoolchildren
☐ You may park on the lines when picking schoolchildren up
☐ You must not wait or park your vehicle here at all
☐ You must stay with your vehicle if you park here

Parking here would block the view of the school entrance and would endanger the lives of children on their way to and from school.

6.77 Mark one answer

You are driving past parked cars. You notice a bicycle wheel sticking out between them. What should you do?

☐ Accelerate past quickly and sound your horn
☐ Slow down and wave the cyclist across
☐ Brake sharply and flash your headlights
☐ Slow down and be prepared to stop for a cyclist

Scan the road as you drive. Try to anticipate hazards by being aware of the places where they are likely to occur. You'll then be able to react in good time, if necessary.

6.78 Mark one answer

You are dazzled at night by a vehicle behind you. You should

☐ set your mirror to anti-dazzle
☐ set your mirror to dazzle the other driver
☐ brake sharply to a stop
☐ switch your rear lights on and off

The interior mirror of most vehicles can be set to the anti dazzle position. You will still be able to see the lights of the traffic behind you, but the dazzle will be greatly reduced.

6.79   Mark one answer

You are driving towards a zebra crossing. A person in a wheelchair is waiting to cross. What should you do?

☐ Continue on your way
☐ Wave to the person to cross
☐ Wave to the person to wait
☐ Be prepared to stop

You should slow down and be prepared to stop as you would with an able-bodied person. Don't wave them across as other traffic may not stop.

6.80   Mark one answer

Yellow zigzag lines on the road outside schools mean

∿-SCHOOL KEEP CLEAR-∿

☐ sound your horn to alert other road users
☐ stop to allow children to cross
☐ you should not park or stop on these lines
☐ you must not drive over these lines

Where there are yellow zigzag markings, you should not park, wait or stop, even to pick up or drop off children. A vehicle parked on the zigzag lines would obstruct children's view of the road and other drivers' view of the pavement. Where there is an upright sign there is mandatory prohibition of stopping during the times shown.

6.81   Mark one answer

What do these road markings outside a school mean?

∿-SCHOOL KEEP CLEAR-∿

☐ You may park here if you are a teacher
☐ Sound your horn before parking
☐ When parking, use your hazard warning lights
☐ You should not wait or park your vehicle here

These markings are used outside schools so that children can see and be seen clearly when crossing the road. Parking here would block people's view of the school entrance. This could endanger the lives of children on their way to and from school.

7.1 Mark one answer

You are about to overtake a slow-moving motorcyclist. Which one of these signs would make you take special care?

☐

☐

☐

☐

In windy weather, watch out for motorcyclists and also cyclists as they can be blown sideways into your path. When you pass them, leave plenty of room and check their position in your mirror before pulling back in.

7.2 Mark one answer

You are waiting to emerge left from a minor road. A large vehicle is approaching from the right. You have time to turn, but you should wait. Why?

☐ The large vehicle can easily hide an overtaking vehicle
☐ The large vehicle can turn suddenly
☐ The large vehicle is difficult to steer in a straight line
☐ The large vehicle can easily hide vehicles from the left

Large vehicles can hide other vehicles that are overtaking, especially motorcycles which may be filtering past queueing traffic.

You need to be aware of the possibility of hidden vehicles and not assume that it is safe to emerge.

7.3 Mark one answer

You are following a long vehicle. It approaches a crossroads and signals left, but moves out to the right. You should

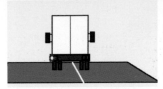

☐ get closer in order to pass it quickly
☐ stay well back and give it room
☐ assume the signal is wrong and it is really turning right
☐ overtake as it starts to slow down

A lorry may swing out to the right as it approaches a left turn. This is to allow the rear wheels to clear the kerb as it turns.

Don't try to filter through if you see a gap on the nearside.

7.4 Mark one answer

You are following a long vehicle approaching a crossroads. The driver signals right but moves close to the left-hand kerb. What should you do?

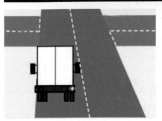

☐ Warn the driver of the wrong signal
☐ Wait behind the long vehicle
☐ Report the driver to the police
☐ Overtake on the right-hand side

When a long vehicle is going to turn right it may need to keep close to the left-hand kerb. This is to prevent the rear end of the trailer cutting the corner. You need to be aware of how long vehicles behave in such situations. Don't overtake the lorry because it could turn as you're alongside. Stay behind and wait for it to turn.

7.5 Mark one answer

You are approaching a mini-roundabout. The long vehicle in front is signalling left but positioned over to the right. You should

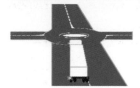

☐ sound your horn
☐ overtake on the left
☐ follow the same course as the lorry
☐ keep well back

At mini-roundabouts there isn't much room for a long vehicle to manoeuvre. It will have to swing out wide so that it can complete the turn safely. Keep well back and don't try to move up alongside it.

7.6 Mark one answer

Before overtaking a large vehicle you should keep well back. Why is this?

☐ To give acceleration space to overtake quickly on blind bends
☐ To get the best view of the road ahead
☐ To leave a gap in case the vehicle stops and rolls back
☐ To offer other drivers a safe gap if they want to overtake you

When following a large vehicle keep well back. If you're too close you won't be able to see the road ahead and the driver of the long vehicle might not be able to see you in their mirrors.

7.7 Mark two answers

You are travelling behind a bus that pulls up at a bus stop. What should you do?

☐ Accelerate past the bus sounding your horn
☐ Watch carefully for pedestrians
☐ Be ready to give way to the bus
☐ Pull in closely behind the bus

There might be pedestrians crossing from in front of the bus. Look out for them if you intend to pass. Consider staying back and waiting.

How many people are waiting to get on the bus? Check the queue if you can. The bus might move off straight away if there is no one waiting to get on.

If a bus is signalling to pull out, give it priority as long as it is safe to do so.

7.8 Mark one answer

You are following a large lorry on a wet road. Spray makes it difficult to see. You should

☐ drop back until you can see better
☐ put your headlights on full beam
☐ keep close to the lorry, away from the spray
☐ speed up and overtake quickly

Large vehicles may throw up a lot of spray when the roads are wet. This will make it difficult for you to see ahead. Dropping back further will
• move you out of the spray and allow you to see further
• increase your separation distance. It takes longer to stop when the roads are wet and you need to allow more room.

Don't
• follow the vehicle in front too closely
• overtake, unless you can see and are sure that the way ahead is clear.

7.9 Mark one answer

You are following a large articulated vehicle. It is going to turn left into a narrow road. What action should you take?

☐ Move out and overtake on the right
☐ Pass on the left as the vehicle moves out
☐ Be prepared to stop behind
☐ Overtake quickly before the lorry moves out

Lorries are larger and longer than other vehicles and this can affect their position when approaching junctions. When turning left they may move out to the right so that they don't cut in and mount the kerb with the rear wheels.

7.10   Mark one answer

You keep well back while waiting to overtake a large vehicle. A car fills the gap. You should

☐ sound your horn
☐ drop back further
☐ flash your headlights
☐ start to overtake

It's very frustrating when your separation distance is shortened by another vehicle. React positively, stay calm and drop further back.

7.11   Mark one answer

You are following a long lorry. The driver signals to turn left into a narrow road. What should you do?

☐ Overtake on the left before the lorry reaches the junction
☐ Overtake on the right as soon as the lorry slows down
☐ Do not overtake unless you can see there is no oncoming traffic
☐ Do not overtake, stay well back and be prepared to stop

When turning into narrow roads articulated and long vehicles will need more room. Initially they will need to swing out in the opposite direction to which they intend to turn. They could mask another vehicle turning out of the same junction. DON'T be tempted to overtake them or pass on the inside.

7.12   Mark one answer

When you approach a bus signalling to move off from a bus stop you should

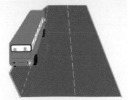

☐ get past before it moves
☐ allow it to pull away, if it is safe to do so
☐ flash your headlights as you approach
☐ signal left and wave the bus on

Try to give way to buses if you can do so safely, especially when they signal to pull away from bus stops. Look out for people who've stepped off the bus or are running to catch it, and may try to cross the road without looking. Don't try to accelerate past before it moves away or flash your lights as other road users may be misled by this signal.

7.13   Mark one answer

You wish to overtake a long, slow-moving vehicle on a busy road. You should

☐ follow it closely and keep moving out to see the road ahead
☐ flash your headlights for the oncoming traffic to give way
☐ stay behind until the driver waves you past
☐ keep well back until you can see that it is clear

If you want to overtake a long vehicle, stay well back so that you can get a better view of the road ahead. The closer you get the less you will be able to see of the road ahead. Be patient, overtaking calls for sound judgement. DON'T take a gamble, only overtake when you are certain that you can complete the manoeuvre safely.

7.14   Mark one answer

Which of these is LEAST likely to be affected by crosswinds?

☐ Cyclists
☐ Motorcyclists
☐ High-sided vehicles
☐ Cars

Although cars are the least likely to be affected, crosswinds can take anyone by surprise. This is most likely to happen, after overtaking a large vehicle, when passing gaps between hedges or buildings, and on exposed sections of road.

7.15   Mark one answer

What should you do as you approach this lorry?

☐ Slow down and be prepared to wait
☐ Make the lorry wait for you
☐ Flash your lights at the lorry
☐ Move to the right-hand side of the road

When turning, long vehicles need much more room on the road than other vehicles.

At junctions they may take up the whole of the road space, so be patient and allow them the room they need.

7.16 Mark one answer

You are following a large vehicle approaching crossroads. The driver signals to turn left. What should you do?

☐ Overtake if you can leave plenty of room
☐ Overtake only if there are no oncoming vehicles
☐ Do not overtake until the vehicle begins to turn
☐ Do not overtake when at or approaching a junction

Hold back and wait until the vehicle has turned before proceeding. Do not overtake because the vehicle turning left could hide a vehicle emerging from the same junction.

7.17 Mark one answer

Powered vehicles, such as wheelchairs or scooters, used by disabled people have a maximum speed of

☐ 8 mph
☐ 12 mph
☐ 16 mph
☐ 20 mph

These are small battery powered vehicles and include wheelchairs and mobility scooters. Some are designed for use on the pavement only and have an upper speed limit of 4 mph (6 km/h). Others can go on the road as well and have a speed limit of 8 mph (12 km/h). They are now very common and are generally used by the elderly, disabled or infirm. Take great care as they are extremely vulnerable because of their low speed and small size.

7.18 Mark one answer

Why is it more difficult to overtake a large vehicle than a car?

☐ It takes longer to pass one
☐ They may suddenly pull up
☐ Their brakes are not as good
☐ They climb hills more slowly

Depending on relevant speed, it will usually take you longer to pass a lorry than other vehicles. Some hazards to watch for include oncoming traffic, junctions ahead, bends or dips which could restrict your view, and signs or road markings that prohibit overtaking. Make sure you can see that it's safe to complete the manoeuvre before you start to overtake.

7.19 Mark one answer

In front of you is a class 3 powered vehicle (powered wheelchair) driven by a disabled person. These vehicles have a maximum speed of

☐ 8 mph (12 km/h)
☐ 18 mph (29 km/h)
☐ 28 mph (45 km/h)
☐ 38 mph (61 km/h)

These vehicles are battery powered and very vulnerable due to their slow speed, small size and low height. Some are designed for pavement and road use and have a maximum speed of 8 mph (12 km/h). Others are for pavement use only and are restricted to 4 mph (6 km/h). Take extra care and be patient if you are following one. Allow plenty of room when overtaking and do not go past unless you can do so safely.

7.20 Mark one answer

It is very windy. You are behind a motorcyclist who is overtaking a high-sided vehicle. What should you do?

☐ Overtake the motorcyclist immediately
☐ Keep well back
☐ Stay level with the motorcyclist
☐ Keep close to the motorcyclist

Motorcyclists are affected more by windy weather than other vehicles. In windy conditions, high-sided vehicles cause air turbulence. You should keep well back as the motorcyclist could be blown off course.

7.21 Mark one answer

It is very windy. You are about to overtake a motorcyclist. You should

☐ overtake slowly
☐ allow extra room
☐ sound your horn
☐ keep close as you pass

Crosswinds can blow a motorcyclist or cyclist across the lane. Passing too close could also cause a draught, unbalancing the rider.

7.22 Mark two answers

You are driving in town. Ahead of you a bus is at a bus stop. Which TWO of the following should you do?

☐ Be prepared to give way if the bus suddenly moves off
☐ Continue at the same speed but sound your horn as a warning
☐ Watch carefully for the sudden appearance of pedestrians
☐ Pass the bus as quickly as you possibly can

As you approach, look out for any signal the driver might make. If you pass the vehicle watch out for pedestrians attempting to cross the road from the other side of the bus. They will be hidden from view until the last moment.

7.23 Mark one answer

You are driving along this road. What should you be prepared to do?

☐ Sound your horn and continue
☐ Slow down and give way
☐ Report the driver to the police
☐ Squeeze through the gap

Sometimes large vehicles may need more space than other road users. If a vehicle needs more time and space to turn be prepared to stop and wait.

7.24 Mark one answer

As a driver why should you be more careful where trams operate?

☐ Because they do not have a horn
☐ Because they do not stop for cars
☐ Because they do not have lights
☐ Because they cannot steer to avoid you

You should take extra care when you first encounter trams. You will have to get used to dealing with a different traffic system.
Be aware that they can accelerate and travel very quickly and that they cannot change direction to avoid obstructions.

7.25 Mark one answer

You are towing a caravan. Which is the safest type of rear-view mirror to use?

☐ Interior wide-angle mirror
☐ Extended-arm side mirrors
☐ Ordinary door mirrors
☐ Ordinary interior mirror

Towing a large trailer or caravan can greatly reduce your view of the road behind. You need to use the correct equipment to make sure you can see clearly behind and down both sides of the caravan or trailer.

7.26 Mark two answers

You are driving in heavy traffic on a wet road. Spray makes it difficult to be seen. You should use your

☐ full beam headlights
☐ rear fog lights if visibility is less than 100 metres (328 feet)
☐ rear fog lights if visibility is more than 100 metres (328 feet)
☐ dipped headlights
☐ sidelights only

You must ensure that you can be seen by others on the road. Use your dipped headlights during the day if the visibility is bad. If you use your rear fog lights, don't forget to turn them off when the visibility improves.

7.27 Mark one answer

It is a very windy day and you are about to overtake a cyclist. What should you do?

☐ Overtake very closely
☐ Keep close as you pass
☐ Sound your horn repeatedly
☐ Allow extra room

Cyclists, and motorcyclists, are very vulnerable in crosswinds. They can easily be blown well off course and veer into your path. Always allow plenty of room when overtaking them. Passing too close could cause a draught and unbalance the rider.

8.1 Mark three answers

In which THREE of these situations may you overtake another vehicle on the left?

☐ When you are in a one-way street
☐ When approaching a motorway slip road where you will be turning off
☐ When the vehicle in front is signalling to turn right
☐ When a slower vehicle is travelling in the right-hand lane of a dual carriageway
☐ In slow-moving traffic queues when traffic in the right-hand lane is moving more slowly

At certain times of the day, traffic might be heavy. If traffic is moving slowly in queues and vehicles in the right-hand lane are moving more slowly, you may overtake on the left. Don't keep changing lanes to try and beat the queue.

8.2 Mark one answer

You are travelling in very heavy rain. Your overall stopping distance is likely to be

☐ doubled
☐ halved
☐ up to ten times greater
☐ no different

As well as visibility being reduced, the road will be extremely wet. This will reduce the grip the tyres have on the road and increase the distance it takes to stop. Double your separation distance.

8.3 Mark two answers

Which TWO of the following are correct? When overtaking at night you should

☐ wait until a bend so that you can see the oncoming headlights
☐ sound your horn twice before moving out
☐ be careful because you can see less
☐ beware of bends in the road ahead
☐ put headlights on full beam

Only overtake the vehicle in front if it's really necessary. At night the risks are increased due to the poor visibility. Don't overtake if there's a possibility of
• road junctions
• bends ahead
• the brow of a bridge or hill, except on a dual carriageway
• pedestrian crossings
• double white lines ahead
• vehicles changing direction
• any other potential hazard.

8.4 Mark one answer

When may you wait in a box junction?

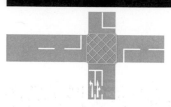

☐ When you are stationary in a queue of traffic
☐ When approaching a pelican crossing
☐ When approaching a zebra crossing
☐ When oncoming traffic prevents you turning right

The purpose of a box junction is to keep the junction clear by preventing vehicles from stopping in the path of crossing traffic.
You must not enter a box junction unless your exit is clear. But, you may enter the box and wait if you want to turn right and are only prevented from doing so by oncoming traffic.

8.5 Mark one answer

Which of these plates normally appear with this road sign?

☐ Humps for ½ mile

☐ Low Bridge

☐ Hump Bridge

☐ Soft Verge

Road humps are used to slow down the traffic. They are found in places where there are often pedestrians, such as
• in shopping areas
• near schools
• in residential areas.
Watch out for people close to the kerb or crossing the road.

8.6   Mark one answer

Traffic calming measures are used to

☐ stop road rage
☐ help overtaking
☐ slow traffic down
☐ help parking

Traffic calming measures are used to make the roads safer for vulnerable road users, such as cyclists, pedestrians and children. These can be designed as chicanes, road humps or other obstacles that encourage drivers and riders to slow down.

8.7   Mark one answer

You are on a motorway in fog. The left-hand edge of the motorway can be identified by reflective studs. What colour are they?

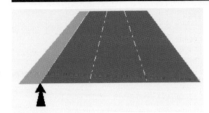

☐ Green
☐ Amber
☐ Red
☐ White

Be especially careful if you're on a motorway in fog. Reflective studs are used to help you in poor visibility. Different colours are used so that you'll know which lane you are in. These are
• red on the left-hand side of the road
• white between lanes
• amber on the right-hand edge of the carriageway
• green between the carriageway and slip roads.

8.8   Mark two answers

A rumble device is designed to

☐ give directions
☐ prevent cattle escaping
☐ alert you to low tyre pressure
☐ alert you to a hazard
☐ encourage you to reduce speed

A rumble device usually consists of raised markings or strips across the road. It gives an audible, visual and tactile warning of a hazard. These strips are found in places where traffic has constantly ignored warning or restriction signs. They are there for a good reason. Slow down and be ready to deal with a hazard.

8.9   Mark one answer

You have to make a journey in foggy conditions. You should

☐ follow other vehicles' tail lights closely
☐ avoid using dipped headlights
☐ leave plenty of time for your journey
☐ keep two seconds behind other vehicles

If you're planning to make a journey when it's foggy, listen to the weather reports on the radio or television. Don't travel if visibility is very poor or your trip isn't necessary.

If you do travel, leave plenty of time for your journey. If someone is expecting you at the other end, let them know that you'll be taking longer than normal to arrive.

8.10   Mark one answer

You are overtaking a car at night. You must be sure that

☐ you flash your headlights before overtaking
☐ you select a higher gear
☐ you have switched your lights to full beam before overtaking
☐ you do not dazzle other road users

To prevent your lights from dazzling the driver of the car in front, wait until you've overtaken before switching to full beam.

8.11 Mark one answer

You are on a road which has speed humps. A driver in front is travelling slower than you. You should

☐ sound your horn
☐ overtake as soon as you can
☐ flash your headlights
☐ slow down and stay behind

Be patient and stay behind the car in front. Normally you should not overtake other vehicles in traffic-calmed areas. If you overtake here your speed may exceed that which is safe along that road, defeating the purpose of the traffic calming measures.

8.12 Mark one answer

You see these markings on the road. Why are they there?

☐ To show a safe distance between vehicles
☐ To keep the area clear of traffic
☐ To make you aware of your speed
☐ To warn you to change direction

These lines may be painted on the road on the approach to a roundabout, village or a particular hazard. The lines are raised and painted yellow and their purpose is to make you aware of your speed. Reduce your speed in good time so that you avoid having to brake harshly over the last few metres before reaching the junction.

8.13 Mark three answers

Areas reserved for trams may have

☐ metal studs around them
☐ white line markings
☐ zigzag markings
☐ a different coloured surface
☐ yellow hatch markings
☐ a different surface texture

Trams can run on roads used by other vehicles and pedestrians. The part of the road used by the trams is known as the reserved area and this should be kept clear.

It has a coloured surface and is usually edged with white road markings. It might also have different surface texture.

8.14 Mark one answer

You see a vehicle coming towards you on a single-track road. You should

☐ go back to the main road
☐ do an emergency stop
☐ stop at a passing place
☐ put on your hazard warning lights

You must take extra care when on single track roads. You may not be able to see around bends due to high hedges or fences. Proceed with caution and expect to meet oncoming vehicles around the next bend. If you do, pull into or opposite a passing place.

8.15 Mark one answer

The road is wet. Why might a motorcyclist steer round drain covers on a bend?

☐ To avoid puncturing the tyres on the edge of the drain covers
☐ To prevent the motorcycle sliding on the metal drain covers
☐ To help judge the bend using the drain covers as marker points
☐ To avoid splashing pedestrians on the pavement

Other drivers or riders may have to change course due to the size or characteristics of their vehicle. Understanding this will help you to anticipate their actions.

Motorcyclists and cyclists will be checking the road ahead for uneven or slippery surfaces, especially in wet weather. They may need to move across their lane to avoid surface hazards such as potholes and drain covers.

8.16 Mark one answer

After this hazard you should test your brakes. Why is this?

☐ You will be on a slippery road
☐ Your brakes will be soaking wet
☐ You will be going down a long hill
☐ You will have just crossed a long bridge

A ford is a crossing over a stream that's shallow enough to go through. After you've gone through a ford or deep puddle the water will affect your brakes. To dry them out apply a light brake pressure while moving slowly. Don't travel at normal speeds until you are sure your brakes are working properly again.

8.17 Mark one answer

Why should you always reduce your speed when travelling in fog?

☐ The brakes do not work as well
☐ You will be dazzled by other headlights
☐ The engine will take longer to warm up
☐ It is more difficult to see events ahead

You won't be able to see as far ahead in fog as you can on a clear day. You will need to reduce your speed so that, if a hazard looms out of the fog, you have the time and space to take avoiding action. Travelling in fog is hazardous. If you can, try and delay your journey until it has cleared.

8.18 Mark two answers

Hills can affect the performance of your vehicle. Which TWO apply when driving up steep hills?

☐ Higher gears will pull better
☐ You will slow down sooner
☐ Overtaking will be easier
☐ The engine will work harder
☐ The steering will feel heavier

The engine will need more power to pull the vehicle up the hill. When approaching a steep hill you should select a lower gear to help maintain your speed. You should do this without hesitation, so that you don't lose too much speed before engaging the lower gear.

8.19 Mark one answer

You are driving on the motorway in windy conditions. When passing high-sided vehicles you should

☐ Increase your speed
☐ be wary of a sudden gust
☐ drive alongside very closely
☐ expect normal conditions

The draught caused by other vehicles could be strong enough to push you out of your lane. Keep both hands on the steering wheel to maintain full control.

8.20 Mark one answer

To correct a rear-wheel skid you should

☐ not steer at all
☐ steer away from it
☐ steer into it
☐ apply your handbrake

Prevention is better than cure, so it's important that you take every precaution to avoid a skid from starting.
If you feel the rear wheels of your vehicle beginning to skid, try to steer in the same direction to recover control. Don't brake suddenly – this will only make the situation worse.

8.21 Mark one answer

You are driving in fog. Why should you keep well back from the vehicle in front?

☐ In case it changes direction suddenly
☐ In case its fog lights dazzle you
☐ In case it stops suddenly
☐ In case its brake lights dazzle you

If you're following another road user in fog stay well back. The driver in front won't be able to see hazards until they're close and might brake suddenly. Another reason why it is important to maintain a good separation distance in fog is that the road surface is likely to be wet and slippery.

8.22 Mark one answer

You should switch your rear fog lights on when visibility drops below

☐ your overall stopping distance
☐ ten car lengths
☐ 200 metres (656 feet)
☐ 100 metres (328 feet)

If visibility falls below 100 metres (328 feet) in fog, switching on your rear fog lights will help following road users to see you. Don't forget to turn them off once visibility improves: their brightness might be mistaken for brake lights and they could dazzle other drivers.

8.23 Mark one answer

Whilst driving, the fog clears and you can see more clearly. You must remember to

☐ switch off the fog lights
☐ reduce your speed
☐ switch off the demister
☐ close any open windows

Bright rear fog lights might be mistaken for brake lights and could be misleading for the traffic behind.

8.24 Mark one answer

You have to park on the road in fog. You should

☐ leave sidelights on
☐ leave dipped headlights and fog lights on
☐ leave dipped headlights on
☐ leave main beam headlights on

If you have to park your vehicle in foggy conditions it's important that it can be seen by other road users. Try to find a place to park off the road. If this isn't possible leave it facing in the same direction as the traffic. Make sure that your lights are clean and that you leave your sidelights on.

8.25 Mark one answer

On a foggy day you unavoidably have to park your car on the road. You should

☐ leave your headlights on
☐ leave your fog lights on
☐ leave your sidelights on
☐ leave your hazard lights on

Ensure that your vehicle can be seen by other traffic. If possible, park your car off the road in a car park or driveway to avoid the extra risk to other road users.

8.26 Mark one answer

You are travelling at night. You are dazzled by headlights coming towards you. You should

☐ pull down your sun visor
☐ slow down or stop
☐ switch on your main beam headlights
☐ put your hand over your eyes

You will have additional hazards to deal with at night. Visibility may be very limited and the lights of oncoming vehicles can often dazzle you. When this happens don't close your eyes, swerve or flash your headlights, as this will also distract other drivers. It may help to focus on the left kerb, verge or lane line.

8.27 Mark one answer

Front fog lights may be used ONLY if

☐ visibility is seriously reduced
☐ they are fitted above the bumper
☐ they are not as bright as the headlights
☐ an audible warning device is used

Your vehicle should have a warning light on the dashboard which illuminates when the fog lights are being used. You need to be familiar with the layout of your dashboard so you are aware if they have been switched on in error, or you have forgotten to switch them off.

8.28 Mark one answer

Front fog lights may be used ONLY if

☐ your headlights are not working
☐ they are operated with rear fog lights
☐ they were fitted by the vehicle manufacturer
☐ visibility is seriously reduced

It is illegal to use fog lights unless visibility is seriously reduced, which is generally when you cannot see for more than 100 metres (328 feet). Check that they have been switched off when conditions improve.

8.29 Mark one answer

You are driving with your front fog lights switched on. Earlier fog has now cleared. What should you do?

☐ Leave them on if other drivers have their lights on
☐ Switch them off as long as visibility remains good
☐ Flash them to warn oncoming traffic that it is foggy
☐ Drive with them on instead of your headlights

Switch off your fog lights if the weather improves, but be prepared to use them again if visibility reduces to less than 100 metres (328 feet).

8.30 Mark one answer

Front fog lights should be used ONLY when

☐ travelling in very light rain
☐ visibility is seriously reduced
☐ daylight is fading
☐ driving after midnight

Fog lights will help others see you, but remember, they must only be used if visibility is seriously reduced to less than 100 metres (328 feet).

8.31 Mark three answers

You forget to switch off your rear fog lights when the fog has cleared. This may

☐ dazzle other road users
☐ reduce battery life
☐ cause brake lights to be less clear
☐ be breaking the law
☐ seriously affect engine power

Don't forget to switch off your fog lights when the weather improves. You could be prosecuted for driving with them on in good visibility. The high intensity of the rear fog lights can look like brake lights, and on a high speed road this can cause other road users to brake unnecessarily.

8.32 Mark one answer

You have been driving in thick fog which has now cleared. You must switch OFF your rear fog lights because

☐ they use a lot of power from the battery
☐ they make your brake lights less clear
☐ they will cause dazzle in your rear view mirrors
☐ they may not be properly adjusted

It is essential that the traffic behind is given a clear warning when you brake. In good visibility, your rear fog lights can make it hard for others to see your brake lights. Make sure you switch off your fog lights when the visibility improves.

8.33 Mark one answer

Front fog lights should be used

☐ when visibility is reduced to 100 metres (328 feet)
☐ as a warning to oncoming traffic
☐ when driving during the hours of darkness
☐ in any conditions and at any time

When visibility is seriously reduced, switch on your fog lights if you have them fitted. It is essential not only that you can see ahead, but also that other road users are able to see you.

8.34 Mark one answer

Using rear fog lights in clear daylight will

☐ be useful when towing a trailer
☐ give extra protection
☐ dazzle other drivers
☐ make following drivers keep back

Rear fog lights shine brighter than normal rear lights so that they show up in reduced visibility. When the weather is clear they could dazzle the driver behind, so switch them off.

8.35 Mark one answer

Using front fog lights in clear daylight will

☐ flatten the battery
☐ dazzle other drivers
☐ improve your visibility
☐ increase your awareness

Fog lights can be brighter than normal dipped headlights. If the weather has improved turn them off to avoid dazzling other road users.

8.36 Mark one answer

You may use front fog lights with headlights ONLY when visibility is reduced to less than

☐ 100 metres (328 feet)
☐ 200 metres (656 feet)
☐ 300 metres (984 feet)
☐ 400 metres (1312 feet)

It is an offence to use fog lights if the visibility is better than 100 metres (328 feet). Switch front fog lights off if the fog clears to avoid dazzling other road users, but be aware that the fog may be patchy.

8.37 Mark one answer

Chains can be fitted to your wheels to help prevent

☐ damage to the road surface
☐ wear to the tyres
☐ skidding in deep snow
☐ the brakes locking

Snow chains can be fitted to your tyres during snowy conditions. They can help you to move off from rest or to keep moving in deep snow. You will still need to adjust your driving according to the road conditions at the time.

8.38 Mark one answer

How can you use the engine of your vehicle to control your speed?

☐ By changing to a lower gear
☐ By selecting reverse gear
☐ By changing to a higher gear
☐ By selecting neutral

You should brake and slow down before selecting a lower gear. The gear can then be used to keep the speed low and help you control the vehicle. This is particularly helpful on long downhill stretches, where brake fade can occur if the brakes overheat.

8.39 Mark one answer

Why could keeping the clutch down or selecting neutral for long periods of time be dangerous?

☐ Fuel spillage will occur
☐ Engine damage may be caused
☐ You will have less steering and braking control
☐ It will wear tyres out more quickly

Letting your vehicle roll or coast in neutral reduces your control over steering and braking. This can be dangerous on downhill slopes where your vehicle could pick up speed very quickly.

8.40 Mark one answer

You are driving on an icy road. What distance should you drive from the car in front?

☐ four times the normal distance
☐ six times the normal distance
☐ eight times the normal distance
☐ ten times the normal distance

Don't travel in icy or snowy weather unless your journey is necessary.

Drive extremely carefully when roads are or may be icy. Stopping distances can be ten times greater than on dry roads.

8.41 Mark one answer

You are on a well-lit motorway at night. You must

☐ use only your sidelights
☐ always use your headlights
☐ always use rear fog lights
☐ use headlights only in bad weather

If you're driving on a motorway at night or in poor visibility, you must always use your headlights, even if the road is well-lit. The other road users in front must be able to see you in their mirrors.

8.42 Mark one answer

You are on a motorway at night with other vehicles just ahead of you. Which lights should you have on?

☐ Front fog lights
☐ Main beam headlights
☐ Sidelights only
☐ Dipped headlights

If you're driving behind other traffic at night on the motorway, leave a two-second time gap and use dipped headlights. Full beam will dazzle the other drivers. Your headlights' beam should fall short of the vehicle in front.

8.43 Mark three answers

Which THREE of the following will affect your stopping distance?

☐ How fast you are going
☐ The tyres on your vehicle
☐ The time of day
☐ The weather
☐ The street lighting

There are several factors that can affect the distance it takes to stop your vehicle. Adjust your driving to take account of how the weather conditions could affect your tyres' grip on the road.

8.44 Mark one answer

You are on a motorway at night. You MUST have your headlights switched on unless

☐ there are vehicles close in front of you
☐ you are travelling below 50 mph
☐ the motorway is lit
☐ your vehicle is broken down on the hard shoulder

Always use your headlights at night on a motorway unless you have stopped on the hard shoulder. If you break down and have to stop on the hard shoulder, switch off the headlights but leave the sidelights on so that other road users can see your vehicle.

8.45 Mark one answer

You will feel the effects of engine braking when you

☐ only use the handbrake
☐ only use neutral
☐ change to a lower gear
☐ change to a higher gear

When going downhill, prolonged use of the brakes can cause them to overheat and lose their effectiveness. Changing to a lower gear will assist your braking.

8.46 Mark one answer

Daytime visibility is poor but not seriously reduced. You should switch on

☐ headlights and fog lights
☐ front fog lights
☐ dipped headlights
☐ rear fog lights

Only use your fog lights when visibility is seriously reduced. Use dipped headlights in poor conditions.

8.47 Mark one answer

Why are vehicles fitted with rear fog lights?

☐ To be seen when driving at high speed
☐ To use if broken down in a dangerous position
☐ To make them more visible in thick fog
☐ To warn drivers following closely to drop back

Rear fog lights make it easier to spot a vehicle ahead in foggy conditions. Avoid the temptation to use other vehicles' lights as a guide, as they may give you a false sense of security.

8.48 Mark one answer

While you are driving in fog, it becomes necessary to use front fog lights. You should

☐ only turn them on in heavy traffic conditions
☐ remember not to use them on motorways
☐ only use them on dual carriageways
☐ remember to switch them off as visibility improves

It is an offence to have your fog lights on in conditions other than seriously reduced visibility, ie less than 100 metres (328 feet).

8.49 Mark one answer

When snow is falling heavily you should

☐ only drive with your hazard lights on
☐ not drive unless you have a mobile phone
☐ only drive when your journey is short
☐ not drive unless it is essential

Consider if the increased risk is worth it. If the weather conditions are bad and your journey isn't essential, then stay at home.

8.50 Mark one answer

You are driving down a long steep hill. You suddenly notice your brakes are not working as well as normal. What is the usual cause of this?

☐ The brakes overheating
☐ Air in the brake fluid
☐ Oil on the brakes
☐ Badly adjusted brakes

This is more likely to happen on vehicles fitted with drum brakes but can apply to disc brakes as well. Using a lower gear will assist the braking and help you to keep control of your vehicle.

8.51 Mark two answers

You have to make a journey in fog. What are the TWO most important things you should do before you set out?

☐ Top up the radiator with anti-freeze
☐ Make sure that you have a warning triangle in the vehicle
☐ Check that your lights are working
☐ Check the battery
☐ Make sure that the windows are clean

Don't drive in fog unless you really have to. Adjust your driving to the conditions. You should always be able to pull up within the distance you can see ahead.

8.52 Mark one answer

You have just driven out of fog. Visibility is now good. You MUST

☐ switch off all your fog lights
☐ keep your rear fog lights on
☐ keep your front fog lights on
☐ leave fog lights on in case fog returns

You MUST turn off your fog lights if visibility is over 100 metres (328 feet). However, be prepared for the fact that the fog may be patchy.

8.53 Mark one answer

You may drive with front fog lights switched on

☐ when visibility is less than 100 metres (328 feet)
☐ at any time to be noticed
☐ instead of headlights on high speed roads
☐ when dazzled by the lights of oncoming vehicles

Only use front fog lights if the distance you are able to see is less than 100 metres (328 feet). Turn off your fog lights as the visibility improves.

8.54 Mark two answers

Why is it dangerous to leave rear fog lights on when they are not needed?

☐ Brake lights are less clear
☐ Following drivers can be dazzled
☐ Electrical systems could be overloaded
☐ Direction indicators may not work properly
☐ The battery could fail

If your rear fog lights are left on when it isn't foggy, the glare they cause makes it difficult for road users behind to know whether you are braking or you have just forgotten to turn off your rear fog lights.

This can be a particular problem on wet roads and on motorways. If you leave your rear fog lights on at night, road users behind you are likely to be dazzled and this could put them at risk.

8.55 Mark one answer

Holding the clutch pedal down or rolling in neutral for too long while driving will

☐ use more fuel
☐ cause the engine to overheat
☐ reduce your control
☐ improve tyre wear

Holding the clutch down or staying in neutral for too long will cause your vehicle to freewheel. This is known as 'coasting' and it is dangerous as it reduces your control of the vehicle.

8.56 Mark one answer

You are driving down a steep hill. Why could keeping the clutch down or rolling in neutral for too long be dangerous?

☐ Fuel consumption will be higher
☐ Your vehicle will pick up speed
☐ It will damage the engine
☐ It will wear tyres out more quickly

Driving in neutral or with the clutch down for long periods is known as 'coasting'.
   There will be no engine braking and your vehicle will pick up speed on downhill slopes. Coasting can be very dangerous because it reduces steering and braking control.

8.57 Mark two answers

What are TWO main reasons why coasting downhill is wrong?

☐ Fuel consumption will be higher
☐ The vehicle will get faster
☐ It puts more wear and tear on the tyres
☐ You have less braking and steering control
☐ It damages the engine

Coasting is when you allow the vehicle to freewheel in neutral or with the clutch pedal depressed. Doing this gives you less control over the vehicle. It's especially important not to let your vehicle coast when approaching hazards such as junctions and bends and when travelling downhill.

8.58 Mark four answers

Which FOUR of the following may apply when dealing with this hazard?

☐ It could be more difficult in winter
☐ Use a low gear and drive slowly
☐ Use a high gear to prevent wheelspin
☐ Test your brakes afterwards
☐ Always switch on fog lamps
☐ There may be a depth gauge

During the winter the stream is likely to flood. It is also possible that in extremely cold weather it could ice over. Assess the situation carefully before you drive through. If you drive a vehicle with low suspension you may have to find a different route.

8.59 Mark one answer

Why is travelling in neutral for long distances (known as coasting) wrong?

☐ It will cause the car to skid
☐ It will make the engine stall
☐ The engine will run faster
☐ There is no engine braking

Try to look ahead and read the road. Plan your approach to junctions and select the correct gear in good time. This will give you the control you need to deal with any hazards that occur.
   You'll coast a little every time you change gear. This can't be avoided, but it should be kept to a minimum.

8.60 Mark one answer

When MUST you use dipped headlights during the day?

☐ All the time
☐ Along narrow streets
☐ In poor visibility
☐ When parking

You MUST use dipped headlights and/or fog lights in fog when visibility is seriously reduced to 100 metres (328 feet) or less. You should use dipped headlights, but NOT fog lights, when visibility is poor, such as in heavy rain.

8.61 Mark one answer

You are braking on a wet road. Your vehicle begins to skid. It does not have anti-lock brakes. What is the FIRST thing you should do?

☐ Quickly pull up the handbrake
☐ Release the footbrake
☐ Push harder on the brake pedal
☐ Gently use the accelerator

If the skid has been caused by braking too hard for the conditions, release the brake. You may then need to reapply and release the brake again. You may need to do this a number of times. This will allow the wheels to turn and so limit the skid. Skids are much easier to get into than they are to get out of. Prevention is better than cure. Stay alert to the road and weather conditions. Drive so that you can stop within the distance you can see to be clear.

8.62 Mark two answers

Using rear fog lights on a clear dry night will

☐ reduce glare from the road surface
☐ make your brake lights less visible
☐ give a better view of the road ahead
☐ dazzle following drivers
☐ help your indicators to be seen more clearly

You should not use rear fog lights unless visibility is seriously reduced. A warning light will show on the dashboard to indicate when your rear fog lights are on. You should know the meaning of all the lights on your dashboard and check them before you move off and as you drive.

Motorway rules

9.1   Mark one answer

When joining a motorway you must always

☐ use the hard shoulder
☐ stop at the end of the acceleration lane
☐ come to a stop before joining the motorway
☐ give way to traffic already on the motorway

You should give way to traffic already on the motorway. Where possible they may move over to let you in but don't force your way into the traffic stream. The traffic may be travelling at high speed so you should match your speed to fit in.

9.2   Mark one answer

What is the national speed limit for cars and motorcycles in the centre lane of a three-lane motorway?

☐ 40 mph
☐ 50 mph
☐ 60 mph
☐ 70 mph

Unless shown otherwise, the speed limit on a motorway applies to all the lanes. Look out for any signs of speed limit changes due to roadworks or traffic flow control.

9.3   Mark one answer

What is the national speed limit on motorways for cars and motorcycles?

☐ 30 mph
☐ 50 mph
☐ 60 mph
☐ 70 mph

Travelling at the national speed limit doesn't allow you to hog the right-hand lane. Always use the left-hand lane whenever possible. When leaving a motorway get into the left-hand lane well before your exit. Reduce your speed on the slip road and look out for sharp bends or curves and traffic queueing at roundabouts.

9.4   Mark one answer

The left-hand lane on a three-lane motorway is for use by

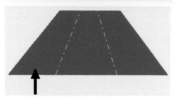

☐ any vehicle
☐ large vehicles only
☐ emergency vehicles only
☐ slow vehicles only

On a motorway all traffic should use the left-hand lane unless overtaking. Use the centre or right-hand lanes if you need to overtake. If you're overtaking a number of slower vehicles move back to the left-hand lane when you're safely past. Check your mirrors frequently and don't stay in the middle or right-hand lane if the left-hand lane is free.

9.5   Mark one answer

Which of these IS NOT allowed to travel in the right-hand lane of a three-lane motorway?

☐ A small delivery van
☐ A motorcycle
☐ A vehicle towing a trailer
☐ A motorcycle and side-car

A vehicle with a trailer is restricted to 60 mph. For this reason it isn't allowed in the right-hand lane as it might hold up the faster-moving traffic that wishes to overtake in that lane.

9.6 Mark one answer

You break down on a motorway. You need to call for help. Why may it be better to use an emergency roadside telephone rather than a mobile phone?

☐ It connects you to a local garage
☐ Using a mobile phone will distract other drivers
☐ It allows easy location by the emergency services
☐ Mobile phones do not work on motorways

On a motorway it is best to use a roadside emergency telephone so that the emergency services are able to locate you easily. The nearest telephone is shown by an arrow on marker posts at the edge of the hard shoulder. If you use a mobile, they will need to know your exact location.

Before you call, find out the number on the nearest marker post. This number will identify your exact location.

9.7 Mark one answer

After a breakdown you need to rejoin the main carriageway of a motorway from the hard shoulder. You should

☐ move out onto the carriageway then build up your speed
☐ move out onto the carriageway using your hazard lights
☐ gain speed on the hard shoulder before moving out onto the carriageway
☐ wait on the hard shoulder until someone flashes their headlights at you

Wait for a safe gap in the traffic before you move out. Indicate your intention and use the hard shoulder to gain speed but don't force your way into the traffic.

9.8 Mark one answer

A crawler lane on a motorway is found

☐ on a steep gradient
☐ before a service area
☐ before a junction
☐ along the hard shoulder

Slow-moving, large vehicles might slow down the progress of other traffic. On a steep gradient this extra lane is provided for these slow-moving vehicles to allow the faster-moving traffic to flow more easily.

9.9 Mark one answer

What do these motorway signs show?

☐ They are countdown markers to a bridge
☐ They are distance markers to the next telephone
☐ They are countdown markers to the next exit
☐ They warn of a police control ahead

The exit from a motorway is indicated by countdown markers. These are positioned 90 metres (100 yards) apart, the first being 270 metres (300 yards) from the start of the slip road. Move into the left-hand lane well before you reach the start of the slip road.

9.10 Mark one answer

On a motorway the amber reflective studs can be found between

☐ the hard shoulder and the carriageway
☐ the acceleration lane and the carriageway
☐ the central reservation and the carriageway
☐ each pair of the lanes

On motorways reflective studs are located into the road to help you in the dark and in conditions of poor visibility. Amber-coloured studs are found on the right-hand edge of the main carriageway, next to the central reservation.

9.11 Mark one answer

What colour are the reflective studs between the lanes on a motorway?

☐ Green
☐ Amber
☐ White
☐ Red

White studs are found between the lanes on motorways. The light from your headlights is reflected back and this is especially useful in bad weather, when visibility is restricted.

9.12 Mark one answer

What colour are the reflective studs between a motorway and its slip road?

☐ Amber
☐ White
☐ Green
☐ Red

The studs between the carriageway and the hard shoulder are normally red. These change to green where there is a slip road. They will help you identify slip roads when visibility is poor or when it is dark.

9.13 Mark one answer

You have broken down on a motorway. To find the nearest emergency telephone you should always walk

☐ with the traffic flow
☐ facing oncoming traffic
☐ in the direction shown on the marker posts
☐ in the direction of the nearest exit

Along the hard shoulder there are marker posts at 100-metre intervals. These will direct you to the nearest emergency telephone.

9.14 Mark one answer

You are joining a motorway. Why is it important to make full use of the slip road?

☐ Because there is space available to turn round if you need to
☐ To allow you direct access to the overtaking lanes
☐ To build up a speed similar to traffic on the motorway
☐ Because you can continue on the hard shoulder

Try to join the motorway without affecting the progress of the traffic already travelling on it. Always give way to traffic already on the motorway. At busy times you may have to slow down to merge into slow-moving traffic.

9.15 Mark one answer

How should you use the emergency telephone on a motorway?

☐ Stay close to the carriageway
☐ Face the oncoming traffic
☐ Keep your back to the traffic
☐ Stand on the hard shoulder

Traffic is passing you at speed. If the draught from a large lorry catches you by surprise it could blow you off balance and even onto the carriageway. By facing the oncoming traffic you can see approaching lorries and so be prepared for their draught. You are also in a position to see other hazards approaching.

9.16 Mark one answer

You are on a motorway. What colour are the reflective studs on the left of the carriageway?

☐ Green
☐ Red
☐ White
☐ Amber

Red studs are placed between the edge of the carriageway and the hard shoulder. Where slip roads leave or join the motorway the studs are green.

9.17 Mark one answer

On a three-lane motorway which lane should you normally use?

☐ Left
☐ Right
☐ Centre
☐ Either the right or centre

On a three-lane motorway you should travel in the left-hand lane unless you're overtaking. This applies regardless of the speed at which you're travelling.

9.18 Mark one answer

When going through a contraflow system on a motorway you should

☐ ensure that you do not exceed 30 mph
☐ keep a good distance from the vehicle ahead
☐ switch lanes to keep the traffic flowing
☐ stay close to the vehicle ahead to reduce queues

There's likely to be a speed restriction in force. Keep to this. Don't
• switch lanes
• get too close to traffic in front of you.
Be aware there will be no permanent barrier between you and the oncoming traffic.

9.19 Mark one answer

You are on a three-lane motorway. There are red reflective studs on your left and white ones to your right. Where are you?

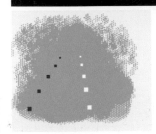

☐ In the right-hand lane
☐ In the middle lane
☐ On the hard shoulder
☐ In the left-hand lane

The colours of the reflective studs on the motorway and their locations are
• red – between the hard shoulder and the carriageway
• white – lane markings
• amber – between the edge of the carriageway and the central reservation
• green – along slip road exits and entrances
• bright green/yellow – roadworks and contraflow systems.

9.20 Mark one answer

You are approaching roadworks on a motorway. What should you do?

☐ Speed up to clear the area quickly
☐ Always use the hard shoulder
☐ Obey all speed limits
☐ Stay very close to the vehicle in front

Collisions can often happen at roadworks. Be aware of the speed limits, slow down in good time and keep your distance from the vehicle in front.

9.21 Mark four answers

Which FOUR of these must NOT use motorways?

☐ Learner car drivers
☐ Motorcycles over 50cc
☐ Double-deck buses
☐ Farm tractors
☐ Horse riders
☐ Cyclists

In addition, motorways MUST NOT be used by, pedestrians, motorcycles under 50 cc, certain slow-moving vehicles without permission, and invalid carriages weighing less than 254 kg (560 lbs).

9.22 Mark four answers

Which FOUR of these must NOT use motorways?

☐ Learner car drivers
☐ Motorcycles over 50cc
☐ Double-deck buses
☐ Farm tractors
☐ Learner motorcyclists
☐ Cyclists

Learner car drivers and motorcyclists are not allowed on the motorway until they have passed their practical test.
Motorways have rules that you need to know before you venture out for the first time. When you've passed your practical test it's a good idea to have some lessons on motorways. Check with your instructor about this.

9.23 Mark one answer

Immediately after joining a motorway you should normally

☐ try to overtake
☐ re-adjust your mirrors
☐ position your vehicle in the centre lane
☐ keep in the left-hand lane

Stay in the left-hand lane long enough to get used to the higher speeds of motorway traffic.

9.24 Mark one answer

What is the right-hand lane used for on a three-lane motorway?

☐ Emergency vehicles only
☐ Overtaking
☐ Vehicles towing trailers
☐ Coaches only

You should keep to the left and only use the right-hand lane if you're passing slower-moving traffic.

9.25 Mark one answer

What should you use the hard shoulder of a motorway for?

☐ Stopping in an emergency
☐ Leaving the motorway
☐ Stopping when you are tired
☐ Joining the motorway

Don't use the hard shoulder for stopping unless it is an emergency. If you want to stop for any other reason go to the next exit or service station.

9.26 Mark one answer

You are in the right-hand lane on a motorway. You see these overhead signs. This means

☐ move to the left and reduce your speed to 50 mph
☐ there are roadworks 50 metres (55 yards) ahead
☐ use the hard shoulder until you have passed the hazard
☐ leave the motorway at the next exit

You MUST obey this sign. There might not be any visible signs of a problem ahead. However, there might be queueing traffic or another hazard which you cannot yet see.

9.27 Mark one answer

You are allowed to stop on a motorway when you

☐ need to walk and get fresh air
☐ wish to pick up hitchhikers
☐ are told to do so by flashing red lights
☐ need to use a mobile telephone

You MUST stop if there are red lights flashing above every lane on the motorway.

However, if any of the other lanes do not show flashing red lights or red cross you may move into that lane and continue if it is safe to do so.

9.28 Mark one answer

You are travelling along the left-hand lane of a three-lane motorway. Traffic is joining from a slip road. You should

☐ race the other vehicles
☐ move to another lane
☐ maintain a steady speed
☐ switch on your hazard flashers

You should move to another lane if it is safe to do so. This can greatly assist the flow of traffic joining the motorway, especially at peak times.

9.29 Mark one answer

A basic rule when on motorways is

☐ use the lane that has least traffic
☐ keep to the left-hand lane unless overtaking
☐ overtake on the side that is clearest
☐ try to keep above 50 mph to prevent congestion

You should normally travel in the left-hand lane unless you are overtaking a slower-moving vehicle. When you are past that vehicle move back into the left-hand lane as soon as it's safe to do so. Don't cut across in front of the vehicle that you're overtaking.

9.30 Mark one answer

On motorways you should never overtake on the left unless

☐ you can see well ahead that the hard shoulder is clear
☐ the traffic in the right-hand lane is signalling right
☐ you warn drivers behind by signalling left
☐ there is a queue of slow-moving traffic to your right that is moving more slowly than you are

Only overtake on the left if traffic is moving slowly in queues and the traffic on your right is moving more slowly than the traffic in your lane.

9.31 Mark one answer　　　　NI EXEMPT

Motorway emergency telephones are usually linked to the police. In some areas they are now linked to

☐ the Highways Agency Control Centre
☐ the Driver Vehicle Licensing Agency
☐ the Driving Standards Agency
☐ the local Vehicle Registration Office

In some areas motorway telephones are now linked to a Highways Agency Control Centre, instead of the police. Highways Agency Traffic Officers work in partnership with the police and assist at motorway emergencies and incidents. They are recognised by a high-visibility orange and yellow jacket and high-visibility vehicle with yellow and black chequered markings.

9.32 Mark one answer
An Emergency Refuge Area is an area

☐ on a motorway for use in cases of emergency or breakdown
☐ for use if you think you will be involved in a road rage incident
☐ on a motorway for a police patrol to park and watch traffic
☐ for construction and road workers to store emergency equipment

Emergency Refuge Areas may be found at the side of the hard shoulder about 500 metres apart. If you break down you should use them rather than the hard shoulder if you are able. When re-joining the motorway you must remember to take extra care especially when the hard shoulder is being used as a running lane within an Active Traffic Management area. Try to match your speed to that of traffic in the lane you are joining.

9.33 Mark one answer
What is an Emergency Refuge Area on a motorway for?

☐ An area to park in when you want to use a mobile phone
☐ To use in cases of emergency or breakdown
☐ For an emergency recovery vehicle to park in a contra-flow system
☐ To drive in when there is queuing traffic ahead

In cases of breakdown or emergency try to get your vehicle into an Emergency Refuge Area. This is safer than just stopping on the hard shoulder as it gives you greater distance from the main carriageway. If you are able to re-join the motorway you must take extra care, especially when the hard shoulder is being used as a running lane.

9.34 Mark one answer   NI EXEMPT
Highways Agency Traffic Officers

☐ will not be able to assist at a breakdown or emergency
☐ are not able to stop and direct anyone on a motorway
☐ will tow a broken down vehicle and it's passengers home
☐ are able to stop and direct anyone on a motorway

Highways Agency Traffic Officers (HATOs) are able to stop and direct traffic on most motorways and some 'A' class roads. They work in partnership with the police at motorway incidents and provide a highly-trained and visible service. Their role is to help keep traffic moving and make your journey as safe and reliable as possible. They are recognised by an orange and yellow jacket and their vehicle has yellow and black markings.

9.35 Mark one answer   NI EXEMPT
You are on a motorway. A red cross is displayed above the hard shoulder. What does this mean?

☐ Pull up in this lane to answer your mobile phone
☐ Use this lane as a running lane
☐ This lane can be used if you need a rest
☐ You should not travel in this lane

Active Traffic Management schemes are being introduced on motorways. Within these areas at certain times the hard shoulder will be used as a running lane. A red cross above the hard shoulder shows that this lane should NOT be used, except for emergencies and breakdowns.

9.36 Mark one answer   NI EXEMPT
You are on a motorway in an Active Traffic Management (ATM) area. A mandatory speed limit is displayed above the hard shoulder. What does this mean?

☐ You should not travel in this lane
☐ The hard shoulder can be used as a running lane
☐ You can park on the hard shoulder if you feel tired
☐ You can pull up in this lane to answer a mobile phone

A mandatory speed limit sign above the hard shoulder shows that it can be used as a running lane between junctions. You must stay within the speed limit. Look out for vehicles that may have broken down and could be blocking the hard shoulder.

9.37 Mark one answer   NI EXEMPT

The aim of an Active Traffic Management scheme on a motorway is to

☐ prevent overtaking
☐ reduce rest stops
☐ prevent tailgating
☐ reduce congestion

Active Traffic Management schemes are intended to reduce congestion and make journey times more reliable. In these areas the hard shoulder may be used as a running lane to ease congestion at peak times or in the event of an incident. It may appear that you could travel faster for a short distance, but keeping traffic flow at a constant speed may improve your journey time.

9.38 Mark one answer   NI EXEMPT

You are in an Active Traffic Management area on a motorway. When the Actively Managed mode is operating

☐ speed limits are only advisory
☐ the national speed limit will apply
☐ the speed limit is always 30 mph
☐ all speed limit signals are set

When an Active Traffic Management (ATM) scheme is operating on a motorway you MUST follow the mandatory instructions shown on the gantries above each lane. This includes the hard shoulder.

9.39 Mark one answer   NI EXEMPT

You are travelling on a motorway. A red cross is shown above the hard shoulder. What does this mean?

☐ Use this lane as a rest area
☐ Use this as a normal running lane
☐ Do not use this lane to travel in
☐ National speed limit applies in this lane

When a red cross is shown above the hard shoulder it should only be used for breakdowns or emergencies. Within Active Traffic Management (ATM) areas the hard shoulder may sometimes be used as a running lane. Speed limit signs directly above the hard shoulder will show that it's open.

9.40 Mark one answer

Why can it be an advantage for traffic speed to stay constant over a longer distance?

☐ You will do more stop-start driving
☐ You will use far more fuel
☐ You will be able to use more direct routes
☐ Your overall journey time will normally improve

When traffic travels at a constant speed over a longer distance, journey times normally improve. You may feel that you could travel faster for short periods but this won't generally improve your overall journey time. Signs will show the maximum speed at which you should travel.

9.41 Mark one answer   NI EXEMPT

You should not normally travel on the hard shoulder of a motorway. When can you use it?

☐ When taking the next exit
☐ When traffic is stopped
☐ When signs direct you to
☐ When traffic is slow moving

Normally you should only use the hard shoulder for emergencies and breakdowns, and at roadworks when signs direct you to do so. Active Traffic Management (ATM) areas are being introduced to ease traffic congestion. In these areas the hard shoulder may be used as a running lane when speed limit signs are shown directly above.

9.42 Mark one answer

For what reason may you use the right-hand lane of a motorway?

☐ For keeping out of the way of lorries
☐ For travelling at more than 70 mph
☐ For turning right
☐ For overtaking other vehicles

The right-hand lane of the motorway is for overtaking.
Sometimes you may be directed into a right-hand lane as a result of roadworks or a traffic incident. This will be indicated by signs or officers directing the traffic.

9.43 Mark one answer
On a motorway what is used to reduce traffic bunching?

☐ Variable speed limits
☐ Contraflow systems
☐ National speed limits
☐ Lane closures

Congestion can be reduced by keeping traffic at a constant speed. At busy times maximum speed limits are displayed on overhead gantries. These can be varied quickly depending on the amount of traffic.

By keeping to a constant speed on busy sections of motorway overall journey times are normally improved.

9.44 Mark three answers
When should you stop on a motorway?

☐ If you have to read a map
☐ When you are tired and need a rest
☐ If red lights show above every lane
☐ When told to by the police
☐ If your mobile phone rings
☐ When signalled by a Highways Agency Traffic Officer

There are some occasions when you may have to stop on the carriageway of a motorway. These include when being signalled by the police or a Highways Agency Traffic Officer, when flashing red lights show above every lane and in traffic jams.

9.45 Mark one answer
When may you stop on a motorway?

☐ If you have to read a map
☐ When you are tired and need a rest
☐ If your mobile phone rings
☐ In an emergency or breakdown

You should not normally stop on a motorway but there may be occasions when you need to do so. If you are unfortunate enough to break down make every effort to pull up on the hard shoulder.

9.46 Mark one answer   NI EXEMPT
You are travelling on a motorway. Unless signs show a lower speed limit you must NOT exceed

☐ 50 mph
☐ 60 mph
☐ 70 mph
☐ 80 mph

The national speed limit for a car or motorcycle on the motorway is 70 mph.

Lower speed limits may be in force, for example at roadworks, so look out for the signs. Variable speed limits operate in some areas to control very busy stretches of motorway. The speed limit may change depending on the volume of traffic.

9.47 Mark one answer
Motorway emergency telephones are usually linked to the police. In some areas they are now linked to

☐ the local ambulance service
☐ a Highways Agency control centre
☐ the local fire brigade
☐ a breakdown service control centre

The controller will ask you
- the make and colour of your vehicle
- whether you are a member of an emergency breakdown service
- the number shown on the emergency telephone casing
- whether you are travelling alone.

9.48 Mark one answer
You are on a motorway. There are red flashing lights above every lane. You must

☐ pull onto the hard shoulder
☐ slow down and watch for further signals
☐ leave at the next exit
☐ stop and wait

Red flashing lights above every lane mean you must not go on any further. You'll also see a red cross illuminated. Stop and wait.

Don't
- change lanes
- continue
- pull onto the hard shoulder (unless in an emergency).

9.49 Mark one answer · NI EXEMPT

You are on a three-lane motorway. A red cross is shown above the hard shoulder and mandatory speed limits above all other lanes. This means

- ☐ the hard shoulder can be used as a rest area if you feel tired
- ☐ the hard shoulder is for emergency or breakdown use only
- ☐ the hard shoulder can be used as a normal running lane
- ☐ the hard shoulder has a speed limit of 50 mph

A red cross above the hard shoulder shows it is closed as a running lane and should only be used for emergencies or breakdowns. At busy times within an Active Traffic Management (ATM) area the hard shoulder may be used as a running lane.

This will be shown by a mandatory speed limit on the gantry above.

9.50 Mark one answer · NI EXEMPT

You are on a three-lane motorway and see this sign. It means you can use

- ☐ any lane except the hard shoulder
- ☐ the hard shoulder only
- ☐ the three right hand lanes only
- ☐ all the lanes including the hard shoulder

Mandatory speed limit signs above all lanes including the hard shoulder, show that you are in an Active Traffic Management (ATM) area. In this case you can use the hard shoulder as a running lane. You must stay within the speed limit shown. Look out for any vehicles that may have broken down and be blocking the hard shoulder.

9.51 Mark one answer

You are travelling on a motorway. You decide you need a rest. You should

- ☐ stop on the hard shoulder
- ☐ pull in at the nearest service area
- ☐ pull up on a slip road
- ☐ park on the central reservation

If you feel tired stop at the nearest service area. If it's too far away leave the motorway at the next exit and find a safe place to stop. You must not stop on the carriageway or hard shoulder of a motorway except in an emergency, in a traffic queue, when signalled to do so by a police or enforcement officer, or by traffic signals. Plan your journey so that you have regular rest stops.

9.52 Mark one answer

You are on a motorway. You become tired and decide you need to rest. What should you do?

- ☐ Stop on the hard shoulder
- ☐ Pull up on a slip road
- ☐ Park on the central reservation
- ☐ Leave at the next exit

Ideally you should plan your journey so that you have regular rest stops. If you do become tired leave at the next exit, or pull in at a service area if this is sooner.

9.53 Mark one answer

You are towing a trailer on a motorway. What is your maximum speed limit?

- ☐ 40 mph
- ☐ 50 mph
- ☐ 60 mph
- ☐ 70 mph

Don't forget that you're towing a trailer. If you're towing a small, light, trailer, it won't reduce your vehicle's performance by very much. However, strong winds or buffeting from large vehicles might cause the trailer to snake from side to side. Be aware of your speed and don't exceed the lower limit imposed.

9.54 Mark one answer

The left-hand lane of a motorway should be used for

☐ breakdowns and emergencies only
☐ overtaking slower traffic in the other lanes
☐ slow vehicles only
☐ normal driving

You should keep to the left-hand lane whenever possible. Only use the other lanes for overtaking or when directed by signals. Using other lanes when the left-hand lane is empty can frustrate drivers behind you.

9.55 Mark one answer

You are driving on a motorway. You have to slow down quickly due to a hazard. You should

☐ switch on your hazard lights
☐ switch on your headlights
☐ sound your horn
☐ flash your headlights

Using your hazard lights, as well as brake lights, will give following traffic an extra warning of the problem ahead. Only use them for long enough to ensure that your warning has been seen.

9.56 Mark one answer

You get a puncture on the motorway. You manage to get your vehicle onto the hard shoulder. You should

☐ change the wheel yourself immediately
☐ use the emergency telephone and call for assistance
☐ try to wave down another vehicle for help
☐ only change the wheel if you have a passenger to help you

Due to the danger from passing traffic you should park as far to the left as you can and leave the vehicle by the nearside door.

Do not attempt even simple repairs. Instead walk to an emergency telephone on your side of the road and phone for assistance.

While waiting for assistance to arrive wait near your car, keeping well away from the carriageway and hard shoulder.

9.57 Mark one answer

You are driving on a motorway. By mistake, you go past the exit that you wanted to take. You should

☐ carefully reverse on the hard shoulder
☐ carry on to the next exit
☐ carefully reverse in the left-hand lane
☐ make a U-turn at the next gap in the central reservation

It is against the law to reverse, cross the central reservation or drive against the traffic flow on a motorway. If you have missed your exit ask yourself if your concentration is fading. It could be that you need to take a rest break before completing your journey.

9.58 Mark one answer

You are driving at 70 mph on a three-lane motorway. There is no traffic ahead. Which lane should you use?

☐ Any lane
☐ Middle lane
☐ Right lane
☐ Left lane

If the left-hand lane is free you should use it, regardless of the speed you're travelling

9.59 Mark one answer

Your vehicle has broken down on a motorway. You are not able to stop on the hard shoulder. What should you do?

☐ Switch on your hazard warning lights
☐ Stop following traffic and ask for help
☐ Attempt to repair your vehicle quickly
☐ Stand behind your vehicle to warn others

If you can't get your vehicle onto the hard shoulder, use your hazard warning lights to warn others. Leave your vehicle only when you can safely get clear of the carriageway.

Do not try to repair the vehicle or attempt to place any warning device on the carriageway.

9.60 Mark one answer

Why is it particularly important to carry out a check on your vehicle before making a long motorway journey?

☐ You will have to do more harsh braking on motorways
☐ Motorway service stations do not deal with breakdowns
☐ The road surface will wear down the tyres faster
☐ Continuous high speeds may increase the risk of your vehicle breaking down

Before you start your journey make sure that your vehicle can cope with the demands of high-speed driving. You should check a number of things, the main ones being oil, water and tyres. You also need to plan rest stops if you're going a long way.

9.61 Mark one answer

You are driving on a motorway. The car ahead shows its hazard lights for a short time. This tells you that

☐ the driver wants you to overtake
☐ the other car is going to change lanes
☐ traffic ahead is slowing or stopping suddenly
☐ there is a police speed check ahead

If the vehicle in front shows its hazard lights there may be an incident or queueing traffic ahead. As well as keeping a safe distance, look beyond it to help you get an early warning of any hazards and a picture of the situation ahead.

9.62 Mark one answer

You are intending to leave the motorway at the next exit. Before you reach the exit you should normally position your vehicle

☐ in the middle lane
☐ in the left-hand lane
☐ on the hard shoulder
☐ in any lane

You'll see the first advance direction sign one mile from the exit. If you're travelling at 60 mph in the right-hand lane you'll only have about 50 seconds before you reach the countdown markers. There will be another sign at the half-mile point. Move in to the left-hand lane in good time. Don't cut across traffic at the last moment and don't risk missing your exit.

9.63 Mark one answer

As a provisional licence holder you should not drive a car

☐ over 30 mph
☐ at night
☐ on the motorway
☐ with passengers in rear seats

When you've passed your practical test ask your instructor to take you for a lesson on the motorway. You'll need to get used to the speed of traffic and how to deal with multiple lanes. The Pass Plus scheme has been created for new drivers, and includes motorway driving. Ask your ADI for details.

9.64 Mark one answer

Your vehicle breaks down on the hard shoulder of a motorway. You decide to use your mobile phone to call for help. You should

☐ stand at the rear of the vehicle while making the call
☐ try to repair the vehicle yourself
☐ get out of the vehicle by the right-hand door
☐ check your location from the marker posts on the left

The emergency services need to know your exact location so they can reach you as quickly as possible. Look for a number on the nearest marker post beside the hard shoulder. Give this number when you call the emergency services as it will help them to locate you. Be ready to describe where you are, for example, by reference to the last junction or service station you passed.

9.65 Mark one answer   NI EXEMPT

You are on a three-lane motorway towing a trailer. You may use the right-hand lane when

☐ there are lane closures
☐ there is slow moving traffic
☐ you can maintain a high speed
☐ large vehicles are in the left and centre lanes

If you are towing a caravan or trailer you must not use the right-hand lane on a motorway with three or more lanes, except in certain circumstances, such as lane closures.

9.66   Mark one answer

You are on a motorway. There is a contraflow system ahead. What would you expect to find?

☐ Temporary traffic lights
☐ Lower speed limits
☐ Wider lanes than normal
☐ Speed humps

When approaching a contraflow system reduce speed in good time and obey all speed limits. You may be travelling in a narrower lane than normal with no permanent barrier between you and the oncoming traffic. Be aware that the hard shoulder may be used for traffic and the road ahead could be obstructed by slow-moving or broken down vehicles.

9.67   Mark one answer

On a motorway you may only stop on the hard shoulder

☐ in an emergency
☐ if you feel tired and need to rest
☐ if you miss the exit that you wanted
☐ to pick up a hitchhiker

You should only stop on the hard shoulder in a genuine emergency. DON'T stop on it to have a rest or picnic, pick up hitchhikers, answer a mobile phone or check a map. If you miss your intended exit carry on to the next, never reverse along the hard shoulder.

10.1 Mark one answer
What is the meaning of this sign?

☐ Local speed limit applies
☐ No waiting on the carriageway
☐ National speed limit applies
☐ No entry to vehicular traffic

This sign doesn't tell you the speed limit in figures. You should know the speed limit for the type of road that you're on. Study your copy of *The Highway Code*.

10.2 Mark one answer
What is the national speed limit for cars and motorcycles on a dual carriageway?

☐ 30 mph
☐ 50 mph
☐ 60 mph
☐ 70 mph

Ensure that you know the speed limit for the road that you're on. The speed limit on a dual carriageway or motorway is 70 mph for cars and motorcycles, unless there are signs to indicate otherwise. The speed limits for different types of vehicles are listed in *The Highway Code*.

10.3 Mark one answer
There are no speed limit signs on the road. How is a 30 mph limit indicated?

☐ By hazard warning lines
☐ By street lighting
☐ By pedestrian islands
☐ By double or single yellow lines

There is usually a 30 mph speed limit where there are street lights unless there are signs showing another limit.

10.4 Mark one answer
Where you see street lights but no speed limit signs the limit is usually

☐ 30 mph
☐ 40 mph
☐ 50 mph
☐ 60 mph

The presence of street lights generally shows that there is a 30 mph speed limit, unless signs tell you otherwise.

10.5 Mark one answer
What does this sign mean?

☐ Minimum speed 30 mph
☐ End of maximum speed
☐ End of minimum speed
☐ Maximum speed 30 mph

A red slash through this sign indicates that the restriction has ended. In this case the restriction was a minimum speed limit of 30 mph.

10.6 Mark one answer
There is a tractor ahead of you. You wish to overtake but you are NOT sure if it is safe to do so. You should

☐ follow another overtaking vehicle through
☐ sound your horn to the slow vehicle to pull over
☐ speed through but flash your lights to oncoming traffic
☐ not overtake if you are in doubt

Never overtake if you're not sure whether it's safe. Can you see far enough down the road to ensure that you can complete the manoeuvre safely? If the answer is no, DON'T GO.

10.7 Mark three answers
Which three of the following are most likely to take an unusual course at roundabouts?

- ☐ Horse riders
- ☐ Milk floats
- ☐ Delivery vans
- ☐ Long vehicles
- ☐ Estate cars
- ☐ Cyclists

Long vehicles might have to take a slightly different position when approaching the roundabout or going around it. This is to stop the rear of the vehicle cutting in and mounting the kerb.

Horse riders and cyclists might stay in the left-hand lane although they are turning right. Be aware of this and allow them room.

10.8 Mark one answer
On a clearway you must not stop

- ☐ at any time
- ☐ when it is busy
- ☐ in the rush hour
- ☐ during daylight hours

Clearways are in place so that traffic can flow without the obstruction of parked vehicles. Just one parked vehicle will cause an obstruction for all other traffic. You MUST NOT stop where a clearway is in force, not even to pick up or set down passengers.

10.9 Mark one answer
What is the meaning of this sign?

- ☐ No entry
- ☐ Waiting restrictions
- ☐ National speed limit
- ☐ School crossing patrol

This sign indicates that there are waiting restrictions. It is normally accompanied by details of when restrictions are in force.

Details of most signs which are in common use are shown in *The Highway Code* and a more comprehensive selection is available in Know Your Traffic Signs.

10.10 Mark one answer
You can park on the right-hand side of a road at night

- ☐ in a one-way street
- ☐ with your sidelights on
- ☐ more than 10 metres (32 feet) from a junction
- ☐ under a lamp-post

Red rear reflectors show up when headlights shine on them. These are useful when you are parked at night but will only reflect if you park in the same direction as the traffic flow. Normally you should park on the left, but if you're in a one-way street you may also park on the right-hand side.

10.11 Mark one answer
On a three-lane dual carriageway the right-hand lane can be used for

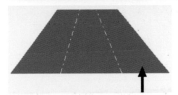

- ☐ overtaking only, never turning right
- ☐ overtaking or turning right
- ☐ fast-moving traffic only
- ☐ turning right only, never overtaking

You should normally use the left-hand lane on any dual carriageway unless you are overtaking or turning right.

When overtaking on a dual carriageway, look for vehicles ahead that are turning right. They're likely to be slowing or stopped. You need to see them in good time so that you can take appropriate action.

10.12 Mark one answer
You are approaching a busy junction. There are several lanes with road markings. At the last moment you realise that you are in the wrong lane. You should

- ☐ continue in that lane
- ☐ force your way across
- ☐ stop until the area has cleared
- ☐ use clear arm signals to cut across

There are times where road markings can be obscured by queueing traffic, or you might be unsure which lane you need to be in.

If you realise that you're in the wrong lane, don't cut across lanes or bully other drivers to let you in. Follow the lane you're in and find somewhere safe to turn around if you need to.

10.13 Mark one answer

Where may you overtake on a one-way street?

☐ Only on the left-hand side
☐ Overtaking is not allowed
☐ Only on the right-hand side
☐ Either on the right or the left

You can overtake other traffic on either side when travelling in a one-way street. Make full use of your mirrors and ensure that it's clear all around before you attempt to overtake. Look for signs and road markings and use the most suitable lane for your destination.

10.14 Mark one answer

When going straight ahead at a roundabout you should

☐ indicate left before leaving the roundabout
☐ not indicate at any time
☐ indicate right when approaching the roundabout
☐ indicate left when approaching the roundabout

When you want to go straight on at a roundabout, don't signal as you approach it, but indicate left just after you pass the exit before the one you wish to take.

10.15 Mark one answer

Which vehicle might have to use a different course to normal at roundabouts?

☐ Sports car
☐ Van
☐ Estate car
☐ Long vehicle

A long vehicle may have to straddle lanes either on or approaching a roundabout so that the rear wheels don't cut in over the kerb.
  If you're following a long vehicle, stay well back and give it plenty of room.

10.16 Mark one answer

You may only enter a box junction when

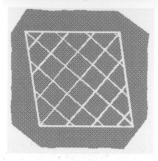

☐ there are less than two vehicles in front of you
☐ the traffic lights show green
☐ your exit road is clear
☐ you need to turn left

Yellow box junctions are marked on the road to prevent the road becoming blocked. Don't enter one unless your exit road is clear. You may only wait in the yellow box if your exit road is clear but oncoming traffic is preventing you from completing the turn.

10.17 Mark one answer

You may wait in a yellow box junction when

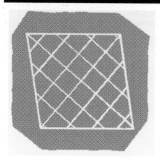

☐ oncoming traffic is preventing you from turning right
☐ you are in a queue of traffic turning left
☐ you are in a queue of traffic to go ahead
☐ you are on a roundabout

The purpose of this road marking is to keep the junction clear of queueing traffic.
  You may only wait in the marked area when you're turning right and your exit lane is clear but you can't complete the turn because of oncoming traffic.

10.18 Mark three answers

You MUST stop when signalled to do so by which THREE of these?

☐ A police officer
☐ A pedestrian
☐ A school crossing patrol
☐ A bus driver
☐ A red traffic light

Looking well ahead and 'reading' the road will help you to anticipate hazards. This will enable you to stop safely at traffic lights or if ordered to do so by an authorised person.

10.19 Mark one answer

Someone is waiting to cross at a zebra crossing. They are standing on the pavement. You should normally

☐ go on quickly before they step onto the crossing
☐ stop before you reach the zigzag lines and let them cross
☐ stop, let them cross, wait patiently
☐ ignore them as they are still on the pavement

By standing on the pavement, the pedestrian is showing an intention to cross. If you are looking well down the road you will give yourself enough time to slow down and stop safely. Don't forget to check your mirrors before slowing down.

10.20 Mark one answer

At toucan crossings, apart from pedestrians you should be aware of

☐ emergency vehicles emerging
☐ buses pulling out
☐ trams crossing in front
☐ cyclists riding across

The use of cycles is being encouraged and more toucan crossings are being installed. These crossings enable pedestrians and cyclists to cross the path of other traffic.
 Watch out as cyclists will approach the crossing faster than pedestrians.

10.21 Mark two answers

Who can use a toucan crossing?

☐ Trains
☐ Cyclists
☐ Buses
☐ Pedestrians
☐ Trams

Toucan crossings are similar to pelican crossings but there is no flashing amber phase. Cyclists share the crossing with pedestrians and are allowed to cycle across when the green cycle symbol is shown.

10.22 Mark one answer

At a pelican crossing, what does a flashing amber light mean?

☐ You must not move off until the lights stop flashing
☐ You must give way to pedestrians still on the crossing
☐ You can move off, even if pedestrians are still on the crossing
☐ You must stop because the lights are about to change to red

If there is no-one on the crossing when the amber light is flashing, you may proceed over the crossing. You don't need to wait for the green light to show.

10.23 Mark one answer

You are waiting at a pelican crossing. The red light changes to flashing amber. This means you must

☐ wait for pedestrians on the crossing to clear
☐ move off immediately without any hesitation
☐ wait for the green light before moving off
☐ get ready and go when the continuous amber light shows

This light allows time for the pedestrians already on the crossing to get to the other side in their own time, without being rushed. Don't rev your engine or start to move off while they are still crossing.

10.24 Mark one answer

When can you park on the left opposite these road markings?

☐ If the line nearest to you is broken
☐ When there are no yellow lines
☐ To pick up or set down passengers
☐ During daylight hours only

You MUST NOT park or stop on a road marked with double white lines (even where one of the lines is broken) except to pick up or set down passengers.

10.25 Mark one answer

You are intending to turn right at a crossroads. An oncoming driver is also turning right. It will normally be safer to

☐ keep the other vehicle to your RIGHT and turn behind it (offside to offside)
☐ keep the other vehicle to your LEFT and turn in front of it (nearside to nearside)
☐ carry on and turn at the next junction instead
☐ hold back and wait for the other driver to turn first

At some junctions the layout may make it difficult to turn offside to offside. If this is the case, be prepared to pass nearside to nearside, but take extra care as your view ahead will be obscured by the vehicle turning in front of you.

10.26 Mark one answer

You are on a road that has no traffic signs. There are street lights. What is the speed limit?

☐ 20 mph
☐ 30 mph
☐ 40 mph
☐ 60 mph

If you aren't sure of the speed limit a good indication is the presence of street lights. If there is street lighting the speed limit will be 30 mph unless otherwise indicated.

10.27 Mark three answers

You are going along a street with parked vehicles on the left-hand side. For which THREE reasons should you keep your speed down?

☐ So that oncoming traffic can see you more clearly
☐ You may set off car alarms
☐ Vehicles may be pulling out
☐ Drivers' doors may open
☐ Children may run out from between the vehicles

Travel slowly and carefully where there are parked vehicles in a built-up area.
Beware of
• vehicles pulling out, especially bicycles and other motorcycles
• pedestrians, especially children, who may run out from between cars
• drivers opening their doors.

10.28 Mark one answer

You meet an obstruction on your side of the road. You should

☐ carry on, you have priority
☐ give way to oncoming traffic
☐ wave oncoming vehicles through
☐ accelerate to get past first

Take care if you have to pass a parked vehicle on your side of the road. Give way to oncoming traffic if there isn't enough room for you both to continue safely.

10.29 Mark two answers

You are on a two-lane dual carriageway. For which TWO of the following would you use the right-hand lane?

☐ Turning right
☐ Normal progress
☐ Staying at the minimum allowed speed
☐ Constant high speed
☐ Overtaking slower traffic
☐ Mending punctures

Normally you should travel in the left-hand lane and only use the right-hand lane for overtaking or turning right. Move back into the left lane as soon as it's safe but don't cut in across the path of the vehicle you've just passed.

10.30 Mark one answer

Who has priority at an unmarked crossroads?

☐ The larger vehicle
☐ No one has priority
☐ The faster vehicle
☐ The smaller vehicle

Practise good observation in all directions before you emerge or make a turn. Proceed only when you're sure it's safe to do so.

10.31 Mark one answer   NI EXEMPT

What is the nearest you may park to a junction?

☐ 10 metres (32 feet)
☐ 12 metres (39 feet)
☐ 15 metres (49 feet)
☐ 20 metres (66 feet)

Don't park within 10 metres (32 feet) of a junction (unless in an authorised parking place). This is to allow drivers emerging from, or turning into, the junction a clear view of the road they are joining. It also allows them to see hazards such as pedestrians or cyclists at the junction.

10.32 Mark three answers   NI EXEMPT

In which THREE places must you NOT park?

☐ Near the brow of a hill
☐ At or near a bus stop
☐ Where there is no pavement
☐ Within 10 metres (32 feet) of a junction
☐ On a 40 mph road

Other traffic will have to pull out to pass you. They may have to use the other side of the road, and if you park near the brow of a hill, they may not be able to see oncoming traffic. It's important not to park at or near a bus stop as this could inconvenience passengers, and may put them at risk as they get on or off the bus.
   Parking near a junction could restrict the view for emerging vehicles.

10.33 Mark one answer

You are waiting at a level crossing. A train has passed but the lights keep flashing. You must

☐ carry on waiting
☐ phone the signal operator
☐ edge over the stop line and look for trains
☐ park and investigate

If the lights at a level crossing continue to flash after a train has passed, you should still wait as there might be another train coming. Time seems to pass slowly when you're held up in a queue. Be patient and wait until the lights stop flashing.

10.34 Mark one answer

At a crossroads there are no signs or road markings. Two vehicles approach. Which has priority?

☐ Neither of the vehicles
☐ The vehicle travelling the fastest
☐ Oncoming vehicles turning right
☐ Vehicles approaching from the right

At a crossroads where there are no 'give way' signs or road markings be very careful. No vehicle has priority, even if the sizes of the roads are different.

10.35 Mark one answer

What does this sign tell you?

☐ That it is a no-through road
☐ End of traffic calming zone
☐ Free parking zone ends
☐ No waiting zone ends

The blue and red circular sign on its own means that waiting restrictions are in force. This sign shows that you are leaving the controlled zone and waiting restrictions no longer apply.

10.36 Mark one answer

You are entering an area of roadworks. There is a temporary speed limit displayed. You should

☐ not exceed the speed limit
☐ obey the limit only during rush hour
☐ ignore the displayed limit
☐ obey the limit except at night

Where there are extra hazards such as roadworks, it's often necessary to slow traffic down by imposing a temporary speed limit. These speed limits aren't advisory, they must be obeyed.

10.37 Mark two answers

In which TWO places should you NOT park?

☐ Near a school entrance
☐ Near a police station
☐ In a side road
☐ At a bus stop
☐ In a one-way street

It may be tempting to park where you shouldn't while you run a quick errand. Careless parking is a selfish act and could endanger other road users.

10.38 Mark one answer

You are travelling on a well-lit road at night in a built-up area. By using dipped headlights you will be able to

- ☐ see further along the road
- ☐ go at a much faster speed
- ☐ switch to main beam quickly
- ☐ be easily seen by others

You may be difficult to see when you're travelling at night, even on a well-lit road. If you use dipped headlights rather than sidelights other road users will see you more easily.

10.39 Mark one answer

The dual carriageway you are turning right onto has a very narrow central reservation. What should you do?

- ☐ Proceed to the central reservation and wait
- ☐ Wait until the road is clear in both directions
- ☐ Stop in the first lane so that other vehicles give way
- ☐ Emerge slightly to show your intentions

When the central reservation is narrow you should treat a dual carriageway as one road. Wait until the road is clear in both directions before emerging to turn right. If you try to treat it as two separate roads and wait in the middle, you are likely to cause an obstruction and possibly a collision.

10.40 Mark one answer

What is the national speed limit on a single carriageway road for cars and motorcycles?

- ☐ 30 mph
- ☐ 50 mph
- ☐ 60 mph
- ☐ 70 mph

Exceeding the speed limit is dangerous and can result in you receiving penalty points on your licence. It isn't worth it. You should know the speed limit for the road that you're on by observing the road signs.

Different speed limits apply if you are towing a trailer.

10.41 Mark one answer

You park at night on a road with a 40 mph speed limit. You should park

- ☐ facing the traffic
- ☐ with parking lights on
- ☐ with dipped headlights on
- ☐ near a street light

You MUST use parking lights when parking at night on a road or lay-by with a speed limit greater than 30 mph. You MUST also park in the direction of the traffic flow and not close to a junction.

10.42 Mark one answer

You will see these red and white markers when approaching

- ☐ the end of a motorway
- ☐ a concealed level crossing
- ☐ a concealed speed limit sign
- ☐ the end of a dual carriageway

If there is a bend just before the level crossing you may not be able to see the level crossing barriers or waiting traffic.

These signs give you an early warning that you may find these hazards just around the bend.

10.43 Mark one answer   NI EXEMPT

You are travelling on a motorway. You MUST stop when signalled to do so by which of these?

- ☐ Flashing amber lights above your lane
- ☐ A Highways Agency Traffic Officer
- ☐ Pedestrians on the hard shoulder
- ☐ A driver who has broken down

You will find Highways Agency Traffic Officers on many of Britain's motorways. They work in partnership with the police, helping to keep traffic moving and to make your journey as safe as possible. It is an offence not to comply with the directions given by a Traffic Officer.

10.44 Mark one answer

At a busy unmarked crossroads, which of the following has priority?

- ☐ Vehicles going straight ahead
- ☐ Vehicles turning right
- ☐ None of the vehicles
- ☐ The vehicles that arrived first

If there are no road signs or markings do not assume that you have priority.

Remember that other drivers may assume they have the right to go. No type of vehicle has priority but it's courteous to give way to large vehicles. Also look out in particular for cyclists and motorcyclists.

10.45 Mark one answer
You are going straight ahead at a roundabout. How should you signal?

☐ Signal right on the approach and then left to leave the roundabout
☐ Signal left after you leave the roundabout and enter the new road
☐ Signal right on the approach to the roundabout and keep the signal on
☐ Signal left just after you pass the exit before the one you will take

To go straight ahead at a roundabout you should normally approach in the left-hand lane. You will not normally need to signal, but look out for the road markings. At some roundabouts the left lane on approach is marked as 'left turn only', so make sure you use the correct lane to go ahead. Signal before you leave as other road users need to know your intentions.

10.46 Mark one answer
You may drive over a footpath

☐ to overtake slow-moving traffic
☐ when the pavement is very wide
☐ if no pedestrians are near
☐ to get into a property

It is against the law to drive on or over a footpath, except to gain access to a property. If you need to cross a pavement, watch for pedestrians in both directions.

10.47 Mark one answer
A single carriageway road has this sign. What is the maximum permitted speed for a car towing a trailer?

☐ 30 mph
☐ 40 mph
☐ 50 mph
☐ 60 mph

When towing trailers, speed limits are also lower on dual carriageways and motorways. These speed limits apply to vehicles pulling all sorts of trailers including caravans, horse boxes etc.

10.48 Mark one answer
You are towing a small caravan on a dual carriageway. You must not exceed

☐ 50 mph
☐ 40 mph
☐ 70 mph
☐ 60 mph

The speed limit is reduced for vehicles towing caravans and trailers, to lessen the risk of the outfit becoming unstable. Due to the increased weight and size of the vehicle and caravan combination, you should plan well ahead. Be extra-careful in windy weather, as strong winds could cause a caravan or large trailer to snake from side to side.

10.49 Mark one answer
You want to park and you see this sign. On the days and times shown you should

Meter
ZONE

Mon - Fri
8.30 am - 6.30 pm
Saturday
8.30 am - 1.30 pm

☐ park in a bay and not pay
☐ park on yellow lines and pay
☐ park on yellow lines and not pay
☐ park in a bay and pay

Parking restrictions apply in a variety of places and situations. Make sure you know the rules and understand where and when restrictions apply. Controlled parking areas will be indicated by signs and road markings. Parking in the wrong place could cause an obstruction and danger to other traffic. It can also result in a fine.

10.50 Mark one answer

You are driving along a road that has a cycle lane. The lane is marked by a solid white line. This means that during its period of operation

☐ the lane may be used for parking your car
☐ you may drive in that lane at any time
☐ the lane may be used when necessary
☐ you must not drive in that lane

Leave the lane free for cyclists. At other times, when the lane is not in operation, you should still be aware that there may be cyclists about. Give them room and don't pass too closely.

10.51 Mark one answer

A cycle lane is marked by a solid white line. You must not drive or park in it

☐ at any time
☐ during the rush hour
☐ if a cyclist is using it
☐ during its period of operation

The cycle lanes are there for a reason. Keep them free and allow cyclists to use them.

It is illegal to drive or park in a cycle lane, marked by a solid white line, during its hours of operation. Parking in a cycle lane will obstruct cyclists and they may move into the path of traffic on the main carriageway as they ride around the obstruction. This could be hazardous for both the cyclist and other road users.

10.52 Mark one answer

While driving, you intend to turn left into a minor road. On the approach you should

☐ keep just left of the middle of the road
☐ keep in the middle of the road
☐ swing out wide just before turning
☐ keep well to the left of the road

Don't swing out into the centre of the road in order to make the turn. This could endanger oncoming traffic and may cause other road users to misunderstand your intentions.

10.53 Mark one answer

You are waiting at a level crossing. The red warning lights continue to flash after a train has passed by. What should you do?

☐ Get out and investigate
☐ Telephone the signal operator
☐ Continue to wait
☐ Drive across carefully

At a level crossing flashing red lights mean you must stop. If the train passes but the lights keep flashing, wait. There may be another train coming.

10.54 Mark one answer

You are driving over a level crossing. The warning lights come on and a bell rings. What should you do?

☐ Get everyone out of the vehicle immediately
☐ Stop and reverse back to clear the crossing
☐ Keep going and clear the crossing
☐ Stop immediately and use your hazard warning lights

Keep going, don't stop on the crossing. If the amber warning lights come on as you're approaching the crossing, you MUST stop unless it is unsafe to do so. Red flashing lights together with an audible signal mean you MUST stop.

10.55 Mark one answer

You are on a busy main road and find that you are travelling in the wrong direction. What should you do?

☐ Turn into a side road on the right and reverse into the main road
☐ Make a U-turn in the main road
☐ Make a 'three-point' turn in the main road
☐ Turn round in a side road

Don't turn round in a busy street or reverse from a side road into a main road. Find a quiet side road and choose a place where you won't obstruct an entrance or exit.

Look out for pedestrians and cyclists as well as other traffic.

10.56 Mark one answer

You may remove your seat belt when carrying out a manoeuvre that involves

☐ reversing
☐ a hill start
☐ an emergency stop
☐ driving slowly

Don't forget to put your seat belt back on when you've finished reversing.

10.57 Mark one answer

You must not reverse

☐ for longer than necessary
☐ for more than a car's length
☐ into a side road
☐ in a built-up area

You may decide to turn your vehicle around by reversing into an opening or side road.

When you reverse, always look behind and all around and watch for pedestrians. Don't reverse from a side road into a main road.

You MUST NOT reverse further than is necessary.

10.58 Mark one answer

When you are NOT sure that it is safe to reverse your vehicle you should

☐ use your horn
☐ rev your engine
☐ get out and check
☐ reverse slowly

If you can't see all around your vehicle get out and have a look. You could also ask someone reliable outside the vehicle to guide you. A small child could easily be hidden directly behind you. Don't take risks.

10.59 Mark one answer

When may you reverse from a side road into a main road?

☐ Only if both roads are clear of traffic
☐ Not at any time
☐ At any time
☐ Only if the main road is clear of traffic

Don't reverse into a main road from a side road. The main road is likely to be busy and the traffic on it moving quickly. Cut down the risks by reversing into a quiet side road.

10.60 Mark one answer

You want to turn right at a box junction. There is oncoming traffic. You should

☐ wait in the box junction if your exit is clear
☐ wait before the junction until it is clear of all traffic
☐ drive on, you cannot turn right at a box junction
☐ drive slowly into the box junction when signalled by oncoming traffic

You can move into the box junction to wait as long as your exit is clear. The oncoming traffic will stop when the traffic lights change, allowing you to proceed.

10.61 Mark one answer

You are reversing your vehicle into a side road. When would the greatest hazard to passing traffic occur?

☐ After you've completed the manoeuvre
☐ Just before you actually begin to manoeuvre
☐ After you've entered the side road
☐ When the front of your vehicle swings out

Always check road and traffic conditions in all directions before reversing into a side road. Keep a good look-out throughout the manoeuvre. Act on what you see and wait if necessary.

10.62 Mark one answer

Where is the safest place to park your vehicle at night?

☐ In a garage
☐ On a busy road
☐ In a quiet car park
☐ Near a red route

If you have a garage, use it. Your vehicle is less likely to be a victim of car crime if it's in a garage. Also in winter the windows will be free from ice and snow.

10.63 Mark one answer

You are driving on an urban clearway. You may stop only to

☐ set down and pick up passengers
☐ use a mobile telephone
☐ ask for directions
☐ load or unload goods

Urban clearways may be in built-up areas and their times of operation will be clearly signed. You should stop only for as long as is reasonable to pick up or set down passengers. You should ensure that you are not causing an obstruction for other traffic.

10.64 Mark one answer

You are looking for somewhere to park your vehicle. The area is full EXCEPT for spaces marked 'disabled use'. You can

☐ use these spaces when elsewhere is full
☐ park if you stay with your vehicle
☐ use these spaces, disabled or not
☐ not park there unless permitted

It is illegal to park in a parking space reserved for disabled users.

These spaces are provided for people with limited mobility, who may need extra space to get in and out of their vehicle.

10.65 Mark one answer

Your vehicle is parked on the road at night. When must you use sidelights?

☐ Where there are continuous white lines in the middle of the road
☐ Where the speed limit exceeds 30 mph
☐ Where you are facing oncoming traffic
☐ Where you are near a bus stop

When parking at night, park in the direction of the traffic. This will enable other road users to see the reflectors on the rear of your vehicle. You MUST use your sidelights when parking on a road, or in a lay-by on a road, where the speed limit is over 30 mph.

10.66 Mark one answer

You are on a road that is only wide enough for one vehicle. There is a car coming towards you. What should you do?

☐ Pull into a passing place on your right
☐ Force the other driver to reverse
☐ Pull into a passing place if your vehicle is wider
☐ Pull into a passing place on your left

Pull into the nearest passing place on the left if you meet another vehicle in a narrow road. If the nearest passing place is on the right, wait opposite it.

10.67 Mark one answer

You are driving at night with full beam headlights on. A vehicle is overtaking you. You should dip your lights

☐ some time after the vehicle has passed you
☐ before the vehicle starts to pass you
☐ only if the other driver dips their headlights
☐ as soon as the vehicle passes you

On full beam your lights could dazzle the driver in front. Make sure that your light beam falls short of the vehicle in front.

10.68 Mark one answer

When may you drive a motor car in this bus lane?

☐ Outside its hours of operation
☐ To get to the front of a traffic queue
☐ You may not use it at any time
☐ To overtake slow-moving traffic

Some bus lanes only operate during peak hours and other vehicles may use them outside these hours. Make sure you check the sign for the hours of operation before driving in a bus lane.

10.69 Mark one answer

Signals are normally given by direction indicators and

☐ brake lights
☐ side lights
☐ fog lights
☐ interior lights

Your brake lights will give an indication to traffic behind that you're slowing down.

Good anticipation will allow you time to check your mirrors before slowing.

10.70 Mark one answer

You are parked in a busy high street. What is the safest way to turn your vehicle around so you can go the opposite way?

☐ Find a quiet side road to turn round in
☐ Drive into a side road and reverse into the main road
☐ Get someone to stop the traffic
☐ Do a U-turn

Make sure you carry out the manoeuvre without causing a hazard to other vehicles.

Choose a place to turn which is safe and convenient for you and for other road users.

10.71 Mark one answer

To help keep your vehicle secure at night, where should you park?

☐ Near a police station
☐ In a quiet road
☐ On a red route
☐ In a well-lit area

Whenever possible park in an area which will be well lit at night

10.72 Mark one answer

You are in the right-hand lane of a dual carriageway. You see signs showing that the right-hand lane is closed 800 yards ahead. You should

☐ keep in that lane until you reach the queue
☐ move to the left immediately
☐ wait and see which lane is moving faster
☐ move to the left in good time

Keep a look-out for traffic signs. If you're directed to change lanes, do so in good time. Don't
- push your way into traffic in another lane
- leave changing lanes until the last moment.

10.73 Mark two answers

You are driving on a road that has a cycle lane. The lane is marked by a broken white line. This means that

☐ you should not drive in the lane unless it is unavoidable
☐ you should not park in the lane unless it is unavoidable
☐ cyclists can travel in both directions in that lane
☐ the lane must be used by motorcyclists in heavy traffic

Where signs or road markings show lanes are for cyclists only, leave them free. Do not drive or park in a cycle lane unless it is unavoidable.

10.74 Mark one answer

What MUST you have to park in a disabled space?

☐ A Blue Badge
☐ A wheelchair
☐ An advanced driver certificate
☐ An adapted vehicle

Don't park in a space reserved for disabled people unless you or your passenger is a disabled badge holder. The badge must be displayed in your vehicle in the bottom left-hand corner of the windscreen.

10.75 Mark three answers

On which THREE occasions MUST you stop your vehicle?

☐ When in an incident where damage or injury is caused
☐ At a red traffic light
☐ When signalled to do so by a police or traffic officer
☐ At a junction with double broken white lines
☐ At a pelican crossing when the amber light is flashing and no pedestrians are crossing

Situations when you MUST stop include the following. When signalled to do so by a, police or traffic officer, traffic warden, school crossing patrol or red traffic light.

You must also stop if you are involved in an incident which causes damage or injury to any other person, vehicle, animal or property.

Road and traffic signs

11.1 Mark one answer
You MUST obey signs giving orders. These signs are mostly in

- ☐ green rectangles
- ☐ red triangles
- ☐ blue rectangles
- ☐ red circles

There are three basic types of traffic sign, those that, warn, inform or give orders.

Generally, triangular signs warn, rectangular ones give information or directions, and circular signs usually give orders. An exception is the eight-sided 'STOP' sign.

11.2 Mark one answer
Traffic signs giving orders are generally which shape?

☐

☐

☐

☐

Road signs in the shape of a circle give orders. Those with a red circle are mostly prohibitive. The 'stop' sign is octagonal to give it greater prominence. Signs giving orders MUST always be obeyed.

11.3 Mark one answer
Which type of sign tells you NOT to do something?

☐

☐

☐

☐

Signs in the shape of a circle give orders. A sign with a red circle means that you aren't allowed to do something. Study Know Your Traffic Signs to ensure that you understand what the different traffic signs mean.

11.4 Mark one answer
What does this sign mean?

- ☐ Maximum speed limit with traffic calming
- ☐ Minimum speed limit with traffic calming
- ☐ '20 cars only' parking zone
- ☐ Only 20 cars allowed at any one time

If you're in places where there are likely to be pedestrians such as outside schools, near parks, residential areas and shopping areas, you should be extra-cautious and keep your speed down.

Many local authorities have taken measures to slow traffic down by creating traffic calming measures such as speed humps.

They are there for a reason; slow down.

11.5 Mark one answer
Which sign means no motor vehicles are allowed?

☐

☐

☐

☐

You would generally see this sign at the approach to a pedestrian-only zone.

11.6 Mark one answer

Which of these signs means no motor vehicles?

If you are driving a motor vehicle or riding a motorcycle you MUST NOT travel past this sign. This area has been designated for use by pedestrians.

11.7 Mark one answer

What does this sign mean?

- ☐ New speed limit 20 mph
- ☐ No vehicles over 30 tonnes
- ☐ Minimum speed limit 30 mph
- ☐ End of 20 mph zone

Where you see this sign the 20 mph restriction ends. Check all around for possible hazards and only increase your speed if it's safe to do so.

11.8 Mark one answer

What does this sign mean?

- ☐ No overtaking
- ☐ No motor vehicles
- ☐ Clearway (no stopping)
- ☐ Cars and motorcycles only

A sign will indicate which types of vehicles are prohibited from certain roads. Make sure that you know which signs apply to the vehicle you're using.

11.9 Mark one answer

What does this sign mean?

- ☐ No parking
- ☐ No road markings
- ☐ No through road
- ☐ No entry

'No entry' signs are used in places such as one-way streets to prevent vehicles driving against the traffic. To ignore one would be dangerous, both for yourself and other road users, as well as being against the law.

11.10 Mark one answer

What does this sign mean?

- ☐ Bend to the right
- ☐ Road on the right closed
- ☐ No traffic from the right
- ☐ No right turn

The 'no right turn' sign may be used to warn road users that there is a 'no entry' prohibition on a road to the right ahead.

11.11 Mark one answer

Which sign means 'no entry'?

Look out for traffic signs. Disobeying or not seeing a sign could be dangerous. It may also be an offence for which you could be prosecuted.

11.12 Mark one answer
What does this sign mean?

☐ Route for trams only
☐ Route for buses only
☐ Parking for buses only
☐ Parking for trams only

Avoid blocking tram routes. Trams are fixed on their route and can't manoeuvre around other vehicles and pedestrians. Modern trams travel quickly and are quiet so you might not hear them approaching.

11.13 Mark one answer
Which type of vehicle does this sign apply to?

☐ Wide vehicles
☐ Long vehicles
☐ High vehicles
☐ Heavy vehicles

The triangular shapes above and below the dimensions indicate a height restriction that applies to the road ahead.

11.14 Mark one answer
Which sign means NO motor vehicles allowed?

☐   ☐

☐   ☐

This sign is used to enable pedestrians to walk free from traffic. It's often found in shopping areas.

11.15 Mark one answer
What does this sign mean?

☐ You have priority
☐ No motor vehicles
☐ Two-way traffic
☐ No overtaking

Road signs that prohibit overtaking are placed in locations where passing the vehicle in front is dangerous. If you see this sign don't attempt to overtake. The sign is there for a reason and you must obey it.

11.16 Mark one answer
What does this sign mean?

☐ Keep in one lane
☐ Give way to oncoming traffic
☐ Do not overtake
☐ Form two lanes

If you're behind a slow-moving vehicle be patient. Wait until the restriction no longer applies and you can overtake safely.

11.17 Mark one answer
Which sign means no overtaking?

☐   ☐

☐   ☐

This sign indicates that overtaking here is not allowed and you could face prosecution if you ignore this prohibition.

11.18 Mark one answer

What does this sign mean?

☐ Waiting restrictions apply
☐ Waiting permitted
☐ National speed limit applies
☐ Clearway (no stopping)

There will be a plate or additional sign to tell you when the restrictions apply.

11.19 Mark one answer

What does this sign mean?

☐ End of restricted speed area
☐ End of restricted parking area
☐ End of clearway
☐ End of cycle route

Even though you have left the restricted area, make sure that you park where you won't endanger other road users or cause an obstruction.

11.20 Mark one answer

Which sign means 'no stopping'?

Stopping where this clearway restriction applies is likely to cause congestion. Allow the traffic to flow by obeying the signs.

11.21 Mark one answer

What does this sign mean?

☐ Roundabout
☐ Crossroads
☐ No stopping
☐ No entry

This sign is in place to ensure a clear route for traffic. Don't stop except in an emergency.

11.22 Mark one answer

You see this sign ahead. It means

☐ national speed limit applies
☐ waiting restrictions apply
☐ no stopping
☐ no entry

Clearways are stretches of road where you aren't allowed to stop unless in an emergency. You'll see this sign. Stopping where these restrictions apply may be dangerous and likely to cause an obstruction. Restrictions might apply for several miles and this may be indicated on the sign.

11.23 Mark one answer

What does this sign mean?

☐ Distance to parking place ahead
☐ Distance to public telephone ahead
☐ Distance to public house ahead
☐ Distance to passing place ahead

If you intend to stop and rest, this sign allows you time to reduce speed and pull over safely.

11.24 Mark one answer
What does this sign mean?

- [ ] Vehicles may not park on the verge or footway
- [ ] Vehicles may park on the left-hand side of the road only
- [ ] Vehicles may park fully on the verge or footway
- [ ] Vehicles may park on the right-hand side of the road only

In order to keep roads free from parked cars, there are some areas where you're allowed to park on the verge. Only do this where you see the sign. Parking on verges or footways anywhere else could lead to a fine.

11.25 Mark one answer
What does this traffic sign mean?

- [ ] No overtaking allowed
- [ ] Give priority to oncoming traffic
- [ ] Two way traffic
- [ ] One-way traffic only

Priority signs are normally shown where the road is narrow and there isn't enough room for two vehicles to pass. These can be at narrow bridges, road works and where there's a width restriction.

Make sure that you know who has priority, don't force your way through. Show courtesy and consideration to other road users.

11.26 Mark one answer
What is the meaning of this traffic sign?

- [ ] End of two-way road
- [ ] Give priority to vehicles coming towards you
- [ ] You have priority over vehicles coming towards you
- [ ] Bus lane ahead

Don't force your way through. Show courtesy and consideration to other road users. Although you have priority, make sure oncoming traffic is going to give way before you continue.

11.27 Mark one answer
What does this sign mean?

- [ ] No overtaking
- [ ] You are entering a one-way street
- [ ] Two-way traffic ahead
- [ ] You have priority over vehicles from the opposite direction

Don't force your way through if oncoming vehicles fail to give way. If necessary, slow down and give way to avoid confrontation or a collision.

11.28 Mark one answer
What shape is a STOP sign at a junction?

- [ ]
- [ ]
- [ ]
- [ ]

To make it easy to recognise, the 'stop' sign is the only sign of this shape. You must stop and take effective observation before proceeding.

11.29 Mark one answer

At a junction you see this sign partly covered by snow. What does it mean?

- ☐ Cross roads
- ☐ Give way
- ☐ Stop
- ☐ Turn right

The STOP sign is the only road sign that is octagonal. This is so that it can be recognised and obeyed even if it is obscured, for example by snow.

11.30 Mark one answer

What does this sign mean?

- ☐ Service area 30 miles ahead
- ☐ Maximum speed 30 mph
- ☐ Minimum speed 30 mph
- ☐ Lay-by 30 miles ahead

This sign is shown where slow-moving vehicles would impede the flow of traffic, for example in tunnels. However, if you need to slow down or even stop to avoid an incident or potential collision, you should do so.

11.31 Mark one answer

What does this sign mean?

- ☐ Give way to oncoming vehicles
- ☐ Approaching traffic passes you on both sides
- ☐ Turn off at the next available junction
- ☐ Pass either side to get to the same destination

These signs are often seen in one-way streets that have more than one lane.

When you see this sign, use the route that's the most convenient and doesn't require a late change of direction.

11.32 Mark one answer

What does this sign mean?

- ☐ Route for trams
- ☐ Give way to trams
- ☐ Route for buses
- ☐ Give way to buses

Take extra care when you encounter trams.

Look out for road markings and signs that alert you to them. Modern trams are very quiet and you may not hear them approaching.

11.33 Mark one answer

What does a circular traffic sign with a blue background do?

- ☐ Give warning of a motorway ahead
- ☐ Give directions to a car park
- ☐ Give motorway information
- ☐ Give an instruction

Signs with blue circles give a positive instruction. These are often found in urban areas and include signs for mini-roundabouts and directional arrows.

11.34 Mark one answer

Where would you see a contraflow bus and cycle lane?

- ☐ On a dual carriageway
- ☐ On a roundabout
- ☐ On an urban motorway
- ☐ On a one-way street

In a contraflow lane the traffic permitted to use it travels in the opposite direction to traffic in the other lanes on the road.

11.35 Mark one answer

What does this sign mean?

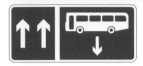

☐ Bus station on the right
☐ Contraflow bus lane
☐ With-flow bus lane
☐ Give way to buses

There will also be markings on the road surface to indicate the bus lane. You must not use this lane for parking or overtaking.

11.36 Mark one answer

What does a sign with a brown background show?

☐ Tourist directions
☐ Primary roads
☐ Motorway routes
☐ Minor routes

Signs with a brown background give directions to places of interest. They will often be seen on a motorway directing you along the easiest route to the attraction.

11.37 Mark one answer

This sign means

☐ tourist attraction
☐ beware of trains
☐ level crossing
☐ beware of trams

These signs indicate places of interest and are designed to guide you by the easiest route. They are particularly useful if you are unfamiliar with the area.

11.38 Mark one answer

What are triangular signs for?

☐ To give warnings
☐ To give information
☐ To give orders
☐ To give directions

This type of sign will warn you of hazards ahead.
Make sure you look at each sign that you pass on the road, so that you do not miss any vital instructions or information.

11.39 Mark one answer

What does this sign mean?

☐ Turn left ahead
☐ T-junction
☐ No through road
☐ Give way

This type of sign will warn you of hazards ahead. Make sure you look at each sign and road markings that you pass, so that you do not miss any vital instructions or information. This particular sign shows there is a T-junction with priority over vehicles from the right.

11.40 Mark one answer

What does this sign mean?

☐ Multi-exit roundabout
☐ Risk of ice
☐ Six roads converge
☐ Place of historical interest

It will take up to ten times longer to stop when it's icy. Where there is a risk of icy conditions you need to be aware of this and take extra care. If you think the road may be icy, don't brake or steer harshly as your tyres could lose their grip on the road.

11.41 Mark one answer
What does this sign mean?

☐ Crossroads
☐ Level crossing with gate
☐ Level crossing without gate
☐ Ahead only

The priority through the junction is shown by the broader line. You need to be aware of the hazard posed by traffic crossing or pulling out onto a major road.

11.42 Mark one answer
What does this sign mean?

☐ Ring road
☐ Mini-roundabout
☐ No vehicles
☐ Roundabout

As you approach a roundabout look well ahead and check all signs. Decide which exit you wish to take and move into the correct position as you approach the roundabout, signalling as required.

11.43 Mark four answers
Which FOUR of these would be indicated by a triangular road sign?

☐ Road narrows
☐ Ahead only
☐ Low bridge
☐ Minimum speed
☐ Children crossing
☐ T-junction

Warning signs are there to make you aware of potential hazards on the road ahead. Act on the signs so you are prepared and can take whatever action is necessary.

11.44 Mark one answer
What does this sign mean?

☐ Cyclists must dismount
☐ Cycles are not allowed
☐ Cycle route ahead
☐ Cycle in single file

Where there's a cycle route ahead, a sign will show a bicycle in a red warning triangle. Watch out for children on bicycles and cyclists rejoining the main road.

11.45 Mark one answer
Which sign means that pedestrians may be walking along the road?

☐   ☐

☐   ☐

When you pass pedestrians in the road, leave plenty of room. You might have to use the right-hand side of the road, so look well ahead, as well as in your mirrors, before pulling out. Take great care if there is a bend in the road obscuring your view ahead.

11.46 Mark one answer
Which of these signs means there is a double bend ahead?

☐   ☐

☐   ☐

Triangular signs give you a warning of hazards ahead. They are there to give you time to prepare for the hazard, for example by adjusting your speed.

381

11.47 Mark one answer
What does this sign mean?

☐ Wait at the barriers
☐ Wait at the crossroads
☐ Give way to trams
☐ Give way to farm vehicles

Obey the 'give way' signs. Trams are unable to steer around you if you misjudge when it is safe to enter the junction.

11.48 Mark one answer
What does this sign mean?

☐ Humpback bridge
☐ Humps in the road
☐ Entrance to tunnel
☐ Soft verges

These have been put in place to slow the traffic down. They're usually found in residential areas. Slow down to an appropriate speed.

11.49 Mark one answer
Which of these signs means the end of a dual carriageway?

☐   ☐

☐   ☐

If you're overtaking make sure you move back safely into the left-hand lane before you reach the end of the dual carriageway.

11.50 Mark one answer
What does this sign mean?

☐ End of dual carriageway
☐ Tall bridge
☐ Road narrows
☐ End of narrow bridge

Don't leave moving into the left-hand lane until the last moment. Plan ahead and don't rely on other traffic letting you in.

11.51 Mark one answer
What does this sign mean?

☐ Crosswinds
☐ Road noise
☐ Airport
☐ Adverse camber

A warning sign with a picture of a windsock will indicate there may be strong crosswinds. This sign is often found on exposed roads.

11.52 Mark one answer

What does this traffic sign mean?

☐ Slippery road ahead
☐ Tyres liable to punctures ahead
☐ Danger ahead
☐ Service area ahead

This sign is there to alert you to the likelihood of danger ahead. It may be accompanied by a plate indicating the type of hazard. Be ready to reduce your speed and take avoiding action.

11.53 Mark one answer

You are about to overtake when you see this sign. You should

Hidden dip

☐ overtake the other driver as quickly as possible
☐ move to the right to get a better view
☐ switch your headlights on before overtaking
☐ hold back until you can see clearly ahead

You won't be able to see any hazards that might be hidden in the dip. As well as oncoming traffic the dip may conceal
• cyclists
• horse riders
• parked vehicles
• pedestrians in the road.

11.54 Mark one answer

What does this sign mean?

☐ Level crossing with gate or barrier
☐ Gated road ahead
☐ Level crossing without gate or barrier
☐ Cattle grid ahead

Some crossings have gates but no attendant or signals. You should, stop, look both ways, listen and make sure that there is no train approaching. If there is a telephone, contact the signal operator to make sure that it's safe to cross.

11.55 Mark one answer

What does this sign mean?

☐ No trams ahead
☐ Oncoming trams
☐ Trams crossing ahead
☐ Trams only

This sign warns you to beware of trams. If you don't usually drive in a town where there are trams, remember to look out for them at junctions and look for tram rails, signs and signals.

11.56 Mark one answer

What does this sign mean?

☐ Adverse camber
☐ Steep hill downwards
☐ Uneven road
☐ Steep hill upwards

This sign will give you an early warning that the road ahead will slope downhill. Prepare to alter your speed and gear. Looking at the sign from left to right will show you whether the road slopes uphill or downhill.

11.57 Mark one answer

What does this sign mean?

☐ Uneven road surface
☐ Bridge over the road
☐ Road ahead ends
☐ Water across the road

This sign is found where a shallow stream crosses the road. Heavy rainfall could increase the flow of water. If the water looks too deep or the stream has spread over a large distance, stop and find another route.

11.58 Mark one answer

What does this sign mean?

☐ Turn left for parking area
☐ No through road on the left
☐ No entry for traffic turning left
☐ Turn left for ferry terminal

If you intend to take a left turn, this sign shows you that you can't get through to another route using the left-turn junction ahead.

11.59 Mark one answer

What does this sign mean?

☐ T-junction
☐ No through road
☐ Telephone box ahead
☐ Toilet ahead

You will not be able to find a through route to another road. Use this road only for access.

11.60 Mark one answer

Which sign means 'no through road'?

This sign is found at the entrance to a road that can only be used for access.

11.61 Mark one answer

Which is the sign for a ring road?

Ring roads are designed to relieve congestion in towns and city centres.

11.62 Mark one answer

What does this sign mean?

☐ The right-hand lane ahead is narrow
☐ Right-hand lane for buses only
☐ Right-hand lane for turning right
☐ The right-hand lane is closed

Yellow and black temporary signs may be used to inform you of roadworks or lane restrictions. Look well ahead. If you have to change lanes, do so in good time.

11.63 Mark one answer

What does this sign mean?

☐ Change to the left lane
☐ Leave at the next exit
☐ Contraflow system
☐ One-way street

If you use the right-hand lane in a contraflow system, you'll be travelling with no permanent barrier between you and the oncoming traffic. Observe speed limits and keep a good distance from the vehicle ahead.

11.64 Mark one answer

What does this sign mean?

☐ Leave motorway at next exit
☐ Lane for heavy and slow vehicles
☐ All lorries use the hard shoulder
☐ Rest area for lorries

Where there's a long, steep, uphill gradient on a motorway, a crawler lane may be provided. This helps the traffic to flow by diverting the slower heavy vehicles into a dedicated lane on the left.

11.65 Mark one answer

A red traffic light means

☐ you should stop unless turning left
☐ stop, if you are able to brake safely
☐ you must stop and wait behind the stop line
☐ proceed with caution

Make sure you learn and understand the sequence of traffic lights. Whatever light appears you will then know what light is going to appear next and be able to take the appropriate action. For example if amber is showing on its own you'll know that red will appear next, giving you ample time to slow and stop safely.

11.66 Mark one answer

At traffic lights, amber on its own means

☐ prepare to go
☐ go if the way is clear
☐ go if no pedestrians are crossing
☐ stop at the stop line

When amber is showing on its own red will appear next. The amber light means STOP, unless you have already crossed the stop line or you are so close to it that pulling up might cause a collision.

11.67 Mark one answer

You are at a junction controlled by traffic lights. When should you NOT proceed at green?

☐ When pedestrians are waiting to cross
☐ When your exit from the junction is blocked
☐ When you think the lights may be about to change
☐ When you intend to turn right

As you approach the lights look into the road you wish to take. Only proceed if your exit road is clear. If the road is blocked hold back, even if you have to wait for the next green signal.

11.68 Mark one answer

You are in the left-hand lane at traffic lights. You are waiting to turn left. At which of these traffic lights must you NOT move on?

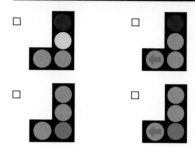

At some junctions there may be a separate signal for different lanes. These are called 'filter' lights. They're designed to help traffic flow at major junctions. Make sure that you're in the correct lane and proceed if the way is clear and the green light shows for your lane.

11.69 Mark one answer

What does this sign mean?

☐ Traffic lights out of order
☐ Amber signal out of order
☐ Temporary traffic lights ahead
☐ New traffic lights ahead

Where traffic lights are out of order you might see this sign. Proceed with caution as nobody has priority at the junction.

11.70 Mark one answer

When traffic lights are out of order, who has priority?

☐ Traffic going straight on
☐ Traffic turning right
☐ Nobody
☐ Traffic turning left

When traffic lights are out of order you should treat the junction as an unmarked crossroads. Be cautious as you may need to give way or stop. Keep a look out for traffic attempting to cross the junction at speed.

11.71 Mark three answers

These flashing red lights mean STOP. In which THREE of the following places could you find them?

☐ Pelican crossings
☐ Lifting bridges
☐ Zebra crossings
☐ Level crossings
☐ Motorway exits
☐ Fire stations

You must always stop when the red lights are flashing, whether or not the way seems to be clear.

11.72 Mark one answer

What do these zigzag lines at pedestrian crossings mean?

☐ No parking at any time
☐ Parking allowed only for a short time
☐ Slow down to 20 mph
☐ Sounding horns is not allowed

The approach to, and exit from, a pedestrian crossing is marked with zigzag lines. You must not park on them or overtake the leading vehicle when approaching the crossing. Parking here would block the view for pedestrians and the approaching traffic.

11.73 Mark one answer
When may you cross a double solid white line in the middle of the road?

☐ To pass traffic that is queueing back at a junction
☐ To pass a car signalling to turn left ahead
☐ To pass a road maintenance vehicle travelling at 10 mph or less
☐ To pass a vehicle that is towing a trailer

You may cross the solid white line to pass a stationary vehicle, pedal cycle, horse or road maintenance vehicle if they are travelling at 10 mph or less. You may also cross the solid line to enter into a side road or access a property.

11.74 Mark one answer
What does this road marking mean?

☐ Do not cross the line
☐ No stopping allowed
☐ You are approaching a hazard
☐ No overtaking allowed

Road markings will warn you of a hazard ahead. A single, broken line along the centre of the road, with long markings and short gaps, is a hazard warning line. Don't cross it unless you can see that the road is clear well ahead.

11.75 Mark one answer
Where would you see this road marking?

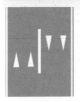

☐ At traffic lights
☐ On road humps
☐ Near a level crossing
☐ At a box junction

Due to the dark colour of the road, changes in level aren't easily seen. White triangles painted on the road surface give you an indication of where there are road humps.

11.76 Mark one answer
Which is a hazard warning line?

☐   ☐

☐   ☐

You need to know the difference between the normal centre line and a hazard warning line. If there is a hazard ahead, the markings are longer and the gaps shorter.

This gives you advanced warning of an unspecified hazard ahead.

11.77 Mark one answer

At this junction there is a stop sign with a solid white line on the road surface. Why is there a stop sign here?

☐ Speed on the major road is derestricted
☐ It is a busy junction
☐ Visibility along the major road is restricted
☐ There are hazard warning lines in the centre of the road

If your view is restricted at a road junction you must stop. There may also be a 'stop' sign. Don't emerge until you're sure there's no traffic approaching.

IF YOU DON'T KNOW, DON'T GO.

11.78 Mark one answer

You see this line across the road at the entrance to a roundabout. What does it mean?

☐ Give way to traffic from the right
☐ Traffic from the left has right of way
☐ You have right of way
☐ Stop at the line

Slow down as you approach the roundabout and check for traffic from the right. If you need to stop and give way, stay behind the broken line until it is safe to emerge onto the roundabout.

11.79 Mark one answer

How will a police officer in a patrol vehicle normally get you to stop?

☐ Flash the headlights, indicate left and point to the left
☐ Wait until you stop, then approach you
☐ Use the siren, overtake, cut in front and stop
☐ Pull alongside you, use the siren and wave you to stop

You must obey signals given by the police. If a police officer in a patrol vehicle wants you to pull over they will indicate this without causing danger to you or other traffic.

11.80 Mark one answer

You approach a junction. The traffic lights are not working. A police officer gives this signal. You should

☐ turn left only
☐ turn right only
☐ stop level with the officer's arm
☐ stop at the stop line

If a police officer or traffic warden is directing traffic you must obey them. They will use the arm signals shown in *The Highway Code*. Learn what these mean and act accordingly.

11.81 Mark one answer

The driver of the car in front is giving this arm signal. What does it mean?

☐ The driver is slowing down
☐ The driver intends to turn right
☐ The driver wishes to overtake
☐ The driver intends to turn left

There might be an occasion where another driver uses an arm signal. This may be because the vehicle's indicators are obscured by other traffic. In order for such signals to be effective all drivers should know the meaning of them. Be aware that the 'left turn' signal might look similar to the 'slowing down' signal.

11.82 Mark one answer

Where would you see these road markings?

☐ At a level crossing
☐ On a motorway slip road
☐ At a pedestrian crossing
☐ On a single-track road

When driving on a motorway or slip road, you must not enter into an area marked with chevrons and bordered by a solid white line for any reason, except in an emergency.

11.83 Mark one answer

What does this motorway sign mean?

☐ Change to the lane on your left
☐ Leave the motorway at the next exit
☐ Change to the opposite carriageway
☐ Pull up on the hard shoulder

On the motorway, signs sometimes show temporary warnings due to traffic or weather conditions. They may be used to indicate

• lane closures
• temporary speed limits
• weather warnings.

11.84 Mark one answer

What does this motorway sign mean?

☐ Temporary minimum speed 50 mph
☐ No services for 50 miles
☐ Obstruction 50 metres (164 feet) ahead
☐ Temporary maximum speed 50 mph

Look out for signs above your lane or on the central reservation. These will give you important information or warnings about the road ahead. Due to the high speed of motorway traffic these signs may light up some distance from any hazard. Don't ignore the signs just because the road looks clear to you.

11.85 Mark one answer

What does this sign mean?

☐ Through traffic to use left lane
☐ Right-hand lane T-junction only
☐ Right-hand lane closed ahead
☐ 11 tonne weight limit

You should move into the lanes as directed by the sign. Here the right-hand lane is closed and the left-hand and centre lanes are available. Merging in turn is recommended when it's safe and traffic is going slowly, for example at road works or a road traffic incident. When vehicles are travelling at speed this is not advisable and you should move into the appropriate lane in good time.

11.86 Mark one answer

On a motorway this sign means

☐ move over onto the hard shoulder
☐ overtaking on the left only
☐ leave the motorway at the next exit
☐ move to the lane on your left

It is important to know and obey temporary signs on the motorway: they are there for a reason. You may not be able to see the hazard straight away, as the signs give warnings well in advance, due to the speed of traffic on the motorway.

11.87 Mark one answer

What does '25' mean on this motorway sign?

☐ The distance to the nearest town
☐ The route number of the road
☐ The number of the next junction
☐ The speed limit on the slip road

Before you set out on your journey use a road map to plan your route. When you see advance warning of your junction, make sure you get into the correct lane in plenty of time. Last-minute harsh braking and cutting across lanes at speed is extremely hazardous.

11.88 Mark one answer

The right-hand lane of a three-lane motorway is

☐ for lorries only
☐ an overtaking lane
☐ the right-turn lane
☐ an acceleration lane

You should stay in the left-hand lane of a motorway unless overtaking. The right-hand lane of a motorway is an overtaking lane and not a 'fast lane'.

After overtaking, move back to the left when it is safe to do so.

11.89 Mark one answer

Where can you find reflective amber studs on a motorway?

☐ Separating the slip road from the motorway
☐ On the left-hand edge of the road
☐ On the right-hand edge of the road
☐ Separating the lanes

At night or in poor visibility reflective studs on the road help you to judge your position on the carriageway.

11.90 Mark one answer

Where on a motorway would you find green reflective studs?

☐ Separating driving lanes
☐ Between the hard shoulder and the carriageway
☐ At slip road entrances and exits
☐ Between the carriageway and the central reservation

Knowing the colours of the reflective studs on the road will help you judge your position, especially at night, in foggy conditions or when visibility is poor.

11.91 Mark one answer

You are travelling along a motorway. You see this sign. You should

☐ leave the motorway at the next exit
☐ turn left immediately
☐ change lane
☐ move onto the hard shoulder

You'll see this sign if the motorway is closed ahead. Pull into the nearside lane as soon as it is safe to do so. Don't leave it to the last moment.

11.92　Mark one answer

What does this sign mean?

☐ No motor vehicles
☐ End of motorway
☐ No through road
☐ End of bus lane

When you leave the motorway make sure that you check your speedometer. You may be going faster than you realise. Slow down and look out for speed limit signs.

11.93　Mark one answer

Which of these signs means that the national speed limit applies?

You should know the speed limit for the road on which you are travelling, and the vehicle that you are driving. The different speed limits are shown in *The Highway Code*.

11.94　Mark one answer

What is the maximum speed on a single carriageway road?

☐ 50 mph
☐ 60 mph
☐ 40 mph
☐ 70 mph

If you're travelling on a dual carriageway that becomes a single carriageway road, reduce your speed gradually so that you aren't exceeding the limit as you enter.

There might not be a sign to remind you of the limit, so make sure you know what the speed limits are for different types of roads and vehicles.

11.95　Mark one answer

What does this sign mean?

☐ End of motorway
☐ End of restriction
☐ Lane ends ahead
☐ Free recovery ends

Temporary restrictions on motorways are shown on signs which have flashing amber lights. At the end of the restriction you will see this sign without any flashing lights.

11.96　Mark one answer

This sign is advising you to

☐ follow the route diversion
☐ follow the signs to the picnic area
☐ give way to pedestrians
☐ give way to cyclists

When a diversion route has been put in place, drivers are advised to follow a symbol which may be a triangle, square, circle or diamond shape on a yellow background.

11.97 Mark one answer

Why would this temporary speed limit sign be shown?

☐ To warn of the end of the motorway
☐ To warn you of a low bridge
☐ To warn you of a junction ahead
☐ To warn of road works ahead

In the interests of road safety, temporary speed limits are imposed at all major road works. Signs like this, giving advanced warning of the speed limit, are normally placed about three quarters of a mile ahead of where the speed limit comes into force.

11.98 Mark one answer

This traffic sign means there is

☐ a compulsory maximum speed limit
☐ an advisory maximum speed limit
☐ a compulsory minimum speed limit
☐ an advised separation distance

The sign gives you an early warning of a speed restriction. If you are travelling at a higher speed, slow down in good time. You could come across queueing traffic due to roadworks or a temporary obstruction.

11.99 Mark one answer

You see this sign at a crossroads. You should

☐ maintain the same speed
☐ carry on with great care
☐ find another route
☐ telephone the police

When traffic lights are out of order treat the junction as an unmarked crossroad. Be very careful as no one has priority and be prepared to stop.

11.100 Mark one answer

You are signalling to turn right in busy traffic. How would you confirm your intention safely?

☐ Sound the horn
☐ Give an arm signal
☐ Flash your headlights
☐ Position over the centre line

In some situations you may feel your indicators cannot be seen by other road users. If you think you need to make your intention more clearly seen, give the arm signal shown in The Highway Code.

11.101 Mark one answer

What does this sign mean?

☐ Motorcycles only
☐ No cars
☐ Cars only
☐ No motorcycles

You must comply with all traffic signs and be especially aware of those signs which apply specifically to the type of vehicle you are using.

11.102 Mark one answer

You are on a motorway. You see this sign on a lorry that has stopped in the right-hand lane. You should

- ☐ move into the right-hand lane
- ☐ stop behind the flashing lights
- ☐ pass the lorry on the left
- ☐ leave the motorway at the next exit

Sometimes work is carried out on the motorway without closing the lanes. When this happens, signs are mounted on the back of lorries to warn other road users of roadworks ahead.

11.103 Mark one answer

You are on a motorway. Red flashing lights appear above your lane only. What should you do?

- ☐ Continue in that lane and look for further information
- ☐ Move into another lane in good time
- ☐ Pull onto the hard shoulder
- ☐ Stop and wait for an instruction to proceed

Flashing red lights above your lane show that your lane is closed. You should move into another lane as soon as you can do so safely.

11.104 Mark one answer

A red traffic light means

- ☐ you must stop behind the white stop line
- ☐ you may go straight on if there is no other traffic
- ☐ you may turn left if it is safe to do so
- ☐ you must slow down and prepare to stop if traffic has started to cross

The white line is generally positioned so that pedestrians have room to cross in front of waiting traffic. Don't move off while pedestrians are crossing, even if the lights change to green.

11.105 Mark one answer

The driver of this car is giving an arm signal. What are they about to do?

- ☐ Turn to the right
- ☐ Turn to the left
- ☐ Go straight ahead
- ☐ Let pedestrians cross

In some situations drivers may need to give arm signals, in addition to indicators, to make their intentions clear. For arm signals to be effective, all road users should know their meaning.

11.106 Mark one answer

When may you sound the horn?

- ☐ To give you right of way
- ☐ To attract a friend's attention
- ☐ To warn others of your presence
- ☐ To make slower drivers move over

Never sound the horn aggressively. You MUST NOT sound it when driving in a built-up area between 11.30 pm and 7.00 am or when you are stationary, an exception to this is when another road user poses a danger. Do not scare animals by sounding your horn.

11.107 Mark one answer

You must not use your horn when you are stationary

- ☐ unless a moving vehicle may cause you danger
- ☐ at any time whatsoever
- ☐ unless it is used only briefly
- ☐ except for signalling that you have just arrived

When stationary only sound your horn if you think there is a risk of danger from another road user. Don't use it just to attract someone's attention. This causes unnecessary noise and could be misleading.

11.108 Mark one answer

What does this sign mean?

- ☐ You can park on the days and times shown
- ☐ No parking on the days and times shown
- ☐ No parking at all from Monday to Friday
- ☐ End of the urban clearway restrictions

Urban clearways are provided to keep traffic flowing at busy times. You may stop only briefly to set down or pick up passengers. Times of operation will vary from place to place so always check the signs.

11.109 Mark one answer

What does this sign mean?

- ☐ Quayside or river bank
- ☐ Steep hill downwards
- ☐ Uneven road surface
- ☐ Road liable to flooding

You should be careful in these locations as the road surface is likely to be wet and slippery. There may be a steep drop to the water, and there may not be a barrier along the edge of the road.

11.110 Mark one answer

Which sign means you have priority over oncoming vehicles?

☐   ☐

☐   ☐

Even though you have priority, be prepared to give way if other drivers don't. This will help to avoid congestion, confrontation or even a collision.

11.111 Mark one answer

A white line like this along the centre of the road is a

- ☐ bus lane marking
- ☐ hazard warning
- ☐ give way marking
- ☐ lane marking

The centre of the road is usually marked by a broken white line, with lines that are shorter than the gaps. When the lines become longer than the gaps this is a hazard warning line. Look well ahead for these, especially when you are planning to overtake or turn off.

11.112 Mark one answer

What is the reason for the yellow criss-cross lines painted on the road here?

- ☐ To mark out an area for trams only
- ☐ To prevent queuing traffic from blocking the junction on the left
- ☐ To mark the entrance lane to a car park
- ☐ To warn you of the tram lines crossing the road

Yellow 'box junctions' like this are often used where it's busy. Their purpose is to keep the junction clear for crossing traffic.

Don't enter the painted area unless your exit is clear. The exception to this is when you are turning right and are only prevented from doing so by oncoming traffic or by other vehicles waiting to turn right.

11.113 Mark one answer

What is the reason for the area marked in red and white along the centre of this road?

- ☐ It is to separate traffic flowing in opposite directions
- ☐ It marks an area to be used by overtaking motorcyclists
- ☐ It is a temporary marking to warn of the roadworks
- ☐ It is separating the two sides of the dual carriageway

Areas of 'hatched markings' such as these are to separate traffic streams which could be a danger to each other. They are often seen on bends or where the road becomes narrow. If the area is bordered by a solid white line, you must not enter it except in an emergency.

11.114 Mark one answer

Other drivers may sometimes flash their headlights at you. In which situation are they allowed to do this?

- ☐ To warn of a radar speed trap ahead
- ☐ To show that they are giving way to you
- ☐ To warn you of their presence
- ☐ To let you know there is a fault with your vehicle

If other drivers flash their headlights this isn't a signal to show priority. The flashing of headlights has the same meaning as sounding the horn, it's a warning of their presence.

11.115 Mark one answer

In some narrow residential streets you may find a speed limit of

- ☐ 20 mph
- ☐ 25 mph
- ☐ 35 mph
- ☐ 40 mph

In some built-up areas, you may find the speed limit reduced to 20 mph. Driving at a slower speed will help give you the time and space to see and deal safely with hazards such as pedestrians and parked cars.

11.116 Mark one answer

At a junction you see this signal. It means

- ☐ cars must stop
- ☐ trams must stop
- ☐ both trams and cars must stop
- ☐ both trams and cars can continue

The white light shows that trams must stop, but the green light shows that other vehicles may go if the way is clear. You may not live in an area where there are trams but you should still learn the signs.

You never know when you may go to a town with trams.

11.117 Mark one answer

Where would you find these road markings?

- ☐ At a railway crossing
- ☐ At a junction
- ☐ On a motorway
- ☐ On a pedestrian crossing

These markings show the direction in which the traffic should go at a mini-roundabout.

11.118 Mark one answer

There is a police car following you. The police officer flashes the headlights and points to the left. What should you do?

- ☐ Turn left at the next junction
- ☐ Pull up on the left
- ☐ Stop immediately
- ☐ Move over to the left

You must pull up on the left as soon as it's safe to do so and switch off your engine.

11.119 Mark one answer

You see this amber traffic light ahead. Which light or lights, will come on next?

☐ Red alone
☐ Red and amber together
☐ Green and amber together
☐ Green alone

At junctions controlled by traffic lights you must stop behind the white line until the lights change to green. Red and amber lights showing together also mean stop.

You may proceed when the light is green unless your exit road is blocked or pedestrians are crossing in front of you.

If you're approaching traffic lights that are visible from a distance and the light has been green for some time they are likely to change. Be ready to slow down and stop.

11.120 Mark one answer

This broken white line painted in the centre of the road means

☐ oncoming vehicles have priority over you
☐ you should give priority to oncoming vehicles
☐ there is a hazard ahead of you
☐ the area is a national speed limit zone

A long white line with short gaps means that you are approaching a hazard. If you do need to cross it, make sure that the road is clear well ahead.

11.121 Mark one answer

You see this signal overhead on the motorway. What does it mean?

☐ Leave the motorway at the next exit
☐ All vehicles use the hard shoulder
☐ Sharp bend to the left ahead
☐ Stop, all lanes ahead closed

You will see this sign if there has been an incident ahead and the motorway is closed.

You MUST obey the sign. Make sure that you prepare to leave as soon as you see the warning sign.

Don't pull over at the last moment or cut across other traffic.

11.122 Mark one answer

What is the purpose of these yellow criss-cross lines on the road?

☐ To make you more aware of the traffic lights
☐ To guide you into position as you turn
☐ To prevent the junction becoming blocked
☐ To show you where to stop when the lights change

You MUST NOT enter a box junction until your exit road or lane is clear. The exception to this is if you want to turn right and are only prevented from doing so by oncoming traffic or by other vehicles waiting to turn right.

11.123 Mark one answer

What MUST you do when you see this sign?

☐ Stop, only if traffic is approaching
☐ Stop, even if the road is clear
☐ Stop, only if children are waiting to cross
☐ Stop, only if a red light is showing

STOP signs are situated at junctions where visibility is restricted or there is heavy traffic. They MUST be obeyed. You MUST stop. Take good all-round observation before moving off.

11.124 Mark one answer

Which shape is used for a 'give way' sign?

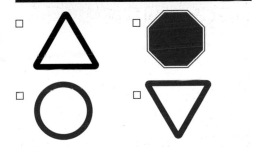

Other warning signs are the same shape and colour, but the 'give way' sign triangle points downwards. When you see this sign you MUST give way to traffic on the road which you are about to enter

11.125 Mark one answer

What does this sign mean?

☐ Buses turning
☐ Ring road
☐ Mini-roundabout
☐ Keep right

When you see this sign, look out for any direction signs and judge whether you need to signal your intentions. Do this in good time so that other road users approaching the roundabout know what you're planning to do.

11.126 Mark one answer

What does this sign mean?

☐ Two-way traffic straight ahead
☐ Two-way traffic crosses a one-way road
☐ Two-way traffic over a bridge
☐ Two-way traffic crosses a two-way road

Be prepared for traffic approaching from junctions on either side of you. Try to avoid unnecessary changing of lanes just before the junction.

11.127 Mark one answer

What does this sign mean?

☐ Two-way traffic ahead across a one-way road
☐ Traffic approaching you has priority
☐ Two-way traffic straight ahead
☐ Motorway contraflow system ahead

This sign may be at the end of a dual carriageway or a one-way street. It is there to warn you of oncoming traffic.

11.128 Mark one answer

What does this sign mean?

☐ Hump-back bridge
☐ Traffic calming hump
☐ Low bridge
☐ Uneven road

You will need to slow down. At humpback bridges your view ahead will be restricted and the road will often be narrow on the bridge. If the bridge is very steep or your view is restricted sound your horn to warn others of your approach. Going too fast over the bridge is highly dangerous to other road users and could even cause your wheels to leave the road, with a resulting loss of control.

11.129 Mark one answer

Which of the following signs informs you that you are coming to a 'no through road'?

This sign is found at the entrance to a road that can only be used for access.

11.130 Mark one answer

What does this sign mean?

☐ Direction to park-and-ride car park
☐ No parking for buses or coaches
☐ Directions to bus and coach park
☐ Parking area for cars and coaches

To ease the congestion in town centres, some cities and towns provide park-and-ride schemes. These allow you to park in a designated area and ride by bus into the centre.

Park-and-ride schemes are usually cheaper and easier than car parking in the town centre.

11.131 Mark one answer

You are approaching traffic lights. Red and amber are showing. This means

☐ pass the lights if the road is clear
☐ there is a fault with the lights – take care
☐ wait for the green light before you cross the stop line
☐ the lights are about to change to red

Be aware that other traffic might still be clearing the junction. Make sure the way is clear before continuing.

11.132 Mark one answer

This marking appears on the road just before a

☐ 'no entry' sign
☐ 'give way' sign
☐ 'stop' sign
☐ 'no through road' sign

Where you see this road marking you should give way to traffic on the main road.

It might not be used at junctions where there is relatively little traffic. However, if there is a double broken line across the junction the 'give way' rules still apply.

11.133 Mark one answer

At a railway level crossing the red light signal continues to flash after a train has gone by. What should you do?

☐ Phone the signal operator
☐ Alert drivers behind you
☐ Wait
☐ Proceed with caution

You MUST always obey red flashing stop lights. If a train passes but the lights continue to flash, another train will be passing soon. Cross only when the lights go off and the barriers open.

11.134 Mark one answer

You are in a tunnel and you see this sign. What does it mean?

☐ Direction to emergency pedestrian exit
☐ Beware of pedestrians, no footpath ahead
☐ No access for pedestrians
☐ Beware of pedestrians crossing ahead

If you have to leave your vehicle in a tunnel and leave by an emergency exit, do so as quickly as you can. Follow the signs directing you to the nearest exit point. If there are several people using the exit, don't panic but try to leave in a calm and orderly manner.

11.135 Mark one answer

Which of these signs shows that you are entering a one-way system?

☐   ☐

☐   ☐

If the road has two lanes you can use either lane and overtake on either side. Use the lane that's more convenient for your destination unless signs or road markings indicate otherwise.

11.136 Mark one answer

What does this sign mean?

☐ With-flow bus and cycle lane
☐ Contraflow bus and cycle lane
☐ No buses and cycles allowed
☐ No waiting for buses and cycles

Buses and cycles can travel in this lane. In this case they will flow in the same direction as other traffic. If it's busy they may be passing you on the left, so watch out for them. Times on the sign will show its hours of operation. No times shown, or no sign at all, means it's 24 hours. In some areas other vehicles, such as taxis and motorcycles, are allowed to use bus lanes. The sign will show these.

11.137 Mark one answer

Which of these signs warns you of a zebra crossing?

☐   ☐

☐   ☐

Look well ahead and check the pavements and surrounding areas for pedestrians.

Look for anyone walking towards the crossing. Check your mirrors for traffic behind, in case you have to slow down or stop.

11.138 Mark one answer

What does this sign mean?

☐ No footpath
☐ No pedestrians
☐ Zebra crossing
☐ School crossing

You need to be aware of the various signs that relate to pedestrians. Some of the signs look similar but have very different meanings. Make sure you know what they all mean and be ready for any potential hazard.

11.139 Mark one answer

What does this sign mean?

☐ School crossing patrol
☐ No pedestrians allowed
☐ Pedestrian zone – no vehicles
☐ Zebra crossing ahead

Look well ahead and be ready to stop for any pedestrians crossing, or about to cross, the road. Also check the pavements for anyone who looks like they might step or run into the road.

11.140 Mark one answer

Which sign means there will be two-way traffic crossing your route ahead?

☐

☐

☐

☐

This sign is found in or at the end of a one-way system. It warns you that traffic will be crossing your path from both directions.

11.141 Mark one answer

Which arm signal tells you that the car you are following is going to pull up?

☐

☐

☐

☐

There may be occasions when drivers need to give an arm signal to confirm an indicator. This could include, in bright sunshine, at a complex road layout, when stopping at a pedestrian crossing or when turning right just after passing a parked vehicle. You should understand what each arm signal means. If you give arm signals, make them clear, correct and decisive.

11.142 Mark one answer

Which of these signs means turn left ahead?

☐

☐

☐

☐

Blue circles tell you what you must do and this sign gives a clear instruction to turn left ahead. You should be looking out for signs at all times and know what they mean.

11.143 Mark one answer

Which sign shows that traffic can only travel in one direction on the road you're on?

This sign means that traffic can only travel in one direction. The others show different priorities on a two-way road.

11.144 Mark one answer

You have just driven past this sign. You should be aware that

☐ it is a single track road
☐ you cannot stop on this road
☐ there is only one lane in use
☐ all traffic is going one way

In a one-way system traffic may be passing you on either side. Always be aware of all traffic signs and understand their meaning.
   Look well ahead and react to them in good time.

11.145 Mark one answer

You are approaching a red traffic light. What will the signal show next?

☐ Red and amber
☐ Green alone
☐ Amber alone
☐ Green and amber

If you know which light is going to show next you can plan your approach accordingly. This can help prevent excessive braking or hesitation at the junction.

11.146 Mark one answer

What does this sign mean?

☐ Low bridge ahead
☐ Tunnel ahead
☐ Ancient monument ahead
☐ Traffic danger spot ahead

When approaching a tunnel switch on your dipped headlights. Be aware that your eyes might need to adjust to the sudden darkness. You may need to reduce your speed.

11.147 Mark one answer

You are approaching a zebra crossing where pedestrians are waiting. Which arm signal might you give?

A 'slowing down' signal will indicate your intentions to oncoming and following vehicles. Be aware that pedestrians might start to cross as soon as they see this signal.

11.148 Mark one answer

The white line along the side of the road

- ☐ shows the edge of the carriageway
- ☐ shows the approach to a hazard
- ☐ means no parking
- ☐ means no overtaking

A continuous white line is used on many roads to indicate the edge of the carriageway. This can be useful when visibility is restricted. The line is discontinued at junctions, lay-bys and entrances and exits from private drives.

11.149 Mark one answer

You see this white arrow on the road ahead. It means

- ☐ entrance on the left
- ☐ all vehicles turn left
- ☐ keep left of the hatched markings
- ☐ road bending to the left

Don't attempt to overtake here, as there might be unseen hazards over the brow of the hill. Keep to the left.

11.150 Mark one answer

How should you give an arm signal to turn left?

☐   ☐

☐   ☐

There may be occasions where other road users are unable to see your indicator, such as in bright sunlight or at a busy, complicated junction. In these cases a hand signal will help others to understand your intentions.

11.151 Mark one answer

You are waiting at a T-junction. A vehicle is coming from the right with the left signal flashing. What should you do?

- ☐ Move out and accelerate hard
- ☐ Wait until the vehicle starts to turn in
- ☐ Pull out before the vehicle reaches the junction
- ☐ Move out slowly

Other road users may give misleading signals. When you're waiting at a junction don't emerge until you're sure of their intentions.

11.152 Mark one answer

When may you use hazard warning lights when driving?

- ☐ Instead of sounding the horn in a built-up area between 11.30 pm and 7 am
- ☐ On a motorway or unrestricted dual carriageway, to warn of a hazard ahead
- ☐ On rural routes, after a warning sign of animals
- ☐ On the approach to toucan crossings where cyclists are waiting to cross

When there's queueing traffic ahead and you have to slow down or even stop, showing your hazard warning lights will alert following traffic to the hazard. Don't forget to switch them off as the queue forms behind you.

11.153 Mark one answer

You are driving on a motorway. There is a slow-moving vehicle ahead. On the back you see this sign. You should

☐ pass on the right
☐ pass on the left
☐ leave at the next exit
☐ drive no further

If a vehicle displaying this sign is in your lane you will have to pass it on the left. Use your mirrors and signal. When it's safe move into the lane on your left. You should always look well ahead so that you can spot any hazards early, giving yourself time to react safely.

11.154 Mark one answer

You should NOT normally stop on these markings near schools

∿-SCHOOL KEEP CLEAR-∿

☐ except when picking up children
☐ under any circumstances
☐ unless there is nowhere else available
☐ except to set down children

At schools you should not stop on yellow zigzag lines for any length of time, not even to set down or pick up children or other passengers.

11.155 Mark one answer

Why should you make sure that your indicators are cancelled after turning?

☐ To avoid flattening the battery
☐ To avoid misleading other road users
☐ To avoid dazzling other road users
☐ To avoid damage to the indicator relay

Leaving your indicators on could confuse other road users and may even lead to a crash. Be aware that if you haven't taken a sharp turn your indicators may not self-cancel and you will need to turn them off manually.

11.156 Mark one answer

You are driving in busy traffic. You want to pull up on the left just after a junction on the left. When should you signal?

☐ As you are passing or just after the junction
☐ Just before you reach the junction
☐ Well before you reach the junction
☐ It would be better not to signal at all

You need to signal to let other drivers know your intentions. However, if you indicate too early they may think you are turning left into the junction. Correct timing of the signal is very important to avoid misleading others.

Documents

12.1 Mark one answer
An MOT certificate is normally valid for

☐ three years after the date it was issued
☐ 10,000 miles
☐ one year after the date it was issued
☐ 30,000 miles

Make a note of the date that your MOT certificate expires. Some garages remind you that your vehicle is due an MOT but not all do. You may take your vehicle for MOT up to to one month in advance and have the certificate post dated.

12.2 Mark one answer
A cover note is a document issued before you receive your

☐ driving licence
☐ insurance certificate
☐ registration document
☐ MOT certificate

Sometimes an insurance company will issue a temporary insurance certificate called a cover note. It gives you the same insurance cover as your certificate, but lasts for a limited period, usually one month.

12.3 Mark two answers
You have just passed your practical test. You do not hold a full licence in another category. Within two years you get six penalty points on your licence. What will you have to do?

☐ Retake only your theory test
☐ Retake your theory and practical tests
☐ Retake only your practical test
☐ Reapply for your full licence immediately
☐ Reapply for your provisional licence

If you accumulate six or more penalty points within two years of gaining your first full licence it will be revoked. The six or more points include any gained due to offences you committed before passing your test. If this happens you may only drive as a learner until you pass both the theory and practical tests again.

12.4 Mark one answer
How long will a Statutory Off Road Notification (SORN) last for?

☐ 12 months
☐ 24 months
☐ 3 years
☐ 10 years

A SORN declaration allows you to keep a vehicle off road and untaxed for 12 months. If you want to keep your vehicle off road beyond that you must send a further SORN form to DVLA, or DVA in Northern Ireland. If the vehicle is sold SORN will end and the new owner becomes responsible immediately.

12.5 Mark one answer   NI EXEMPT
What is a Statutory Off Road Notification (SORN) declaration?

☐ A notification to tell VOSA that a vehicle does not have a current MOT
☐ Information kept by the police about the owner of the vehicle
☐ A notification to tell DVLA that a vehicle is not being used on the road
☐ Information held by insurance companies to check the vehicle is insured

If you want to keep a vehicle off the public road you must declare SORN. It is an offence not to do so. You then won't have to pay road tax. If you don't renew the SORN declaration or re-license the vehicle, you will incur a penalty.

12.6 Mark one answer   NI EXEMPT
A Statutory Off Road Notification (SORN) declaration is

☐ to tell DVLA that your vehicle is being used on the road but the MOT has expired
☐ to tell DVLA that you no longer own the vehicle
☐ to tell DVLA that your vehicle is not being used on the road
☐ to tell DVLA that you are buying a personal number plate

This will enable you to keep a vehicle off the public road for 12 months without having to pay road tax. You must send a further SORN declaration after 12 months.

12.7 Mark one answer
A Statutory Off Road Notification (SORN) is valid

☐ for as long as the vehicle has an MOT
☐ for 12 months only
☐ only if the vehicle is more than 3 years old
☐ provided the vehicle is insured

If you want to keep a vehicle off the public road you must declare SORN. It is an offence not to do so. You then won't have to pay road tax for that vehicle. You will incur a penalty after 12 months if you don't renew the SORN declaration, or re-license the vehicle. If you sell the vehicle the SORN declaration ends and the new owner should declare SORN or re-license the vehicle.

12.8 Mark one answer
A Statutory Off Road Notification (SORN) will last

☐ for the life of the vehicle
☐ for as long as you own the vehicle
☐ for 12 months only
☐ until the vehicle warranty expires

If you are keeping a vehicle, or vehicles, off road and don't want to pay road tax you must declare SORN. You must still do this even if the vehicle is incapable of being used, for example it may be under restoration or being stored. After 12 months you must send another SORN declaration or re-license your vehicle. You will be fined if you don't do this. The SORN will end if you sell the vehicle and the new owner will be responsible immediately.

12.9 Mark one answer
What is the maximum specified fine for driving without insurance?

☐ 50
☐ £500
☐ £1,000
☐ £5,000

It is a serious offence to drive without insurance. As well as a heavy fine you may be disqualified or incur penalty points.

12.10 Mark one answer
Who is legally responsible for ensuring that a Vehicle Registration Certificate (V5C) is updated?

☐ The registered vehicle keeper
☐ The vehicle manufacturer
☐ Your insurance company
☐ The licensing authority

It is your legal responsibility to keep the details of your Vehicle Registration Certificate (V5C) up to date. You should tell the licensing authority of any changes. These include your name, address, or vehicle details. If you don't do this you may have problems when you sell your vehicle.

12.11 Mark one answer
For which of these MUST you show your insurance certificate?

☐ When making a SORN declaration
☐ When buying or selling a vehicle
☐ When a police officer asks you for it
☐ When having an MOT inspection

You MUST be able to produce your valid insurance certificate when requested by a police officer. If you can't do this immediately you may be asked to take it to a police station. Other documents you may be asked to produce are your driving licence and MOT certificate.

12.12 Mark one answer
You must have valid insurance before you can

☐ make a SORN declaration
☐ buy or sell a vehicle
☐ apply for a driving licence
☐ obtain a tax disc

You MUST have valid insurance before you can apply for a tax disc. Your vehicle will also need to have a valid MOT certificate, if applicable. You can apply on-line, at certain post offices or by post. It is illegal and can be dangerous to drive without valid insurance or an MOT.

12.13 Mark one answer
Your vehicle needs a current MOT certificate. Until you have one you will NOT be able to

☐ renew your driving licence
☐ change your insurance company
☐ renew your road tax disc
☐ notify a change of address

If your vehicle is required to have an MOT certificate you will need to make sure this is current before you are able to renew your tax disc (also known as vehicle excise duty). You can renew online, by phone or by post.

12.14 Mark three answers

Which THREE of these do you need before you can use a vehicle on the road legally?

☐ A valid driving licence
☐ A valid tax disc clearly displayed
☐ Proof of your identity
☐ Proper insurance cover
☐ Breakdown cover
☐ A vehicle handbook

Using a vehicle on the road illegally carries a heavy fine and can lead to penalty points on your licence. Things you MUST have include, a valid driving licence, a current valid tax disc, and proper insurance cover.

12.15 Mark one answer

When you apply to renew your Vehicle Excise Duty (tax disc) you must have

☐ valid insurance
☐ the old tax disc
☐ the handbook
☐ a valid driving licence

Tax discs can be renewed at post offices, vehicle registration offices, online, or by post. When applying make sure you have all the relevant valid documents, including MOT where applicable.

12.16 Mark one answer

A police officer asks to see your documents. You do not have them with you. You may be asked to take them to a police station within

☐ 5 days
☐ 7 days
☐ 14 days
☐ 21 days

You don't have to carry the documents for your vehicle around with you. If a police officer asks to see them and you don't have them with you, you may be asked to produce them at a police station within seven days.

12.17 Mark one answer

When you apply to renew your vehicle excise licence (tax disc) what must you have?

☐ Valid insurance
☐ The old tax disc
☐ The vehicle handbook
☐ A valid driving licence

Tax discs can be renewed, online, at most post offices, your nearest vehicle registration office or by post to the licensing authority. Make sure you have or take all the relevant documents with your application.

12.18 Mark one answer

When should you update your Vehicle Registration Certificate?

☐ When you pass your driving test
☐ When you move house
☐ When your vehicle needs an MOT
☐ When you have a collision

As the registered keeper of a vehicle it is up to you to inform DVLA (DVA in Northern Ireland) of any changes in your vehicle or personal details, for example, change of name or address. You do this by completing the relevant section of the Registration Certificate and sending it to them.

12.19 Mark one answer

To drive on the road learners MUST

☐ have NO penalty points on their licence
☐ have taken professional instruction
☐ have a signed, valid provisional licence
☐ apply for a driving test within 12 months

Before you drive on the road you MUST have a valid provisional licence, for the category of vehicle that you're driving. It must show your signature, it isn't valid without it.

12.20 Mark one answer

Before driving anyone else's motor vehicle you should make sure that

☐ the vehicle owner has third party insurance cover
☐ your own vehicle has insurance cover
☐ the vehicle is insured for your use
☐ the owner has left the insurance documents in the vehicle

Driving a vehicle without insurance cover is illegal. If you cause injury to anyone or damage to property, it could be very expensive and you could also be subject to a criminal prosecution. You can arrange insurance cover with, an insurance company, a broker and some motor manufacturers or dealers.

12.21 Mark one answer

Your car needs an MOT certificate. If you drive without one this could invalidate your

☐ vehicle service record
☐ insurance
☐ road tax disc
☐ vehicle registration document

If your vehicle requires an MOT certificate, it's illegal to drive it without one. The only exceptions are that you may drive to a prearranged MOT test appointment, or to a garage for repairs required for the test. As well as being illegal, the vehicle may also be unsafe for use on the road and could endanger you, any passengers, and other road users.

12.22 Mark one answer

How old must you be to supervise a learner driver?

☐ 18 years old
☐ 19 years old
☐ 20 years old
☐ 21 years old

As well as being at least 21 years old you must hold a full EC/EEA driving licence for the category of vehicle being driven and have held that licence for at least three years.

12.23 Mark one answer

A newly qualified driver must

☐ display green 'L' plates
☐ not exceed 40 mph for 12 months
☐ be accompanied on a motorway
☐ have valid motor insurance

It is your responsibility to make sure you are properly insured for the vehicle you are driving.

12.24 Mark three answers

You have third party insurance. What does this cover?

☐ Damage to your own vehicle
☐ Damage to your vehicle by fire
☐ Injury to another person
☐ Damage to someone's property
☐ Damage to other vehicles
☐ Injury to yourself

Third party insurance doesn't cover damage to your own vehicle or injury to yourself. If you have a crash and your vehicle is damaged you might have to carry out the repairs at your own expense.

12.25 Mark one answer

Vehicle excise duty is often called 'Road Tax' or 'The Tax Disc'. You must

☐ keep it with your registration document
☐ display it clearly on your vehicle
☐ keep it concealed safely in your vehicle
☐ carry it on you at all times

The tax disc should be displayed at the bottom of the windscreen on the nearside (left-hand side). This allows it to be easily seen from the kerbside. It must be current, and you can't transfer the disc from vehicle to vehicle.

12.26 Mark one answer

Your vehicle needs a current MOT certificate. You do not have one. Until you do have one you will not be able to renew your

☐ driving licence
☐ vehicle insurance
☐ road tax disc
☐ vehicle registration document

When you renew your road tax disc you need to produce a current, valid MOT certificate for your vehicle.

12.27 Mark three answers

Which THREE pieces of information are found on a vehicle registration document?

☐ Registered keeper
☐ Make of the vehicle
☐ Service history details
☐ Date of the MOT
☐ Type of insurance cover
☐ Engine size

Every vehicle used on the road has a registration certificate. This is issued by the Driver and Vehicle Licensing Agency (DVLA) or Driver and Vehicle Agency (DVA) in Northern Ireland. The document shows vehicle details including, date of first registration, registration number, previous keeper, registered keeper, make of vehicle, engine size and chassis number, year of manufacture and colour.

12.28 Mark three answers

You have a duty to contact the licensing authority when

☐ you go abroad on holiday
☐ you change your vehicle
☐ you change your name
☐ your job status is changed
☐ your permanent address changes
☐ your job involves travelling abroad

The licensing authority need to keep their records up to date. They send out a reminder when your road tax is due and need your current address to send this to you. Every vehicle in the country is registered, so it's possible to trace its history.

12.29 Mark three answers

You must notify the licensing authority when

☐ your health affects your driving
☐ your eyesight does not meet a set standard
☐ you intend lending your vehicle
☐ your vehicle requires an MOT certificate
☐ you change your vehicle

The Driver and Vehicle Licensing Agency (DVLA) hold the records of all vehicles and drivers in Great Britain (DVA in Northern Ireland). They need to know of any change in circumstances so that they can keep their records up to date. Your health might affect your ability to drive safely. Don't risk endangering your own safety or that of other road users.

12.30 Mark one answer   NI EXEMPT

The cost of your insurance may reduce if you

☐ are under 25 years old
☐ do not wear glasses
☐ pass the driving test first time
☐ take the Pass Plus scheme

The cost of insurance varies with your age and how long you have been driving.

Usually, the younger you are the more expensive it is, especially if you are under 25 years of age.

The Pass Plus scheme provides additional training to newly qualified drivers. Pass Plus is recognised by many insurance companies and taking this extra training could give you reduced insurance premiums, as well as improving your skills and experience.

12.31 Mark one answer   NI EXEMPT

Which of the following may reduce the cost of your insurance?

☐ Having a valid MOT certificate
☐ Taking a Pass Plus course
☐ Driving a powerful car
☐ Having penalty points on your licence

The aim of the Pass Plus course is to build up your skills and experience. It is recognised by some insurance companies, who reward people completing the scheme with cheaper insurance premiums.

12.32 Mark two answers

To supervise a learner driver you must

☐ have held a full licence for at least 3 years
☐ be at least 21 years old
☐ be an approved driving instructor
☐ hold an advanced driving certificate

Don't just take someone's word that they are qualified to supervise you. The person who sits alongside you while you are learning should be a responsible adult and an experienced driver.

12.33 Mark one answer   NI EXEMPT

When is it legal to drive a car over three years old without an MOT certificate?

☐ Up to seven days after the old certificate has run out
☐ When driving to an MOT centre to arrange an appointment
☐ Just after buying a second-hand car with no MOT
☐ When driving to an appointment at an MOT centre

Any car over three years old MUST have a valid MOT certificate before it can be used on the road. Exceptionally, you may drive to a pre-arranged test appointment or to a garage for repairs required for the test. However you should check this with your insurance company. Driving an un-roadworthy vehicle may invalidate your insurance.

12.34 Mark one answer   NI EXEMPT

Motor cars must first have an MOT test certificate when they are

☐ one year old
☐ three years old
☐ five years old
☐ seven years old

The vehicle you drive MUST be roadworthy and in good condition. If it's over three years old it MUST have a valid MOT test certificate. The MOT test ensures that a vehicle meets minimum legal standards in terms of safety, components and environmental impact at the time it is tested.

12.35 Mark one answer NI EXEMPT

The Pass Plus scheme has been created for new drivers. What is its main purpose?

☐ To allow you to drive faster
☐ To allow you to carry passengers
☐ To improve your basic skills
☐ To let you drive on motorways

New drivers are far more vulnerable on the road and more likely to be involved in incidents and collisions. The Pass Plus scheme has been designed to improve new drivers' basic skills and help widen their driving experience.

12.36 Mark two answers

Your vehicle is insured third party only. This covers

☐ damage to your vehicle
☐ damage to other vehicles
☐ injury to yourself
☐ injury to others
☐ all damage and injury

This type of insurance cover is usually cheaper than comprehensive. However, it does not cover any damage to your own vehicle or property. It only covers damage and injury to others.

12.37 Mark one answer

What is the legal minimum insurance cover you must have to drive on public roads?

☐ Third party, fire and theft
☐ Comprehensive
☐ Third party only
☐ Personal injury cover

The minimum insurance required by law is third party cover. This covers others involved in a collision but not damage to your vehicle. Basic third party insurance won't cover theft or fire damage. Check with your insurance company for advice on the best cover for you and make sure that you read the policy carefully.

12.38 Mark one answer

You claim on your insurance to have your car repaired. Your policy has an excess of £100. What does this mean?

☐ The insurance company will pay the first £100 of any claim
☐ You will be paid £100 if you do not claim within one year
☐ Your vehicle is insured for a value of £100 if it is stolen
☐ You will have to pay the first £100 of the cost of repair to your car

Having an excess on your policy will help to keep down the premium, but if you make a claim you will have to pay the excess yourself, in this case £100.

12.39 Mark one answer NI EXEMPT

The Pass Plus scheme is designed to

☐ give you a discount on your MOT
☐ improve your basic driving skills
☐ increase your mechanical knowledge
☐ allow you to drive anyone else's vehicle

After passing your practical driving test you can take further training. This is known as the Pass Plus scheme. It is designed to improve your basic driving skills and involves a series of modules including night time and motorway driving. The sort of things you may not have covered whilst learning.

12.40 Mark one answer NI EXEMPT

By taking part in the Pass Plus scheme you will

☐ never get any points on your licence
☐ be able to service your own car
☐ allow you to drive anyone else's vehicle
☐ improve your basic driving skills

The Pass Plus scheme can be taken after you've passed your practical driving test.
Ask your ADI for details. It is designed to improve your basic driving skills. By successfully completing the course you may get a discount on your insurance.

12.41 Mark one answer · NI EXEMPT

The Pass Plus scheme is aimed at all newly qualified drivers. It enables them to

☐ widen their driving experience
☐ supervise a learner driver
☐ increase their insurance premiums
☐ avoid mechanical breakdowns

The Pass Plus scheme was created by DSA for newly qualified drivers. It aim's to widen their driving experience and improve basic skills. After passing the practical driving test additional professional training can be taken with an Approved Driving Instructor (ADI). Some insurance companies also offer discounts to holders of a Pass Plus certificate. You will find more information in *Drive On* magazine.

12.42 Mark two answers · NI EXEMPT

New drivers can take further training after passing the practical test. A Pass Plus course will help to

☐ improve your basic skills
☐ widen your experience
☐ increase your insurance premiums
☐ get cheaper road tax

Novice drivers are in much more danger than experienced drivers. They can often be involved in collisions soon after passing their test, sometimes with tragic results.

The Pass Plus scheme gives structured training to help new drivers improve basic skills and widen their experience. Approved Driving Instructors (ADIs) will be able to advise of the benefits.

12.43 Mark one answer · NI EXEMPT

The Pass Plus Scheme is operated by DSA for newly qualified drivers. It is intended to

☐ improve your basic skills
☐ reduce the cost of your driving licence
☐ prevent you from paying congestion charges
☐ allow you to supervise a learner driver

The Pass Plus scheme provides a wide range of driving experience accompanied by a qualified instructor. There is no test and when completed you may get a reduction in insurance costs. It can help to improve basic skills, reduce the risk of having a collision and make you a safer driver.

12.44 Mark one answer

For which of these must you show your motor insurance certificate?

☐ When you are taking your driving test
☐ When buying or selling a vehicle
☐ When a police officer asks you for it
☐ When having an MOT inspection

When you take out motor insurance you'll be issued with a certificate. This contains details explaining who and what is insured. If a police officer asks to see your insurance certificate you must produce it at the time or at a police station within a specified period. You also need to have current valid insurance when renewing your vehicle excise duty (road tax).

12.45 Mark three answers

Which THREE of these do you need before you can drive legally?

☐ A valid driving licence
☐ A valid tax disc displayed on your vehicle
☐ A vehicle service record
☐ Proper insurance cover
☐ Breakdown cover
☐ A vehicle handbook

Make sure that you have a valid driving licence and proper insurance cover before driving any vehicle. These are legal requirements, as is displaying a valid tax disc in the vehicle.

12.46 Mark one answer

A friend wants to help you learn to drive. They must be

☐ at least 21 and have held a full licence for at least one year
☐ over 18 and hold an advanced driver's certificate
☐ over 18 and have fully comprehensive insurance
☐ at least 21 and have held a full licence for at least three years

Helping someone to drive is a responsible task. Before learning to drive you're advised to find a qualified Approved Driving Instructor (ADI) to teach you. This will ensure that you're taught the correct procedures from the start.

12.47 Mark one answer

Your motor insurance policy has an excess of £100. What does this mean?

☐ The insurance company will pay the first £100 of any claim
☐ You will be paid £100 if you do not have a crash
☐ Your vehicle is insured for a value of £100 if it is stolen
☐ You will have to pay the first £100 of any claim

This is a method used by insurance companies to keep annual premiums down. Generally, the higher the excess you choose to pay, the lower the annual premium you will be charged.

Incidents, accidents and emergencies

13.1 Mark one answer

You see a car on the hard shoulder of a motorway with a HELP pennant displayed. This means the driver is most likely to be

☐ a disabled person
☐ first aid trained
☐ a foreign visitor
☐ a rescue patrol person

If a disabled driver's vehicle breaks down and they are unable to walk to an emergency phone, they are advised to stay in their car and switch on the hazard warning lights. They may also display a 'Help' pennant in their vehicle.

13.2 Mark two answers

For which TWO should you use hazard warning lights?

☐ When you slow down quickly on a motorway because of a hazard ahead
☐ When you have broken down
☐ When you wish to stop on double yellow lines
☐ When you need to park on the pavement

Hazard warning lights are fitted to all modern cars and some motorcycles. They should only be used to warn other road users of a hazard ahead.

13.3 Mark one answer

When are you allowed to use hazard warning lights?

☐ When stopped and temporarily obstructing traffic
☐ When travelling during darkness without headlights
☐ When parked for shopping on double yellow lines
☐ When travelling slowly because you are lost

You must not use hazard warning lights when moving, except when slowing suddenly on a motorway or unrestricted dual carriageway to warn the traffic behind. Never use hazard warning lights to excuse dangerous or illegal parking.

13.4 Mark one answer

You are going through a congested tunnel and have to stop. What should you do?

☐ Pull up very close to the vehicle in front to save space
☐ Ignore any message signs as they are never up to date
☐ Keep a safe distance from the vehicle in front
☐ Make a U-turn and find another route

It's important to keep a safe distance from the vehicle in front at all times. This still applies in congested tunnels even if you are moving very slowly or have stopped. If the vehicle in front breaks down you may need room to manoeuvre past it.

13.5 Mark one answer

On the motorway, the hard shoulder should be used

☐ to answer a mobile phone
☐ when an emergency arises
☐ for a short rest when tired
☐ to check a road atlas

Pull onto the hard shoulder and use the emergency telephone to report your problem. This lets the emergency services know your exact location so they can send help. Never cross the carriageway to use the telephone on the other side.

13.6 Mark one answer

You arrive at the scene of a crash. Someone is bleeding badly from an arm wound. There is nothing embedded in it. What should you do?

☐ Apply pressure over the wound and keep the arm down
☐ Dab the wound
☐ Get them a drink
☐ Apply pressure over the wound and raise the arm

If possible, lay the casualty down. Check for anything that may be in the wound. Apply firm pressure to the wound using clean material, without pressing on anything which might be in it. Raising the arm above the level of the heart will also help to stem the flow of blood.

13.7 Mark one answer

You are at an incident where a casualty is unconscious. Their breathing should be checked. This should be done for at least

☐ 2 seconds
☐ 10 seconds
☐ 1 minute
☐ 2 minutes

Once the airway is open, check breathing. Listen and feel for breath. Do this by placing your cheek over their mouth and nose, and look to see if the chest rises. This should be done for up to 10 seconds.

13.8 Mark one answer

Following a collision someone has suffered a burn. The burn needs to be cooled. What is the shortest time it should be cooled for?

☐ 5 minutes
☐ 10 minutes
☐ 15 minutes
☐ 20 minutes

Check the casualty for shock and if possible try to cool the burn for at least ten minutes. Use a clean, cold non-toxic liquid preferably water.

13.9 Mark one answer

After a collision someone has suffered a burn. The burn needs to be cooled. What is the shortest time it should be cooled for?

☐ 30 seconds
☐ 60 seconds
☐ 5 minutes
☐ 10 minutes

It's important to cool a burn for at least ten minutes. Use a clean, cold non-toxic liquid preferably water. Bear in mind the person may also be in shock.

13.10 Mark one answer

A casualty is not breathing normally. Chest compressions should be given. At what rate?

☐ 50 per minute
☐ 100 per minute
☐ 200 per minute
☐ 250 per minute

If a casualty is not breathing normally chest compressions may be needed to maintain circulation. Place two hands on the centre of the chest and press down about 4–5 centimetres, at the rate of 100 per minute.

13.11 Mark one answer

A person has been injured. They may be suffering from shock. What are the warning signs to look for?

☐ Flushed complexion
☐ Warm dry skin
☐ Slow pulse
☐ Pale grey skin

The effects of shock may not be immediately obvious. Warning signs are rapid pulse, sweating, pale grey skin and rapid shallow breathing.

13.12 Mark one answer

You suspect that an injured person may be suffering from shock. What are the warning signs to look for?

☐ Warm dry skin
☐ Sweating
☐ Slow pulse
☐ Skin rash

Sometimes you may not realise that someone is in shock. The signs to look for are rapid pulse, sweating, pale grey skin and rapid shallow breathing.

13.13 Mark one answer

An injured person has been placed in the recovery position. They are unconscious but breathing normally. What else should be done?

☐ Press firmly between the shoulders
☐ Place their arms by their side
☐ Give them a hot sweet drink
☐ Check the airway is clear

After a casualty has been placed in the recovery position, their airway should be checked to make sure it's clear. Don't leave them alone until medical help arrives. Where possible do NOT move a casualty unless there's further danger.

13.14 Mark one answer

An injured motorcyclist is lying unconscious in the road. You should always

☐ remove the safety helmet
☐ seek medical assistance
☐ move the person off the road
☐ remove the leather jacket

If someone has been injured, the sooner proper medical attention is given the better.
Send someone to phone for help or go yourself. An injured person should only be moved if they're in further danger. An injured motorcyclist's helmet should NOT be removed unless it is essential.

13.15 Mark one answer

You are on a motorway. A large box falls onto the road from a lorry. The lorry does not stop. You should

☐ go to the next emergency telephone and report the hazard
☐ catch up with the lorry and try to get the driver's attention
☐ stop close to the box until the police arrive
☐ pull over to the hard shoulder, then remove the box

Lorry drivers can be unaware of objects falling from their vehicles. If you see something fall onto a motorway look to see if the driver pulls over. If they don't stop, do not attempt to retrieve it yourself. Pull on to the hard shoulder near an emergency telephone and report the hazard. You will be connected to the police or a Highways Agency control centre.

13.16 Mark one answer

You are going through a long tunnel. What will warn you of congestion or an incident ahead?

☐ Hazard warning lines
☐ Other drivers flashing their lights
☐ Variable message signs
☐ Areas marked with hatch markings

Follow the instructions given by the signs or by tunnel officials.
In congested tunnels a minor incident can soon turn into a major one with serious or even fatal results.

13.17 Mark one answer

An adult casualty is not breathing. To maintain circulation, compressions should be given. What is the correct depth to press?

☐ 1 to 2 centimetres
☐ 4 to 5 centimetres
☐ 10 to 15 centimetres
☐ 15 to 20 centimetres

An adult casualty is not breathing normally. To maintain circulation place two hands on the centre of the chest. Then press down 4 – 5 centimetres at a rate of 100 times per minute.

13.18 Mark two answers

You are the first to arrive at the scene of a crash. Which TWO of these should you do?

☐ Leave as soon as another motorist arrives
☐ Make sure engines are switched off
☐ Drag all casualties away from the vehicles
☐ Call the emergency services promptly

At a crash scene you can help in practical ways, even if you aren't trained in first aid. Make sure you do not put yourself or anyone else in danger. The safest way to warn other traffic is by switching on your hazard warning lights.

13.19 Mark one answer

At the scene of a traffic incident you should

☐ not put yourself at risk
☐ go to those casualties who are screaming
☐ pull everybody out of their vehicles
☐ leave vehicle engines switched on

It's important that people at the scene of a collision do not create further risk to themselves or others. If the incident is on a motorway or major road, traffic will be approaching at speed. Do not put yourself at risk when trying to help casualties or warning other road users.

13.20 Mark three answers

You are the first person to arrive at an incident where people are badly injured. Which THREE should you do?

☐ Switch on your own hazard warning lights
☐ Make sure that someone telephones for an ambulance
☐ Try and get people who are injured to drink something
☐ Move the people who are injured clear of their vehicles
☐ Get people who are not injured clear of the scene

If you're the first to arrive at a crash scene the first concerns are the risk of further collision and fire. Ensuring that vehicle engines are switched off will reduce the risk of fire. Use hazard warning lights so that other traffic knows there's a need for caution. Make sure the emergency services are contacted, don't assume this has already been done.

13.21 Mark one answer

You arrive at the scene of a motorcycle crash. The rider is injured. When should the helmet be removed?

☐ Only when it is essential
☐ Always straight away
☐ Only when the motorcyclist asks
☐ Always, unless they are in shock

DO NOT remove a motorcyclist's helmet unless it is essential. Remember they may be suffering from shock. Don't give them anything to eat or drink but do reassure them confidently.

13.22 Mark three answers

You arrive at a serious motorcycle crash. The motorcyclist is unconscious and bleeding. Your THREE main priorities should be to

☐ try to stop the bleeding
☐ make a list of witnesses
☐ check their breathing
☐ take the numbers of other vehicles
☐ sweep up any loose debris
☐ check their airways

Further collisions and fire are the main dangers immediately after a crash. If possible get others to assist you and make the area safe. Help those involved and remember, DR ABC, Danger, Response, Airway, Breathing, Compressions. This will help when dealing with any injuries.

13.23 Mark one answer

You arrive at an incident. A motorcyclist is unconscious. Your FIRST priority is the casualty's

☐ breathing
☐ bleeding
☐ broken bones
☐ bruising

At the scene of an incident always be aware of danger from further collisions or fire. The first priority when dealing with an unconscious person is to ensure they can breathe. This may involve clearing their airway if you can see an obstruction, or if they're having difficulty breathing.

13.24 Mark three answers

At an incident a casualty is unconscious. Which THREE of these should you check urgently?

☐ Circulation
☐ Airway
☐ Shock
☐ Breathing
☐ Broken bones

Remember DR ABC. An unconscious casualty may have difficulty breathing.
Check that their airway is clear by tilting the head back gently and unblock it if necessary. Then make sure they are breathing. If there is bleeding, stem the flow by placing clean material over any wounds but without pressing on any objects in the wound. Compressions may need to be given to maintain circulation.

13.25 Mark three answers

You arrive at the scene of an incident. It has just happened and someone is unconscious. Which THREE of these should be given urgent priority to help them?

☐ Clear the airway and keep it open
☐ Try to get them to drink water
☐ Check that they are breathing
☐ Look for any witnesses
☐ Stop any heavy bleeding
☐ Take the numbers of vehicles involved

Make sure that the emergency services are called immediately. Once first aid has been given, stay with the casualty.

13.26 Mark three answers

At an incident someone is unconscious. Your THREE main priorities should be to

☐ sweep up the broken glass
☐ take the names of witnesses
☐ count the number of vehicles involved
☐ check the airway is clear
☐ make sure they are breathing
☐ stop any heavy bleeding

Remember this procedure by saying DR ABC. This stands for, Danger, Response, Airway, Breathing, Compressions.

13.27 Mark three answers

You have stopped at an incident to give help. Which THREE things should you do?

☐ Keep injured people warm and comfortable
☐ Keep injured people calm by talking to them reassuringly
☐ Keep injured people on the move by walking them around
☐ Give injured people a warm drink
☐ Make sure that injured people are not left alone

There are a number of things you can do to help, even without expert training. Be aware of further danger and fire, make sure the area is safe. People may be in shock. Don't give them anything to eat or drink.
Keep them warm and comfortable and reassure them. Don't move injured people unless there is a risk of further danger.

13.28 Mark three answers

You arrive at an incident. It has just happened and someone is injured. Which THREE should be given urgent priority?

☐ Stop any severe bleeding
☐ Give them a warm drink
☐ Check they are breathing
☐ Take numbers of vehicles involved
☐ Look for witnesses
☐ Clear their airway and keep it open

The first priority with a casualty is to make sure their airway is clear and they are breathing. Any wounds should be checked for objects and then bleeding stemmed using clean material. Ensure the emergency services are called, they are the experts. If you're not first aid trained consider getting training. It might save a life.

13.29 Mark one answer

Which of the following should you NOT do at the scene of a collision?

☐ Warn other traffic by switching on your hazard warning lights
☐ Call the emergency services immediately
☐ Offer someone a cigarette to calm them down
☐ Ask drivers to switch off their engines

Keeping casualties or witnesses calm is important, but never offer a cigarette because of the risk of fire. Bear in mind they may be in shock. Don't offer an injured person anything to eat or drink. They may have internal injuries or need surgery.

13.30 Mark two answers

There has been a collision. A driver is suffering from shock. What TWO of these should you do?

☐ Give them a drink
☐ Reassure them
☐ Not leave them alone
☐ Offer them a cigarette
☐ Ask who caused the incident

Be aware they could have an injury that is not immediately obvious. Ensure the emergency services are called. Reassure and stay with them until the experts arrive.

13.31 Mark one answer

You have to treat someone for shock at the scene of an incident. You should

☐ reassure them constantly
☐ walk them around to calm them down
☐ give them something cold to drink
☐ cool them down as soon as possible

Stay with the casualty and talk to them quietly and firmly to calm and reassure them. Avoid moving them unnecessarily in case they are injured. Keep them warm, but don't give them anything to eat or drink.

13.32 Mark one answer

You arrive at the scene of a motorcycle crash. No other vehicle is involved. The rider is unconscious and lying in the middle of the road. The FIRST thing you should do is

☐ move the rider out of the road
☐ warn other traffic
☐ clear the road of debris
☐ give the rider reassurance

The motorcyclist is in an extremely vulnerable position, exposed to further danger from traffic. Approaching vehicles need advance warning in order to slow down and safely take avoiding action or stop. Don't put yourself or anyone else at risk. Use the hazard warning lights on your vehicle to alert other road users to the danger.

13.33 Mark one answer

At an incident a small child is not breathing. To restore normal breathing you should breathe into their mouth

☐ sharply
☐ gently
☐ heavily
☐ rapidly

If a young child has stopped breathing, first check that the airway is clear. Then give compressions to the chest using one hand (two fingers for an infant) and begin mouth to mouth resuscitation. Breathe very gently and continue the procedure until they can breathe without help.

13.34 Mark three answers

At an incident a casualty is not breathing. To start the process to restore normal breathing you should

☐ tilt their head forward
☐ clear the airway
☐ turn them on their side
☐ tilt their head back gently
☐ pinch the nostrils together
☐ put their arms across their chest

It's important to ensure that the airways are clear before you start mouth to mouth resuscitation. Gently tilt their head back and use your finger to check for and remove any obvious obstruction in the mouth.

13.35 Mark one answer

You arrive at an incident. There has been an engine fire and someone's hands and arms have been burnt. You should NOT

☐ douse the burn thoroughly with clean cool non-toxic liquid
☐ lay the casualty down on the ground
☐ remove anything sticking to the burn
☐ reassure them confidently and repeatedly

This could cause further damage and infection to the wound. Your first priority is to cool the burn with a clean, cool, non-toxic liquid, preferably water. Don't forget the casualty may be in shock.

13.36 Mark one answer

You arrive at an incident where someone is suffering from severe burns. You should

☐ apply lotions to the injury
☐ burst any blisters
☐ remove anything stuck to the burns
☐ douse the burns with clean cool non-toxic liquid

Use a liquid that is clean, cold and non-toxic, preferably water. Its coolness will help take the heat out of the burn and relieve the pain. Keep the wound doused for at least ten minutes. If blisters appear don't attempt to burst them as this could lead to infection.

13.37 Mark two answers

You arrive at an incident. A pedestrian has a severe bleeding leg wound. It is not broken and there is nothing in the wound. What TWO of these should you do?

☐ Dab the wound to stop bleeding
☐ Keep both legs flat on the ground
☐ Apply firm pressure to the wound
☐ Raise the leg to lessen bleeding
☐ Fetch them a warm drink

First check for anything that may be in the wound such as glass. If there's nothing in it apply a pad of clean cloth or bandage.
Raising the leg will lessen the flow of blood. Don't tie anything tightly round the leg. This will restrict circulation and can result in long-term injury.

13.38 Mark one answer

At an incident a casualty is unconscious but still breathing. You should only move them if

☐ an ambulance is on its way
☐ bystanders advise you to
☐ there is further danger
☐ bystanders will help you to

Do not move a casualty unless there is further danger, for example, from other traffic or fire. They may have unseen or internal injuries. Moving them unnecessarily could cause further injury. Do NOT remove a motorcyclist's helmet unless it's essential.

13.39 Mark one answer

At a collision you suspect a casualty has back injuries. The area is safe. You should

☐ offer them a drink
☐ not move them
☐ raise their legs
☐ not call an ambulance

Talk to the casualty and keep them calm. Do not attempt to move them as this could cause further injury. Call an ambulance at the first opportunity.

13.40 Mark one answer

At an incident it is important to look after any casualties. When the area is safe, you should

☐ get them out of the vehicle
☐ give them a drink
☐ give them something to eat
☐ keep them in the vehicle

When the area is safe and there's no danger from other traffic or fire it's better not to move casualties. Moving them may cause further injury.

13.41 Mark one answer

A tanker is involved in a collision. Which sign shows that it is carrying dangerous goods?

There will be an orange label on the side and rear of the tanker. Look at this carefully and report what it says when you phone the emergency services. Details of hazard warning plates are given in *The Highway Code*.

13.42 Mark three answers

You are involved in a collision. Because of this which THREE of these documents may the police ask you to produce?

☐ Vehicle registration document
☐ Driving licence
☐ Theory test certificate
☐ Insurance certificate
☐ MOT test certificate
☐ Vehicle service record

You MUST stop if you have been involved in a collision which results in injury or damage. The police may ask to see your documents at the time or later at a police station.

13.43 Mark one answer

After a collision someone is unconscious in their vehicle. When should you call the emergency services?

☐ Only as a last resort
☐ As soon as possible
☐ After you have woken them up
☐ After checking for broken bones

It is important to make sure that emergency services arrive on the scene as soon as possible. When a person is unconscious, they could have serious injuries that are not immediately obvious.

13.44 Mark one answer

A casualty has an injured arm. They can move it freely but it is bleeding. Why should you get them to keep it in a raised position?

☐ Because it will ease the pain
☐ It will help them to be seen more easily
☐ To stop them touching other people
☐ It will help to reduce the blood flow

If a casualty is bleeding heavily, raise the limb to a higher position. This will help to reduce the blood flow. Before raising the limb you should make sure that it is not broken.

13.45 Mark one answer

You are going through a tunnel. What systems are provided to warn of any incidents, collisions or congestion?

☐ Double white centre lines
☐ Variable message signs
☐ Chevron 'distance markers'
☐ Rumble strips

Take notice of any instructions given on variable message signs or by tunnel officials. They will warn you of any incidents or congestion ahead and advise you what to do.

13.46 Mark one answer

A collision has just happened. An injured person is lying in a busy road. What is the FIRST thing you should do to help?

☐ Treat the person for shock
☐ Warn other traffic
☐ Place them in the recovery position
☐ Make sure the injured person is kept warm

The most immediate danger is further collisions and fire. You could warn other traffic by displaying an advance warning triangle or sign (but not on a motorway), switching on hazard warning lights or by any other means that does not put you or others at risk.

13.47 Mark two answers

At an incident a casualty has stopped breathing. You should

☐ remove anything that is blocking the mouth
☐ keep the head tilted forwards as far as possible
☐ raise the legs to help with circulation
☐ try to give the casualty something to drink
☐ tilt the head back gently to clear the airway

Unblocking the airway and gently tilting the head back will help the casualty to breathe.
   They will then be in the correct position if mouth-to-mouth resuscitation is required.
   Don't move a casualty unless there's further danger.

13.48 Mark four answers

You are at the scene of an incident. Someone is suffering from shock. You should

☐ reassure them constantly
☐ offer them a cigarette
☐ keep them warm
☐ avoid moving them if possible
☐ avoid leaving them alone
☐ give them a warm drink

The signs of shock may not be immediately obvious. Prompt treatment can help to minimise the effects. Lay the casualty down, loosen tight clothing, call an ambulance and check their breathing and pulse.

13.49 Mark one answer

There has been a collision. A motorcyclist is lying injured and unconscious. Unless it's essential, why should you usually NOT attempt to remove their helmet?

☐ Because they may not want you to
☐ This could result in more serious injury
☐ They will get too cold if you do this
☐ Because you could scratch the helmet

When someone is injured, any movement which is not absolutely necessary should be avoided since it could make injuries worse. Unless it is essential, it's generally safer to leave a motorcyclist's helmet in place.

13.50 Mark one answer

You have broken down on a two-way road. You have a warning triangle. You should place the warning triangle at least how far from your vehicle?

☐ 5 metres (16 feet)
☐ 25 metres (82 feet)
☐ 45 metres (147 feet)
☐ 100 metres (328 feet)

Advance warning triangles fold flat and don't take up much room. Use it to warn other road users if your vehicle has broken down or there's been an incident. Place it at least 45 metres (147 feet) behind your vehicle or incident on the same side of the road or verge. Place it further back if the scene is hidden by, for example, a bend, hill or dip in the road. Don't use them on motorways.

13.51 Mark three answers

You break down on a level crossing. The lights have not yet begun to flash. Which THREE things should you do?

☐ Telephone the signal operator
☐ Leave your vehicle and get everyone clear
☐ Walk down the track and signal the next train
☐ Move the vehicle if a signal operator tells you to
☐ Tell drivers behind what has happened

If your vehicle breaks down on a level crossing, your first priority is to get everyone out of the vehicle and clear of the crossing. Then use the railway telephone, if there is one, to tell the signal operator. If you have time before the train arrives, move the vehicle clear of the crossing, but only do this if alarm signals are not on.

13.52 Mark two answers

Your tyre bursts while you are driving. Which TWO things should you do?

☐ Pull on the handbrake
☐ Brake as quickly as possible
☐ Pull up slowly at the side of the road
☐ Hold the steering wheel firmly to keep control
☐ Continue on at a normal speed

A tyre bursting can lead to a loss of control, especially if you're travelling at high speed.
   Using the correct procedure should help you to stop the vehicle safely.

13.53 Mark two answers

Which TWO things should you do when a front tyre bursts?

☐ Apply the handbrake to stop the vehicle
☐ Brake firmly and quickly
☐ Let the vehicle roll to a stop
☐ Hold the steering wheel lightly
☐ Grip the steering wheel firmly

Try not to react by applying the brakes harshly. This could lead to further loss of steering control. Indicate your intention to pull up at the side of the road and roll to a stop.

13.54 Mark one answer

Your vehicle has a puncture on a motorway. What should you do?

☐ Drive slowly to the next service area to get assistance
☐ Pull up on the hard shoulder. Change the wheel as quickly as possible
☐ Pull up on the hard shoulder. Use the emergency phone to get assistance
☐ Switch on your hazard lights. Stop in your lane

Pull up on the hard shoulder and make your way to the nearest emergency telephone to call for assistance.
   Do not attempt to repair your vehicle while it is on the hard shoulder because of the risk posed by traffic passing at high speeds.

13.55 Mark one answer

You have stalled in the middle of a level crossing and cannot restart the engine. The warning bell starts to ring. You should

☐ get out and clear of the crossing
☐ run down the track to warn the signal operator
☐ carry on trying to restart the engine
☐ push the vehicle clear of the crossing

Try to stay calm, especially if you have passengers on board. If you can't restart your engine before the warning bells ring, leave the vehicle and get yourself and any passengers well clear of the crossing.

13.56 Mark two answers

You are on a motorway. When can you use hazard warning lights?

☐ When a vehicle is following too closely
☐ When you slow down quickly because of danger ahead
☐ When you are towing another vehicle
☐ When driving on the hard shoulder
☐ When you have broken down on the hard shoulder

Hazard warning lights will warn the traffic travelling behind you that there is a hazard ahead.

13.57 Mark three answers

You have broken down on a motorway. When you use the emergency telephone you will be asked

☐ for the number on the telephone that you are using
☐ for your driving licence details
☐ for the name of your vehicle insurance company
☐ for details of yourself and your vehicle
☐ whether you belong to a motoring organisation

Have these details ready before you use the emergency telephone and be sure to give the correct information. For your own safety always face the traffic when you speak on a roadside telephone.

13.58 Mark one answer

Before driving through a tunnel what should you do?

☐ Switch your radio off
☐ Remove any sunglasses
☐ Close your sunroof
☐ Switch on windscreen wipers

If you are wearing sunglasses you should remove them before driving into a tunnel. If you don't, your vision will be restricted, even in tunnels that appear to be well-lit.

13.59 Mark one answer

You are driving through a tunnel and the traffic is flowing normally. What should you do?

☐ Use parking lights
☐ Use front spot lights
☐ Use dipped headlights
☐ Use rear fog lights

Before entering a tunnel you should switch on your dipped headlights, as this will allow you to see and be seen. In many tunnels it is a legal requirement.
   Don't wear sunglasses while driving in a tunnel. You may wish to tune your radio into a local channel.

13.60 Mark one answer

You are driving through a tunnel. Your vehicle breaks down. What should you do?

☐ Switch on hazard warning lights
☐ Remain in your vehicle
☐ Wait for the police to find you
☐ Rely on CCTV cameras seeing you

If your vehicle breaks down in a tunnel it could present a danger to other traffic. First switch on your hazard warning lights and then call for help from an emergency telephone point.
   Don't rely on being found by the police or being seen by a CCTV camera. The longer the vehicle stays in an exposed position, the more danger it poses to other drivers.

13.61 Mark one answer

When driving through a tunnel you should

☐ Look out for variable message signs
☐ Use your air conditioning system
☐ Switch on your rear fog lights
☐ Always use your windscreen wipers

A minor incident in a tunnel can quickly turn into a major disaster. Variable message signs are provided to warn of any incidents or congestion. Follow their advice.

13.62 Mark two answers

What TWO safeguards could you take against fire risk to your vehicle?

☐ Keep water levels above maximum
☐ Carry a fire extinguisher
☐ Avoid driving with a full tank of petrol
☐ Use unleaded petrol
☐ Check out any strong smell of petrol
☐ Use low octane fuel

The fuel in your vehicle can be a dangerous fire hazard. Never
• use a naked flame near the vehicle if you can smell fuel
• smoke when refuelling your vehicle.

13.63 Mark one answer

You are on the motorway. Luggage falls from your vehicle. What should you do?

☐ Stop at the next emergency telephone and contact the police
☐ Stop on the motorway and put on hazard lights while you pick it up
☐ Walk back up the motorway to pick it up
☐ Pull up on the hard shoulder and wave traffic down

If any object falls onto the motorway carriageway from your vehicle pull over onto the hard shoulder near an emergency telephone and phone for assistance. You will be connected to the police or a Highways Agency control centre. Don't stop on the carriageway or attempt to retrieve anything.

13.64 Mark one answer

While driving, a warning light on your vehicle's instrument panel comes on. You should

☐ continue if the engine sounds all right
☐ hope that it is just a temporary electrical fault
☐ deal with the problem when there is more time
☐ check out the problem quickly and safely

Make sure you know what the different warning lights mean. An illuminated warning light could mean that your car is unsafe to drive. Don't take risks. If you aren't sure about the problem get a qualified mechanic to check it.

13.65 Mark one answer

You have broken down on a two-way road. You have a warning triangle. It should be displayed

☐ on the roof of your vehicle
☐ at least 150 metres (492 feet) behind your vehicle
☐ at least 45 metres (147 feet) behind your vehicle
☐ just behind your vehicle

If you need to display a warning triangle make sure that it can be clearly seen by other road users. Place it on the same side of the road as the broken down vehicle and away from any obstruction that would make it hard to see.

13.66 Mark one answer

Your engine catches fire. What should you do first?

☐ Lift the bonnet and disconnect the battery
☐ Lift the bonnet and warn other traffic
☐ Call a breakdown service
☐ Call the fire brigade

If you suspect a fire in the engine compartment you should pull up as safely and as quickly as possible. DO NOT open the bonnet as this will fuel the fire further. Get any passengers out of the vehicle and dial 999 immediately to contact the fire brigade.

13.67 Mark one answer

Your vehicle breaks down in a tunnel. What should you do?

☐ Stay in your vehicle and wait for the police
☐ Stand in the lane behind your vehicle to warn others
☐ Stand in front of your vehicle to warn oncoming drivers
☐ Switch on hazard lights then go and call for help immediately

A broken-down vehicle in a tunnel can cause serious congestion and danger to other road users. If your vehicle breaks down, get help without delay. Switch on your hazard warning lights, then go to an emergency telephone point to call for help.

13.68 Mark one answer

Your vehicle catches fire while driving through a tunnel. It is still driveable. What should you do?

☐ Leave it where it is with the engine running
☐ Pull up, then walk to an emergency telephone point
☐ Park it away from the carriageway
☐ Drive it out of the tunnel if you can do so

If it's possible, and you can do so without causing further danger, it may be safer to drive a vehicle which is on fire out of a tunnel. The greatest danger in a tunnel fire is smoke and suffocation.

13.69 Mark one answer

You are driving through a tunnel. Your vehicle catches fire. What should you do?

☐ Continue through the tunnel if you can
☐ Turn your vehicle around immediately
☐ Reverse out of the tunnel
☐ Carry out an emergency stop

The main dangers in a tunnel fire are suffocation and smoke. If you can do so safely it's better to drive a burning vehicle out of a tunnel. If you can't do this, pull over, switch off the engine, use hazard warning lights and phone immediately for help. It may be possible to put out a small fire but if it seems large do NOT tackle it!

13.70 Mark two answers

You are in a tunnel. Your vehicle is on fire and you CANNOT drive it. What should you do?

☐ Stay in the vehicle and close the windows
☐ Switch on hazard warning lights
☐ Leave the engine running
☐ Try and put out the fire
☐ Switch off all of your lights
☐ Wait for other people to phone for help

It's usually better to drive a burning vehicle out of a tunnel. If you can't do this pull over and stop at an emergency point if possible.

Switch off the engine, use hazard warning lights, and leave the vehicle immediately.

Call for help from the nearest emergency point. If you have an extinguisher it may help to put out a small fire but do NOT try to tackle a large one.

13.71 Mark one answer

When approaching a tunnel it is good advice to

☐ put on your sunglasses and use the sun visor
☐ check your tyre pressures
☐ change down to a lower gear
☐ make sure your radio is tuned to the frequency shown

On the approach to tunnels a sign will usually show a local radio channel. It should give a warning of any incidents or congestion in the tunnel ahead. Many radios can be set to automatically pick up traffic announcements and local frequencies. If you have to tune the radio manually don't be distracted while doing so. Incidents in tunnels can lead to serious casualties. The greatest hazard is fire.

Getting an advance warning of problems could save your life and others.

13.72 Mark one answer

Your vehicle has broken down on an automatic railway level crossing. What should you do FIRST?

☐ Get everyone out of the vehicle and clear of the crossing
☐ Telephone your vehicle recovery service to move it
☐ Walk along the track to give warning to any approaching trains
☐ Try to push the vehicle clear of the crossing as soon as possible

Firstly get yourself and anyone else well away from the crossing. If there's a railway phone use that to get instructions from the signal operator. Then if there's time move the vehicle clear of the crossing.

13.73 Mark three answers

Which THREE of these items should you carry for use in the event of a collision?

☐ Road map
☐ Can of petrol
☐ Jump leads
☐ Fire extinguisher
☐ First aid kit
☐ Warning triangle

Used correctly, these items can provide invaluable help in the event of a collision or breakdown. They could even save a life.

13.74 Mark one answer

You have a collision whilst your car is moving. What is the FIRST thing you must do?

☐ Stop only if someone waves at you
☐ Call the emergency services
☐ Stop at the scene of the incident
☐ Call your insurance company

If you are in a collision that causes damage or injury to any other person, vehicle, animal or property, by law you MUST STOP. Give your name, the vehicle owner's name and address, and the vehicle's registration number to anyone who has reasonable grounds for requiring them.

13.75 Mark four answers

You are in collision with another moving vehicle. Someone is injured and your vehicle is damaged. Which FOUR of the following should you find out?

☐ Whether the driver owns the other vehicle involved
☐ The other driver's name, address and telephone number
☐ The make and registration number of the other vehicle
☐ The occupation of the other driver
☐ The details of the other driver's vehicle insurance
☐ Whether the other driver is licensed to drive

Try to keep calm and don't rush. Ensure that you have all the details before you leave the scene. If possible take pictures and note the positions of all the vehicles involved.

13.76 Mark one answer   NI EXEMPT

You lose control of your car and damage a garden wall. No one is around. What must you do?

☐ Report the incident to the police within 24 hours
☐ Go back to tell the house owner the next day
☐ Report the incident to your insurance company when you get home
☐ Find someone in the area to tell them about it immediately

If the property owner is not available at the time, you MUST inform the police of the incident. This should be done as soon as possible, and within 24 hours.

13.77 Mark one answer

You are in a collision on a two-way road. You have a warning triangle with you. At what distance before the obstruction should you place the warning triangle?

☐ 25 metres (82 feet)
☐ 45 metres (147 feet)
☐ 100 metres (328 feet)
☐ 150 metres (492 feet)

This is the minimum distance to place the triangle from the obstruction. If there's a bend or hump in the road place it so that approaching traffic has plenty of time to react to the warning and slow down. You may also need to use your hazard warning lights, especially in poor visibility or at night.

13.78 Mark one answer

You have a collision while driving through a tunnel. You are not injured but your vehicle cannot be driven. What should you do FIRST?

☐ Rely on other drivers phoning for the police
☐ Switch off the engine and switch on hazard lights
☐ Take the names of witnesses and other drivers
☐ Sweep up any debris that is in the road

If you are involved in a collision in a tunnel be aware of the danger this can cause to other traffic. The greatest danger is fire. Put on your hazard warning lights straight away and switch off your engine. Then call for help from an emergency telephone point.

13.79 Mark one answer

You are driving through a tunnel. There has been a collision and the car in front is on fire and blocking the road. What should you do?

☐ Overtake and continue as quickly as you can
☐ Lock all the doors and windows
☐ Switch on hazard warning lights
☐ Stop, then reverse out of the tunnel

If the vehicle in front is on fire, you should pull over to the side and stop. Switch on your warning lights and switch off your engine. If you can locate a fire extinguisher use it to put out the fire, taking great care.

Do NOT open the bonnet. Always call for help from the nearest emergency point and if possible give first aid to anyone who is injured.

14.1 Mark two answers

You are towing a small trailer on a busy three-lane motorway. All the lanes are open. You must

☐ not exceed 60 mph
☐ not overtake
☐ have a stabiliser fitted
☐ use only the left and centre lanes

You should be aware of the motorway regulations for vehicles towing trailers. These state that a vehicle towing a trailer must not
• use the right-hand lane of a three-lane motorway unless directed to do so, for example, at roadworks or due to a lane closure
• exceed 60 mph.

14.2 Mark one answer

If a trailer swerves or snakes when you are towing it you should

☐ ease off the accelerator and reduce your speed
☐ let go of the steering wheel and let it correct itself
☐ brake hard and hold the pedal down
☐ increase your speed as quickly as possible

Strong winds or buffeting from large vehicles can cause a trailer or caravan to snake or swerve. If this happens, ease off the accelerator. Don't brake harshly, steer sharply or increase your speed.

14.3 Mark one answer

How can you stop a caravan snaking from side to side?

☐ Turn the steering wheel slowly to each side
☐ Accelerate to increase your speed
☐ Stop as quickly as you can
☐ Slow down very gradually

Keep calm and don't brake harshly or you could lose control completely. Ease off the accelerator until the unit is brought back under control. The most dangerous time is on long downhill gradients.

14.4 Mark two answers

On which TWO occasions might you inflate your tyres to more than the recommended normal pressure?

☐ When the roads are slippery
☐ When driving fast for a long distance
☐ When the tyre tread is worn below 2mm
☐ When carrying a heavy load
☐ When the weather is cold
☐ When the vehicle is fitted with anti-lock brakes

Check the vehicle handbook. This should give you guidance on the correct tyre pressures for your vehicle and when you may need to adjust them. If you are carrying a heavy load you may need to adjust the headlights as well. Most cars have a switch on the dashboard to do this.

14.5 Mark one answer

A heavy load on your roof rack will

☐ improve the road holding
☐ reduce the stopping distance
☐ make the steering lighter
☐ reduce stability

A heavy load on your roof rack will reduce the stability of the vehicle because it moves the centre of gravity away from that designed by the manufacturer. Be aware of this when you negotiate bends and corners.

If you change direction at speed, your vehicle and/or load could become unstable and you could lose control.

14.6 Mark one answer

You are towing a caravan along a motorway. The caravan begins to swerve from side to side. What should you do?

☐ Ease off the accelerator slowly
☐ Steer sharply from side to side
☐ Do an emergency stop
☐ Speed up very quickly

Try not to brake or steer heavily as this will only make matters worse and you could lose control altogether. Keep calm and regain control by easing off the accelerator.

14.7 Mark two answers

Overloading your vehicle can seriously affect the

☐ gearbox
☐ steering
☐ handling
☐ battery life
☐ journey time

Any load will have an effect on the handling of your vehicle and this becomes worse as you increase the load. Any change in the centre of gravity or weight the vehicle is carrying will affect its braking and handling on bends.

You need to be aware of this when carrying passengers, heavy loads, fitting a roof rack or towing a trailer.

14.8 Mark one answer

Who is responsible for making sure that a vehicle is not overloaded?

☐ The driver of the vehicle
☐ The owner of the items being carried
☐ The person who loaded the vehicle
☐ The licensing authority

Your vehicle must not be overloaded. Carrying heavy loads will affect control and handling characteristics. If your vehicle is overloaded and it causes a crash, you'll be held responsible.

14.9 Mark one answer

You are planning to tow a caravan. Which of these will mostly help to aid the vehicle handling?

☐ A jockey wheel fitted to the towbar
☐ Power steering fitted to the towing vehicle
☐ Anti-lock brakes fitted to the towing vehicle
☐ A stabiliser fitted to the towbar

Towing a caravan or trailer affects the way the tow vehicle handles. It is highly recommended that you take a caravan manoeuvring course. These are provided by various organisations for anyone wishing to tow a trailer.

14.10 Mark one answer

Are passengers allowed to ride in a caravan that is being towed?

☐ Yes, if they are over fourteen
☐ No, not at any time
☐ Only if all the seats in the towing vehicle are full
☐ Only if a stabiliser is fitted

Riding in a towed caravan is highly dangerous. The safety of the entire unit is dependent on the stability of the trailer.

Moving passengers would make the caravan unstable and could cause loss of control.

14.11 Mark one answer

A trailer must stay securely hitched up to the towing vehicle. What additional safety device can be fitted to the trailer braking system?

☐ Stabiliser
☐ Jockey wheel
☐ Corner steadies
☐ Breakaway cable

In the event of a towbar failure the cable activates the trailer brakes, then snaps. This allows the towing vehicle to get free of the trailer and out of danger.

14.12 Mark one answer

Why would you fit a stabiliser before towing a caravan?

☐ It will help with stability when driving in crosswinds
☐ It will allow heavy items to be loaded behind the axle
☐ It will help you to raise and lower the jockey wheel
☐ It will allow you to tow without the breakaway cable

Fitting a stabiliser to your tow bar will help to reduce snaking by the caravan especially where there are crosswinds. However, this does not take away your responsibility to ensure that your vehicle/caravan combination is loaded correctly.

14.13 Mark one answer

You wish to tow a trailer. Where would you find the maximum noseweight of your vehicle's tow ball?

☐ In the vehicle handbook
☐ In The Highway Code
☐ In your vehicle registration certificate
☐ In your licence documents

You must know how to load your trailer or caravan so that the hitch exerts a downward force onto the tow ball. This information can be found in your vehicle handbook or from your vehicle manufacturer's agent.

14.14   Mark one answer

Any load that is carried on a roof rack should be

☐ securely fastened when driving
☐ loaded towards the rear of the vehicle
☐ visible in your exterior mirror
☐ covered with plastic sheeting

The safest way to carry items on the roof is in a specially designed roof box. This will help to keep your luggage secure and dry, and also has less wind resistance than loads carried on a roof rack.

14.15   Mark one answer

You are carrying a child in your car. They are under three years of age. Which of these is a suitable restraint?

☐ A child seat
☐ An adult holding a child
☐ An adult seat belt
☐ An adult lap belt

It's your responsibility to ensure that all children in your car are secure. Suitable restraints include a child seat, baby seat, booster seat or booster cushion. It's essential that any restraint used should be suitable for the child's size and weight, and fitted to the manufacturer's instructions.

Section One
Alertness

1.1 look over your shoulder for a
final check
1.2 slow down
consider using your horn
beware of pedestrians
1.3 Approaching a dip in the road
1.4 overtaking drivers to move back to the left
1.5 pull up in a suitable place
1.6 To make you aware of your speed
1.7 be ready to stop
1.8 Use the mirrors
1.9 allows the driver to see you in the mirrors
1.10 To assess how your actions will affect following traffic
1.11 Stop and then move forward slowly and carefully for a
proper view
1.12 restrict your view
distract your attention
1.13 Loud music
Arguing with a passenger
Using a mobile phone
Putting in a cassette tape
1.14 leave the motorway and find a safe place to stop
ensure a supply of fresh air into your vehicle
1.15 even when street lights are not lit
so others can see you
1.16 use a mobile phone
listen to very loud music
1.17 Using a mobile phone
Talking into a microphone
Tuning your car radio
Looking at a map
1.18 suitably parked
1.19 keep both hands on the wheel
1.20 look round before you move off
use all the mirrors on the vehicle
give a signal if necessary
1.21 slowly, leaving plenty of room
1.22 find a safe place to stop
1.23 stop in a proper and convenient place
1.24 Turn into a side road, stop and check a map
1.25 approaching bends and junctions
1.26 Ask someone to guide you
1.27 An area not covered by your mirrors
1.28 could distract your attention from the road
1.29 divert your attention
1.30 Find a suitable place to stop
1.31 stop in a safe place
1.32 Check that the central reservation is wide enough for
your vehicle
1.33 Motorcyclists
1.34 Windscreen pillars
1.35 Stop in a safe place before using the system
1.36 Leave the motorway and stop in a safe place
1.37 is still likely to distract your attention from the road

Section Two
Attitude

2.1 give way to pedestrians already on the crossing
2.2 there may be another vehicle coming
2.3 following another vehicle too closely
2.4 your view ahead is reduced
2.5 four seconds
2.6 Slow down
2.7 Bomb disposal
Blood transfusion
Police patrol
2.8 Coastguard
Bomb disposal
Mountain rescue
2.9 pull over as soon as safely possible to let it pass
2.10 Doctor's car
2.11 doctor on an emergency call
2.12 tram drivers
2.13 Cycles
2.14 To alert others to your presence
2.15 in the right-hand lane
2.16 To help other road users know what you intend to do
2.17 Toucan
2.18 allow the vehicle to overtake
2.19 to let them know that you are there
2.20 Slow down and look both ways
2.21 give way to pedestrians who are crossing
2.22 to keep a safe gap from the vehicle in front
2.23 Steady amber
2.24 Slow down, gradually increasing the gap between you
and the vehicle in front
2.25 A doctor is answering an emergency call
2.26 slow down and give way if it is safe to do so
2.27 Dipped headlights
2.28 slow down and let the vehicle turn
2.29 Drop back to leave the correct separation distance
2.30 apply the handbrake only
2.31 keep a steady course and allow the driver behind to
overtake
2.32 in operation 24 hours a day
2.33 Drive slowly past
Give plenty of room
2.34 stop and switch off your engine
2.35 go past slowly and carefully
2.36 slow down and prepare to stop
2.37 Slow down and be ready to stop
2.38 Be patient and wait
2.39 give you a good view of the road ahead
2.40 the pedestrians have reached a safe position
2.41

2.42 Flashing amber
2.43 good
2.44 use dipped beam headlights
2.45 pull in safely when you can, to let following vehicles
overtake

2.46 waste fuel and money
make roads slippery for other road users
2.47 your filler cap is securely fastened
2.48 slippery
2.49 Competitive
2.50 showing off and being competitive

Section Three
Safety and your vehicle

3.1 Braking
Steering
3.2 between 11.30 pm and 7 am in a built-up area
3.3 reduces noise pollution
uses electricity
reduces town traffic
3.4 they use electric power
3.5 help the traffic flow
3.6 traffic calming measures
3.7 toxic exhaust gases
3.8 exhaust fumes cleaner
3.9 When tyres are cold
3.10 Between 11.30 pm and 7 am
3.11 under-inflated
3.12 Take it to a local authority site
Take it to a garage
3.13 Harsh braking and accelerating
3.14 Distilled water
3.15 Where the speed limit exceeds 30 mph
3.16 air pollution
damage to buildings
using up of natural resources
3.17 The braking system
Wheel alignment
The suspension
3.18 Just above the cell plates
3.19 left with parking lights on
3.20 Look at a map
3.21 a motoring organisation
3.22 Use a route planner on the internet
3.23 Print or write down the route
3.24 You will have an easier journey
3.25 you will have a more pleasant journey
3.26 it will help to ease congestion
3.27 you are less likely to be delayed
3.28 Your original route may be blocked
3.29 Your first route may be blocked
3.30 allow plenty of time for your journey
3.31 increased fuel consumption
3.32 20%
3.33 Brake fluid level
3.34 reduce harmful exhaust emissions
3.35 Under-inflated tyres
3.36 fuel consumption
braking
3.37 braking system
suspension
3.38 the brakes overheating
3.39 have the brakes checked immediately
3.40 a fault in the braking system
3.41 To maintain control of the pedals
3.42 A properly adjusted head restraint
3.43 Worn shock absorbers
3.44 increase fuel consumption
3.45 have a large deep cut in the side wall
3.46 1.6 mm
3.47 You, the driver
3.48 It will waste fuel

3.49 By reducing your speed
By gentle acceleration
By servicing your vehicle properly
3.50 having your vehicle properly serviced
making sure your tyres are correctly inflated
not over-revving in the lower gears
3.51 use public transport more often
share a car when possible
walk or cycle on short journeys
3.52 Carrying unnecessary weight
Under-inflated tyres
A fitted, empty roof rack
3.53 Cycle when possible
Have your vehicle properly tuned and serviced
Watch the traffic and plan ahead
3.54 use your car for very short journeys
3.55 Headlights
Windscreen
Seat belts
3.56 30%
3.57 consult your garage as soon as possible
3.58 the steering to vibrate
3.59 steering
tyres
3.60 lock them out of sight
3.61 Lock valuables out of sight
3.62 Etching the car number on the windows
3.63 The vehicle documents
3.64 Remove all valuables
3.65 An immobiliser
3.66 engage the steering lock
3.67 remove the key and lock it
3.68 Reducing your road speed
Planning well ahead
3.69 Take it to a local authority site
3.70 To help protect the environment against pollution
3.71 avoid harsh acceleration
brake in good time
anticipate well ahead
3.72 exhaust emissions
3.73 better fuel economy
cleaner exhaust emissions
3.74 Maintain a reduced speed throughout
3.75 Before a long journey
3.76 No, not in any circumstances
3.77 lock it and remove the key
3.78 lock it and remove the key
3.79 In a secure car park
3.80 In front of a property entrance
At or near a bus stop
On the approach to a level crossing
3.81 Near the brow of a hill
Where the kerb has been lowered for wheelchairs
At or near a bus stop
3.82 In a secure car park
3.83 help you to avoid neck injury
3.84 making a lot of short journeys
accelerating as quickly as possible
3.85 walking or cycling
3.86 Take all valuables with you
3.87 Install a security-coded radio
3.88 Lock them out of sight
3.89 Park in a well-lit area
3.90 Leave it in a well-lit area
3.91 vehicle watch scheme
3.92 On the exhaust system
3.93 lock it and remove the key
3.94 reduce fuel consumption by about 15%
3.95 missing out some gears

3.96 By reducing exhaust emissions
3.97 Improved road safety
3.98 By reducing the amount of time you are accelerating
3.99 accelerating
3.100 1.6 mm
3.101 accelerating
3.102 exempt for medical reasons
3.103 exempt for medical reasons
3.104 You, the driver
3.105 Oil leaks
3.106 use an adult seat belt
3.107 Make sure any front passenger airbag is deactivated
3.108 a suitable child restraint is available
3.109 Switch off the engine
3.110 Deactivate the airbag
3.111 a correct child restraint is not available
3.112 Never if you are away from the vehicle

Section Four
Safety margins

4.1 ten times the normal distance
4.2 ten times
4.3 passing pedal cyclists
4.4 To improve your view of the road
4.5 go slowly while gently applying the brakes
4.6 The grip of the tyres
The braking
4.7 On an open stretch of road
4.8 96 metres (315 feet)
4.9 73 metres (240 feet)
4.10 Drop back to regain a safe distance
4.11 53 metres (175 feet)
4.12 36 metres (118 feet)
4.13 Pass wide
4.14 Allow extra room
4.15 38 metres (125 feet)
4.16 Increase your distance from the vehicle in front
4.17 Reduce your speed and increase the gap in front
4.18 reduce speed in good time
choose an appropriate lane in good time
keep the correct separation distance
4.19 Driver error
4.20 Drive at a slow speed in as high a gear as possible
4.21 the driver
4.22 Slow down before you reach the bend
Avoid sudden steering movements
4.23 steer carefully to the right
4.24 windows
lights
mirrors
number plates
4.25 the highest gear you can
4.26 brake gently in plenty of time
4.27 road holding
4.28 select a low gear and use the brakes carefully
4.29 Turn the steering wheel towards the kerb
Put the handbrake on firmly
4.30 slow your vehicle right down
4.31 Select a lower gear
4.32 skid
4.33 braking in an emergency
4.34 can be steered while you are braking
4.35 loose
wet
4.36 braking excessively
4.37 steer and brake at the same time
4.38 steering control when braking

4.39 rapidly and firmly
4.40 on surface water
on loose road surfaces
4.41 test your brakes
4.42 ease off the accelerator
4.43 in the highest gear possible
4.44 The steering will feel very light
4.45 The tyres make hardly any noise
The steering becomes lighter
4.46 The steering will feel very light
4.47 in the rain
4.48 Test your brakes
4.49 a two-second time gap
4.50 By changing to a lower gear
4.51 brake promptly and firmly until you have slowed down
4.52 press the brake pedal promptly and firmly until you have stopped
4.53 Just as the wheels are about to lock
4.54 maximum brake pressure has been applied
4.55 dipped headlights
4.56 brake rapidly and firmly without releasing the brake pedal
4.57 reduces the driver's control
4.58 Your steering feels light
4.59 Use dipped headlights
Allow more time for your journey
Slow down

Section Five
Hazard awareness

5.1 On a large goods vehicle
On a builder's skip placed on the road
5.2 The cyclist crossing the road
5.3 The parked car (arrowed A)
5.4 Slow down and get ready to stop
5.5 Pedestrians stepping out between cars
Doors opening on parked cars
Cars leaving parking spaces
5.6 bend sharply to the left
5.7 slow down and allow the cyclist to turn
5.8 There is reduced visibility
5.9 buses
5.10 Lorry
5.11 behind the line, then edge forward to see clearly
5.12 ignore the error and stay calm
5.13 react very quickly
5.14 A school crossing patrol
5.15 Yes, regular stops help concentration
5.16 try not to react
5.17 Stop before the barrier
5.18 Be prepared to stop for any traffic
5.19 Wait for the pedestrian in the road to cross
5.20 Stay behind until you are past the junction
5.21 Be prepared to give way to large vehicles in the middle of the road
5.22 They give a wider field of vision
5.23 approach with care and keep to the left of the lorry
5.24 stay behind and not overtake
5.25 The bus may move out into the road
5.26 a school bus
5.27 Car doors opening suddenly
Children running out from between vehicles
5.28 The cyclist may swerve out into the road
5.29 stop and take a break
5.30 travel at a reduced speed
5.31 Because of the bend
Because of the level crossing
5.32 To enable you to change lanes early

5.33 Traffic in both directions can use the middle lane to overtake

5.34 A disabled person's vehicle

5.35 Stop

5.36 It may suddenly move off
People may cross the road in front of it

5.37 If you are turning left shortly afterwards
When you are approaching a junction
When your view ahead is blocked

5.38 Less control
A false sense of confidence
Poor judgement of speed

5.39 Edge of the carriageway

5.40 A steady amber light

5.41 Allow the cyclist time and room

5.42 slow, but continue around the bend

5.43 wait for the cyclist to pull away

5.44 check for bicycles on your left

5.45 there is a staggered junction ahead

5.46 reduce your speed

5.47 Traffic will move into the left-hand lane

5.48 The two left lanes are open

5.49 Not drink any alcohol at all

5.50 Insurance premiums

5.51 Go home by public transport

5.52 after checking with your doctor

5.53 not drive yourself

5.54 be medically fit to drive
not drive after taking certain medicines

5.55 stop and rest as soon as possible
make sure you have a good supply of fresh air

5.56 stop at the next service area and rest
leave the motorway at the next exit and rest

5.57 Seek medical advice before driving

5.58 wait until you are fit and well before driving

5.59 ensure a supply of fresh air

5.60 stopping every so often for a walk
opening a window for some fresh air
ensuring plenty of refreshment breaks

5.61 Avoid drinking alcohol completely

5.62 Check the label to see if the medicine will affect your driving

5.63 continue to the end of the road

5.64 Looking at road maps
Listening to loud music
Using a mobile phone

5.65 sound your horn and be prepared to stop

5.66 calm down before you start to drive

5.67 Pull over at a safe place to rest

5.68 There are roadworks ahead of you

5.69 keep a safe gap

5.70 find a way of getting home without driving

5.71 Reduced co-ordination
Increased confidence
Poor judgement

5.72 It reduces your concentration

5.73 Some types of medicine can cause your reactions to slow down

5.74 leave the motorway at the next exit

5.75 At all times when driving

5.76 Making sure that you get plenty of fresh air
Making regular stops for refreshments

5.77 Tinted

5.78 slow down your reactions to hazards
worsen your judgement of speed
give a false sense of confidence

5.79 Drugs
Tiredness
Loud music

5.80 the licensing authority

5.81 When your vehicle has broken down and is causing an obstruction

5.82 Approach slowly and edge out until you can see more clearly

5.83 When you have broken down

5.84 broken down and causing an obstruction

5.85 Quick acceleration

5.86 allow at least a four-second gap
be aware of spray reducing your vision

5.87 Pedestrians walking towards you

5.88 be wary of cars on your right cutting in
slow down, keeping a safe separation distance

5.89 on your own
on the motorway

5.90 Ask your doctor
Check the medicine label

5.91 When driving on a motorway to warn traffic behind of a hazard ahead

5.92 Reflections of traffic in shop windows

5.93 inform the licensing authority

5.94 To allow vehicles to enter and emerge

5.95 Open a window and stop as soon as it's safe and legal

5.96 Briefly use the hazard warning lights

Section Six
Vulnerable road users

6.1

6.2 give way to them

6.3 wait and allow them to cross

6.4 give way to the pedestrians who are already crossing

6.5 Pedestrians

6.6 overtaking on your right

6.7 cyclists can use it

6.8 By displaying a stop sign

6.9 On the rear of a school bus or coach

6.10

6.11 A route for pedestrians and cyclists

6.12 deaf and blind

6.13 Be patient and allow them to cross in their own time

6.14 be careful, they may misjudge your speed

6.15 Give the cyclist plenty of room

6.16 Motorcycles
Bicycles

6.17 They are harder to see

6.18 Motorcycles are small and hard to see

6.19 So that the rider can be seen more easily

6.20 drivers often do not see them

6.21 stay behind

6.22 they need to check for traffic in their blind area

6.23 Cyclists
Motorcyclists
Pedestrians

6.24 when approaching junctions

6.25 be prepared to stop
give them plenty of room

6.26 wait because they will take longer to cross

6.27 Reduce speed until you are clear of the area

6.28	a clear view of the crossing area
6.29	On a school bus
6.30	Any direction
6.31	stay behind until the moped has passed the junction
6.32	stay well back
6.33	Be patient and prepare for them to react more slowly
6.34	be patient as you expect them to make mistakes
6.35	Pedestrians
6.36	wait for them to cross
6.37	be aware that the driver's reactions may not be as fast as yours
6.38	hold back until the cyclist has passed the junction
6.39	go in any direction
6.40	They will have a flashing amber light
6.41	just before you turn left
6.42	slow moving
6.43	With-flow pedal cycle lane
6.44	Slow down and be ready to stop
6.45	children's view of the crossing area
6.46	Watch out for pedestrians walking in the road
6.47	allow extra room in case they swerve to avoid potholes
6.48	Cycle route ahead
6.49	The cyclist is slower and more vulnerable
6.50	prepare to slow down and stop
6.51	deaf
6.52	pedestrians and cyclists may cross
6.53	To allow cyclists to position in front of other traffic
6.54	To allow cyclists to position in front of other traffic
6.55	The cyclist might swerve
6.56	Allow plenty of room
	Go very slowly
	Be ready to stop
6.57	You are approaching an organised walk
6.58	By taking further training
6.59	Get out and check
6.60	give way to the pedestrian
6.61	Children
6.62	Stop and give way
6.63	Stop, then move slowly forward until you have a clear view
6.64	To check for overtaking vehicles
6.65	Give way to any pedestrians on the crossing
6.66	allow the person to cross
	be patient
6.67	Slow down and be prepared to stop for children
6.68	check for traffic overtaking on your right
6.69	look for motorcyclists filtering through the traffic
6.70	Pedestrians may come from behind the bus
6.71	Drive slowly and leave plenty of room
6.72	check for traffic overtaking on your right
6.73	The rider may be blown across in front of you
6.74	At a road junction
6.75	At junctions
6.76	You must not wait or park your vehicle here at all
6.77	Slow down and be prepared to stop for a cyclist
6.78	set your mirror to anti-dazzle
6.79	Be prepared to stop
6.80	you should not park or stop on these lines
6.81	You should not wait or park your vehicle here

Section Seven
Other types of vehicle

7.1

7.2	The large vehicle can easily hide an overtaking vehicle
7.3	stay well back and give it room
7.4	Wait behind the long vehicle
7.5	keep well back
7.6	To get the best view of the road ahead
7.7	Watch carefully for pedestrians
	Be ready to give way to the bus
7.8	drop back until you can see better
7.9	Be prepared to stop behind
7.10	drop back further
7.11	Do not overtake, stay well back and be prepared to stop.
7.12	allow it to pull away, if it is safe to do so
7.13	keep well back until you can see that it is clear
7.14	Cars
7.15	Slow down and be prepared to wait
7.16	Do not overtake when at or approaching a junction.
7.17	8 mph
7.18	It takes longer to pass one
7.19	8 mph (12 km/h)
7.20	Keep well back
7.21	allow extra room
7.22	Be prepared to give way if the bus suddenly moves off
	Watch carefully for the sudden appearance of pedestrians
7.23	Slow down and give way
7.24	Because they cannot steer to avoid you
7.25	Extended-arm side mirrors
7.26	rear fog lights if visibility is less than 100 metres (328 feet)
	dipped headlights
7.27	Allow extra room

Section Eight
Vehicle handling

8.1	When you are in a one-way street
	When the vehicle in front is signalling to turn right
	In slow-moving traffic queues when traffic in the right-hand lane is moving more slowly
8.2	doubled
8.3	be careful because you can see less
	beware of bends in the road ahead
8.4	When oncoming traffic prevents you turning right
8.5	**Humps for ½ mile**
8.6	slow traffic down
8.7	Red
8.8	alert you to a hazard
	encourage you to reduce speed
8.9	leave plenty of time for your journey
8.10	you do not dazzle other road users
8.11	slow down and stay behind
8.12	To make you aware of your speed
8.13	white line markings
	a different coloured surface
	a different surface texture
8.14	stop at a passing place
8.15	To prevent the motorcycle sliding on the metal drain covers
8.16	Your brakes will be soaking wet
8.17	It is more difficult to see events ahead
8.18	You will slow down sooner
	The engine will work harder
8.19	be wary of a sudden gust
8.20	steer into it
8.21	In case it stops suddenly
8.22	100 metres (328 feet)
8.23	switch off the fog lights

8.24	leave sidelights on	9.14	To build up a speed similar to traffic on the
8.25	leave your sidelights on		motorway
8.26	slow down or stop	9.15	Face the oncoming traffic
8.27	visibility is seriously reduced	9.16	Red
8.28	visibility is seriously reduced	9.17	Left
8.29	Switch them off as long as visibility remains good	9.18	keep a good distance from the vehicle ahead
8.30	visibility is seriously reduced	9.19	In the left-hand lane
8.31	dazzle other road users	9.20	Obey all speed limits
	cause brake lights to be less clear	9.21	Learner car drivers
	be breaking the law		Farm tractors
8.32	they make your brake lights less clear		Horse riders
8.33	when visibility is reduced to 100 metres (328 feet)		Cyclists
8.34	dazzle other drivers	9.22	Learner car drivers
8.35	dazzle other drivers		Farm tractors
8.36	100 metres (328 feet)		Learner motorcyclists
8.37	skidding in deep snow		Cyclists
8.38	By changing to a lower gear	9.23	keep in the left-hand lane
8.39	You will have less steering and braking control	9.24	Overtaking
8.40	ten times the normal distance	9.25	Stopping in an emergency
8.41	always use your headlights	9.26	move to the left and reduce your speed to 50 mph
8.42	Dipped headlights	9.27	are told to do so by flashing red lights
8.43	How fast you are going	9.28	move to another lane
	The tyres on your vehicle	9.29	keep to the left-hand lane unless overtaking
	The weather	9.30	there is a queue of slow-moving traffic to your right that is
8.44	your vehicle is broken down on the hard shoulder		moving more slowly than you are
8.45	change to a lower gear	9.31	the Highways Agency Control Centre
8.46	dipped headlights	9.32	on a motorway for use in cases of emergency or
8.47	To make them more visible in thick fog		breakdown
8.48	remember to switch them off as visibility improves	9.33	To use in cases of emergency or breakdown
8.49	not drive unless it is essential	9.34	are able to stop and direct anyone on a
8.50	The brakes overheating		motorway
8.51	Check that your lights are working	9.35	You should not travel in this lane
	Make sure that the windows are clean	9.36	The hard shoulder can be used as a running lane
8.52	switch off all your fog lights	9.37	reduce congestion
8.53	when visibility is less than 100 metres (328 feet)	9.38	all speed limit signals are set
8.54	Brake lights are less clear	9.39	Do not use this lane to travel in
	Following drivers can be dazzled	9.40	Your overall journey time will normally improve
8.55	reduce your control	9.41	When signs direct you to
8.56	Your vehicle will pick up speed	9.42	For overtaking other vehicles
8.57	The vehicle will get faster	9.43	Variable speed limits
	You have less braking and steering control	9.44	If red lights show above every lane
8.58	It could be more difficult in winter		When told to by the police
	Use a low gear and drive slowly		When signalled by a Highways Agency Traffic Officer
	Test your brakes afterwards	9.45	In an emergency or breakdown
	There may be a depth gauge	9.46	70 mph
8.59	There is no engine braking	9.47	a Highways Agency control centre
8.60	In poor visibility	9.48	stop and wait
8.61	Release the footbrake	9.49	the hard shoulder is for emergency or breakdown use
8.62	make your brake lights less visible		only
	dazzle following drivers	9.50	all the lanes including the hard shoulder
		9.51	pull in at the nearest service area
		9.52	Leave at the next exit

Section Nine
Motorway rules

		9.53	60 mph
		9.54	normal driving
9.1	give way to traffic already on the motorway	9.55	switch on your hazard lights
9.2	70 mph	9.56	use the emergency telephone and call for
9.3	70 mph		assistance
9.4	any vehicle	9.57	carry on to the next exit
9.5	A vehicle towing a trailer	9.58	Left lane
9.6	It allows easy location by the emergency services	9.59	Switch on your hazard warning lights
9.7	gain speed on the hard shoulder before moving out onto	9.60	Continuous high speeds may increase the risk of your
	the carriageway		vehicle breaking down
9.8	on a steep gradient	9.61	traffic ahead is slowing or stopping suddenly
9.9	They are countdown markers to the next exit	9.62	in the left-hand lane
9.10	the central reservation and the carriageway	9.63	on the motorway
9.11	White	9.64	check your location from the marker posts on the left
9.12	Green	9.65	there are lane closures
9.13	in the direction shown on the marker posts	9.66	Lower speed limits
		9.67	in an emergency

Section Ten
Rules of the road

10.1 National speed limit applies
10.2 70 mph
10.3 By street lighting
10.4 30 mph
10.5 End of minimum speed
10.6 not overtake if you are in doubt
10.7 Horse riders
Long vehicles
Cyclists
10.8 at any time
10.9 Waiting restrictions
10.10 in a one-way street
10.11 overtaking or turning right
10.12 continue in that lane
10.13 Either on the right or the left
10.14 indicate left before leaving the roundabout
10.15 Long vehicle
10.16 your exit road is clear
10.17 oncoming traffic is preventing you from turning right
10.18 A police officer
A school crossing patrol
A red traffic light
10.19 stop, let them cross, wait patiently
10.20 cyclists riding across
10.21 Cyclists
Pedestrians
10.22 You must give way to pedestrians still on the crossing
10.23 wait for pedestrians on the crossing to clear
10.24 To pick up or set down passengers
10.25 keep the other vehicle to your RIGHT and turn behind it (offside to offside)
10.26 30 mph
10.27 Vehicles may be pulling out
Drivers' doors may open
Children may run out from between the vehicles
10.28 give way to oncoming traffic
10.29 Turning right
Overtaking slower traffic
10.30 No one has priority
10.31 10 metres (32 feet)
10.32 Near the brow of a hill
At or near a bus stop
Within 10 metres (32 feet) of a junction
10.33 carry on waiting
10.34 Neither of the vehicles
10.35 No waiting zone ends
10.36 not exceed the speed limit
10.37 Near a school entrance
At a bus stop
10.38 be easily seen by others
10.39 Wait until the road is clear in both directions
10.40 60 mph
10.41 with parking lights on
10.42 a concealed level crossing
10.43 A Highways Agency Traffic Officer
10.44 None of the vehicles
10.45 Signal left just after you pass the exit before the one you will take
10.46 to get into a property
10.47 50 mph
10.48 60 mph
10.49 park in a bay and pay
10.50 you must not drive in that lane
10.51 during its period of operation

10.52 keep well to the left of the road
10.53 Continue to wait
10.54 Keep going and clear the crossing
10.55 Turn round in a side road
10.56 reversing
10.57 for longer than necessary
10.58 get out and check
10.59 Not at any time
10.60 wait in the box junction if your exit is clear
10.61 When the front of your vehicle swings out
10.62 In a garage
10.63 set down and pick up passengers
10.64 not park there unless permitted
10.65 Where the speed limit exceeds 30 mph
10.66 Pull into a passing place on your left
10.67 as soon as the vehicle passes you
10.68 Outside its hours of operation
10.69 brake lights
10.70 Find a quiet side road to turn round in
10.71 In a well-lit area
10.72 move to the left in good time
10.73 you should not drive in the lane unless it is unavoidable
you should not park in the lane unless it is unavoidable
10.74 A Blue Badge
10.75 When in an incident where damage or injury is caused
At a red traffic light
When signalled to do so by a police or traffic officer

Section Eleven
Road and traffic signs

11.1 red circles
11.2

11.3

11.4 Maximum speed limit with traffic calming
11.5

11.6

11.7 End of 20 mph zone
11.8 No motor vehicles
11.9 No entry
11.10 No right turn

11.11

11.12 Route for trams only
11.13 High vehicles
11.14

11.15 No overtaking
11.16 Do not overtake
11.17
11.18

11.19 End of restricted parking area
11.20
11.21 No stopping
11.22

11.23 Distance to parking place ahead
11.24 Vehicles may park fully on the verge or footway
11.25 Give priority to oncoming traffic
11.26 You have priority over vehicles coming towards you
11.27 You have priority over vehicles from the opposite direction
11.28
11.29 Stop
11.30 Minimum speed 30 mph
11.31

Pass either side to get to the same destination
11.32 Route for trams
11.33 Give an instruction
11.34 On a one-way street
11.35 Contraflow bus lane
11.36 Tourist directions
11.37 tourist attraction
11.38 To give warnings
11.39 T-junction
11.40 Risk of ice
11.41 Crossroads
11.42 Roundabout
11.43 Road narrows
Low bridge
Children crossing
T-junction
11.44 Cycle route ahead

11.45

11.46

11.47 Give way to trams
11.48 Humps in the road
11.49

11.50 End of dual carriageway
11.51 Crosswinds
11.52 Danger ahead
11.53 hold back until you can see clearly ahead
11.54 Level crossing with gate or barrier
11.55 Trams crossing ahead
11.56 Steep hill downwards
11.57 Water across the road
11.58 No through road on the left
11.59 No through road
11.60

11.61

11.62 The right-hand lane is closed
11.63 Contraflow system
11.64 Lane for heavy and slow vehicles
11.65 you must stop and wait behind the stop line
11.66 stop at the stop line
11.67 When your exit from the junction is blocked
11.68

11.69 Traffic lights out of order
11.70 Nobody
11.71 Lifting bridges
Level crossings
Fire stations
11.72 No parking at any time
11.73 To pass a road maintenance vehicle travelling at 10 mph or less
11.74 You are approaching a hazard

434

11.75 On road humps
11.76

11.77 Visibility along the major road is restricted
11.78 Give way to traffic from the right
11.79 Flash the headlights, indicate left and point to the left
11.80 stop at the stop line
11.81 The driver intends to turn left
11.82 On a motorway slip road
11.83 Change to the lane on your left
11.84 Temporary maximum speed 50 mph
11.85 Right-hand lane closed ahead
11.86 move to the lane on your left
11.87 The number of the next junction
11.88 an overtaking lane
11.89 On the right-hand edge of the road
11.90 At slip road entrances and exits
11.91 leave the motorway at the next exit
11.92 End of motorway
11.93

11.94 60 mph
11.95 End of restriction
11.96 follow the route diversion
11.97 To warn of road works ahead
11.98 a compulsory maximum speed limit
11.99 carry on with great care
11.100 Give an arm signal
11.101 No motorcycles
11.102 pass the lorry on the left
11.103 Move into another lane in good time
11.104 you must stop behind the white stop line
11.105 Turn to the left
11.106 To warn others of your presence
11.107 unless a moving vehicle may cause you danger
11.108 No parking on the days and times shown
11.109 Quayside or river bank
11.110

11.111 hazard warning
11.112 To prevent queueing traffic from blocking the junction on the left
11.113 It is to separate traffic flowing in opposite directions
11.114 To warn you of their presence
11.115 20 mph
11.116 trams must stop
11.117 At a junction
11.118 Pull up on the left
11.119 Red alone
11.120 there is a hazard ahead of you
11.121 Leave the motorway at the next exit
11.122 To prevent the junction becoming blocked
11.123 Stop, even if the road is clear

11.124

11.125 Mini-roundabout
11.126 Two-way traffic crosses a one-way road
11.127 Two-way traffic straight ahead
11.128 Hump-back bridge
11.129

11.130 Direction to park-and-ride car park
11.131 wait for the green light before you cross the stop line
11.132 'give way' sign
11.133 Wait
11.134 Direction to emergency pedestrian exit
11.135

11.136 With-flow bus and cycle lane
11.137

11.138 Zebra crossing
11.139 Zebra crossing ahead
11.140

11.141

11.142

11.143

11.144 all traffic is going one way
11.145 Red and amber
11.146 Tunnel ahead
11.147

11.148 shows the edge of the carriageway
11.149 keep left of the hatched markings
11.150

11.151 Wait until the vehicle starts to turn in
11.152 On a motorway or unrestricted dual carriageway, to warn of a hazard ahead
11.153 pass on the left
11.154 under any circumstances
11.155 To avoid misleading other road users
11.156 As you are passing or just after the junction

Section Twelve
Documents

12.1 one year after the date it was issued
12.2 insurance certificate
12.3 Retake your theory and practical tests
Reapply for your provisional licence
12.4 12 months
12.5 A notification to tell DVLA that a vehicle is not being used on the road
12.6 to tell DVLA that your vehicle is not being used on the road
12.7 for 12 months only
12.8 for 12 months only
12.9 £5,000
12.10 The registered vehicle keeper
12.11 When a police officer asks you for it
12.12 obtain a tax disc
12.13 renew your road tax disc
12.14 A valid driving licence
A valid tax disc clearly displayed
Proper insurance cover
12.15 valid insurance
12.16 7 days
12.17 Valid insurance
12.18 When you move house
12.19 have a signed, valid provisional licence
12.20 the vehicle is insured for your use
12.21 insurance
12.22 21 years old
12.23 have valid motor insurance
12.24 Injury to another person
Damage to someone's property
Damage to other vehicles
12.25 display it clearly on your vehicle
12.26 road tax disc
12.27 Registered keeper
Make of the vehicle
Engine size
12.28 you change your vehicle
you change your name
your permanent address changes

12.29 your health affects your driving
your eyesight does not meet a set standard
you change your vehicle
12.30 take the Pass Plus scheme
12.31 Taking a Pass Plus course
12.32 have held a full licence for at least 3 years
be at least 21 years old
12.33 When driving to an appointment at an MOT centre
12.34 three years old
12.35 To improve your basic skills
12.36 damage to other vehicles
injury to others
12.37 Third party only
12.38 You will have to pay the first £100 of the cost of repair to your car
12.39 improve your basic driving skills
12.40 improve your basic driving skills
12.41 widen their driving experience
12.42 improve your basic skills
widen your experience
12.43 improve your basic skills
12.44 When a police officer asks you for it
12.45 A valid driving licence
A valid tax disc displayed on your vehicle
Proper insurance cover
and have held a full licence for at least three years
12.46 at least 21
12.47 You will have to pay the first £100 of any claim

Section Thirteen
Incidents, accidents and emergencies

13.1 a disabled person
13.2 When you slow down quickly on a motorway because of a hazard ahead
When you have broken down
13.3 When stopped and temporarily obstructing traffic
13.4 Keep a safe distance from the vehicle in front
13.5 when an emergency arises
13.6 Apply pressure over the wound and raise the arm
13.7 10 seconds
13.8 10 minutes
13.9 10 minutes
13.10 100 per minute
13.11 Pale grey skin
13.12 Sweating
13.13 Check the airway is clear
13.14 seek medical assistance
13.15 go to the next emergency telephone and report the hazard
13.16 Variable message signs
13.17 4 to 5 centimetres
13.18 Make sure engines are switched off
Call the emergency services promptly
13.19 not put yourself at risk
13.20 Switch on your own hazard warning lights
Make sure that someone telephones for an ambulance
Get people who are not injured clear of the scene
13.21 Only when it is essential
13.22 try to stop the bleeding
check their breathing
check their airways
13.23 breathing
13.24 Circulation
Airway
Breathing

13.25 Clear the airway and keep it open
Check that they are breathing
Stop any heavy bleeding
13.26 check the airway is clear
make sure they are breathing
stop any heavy bleeding
13.27 Keep injured people warm and comfortable
Keep injured people calm by talking to them reassuringly
Make sure that injured people are not left alone
13.28 Stop any severe bleeding
Check they are breathing
Clear their airway and keep it open
13.29 Offer someone a cigarette to calm them down
13.30 Reassure them
Not leave them alone
13.31 reassure them constantly
13.32 warn other traffic
13.33 gently
13.34 clear the airway
tilt their head back gently
pinch the nostrils together
13.35 remove anything sticking to the burn
13.36 douse the burns with clean, cool, non-toxic liquid
13.37 Apply firm pressure to the wound
Raise the leg to lessen bleeding
13.38 there is further danger
13.39 not move them
13.40 keep them in the vehicle
13.41

13.42 Driving licence
Insurance certificate
MOT test certificate
13.43 As soon as possible
13.44 It will help to reduce the blood flow
13.45 Variable message signs
13.46 Warn other traffic
13.47 remove anything that is blocking the mouth
tilt the head back gently to clear the airway
13.48 reassure them constantly
keep them warm
avoid moving them if possible
avoid leaving them alone
13.49 This could result in more serious injury
13.50 45 metres (147 feet)
13.51 Telephone the signal operator
Leave your vehicle and get everyone clear
Move the vehicle if a signal operator tells you to
13.52 Pull up slowly at the side of the road
Hold the steering wheel firmly to keep control
13.53 Let the vehicle roll to a stop
Grip the steering wheel firmly
13.54 Pull up on the hard shoulder
Use the emergency phone to get assistance
13.55 get out and clear of the crossing
13.56 When you slow down quickly because of danger ahead
When you have broken down on the hard shoulder
13.57 for the number on the telephone that you are using
for details of yourself and your vehicle
whether you belong to a motoring organisation
13.58 Remove any sunglasses
13.59 Use dipped headlights
13.60 Switch on hazard warning lights
13.61 Look out for variable message signs

13.62 Carry a fire extinguisher
Check out any strong smell of petrol
13.63 Stop at the next emergency telephone and contact the police
13.64 check out the problem quickly and safely
13.65 at least 45 metres (147 feet) behind your vehicle
13.66 Call the fire brigade
13.67 Switch on hazard lights then go and call for help immediately
13.68 Drive it out of the tunnel if you can do so
13.69 Continue through the tunnel if you can
13.70 Switch on hazard warning lights
Try and put out the fire
13.71 make sure your radio is tuned to the frequency shown
13.72 Get everyone out of the vehicle and clear of the crossing
13.73 Fire extinguisher
First aid kit
Warning triangle
13.74 Stop at the scene of the incident
13.75 Whether the driver owns the other vehicle involved
The other driver's name, address and telephone number
The make and registration number of the other vehicle
The details of the other driver's vehicle insurance
13.76 Report the incident to the police within 24 hours
13.77 45 metres (147 feet)
13.78 Switch off the engine and switch on hazard lights
13.79 Switch on hazard warning lights

Section Fourteen
Vehicle loading

14.1 not exceed 60 mph
use only the left and centre lanes
14.2 ease off the accelerator and reduce your speed
14.3 Slow down very gradually
14.4 When driving fast for a long distance
When carrying a heavy load
14.5 reduce stability
14.6 Ease off the accelerator slowly
14.7 steering
handling
14.8 The driver of the vehicle
14.9 A stabiliser fitted to the towbar
14.10 No, not at any time
14.11 Breakaway cable
14.12 It will help with stability when driving in crosswinds
14.13 In the vehicle handbook
14.14 securely fastened when driving
14.15 A child seat

Index